D1187013

Au

Titl

Access

Beyond the numbers game

a reader in educational evaluation

Edited by David Hamilton, David Jenkins, Christine King,
Barry MacDonald and Malcolm Parlett

Macmillan Education

First published 1977

Published by
MACMILLAN EDUCATION LTD
Houndmills Basingstoke Hampshire RG21 2XS
and London
Associated companies in New York Dublin
Melbourne Johannesburg and Delhi

Printed in Great Britain by A. Wheaton & Co., Exeter

Beyond the numbers game: a reader in educational
    evaluation.
Bibl.
ISBN 0-333-19872-7
ISBN 0-333-21274-6   Pbk
1. Hamilton, David, b. 1943
375'. 006'08   LB1027
Curriculum evaluation—Addresses, essays, lectures

Contents

iv Contents

Preface

In December 1972 a small working conference took place at Churchill College, Cambridge, financed by the Nuffield Foundation. Its aim was to explore 'non-traditional' modes of curriculum evaluation and to set out guidelines for future developments in this field. Participants were chosen for their known reservations about established evaluation practice, or because they had suggested or experimented with new approaches. The conference participants were as follows:[1]

Myron Atkin, University of Illinois
John Banks, Department of Education and Science
Tony Becher, Nuffield Foundation
Alan Gibson, Department of Education and Science
David Hamilton, University of Glasgow
David Jenkins, Open University
Barry MacDonald, University of East Anglia
Tim McMullen, Centre for Research and Innovation in Education, OECD
Malcolm Parlett, University of Edinburgh
· Louis Smith, Washington University of St Louis
Robert Stake, University of Illinois
David Tawney, University of Keele
Kim Taylor, Centre for Research and Innovation in Education, OECD
Erik Wallin, Pedagogiska Institutionen, Goteborg.

At the end of the conference, members decided that it might be useful to make available an agreed summary of their conclusions, in the form of a manifesto. Read today, several years later, the 'call to arms' has a distinctly historical ring to it — the battle is well and truly joined. But the points it makes are enduring ones, hurried though the resulting draft was.

On 20 December, 1972 at Churchill College, Cambridge, the following conference participants concluded a discussion of the aims and procedures of evaluating educational practices and agreed:

I That past efforts to evaluate these practices have, on the whole, not adequately served the needs of those who require evidence of the effects of such practices, because of:

(a) an under-attention to educational processes including those of the learning milieu;

---

1 Several of the conference participants have subsequently changed jobs.

(*b*) an over-attention to psychometrically measurable changes in student behaviour (that to an extent represent the outcomes of the practice, but which are a misleading over-simplification of the complex changes that occur in students); and

(*c*) the existence of an educational research climate that rewards accuracy of measurement and generality of theory but overlooks both mismatch between school problems and research issues and tolerates ineffective communication between researchers and those outside the research community.

II   That future efforts to evaluate these practices be designed so as to be:

(*a*) responsive to the needs and perspectives of differing audiences;

(*b*) illuminative of the complex organisational, teaching and learning processes at issue;

(*c*) relevant to public and professional decisions forthcoming; and

(*d*) reported in language which is accessible to their audiences.

III   More specifically they recommended that, increasingly,

(*a*) observational data, carefully validated, be used (sometimes in substitute for data from questioning and testing);

(*b*) the evaluation be designed so as to be flexible enough to allow for response to unanticipated events (progressive focusing rather than pre-ordinate design); and that

(*c*) the value positions of the evaluator, whether highlighted or constrained by the design, be made evident to the sponsors and audiences of the evaluation.

IV   Though without consensus on the issues themselves, it was agreed that considered attention by those who design evaluation studies should be given to such issues as the following:

(*a*) the sometimes conflicting roles of the same evaluator as expert, scientist, guide and teacher of decision-makers on the one hand, and as technical specialist, employee and servant of decision-makers on the other;

(*b*) the degree to which the evaluator, his sponsors and his subjects, should specify in advance the limits of inquiry, the circulation of findings, and such matters as may become controversial later;

(*c*) the advantages and disadvantages of intervening in educational practices for the purpose of gathering data or of controlling the variability of certain features in order to increase the generalisability of the findings;

(*d*) the complexity of educational decisions which, as a matter of rule, have political, social and economic implications; and the responsibility that the evaluator may or may not have for exploring these implications;

(*e*) the degree to which the evaluator should interpret his observations rather than leave them for different audiences to interpret.

It was acknowledged that different evaluation designs will serve different purposes and that even for a single educational programme many different designs could be used.

The conference also felt that it would be useful to have generally available a reader in 'alternative' or 'illuminative' curriculum evaluation to further the aims implicit in the conference and the manifesto. This volume is the result. In spite of a strong central theme arising out of the circumstances of its commission, the book contains intact a number of skirmishes and internal debates that are current among illuminative evaluators.

Section 1
Introduction

Introduction

Near the top of our lists of 'books we would like to have had some part in writing' comes the Webb et al. *latter-day classic* Unobtrusive Measures: Nonreactive Research in the Social Sciences. *Yet the preface to that splendidly imaginative book displays an uncharacteristic failure of nerve. The authors write:*

This monograph has had a series of working titles, and we should identify them for the benefit of our friends who shared early drafts. To some, this is The Bullfighter's Beard—*a provocative, if uncommunicative, title. . . .*

This title lasted for a while, but the occasionally bizarre content of the material shifted the working title to Oddball Research, Oddball Measures, *and the like. Most of our friends have known the manuscript under one of the 'oddball' labels, and it is only a fear of librarians that has caused us to drop it.*[1]

This volume too has had a series of working titles, and as some of these have appeared in pre-emptive bibliographies it is necessary that we travel recognised, albeit incognito. One of the working titles, Evaluation on the Run, *sounded possible in the UK, but our American friends warned of semantic jet-lag. The main working title (which as with one of those pornographic movies in which even the title is censored we cannot reproduce in full) was* Whatever Happened to You-Know-Who? *This was dropped following threats of litigation and licking of wounds all round.*

But the intention in giving the now-abandoned detective-thriller-sounding title was a good one. The book tells a story with a number of twists and turns. We have allowed ourselves a few chalk marks on the library floor but haven't removed the corpse. There is consequently an invitation to the reader to become himself the detective, to adjudicate, to weigh evidence, to detect paradox or corroboration, to perceive motivation, and to allocate praise or blame.

The cynic may seek to falsify these claims by pointing to the implicit polemicism of the editors, and their obtrusive commentary. This is arguable, although it is not how we see our contribution. In the same way as the detective novel deliberately offers opportunities for alternative interpretations of the circumstantial evidence of the plot, so we keep open the dialogue between interpretation and evidence.

1 Eugene J. Webb, Donald T. Campbell, Richard D. Schwartz and Lee Sechrest (1966). *Unobtrusive Measures: Nonreactive Research in the Social Sciences.* Chicago: Rand McNally, p.v.

Beyond the Numbers Game *is, however, a much more accurate title for a book charting a paradigm shift from an evaluation methodology valuing numeracy to one valuing literacy. But the social irony is not accidental. The real 'numbers game', like psychometric evaluation, is in cultural terms as American as violence or apple pie.*

Evaluation as illumination

At the risk of engendering a misleadingly polarised perception of the alternatives facing curriculum evaluators, our starting point is one of the papers discussed at the Cambridge conference, Malcolm Parlett and David Hamilton's 'Evaluation as illumination: a new approach to the study of innovatory programmes'. At the time of writing, both authors were based at the newly-established Centre for Research in the Educational Sciences, at the University of Edinburgh.

The Parlett/Hamilton collaboration derived from a convergence of research interest. David Hamilton—a teacher by training—was dissatisfied with the available methods of analysing classroom behaviour. Malcolm Parlett, a lapsed positivist, mercifully with a Cambridge research degree in short-term memory, was evolving new approaches towards evaluating innovations in teaching. This arose in part out of his involvement in the Nuffield Resources for Learning Project. Thus both Parlett and Hamilton were interested in opening up the classroom to scrutiny, and this interest was both methodological and theoretical. The initial drafting of 'Evaluation as illumination' took place in April 1971. After many revisions it was completed in September 1972. Like all close collaborations their joint statement raises intriguing questions about the mechanisms of co-authorship, particularly as at the time Parlett was Hamilton's research tutor. Some who know both of them well surmise, perhaps a little unkindly, that Malcolm Parlett wrote the text and David Hamilton the footnotes.

'Evaluation as illumination' advocates a total reappraisal of the rationale and techniques of programme evaluation. Characteristically, conventional approaches have followed the experimental and psychometric traditions dominant in educational research. Their aim [unfulfilled] of achieving fully 'objective methods' has led to studies that are artificial and restricted in scope. The authors argue that such evaluations are inadequate for elucidating the complex problem areas they confront, and as a result provide little effective input to the decision-making process.

Illuminative evaluation is introduced as belonging to a contrasting 'anthropological' research paradigm. Attempted measurement of 'educational products' is abandoned for intensive study of the programme as a whole: its rationale and evolution, its operations, achievements and difficulties. The innovation is not examined in isolation, but in the school context or 'learning milieu'. The paper then describes the methodological strategies of illuminative evaluation. Observation, interviews with partici-pants [students, instructors, administrators and others], questionnaires and analysis of documents and background information are all combined to help 'illuminate' problems, issues and significant programme features.

The paper concludes with a discussion of the problems and potentialities of the new approach: its range of applicability; the validity and generalisability of evidence; the professional skills and obligations of the research worker; how explorations of the learning milieu can meet the need for theoretical advance; and how the illuminative approach can clarify and interpret the programme for the various groups of decision-makers who look to the evaluation study for assistance in their tasks.

BEYOND THE NUMBER GAME.   1977
MACMILLAN ED LTD.

1.1 Malcolm Parlett and David Hamilton
Evaluation as illumination: a new approach to the study of innovatory programmes

Innovation is now a major educational priority. For nearly two decades it has expanded and proliferated. It absorbs increasing sums of public and private money. Its impact is felt throughout the world.[1] Curricula are restructured, new devices introduced, forms of teaching permuted. But decisions to change are more than educational: questions of politics, ideology, fashion and finance also intervene.

More recently—to aid decision-making—innovation has been joined by evaluation. Increasingly, committees and foundations fund evaluation studies as an integral part of innovation programmes. Like innovation itself, evaluation has rapidly developed a legitimacy and importance of its own: professional journals have been launched and research centres established. The 'evaluator' has emerged as a new and influential figure. In short, both innovation and evaluation have become 'big science'.[2]

As a new field, programme evaluation has encountered a wide range of problems, both theoretical and methodological. Current concerns[3] include the 'roles' of evaluation;[4] the neutrality of the evaluator;[5] the value of class-room observation;[6] the function of 'formative' evaluation;[7] the use of 'objectives';[8] and the value of long-term studies.[9] Confusion is engendered as rival proposals, models and terminologies are voiced and then rapidly countered. As a developing field of study, evaluation proceeds in the absence of coherent or agreed frames of reference.

1 See for example the series of reports: *Innovation in Education* 1971 Paris: OECD Centre for Educational Research and Innovation, which reviews developments in member countries.

2 D. J. de S. Price (1963). *Little Science, Big Science.* Columbia: Columbia University Press.

3 Much of this debate has been monitored by the AERA Monograph Series on Curriculum Evaluation, Chicago: Rand McNally, 1967 onwards.

4 M. Scriven (1967). 'The methodology of evaluation'. In R. Tyler *et al., Perspectives of Curriculum Evaluation.* AERA Monograph Series on Curriculum Evaluation No. 1, pp. 39-83.

5 F. G. Caro (1971). 'Issues in the evaluation of social programs', *Review of Educational Research,* 41, pp. 87-114.

6 R. J. Light & P. V. Smith (1970). 'Choosing a future: strategies for designing and evaluating new programs'. *Harvard Educational Review,* 40, Winter, pp. 1-28.

7 L. M. Smith (1971). 'Participant observation and evaluation strategies'. Paper presented to AERA symposium on 'Participant Observation and Curriculum: Research and Evaluation'. New York, February 1971.

8 J. Popham *et al.,* 1969. *Instructional Objectives,* AERA Monograph Series on Curriculum Evaluation, No. 3. Chicago: Rand McNally.

9 F. G. Caro, *op cit.*

Source: M. Parlett and D. Hamilton (1972). 'Evaluation as illumination: a new approach to the study of innovatory programmes'. Occasional Paper 9, Centre for Research in the Educational Sciences, University of Edinburgh.

More generally within educational research two distinct paradigms[10] can be discerned. Each has its own strategies, foci and assumptions. Dominant is the 'classical' or 'agricultural-botany'[11] paradigm, which utilises a hypothetico-deductive methodology derived from the experimental and mental-testing traditions in psychology. Almost all evaluation studies have resided within this traditional paradigm.

More recently, a small number of empirical studies have been conceived outside the agricultural-botany framework, and relate instead to social anthropology, psychiatry and participant observation research in sociology.[12] Such research can be thought of as representing a second and contrasting paradigm, with a fundamentally different research style and methodology from that of mainstream educational research. We outline here an approach to evaluation that belongs to this alternative, or 'social anthropology' paradigm.[13]

Traditional evaluation and the agricultural-botany paradigm

The most common form of agricultural-botany type evaluation is presented as an assessment of the effectiveness of an innovation by examining whether or not it has reached required standards on pre-specified criteria.[14] Students —rather like plant crops—are given pre-tests (the seedlings are weighed or measured) and then submitted to different experiences (treatment conditions). Subsequently, after a period of time, their attainment (growth or yield) is measured to indicate the relative efficiency of the methods (fertilisers) used. Studies of this kind are designed to yield data of one particular type, i.e. 'objective' numerical data that permit statistical

10   The term paradigm as used by T. S. Kuhn (1970). *The Structure of Scientific Revolutions.* Chicago: University of Chicago Press, 2nd ed., is an overarching concept similar in meaning to 'world-view', 'philosophy' or even 'intellectual orthodoxy'. A paradigm prescribes problem fields, research methods and acceptable standards of solution and explanation for the academic community it embraces.

11   M. Parlett (1972). 'Evaluating innovations in teaching', in H. J. Butcher and E. Rudd (eds.). *Contemporary Problems in Higher Education,* London: McGraw-Hill. The designation 'agricultural-botany' is not fortuitous. Many of the statistical and experimental techniques used in educational research were originally developed (e.g. by Fisher) for use in agricultural experimentation.

12   See, for example, J. Henry (1971). *Essays on Education.* Harmondsworth: Penguin Books; P. W. Jackson (1968). *Life in Classrooms.* New York: Holt, Rinehart & Winston and M. F. D. Young (ed.) (1971). *Knowledge and Control.* London: Crowell Collier-Macmillan.

13   M. Parlett, *op. cit.*

14   For instance within this framework Lindvall and Cox have argued that the 'effectiveness' of an innovation is 'determined' by the answers to four basic questions: (1) What goals should the programme achieve? (2) What is the plan for achieving these goals? (3) Does the operating programme represent a true implementation of the plan? (4) Does the programme, when developed and put into operation, achieve the desired goals? (C. M. Lindvall & R. C. Cox, (1970), *The IPI Evaluation Program,* AERA Monograph Series on Curriculum Evaluation, No. 5. Chicago: Rand McNally, pp. 5-6.) At face value these questions seem reasonable. But they embody problematic assumptions. For example, programmes rarely have clearly specified and commonly agreed 'desired goals'. Measurement of 'goal achievement' is never unequivocal. To speak of a 'true implementation' is utopian, even nonsensical in terms of educational practice.

analyses.[15] Isolated variables like IQ, social class, test scores, personality profiles and attitude ratings are codified and processed to indicate the efficiency of new curricula, media or methods.

Recently, however, there has been increasing resistance to evaluations of this type.[16] The more notable shortcomings may be summarised as follows:

1   Educational situations are characterised by numerous relevant parameters. Within the terms of the agricultural - botany paradigm these must be randomised using very large samples; or otherwise strictly controlled. The former approach entails a major data-collection exercise and is expensive in time and resources. It also runs counter to the need, widely acknowledged, for evaluation before large-scale application rather than after it. The latter procedure — of strict control — is rarely followed. To attempt to simulate laboratory conditions by 'manipulating educational personnel' is not only dubious ethically, but also leads to gross administrative and personal inconvenience. Even if a situation could be so unnervingly controlled, its artificiality would render the exercise irrelevant; rarely can 'tidy' results be generalised to an 'untidy' reality. Whichever approach is used, there is a tendency for the investigator to think in terms of 'parameters' and 'factors' rather than 'individuals' and 'institutions'. Again, this divorces the study from the real world.

2   Before-and-after research designs assume that innovatory programmes undergo little or no change during the period of study. This built-in premise is rarely upheld in practice. Yet it remains fundamental to the design, constraining the researchers from adapting to the changed circumstances that so frequently arise.[17] It may even have a deleterious effect on the

15   Again, within this framework, it has been proposed that 'the search for (compensatory) programmes which are working well should become a three-step procedure: (1) first, locate the best recreatable centres, employing techniques which use estimates of average random variation require analysis of variance, followed by multiple comparison procedures; (2) estimate, separately, the impact of random factors upon only the best-performing centres; (3) use this selective estimate of random variation to test whether these best centres are out-performing chance, and are worth recreating'. (R. J. Light & P. V. Smith, op. cit., p. 18.) The evaluation suggested by Light and Smith is based purely on numerical results; no other data would be collected or eligible for consideration.

16   The objections are developed more extensively in M. Guttentag (1971). 'Models and methods in evaluation research'. J. Theory Soc. Behavior, 1, pp. 75-95; R. E. Stake (1973). 'Measuring what learners learn (with a special look at performance contracting)', in E. House (ed.) School Evaluation. Berkeley: McCutchan; B. MacDonald, 'The evaluation of the Humanities Curriculum Project: a wholistic approach', University of East Anglia, Norwich: Centre for Applied Research in Education, n.d.; S. Messick. 'Evaluation of educational programmes as research on educational process'. Princeton: Educational Testing Service, n.d.; L. C. Taylor (1971). Resources for Learning. Harmondsworth: Penguin Books; and M. Parlett, op. cit.

17   During the long-term evaluation of a Swedish individualised maths programme (IMU), teachers who wished to transfer students from one class to another were actively discouraged by the evaluator from doing so, on the grounds that it would render interclass comparisons invalid. Teachers also requested separate diagnostic tests for less able children. But again, this educational need was subordinated to the evaluator's requirements. The British evaluation of the initial teaching alphabet (i.t.a.), set up to compare pupil progress with i.t.a. and traditional orthography (t.o.) over a five-year period, provides a second example. Early before-and-after test results indicated that a major educational difficulty was faced by children transferring from i.t.a. to t.o. But nothing was done to focus attention on this problem: the research die had already been cast. (See J. Downing (ed.) (1967). The i.t.a. Symposium, London: National Foundation for Educational Research.)

programme itself, by discouraging new developments and redefinitions mid-stream. Longitudinal studies, for these reasons, can rarely serve an effective 'formative' or cybernetic function.[18]

3 The methods used in traditional evaluations impose artificial and arbitrary restrictions on the scope of the study. For instance, the concentration on seeking quantitative information by objective means can lead to neglect of other data, perhaps more salient to the innovation, but which are disregarded as 'subjective', 'anecdotal' or 'impressionistic'. However, the evaluator is likely to be forced to utilise information of this sort if he is satisfactorily to explain his findings, weight their importance and place them in context.

4 Research of this type, by employing large samples and seeking statistical generalisations, tends to be insensitive to local perturbations and unusual effects. Atypical results are seldom studied in detail. Despite their significance for the innovation, or possible importance to the individuals and institutions concerned, they are ironed out and lost to discussion.

5 Finally, this type of evaluation often fails to articulate with the varied concerns and questions of participants, sponsors and other interested parties. Since classical evaluators believe in an 'objective truth' equally relevant to all parties, their studies rarely acknowledge the diversity of questions posed by different interest-groups.

These points suggest that applying the agricultural-botany paradigm to the study of innovations is often a cumbersome and inadequate procedure.[19] The evaluation falls short of its own tacit claims to be controlled, exact and unambiguous. Rarely, if ever, can educational programmes be subject to strict enough control to meet the design's requirements. Innovations, in particular, are vulnerable to manifold extraneous influences. Yet the traditional evaluator ignores these. He is restrained by the dictates of his paradigm to seek generalised findings along pre-ordained lines. His definition of empirical reality is narrow. One effect of this is that it diverts attention away from questions of educational practice towards more centralised bureaucratic concerns.

Illuminative evaluation and the social-anthropological paradigm

Although traditional forms of evaluation have been criticised in this way, little attempt has been made to develop alternative models. The model

18 Because the prespecification of parameters, by definition, occurs at the outset, variables which emerge during the study are likely to be left out of the analysis. In an extreme case this neglect of 'new' variables may negate an entire evaluation study. After criticism that it had not controlled for the Hawthorne effect, the i.t.a. experiment was restarted after two years.

19 We are not, of course, arguing here against the use of experimental longitudinal or survey research methods as such. Rather, for the reasons suggested, we submit that they are usually inappropriate, ineffective or insufficient for programme evaluation purposes.

described here, *illuminative evaluation*,[20] takes account of the wider contexts in which educational programmes function. Its primary concern is with description and interpretation rather than measurement and prediction.[21] It stands unambiguously within the alternative anthropological paradigm. The aims of illuminative evaluation are to study the innovatory programme: how it operates; how it is influenced by the various school situations in which it is applied; what those directly concerned regard as its advantages and disadvantages; and how students' intellectual tasks and academic experiences are most affected. It aims to discover and document what it is like to be participating in the scheme, whether as teacher or pupil; and, in addition, to discern and discuss the innovation's most significant features, recurring concomitants and critical processes. In short, it seeks to address and to illuminate a complex array of questions: 'Research on innovation can be enlightening to the innovator and to the whole academic community by clarifying the processes of education and by helping the innovator and other interested parties to identify those procedures, those elements in the educational effort, which seem to have had desirable results.'[22]

The paradigm shift entailed in adopting illuminative evaluation requires more than an exchange of methodologies: it also involves new suppositions, concepts and terminology. Central to an understanding of illuminative evaluation are two concepts: the 'instructional system' and the 'learning milieu'.

The instructional system

Educational catalogues, prospectuses and reports characteristically contain a variety of formalised plans and statements which relate to particular teaching arrangements. Each of these summaries can be said to constitute or define an instructional system, and includes, say, a set of pedagogic assumptions, a new syllabus and details of techniques and equipment. This 'catalogue description' is an idealised specification of the scheme: a set of elements arranged to a coherent plan. Despite their immense variation, the Dalton Plan, performance contracting, programmed learning, the integrated day,

20   The term 'illuminative research' is drawn from M. A. Trow (1970). 'Methodological problems in the evaluation of innovation', in M. C. Wittrock & D. E. Wiley (eds.), *The Evaluation of Instruction*. New York: Holt, Rinehart & Winston, pp. 289-305. The approach to evaluation described here grew out of research at MIT in association with B. R. Snyder and M. J. Kahne. (See M. Parlett (1969). 'Undergraduate teaching observed', *Nature*, **223**, pp. 1102-4.)

21   For three published reports which approach the style advocated here see: J. P. Hanley *et al.* (1969). *Curiosity, Competence, Community.* Cambridge, Mass.: Educational Development Center Inc.; L. M. Smith & P. A. Pohland (1974). 'Education, technology and the rural highlands.' In Four Evaluation Examples: Anthropological, Economic, Narrative and Portrayal, AERA Monograph Series on Curriculum Evaluation, No. 7. Chicago: Rand McNally, pp. 5-54; M. Parlett & J. G. King (1971). *Concentrated Study.* Research in Higher Education Monograph No. 14. London: Society for Research in Higher Education.

22   M. A. Trow, *op. cit.* p. 302.

team teaching, *Sesame Street* and *Man: A Course of Study* can all be considered as instructional systems in these terms.

The traditional evaluator builds his study around innovations defined in this way. He examines the blueprint or formalised plan and extracts the programmes' goals, objectives or desired outcomes. From these, in turn, he derives the tests and attitude inventories he will administer. His aim is to evaluate the instructional system by examining whether, for example, it has 'attained its objectives' or met its 'performance criteria'.

This technological approach fails to recognise the catalogue description for what it is. It ignores the fact that an instructional system, when adopted, undergoes modifications that are rarely trivial. The instructional system may remain as a shared idea, abstract model, slogan or shorthand, but it assumes a different form in every situation. Its constituent elements are emphasised or de-emphasised, expanded or truncated, as teachers, administrators, technicians and students interpret and reinterpret the instructional system for their particular setting. In practice, objectives are commonly reordered, redefined, abandoned or forgotten. The original 'ideal' formulation ceases to be accurate, or indeed, of much relevance. Few in practice take catalogue descriptions and lists of objectives very seriously, save — it seems — for the traditional evaluator.

To switch from discussing the instructional system in abstract form to describing the details of its implementation is to cross into another realm. Here the second new concept is required.

The learning milieu

This is the social-psychological and material environment in which students and teachers work together. The learning milieu represents a network or nexus of cultural, social, institutional and psychological variables. These interact in complicated ways to produce, in each class or course, a unique pattern of circumstances, pressures, customs, opinions and work-styles which suffuse the teaching and learning that occur there. The configuration of the learning milieu, in any particular classroom, depends on the interplay of numerous different factors. For instance, there are numerous constraints (legal, administrative, occupational, architectural and financial) on the organisation of teaching in schools; there are pervasive operating assumptions (about the arrangement of subjects, curricula, teaching methods and student evaluation) held by faculty; there are the individual teacher's characteristics (teaching-style, experience, professional orientation and private goals); and there are student perspectives and preoccupations.

Acknowledging the diversity and complexity of learning milieux is an essential prerequisite for the serious study of educational programmes. The argument advanced here is that innovatory programmes, even for research purposes, cannot sensibly be separated from the learning milieux of which they become part. If an evaluation study hinges on the supposed perpetuation of the instructional system in more or less its original form, it makes an arbitrary and artificial distinction: it treats the innovation as a self-contained and independent system, which in practice it manifestly is not.

The introduction of an innovation sets off a chain of repercussions throughout the learning milieu. In turn these unintended consequences are likely to affect the innovation itself, changing its form and moderating its impact. For example, at the Massachusetts Institute of Technology it was found that switching from 'distributed' to 'concentrated' study (a change from students taking several subjects concurrently to intensive full-time study of a single subject) was, in the event, far more than a rescheduling arrangement.[23] It demanded new pedagogic forms (continuous lecturing would have led to 'overload'); it resulted in new role-relationships between faculty and students (daily contact encouraged a degree of informality impossible with two meetings a week of one hour each); and it changed peer relations between students (their working alongside the same students continously led to much greater interaction than is usual in MIT sophomore classes). Such profound shifts in the learning milieu produced a further range of important secondary effects, apparently far removed from the innovation as such, but ultimately deriving from it.

To attempt to gauge the impact of the innovation (in this instance 'concentrated study') without paying attention to factors such as these, would clearly be absurd. In the above study it was possible to trace how each of these milieu effects had its corollary in the intellectual sphere: e.g. the informality encouraged normally silent students to ask questions; and though the range of different learning activities was regarded as excellent for achieving basic comprehension of the subject-matter, it might have put the students at a disadvantage in a conventional exam.

Connecting changes in the learning milieu with intellectual experiences of students is one of the chief concerns for illuminative evaluation. Students do not confront 'knowledge' in naked form; it comes to them clothed in texts, lectures, tape-loops, etc. These form part of a wider set of arrangements for instructing, assessing and counselling which embody core assumptions about how knowledge and pedagogy should be organised. This 'management' framework, in turn, is embedded within wider departmental and institutional structures, each with its own set of procedures, and professional and societal allegiances. Though apparently far removed from the assimilation and schematisation of knowledge at the classroom level, these 'higher-order' aspects of the school or college environment cannot be ignored. To take an example: teaching and learning in a particular setting are profoundly influenced by the type of assessment procedures in use; by constraints of scheduling; by the size and

---

23 M. Parlett & J. G. King, *op. cit.*

diversity of classes; by the availability of teaching assistants, library, computing and copying facilities. These, in turn, are dependent on departmental priorities; on policies of faculty promotion; on institutional myths and traditions; and on local and national pressures.

The learning milieu concept is necessary for analysing the interdependence of learning and teaching, and for relating the organisation and practices of instruction with the immediate and long-term responses of students. For instance, students' intellectual development cannot be understood in isolation but only within a particular school or college milieu. Equally, there are phenomena of crucial educational significance (such as boredom, interest, concentration, 'floundering' and intellectual dependency) that make nonsense of the traditional psychological distinction between 'cognitive' and 'affective', and which customarily arise as responses to the total learning milieu, not to single components of it. Students do not respond merely to presented content and to tasks assigned. Rather, they adapt to and work within the learning milieu taken as an interrelated whole. They pay close attention to 'hidden'[24] as well as 'visible' curricula. Besides acquiring particular habits of studying, reading and responding, they also assimilate the conventions, beliefs and models of reality that are constantly and inevitably transmitted through the total teaching process.[25]

Organisation and methods of illuminative evaluation

Illuminative evaluations — like the innovations and learning milieux that they study — come in diverse forms. The size, aims and techniques of the evaluation depend on many factors: the sponsors' preoccupations; the exact nature and stage of the innovation; the number of institutions, teachers and students involved; the level of cooperation and the degree of access to relevant information; the extent of the investigator's previous experience; the time available for data collection; the format of the required report; and, not least, the size of the evaluation budget.

Illuminative evaluation is not a standard methodological package, but a general research strategy. It aims to be both adaptable and eclectic. The choice of research tactics follows not from research doctrine, but from decisions in each case as to the best available techniques: the problem defines the methods used, not *vice versa*. Equally, no method (with its own built-in limitations) is used exclusively or in isolation; different techniques are combined to throw light on a common problem. Besides viewing the

24 B. R. Snyder (1971). *The Hidden Curriculum*. New York: Knopf.
25 For studies that examine various aspects of this 'secondary' learning and its relationship to intellectual development and social context see H. S. Becker *et al.* (1968). *Making the Grade*. New York: Wiley & Sons; W. G. Perry (1968). *Forms of Intellectual and Ethical Development in the College Years*. New York: Holt, Rinehart & Winston; and M. F. D. Young, *op. cit.*

problem from a number of angles, this 'triangulation'[26] approach also facilitates the cross-checking of otherwise tentative findings.

At the outset, the researcher is concerned to familiarise himself thoroughly with the day-to-day reality of the setting or settings he is studying. In this he is similar to social anthropologists or to natural historians. Like them he makes no attempt to manipulate, control or eliminate situational variables, but takes as given the complex scene he encounters. His chief task is to unravel it; isolate its significant features; delineate cycles of cause and effect; and comprehend relationships between beliefs and practices and between organisational patterns and the responses of individuals. Since illuminative evaluation concentrates on examining the innovation as an integral part of the learning milieu, there is a definite emphasis both on observation at the classroom level and on interviewing participating instructors and students.

In illuminative evaluation there are three characteristic stages: investigators observe; inquire further; and then seek to explain. Thus, in our study of a pilot project in independent learning in British secondary schools[27] early visits to the participating schools yielded a number of common incidents, recurring trends and issues frequently raised in discussion. These we either observed ourselves, or heard about from teachers and pupils. For example, we noticed that teachers spoke in different ways about the independent learning materials provided for use with their classes. While some regarded the sets of materials as constituting, collectively, a course of study, others saw the same materials as having a supplementary or ancillary function; to be used simply as a collection of resources to draw upon as, when, or if necessary.

The second stage began with the selection of a number of such phenomena, occurrences or groups of opinions as a topic for more sustained and intensive inquiry. A change of emphasis accompanied this development. During the first, exploratory stage, we had become 'knowledgeable' about the scheme. At the second stage this enabled our questioning to be more focused, communication to be more coherent and relaxed, and, in general, observation and inquiry to be more directed, systematic and selective. (Thus—in our contacts with the teachers—we sought to find out more about the status they assigned to the independent learning materials, and the extent to which they integrated them with others.)

The third stage consisted in seeking general principles underlying the organisation of the programme; spotting patterns of cause and effect within its operation; and placing individual findings within a broader explanatory context. It began with our weighing alternative interpreta-

26   E. J. Webb *et al.* (1966). *Unobtrusive Measures: Nonreactive Research in the Social Sciences.* Chicago: Rand McNally.

27   The Nuffield Foundation Resources for Learning Project. The background to this is described in L. C. Taylor (*op. cit*).

tions in the light of information obtained. Thus, why did teachers differ in their attitudes towards the materials? It seemed, in general, that teachers' views depended on the availability of related materials in the school; on their previous experience with similar methods; and, most critically, on whether or not they saw the material as 'displacing' or as 'supporting' the teacher. A number of other lines of investigation led to the same central issue: that of the changed role of the teacher in an independent learning setting.

Obviously the three stages overlap and interrelate functionally. The transition from stage to stage, as the investigation unfolds, occurs as problem areas become progressively clarified and redefined. The course of the study cannot be charted in advance. Beginning with an extensive data base, the researchers systematically reduce the breadth of their inquiry to give more concentrated attention to the emerging issues. This 'progressive focusing' permits unique and unpredicted phenomena to be given due weight. It reduces the problem of data overload, and prevents the accumulation of a mass of unanalysed material.

Within this three-stage framework, an information profile is assembled using data collected from four areas: observation, interviews, questionnaires and tests, documentary and background sources.

Observation

As noted above, the observation phase occupies a central place in illuminative evaluation. The investigator builds up a continuous record of on-going events, transactions and informal remarks.[28] At the same time he seeks to organise this data at source, adding interpretative comments on both manifest and latent features of the situation. In addition to observing and documenting day-to-day activities of the programme, the investigator may also be present at a wide variety of other events (e.g. faculty and student meetings, open days, examiners' meetings, etc.).[29]

Much of the on-site observation involves recording discussions with and between participants. These provide additional information which might not otherwise be apparent or forthcoming from more formal interviews. The language conventions, slang, jargon and metaphors that characterise conversation within each learning milieu can reveal tacit assumptions, interpersonal relationships and status differentials.

Finally, there is a place for codified observation, using schedules for recording patterns of attendance, seating, utilisation of time and facilities, teacher-pupil interaction, etc.[30] The illuminative evaluator is cautious in

28 A useful source of participant observation research methods is G. J. McCall and J. L. Simmons (1969). *Issues in Participant Observation*. London: Addison-Wesley.

29 For a research study that draws extensively on non-official, 'back-of-the-shop' settings see L. M. Smith & P. M. Keith (1971). *Anatomy of Educational Innovation*. New York: John Wiley.

30 For a discussion of classroom 'observation systems' see G. A. Nuthall, (1970). 'A review of some selected recent studies of classroom interaction and teaching behavior'. In J. J. Gallagher *et al. Classroom Observation*, AERA Monograph Series on Curriculum Evaluation, No. 6. Chicago: Rand McNally, pp. 6-29.

the deployment of such techniques. In that they record only surface behaviour they do not facilitate the uncovering of underlying, more meaningful features.

Interviews

Discovering the views of participants is crucial to assessing the impact of an innovation.[31] Instructors and students are asked about their work, what they think of it, how it compares with their previous experience, and also to comment on the use and value of the innovation. Interviews vary as to the type of information or comment that is sought. While brief, structured interviews are convenient for obtaining biographical, historical or factual information, more open-ended and discursive forms are suitable for less straightforward topics (e.g. career ambitions and anxieties).

Though desirable, it is rarely possible to interview every participant, except in small innovatory programmes or with large research teams. Interviewees, therefore, must usually be selected randomly or by 'theoretical' sampling.[32] This latter mode requires seeking out informants or particular groups who have special insight or whose position makes their viewpoints noteworthy (e.g. students who have won prizes or failed altogether; marginal faculty members, who may have close knowledge of the innovation but have stayed outside it; young assistants teaching in their first semester, etc.). Those interviewed can also include more distant but equally relevant figures: e.g. at the college level, deans, administrators and student counsellors; and, beyond the college, curriculum developers and foundation officials from whom the innovation stemmed.

Questionnaire and test data

While concentrating on observation and interview, the illuminative evaluator does not eschew paper and pencil techniques. Their advantage in larger-scale illuminative studies is especially evident. Also survey-type questionnaires used late in a study can sustain or qualify earlier tentative findings. Free and fixed response formats can be included to obtain both quantitative summary data and also open-ended, and perhaps new and unexpected comment.[33]

There are, of course, several valid objections to questionnaires, particularly if they are used in isolation. Unless most carefully prepared,

---

31   Various approaches to interviewing can be found in the social sciences. Contrast the opposing perspectives presented by H. H. Hyman *et al.* (1954). *Interviewing in Social Research*. Chicago: University of Chicago Press; and A. V. Cicourel (1967). *Method and Measurement in Sociology*. New York: Free Press. In that it is more characteristic of the 'anthropological' paradigm, illuminative evaluation favours the latter approach.

32   B. Glaser and A. Strauss (1967). *The Discovery of Grounded Theory*. New York: Aldine.

33   If necessary, this qualitative data can be content analysed, to furnish further numerical results.

questionnaires can lead to mindless accumulations of uninterpretable data. Expensive in time and resources, such careful preparation must be weighed against the benefits likely to accrue. A second drawback is that many recipients regard questionnaires as impersonal and intrusive. Others, keen to express their complicated views, find the questionnaire a frustrating, indeed trivialising, medium. From these dissatisfied groups, some do not reply; yet these non-respondents may be the most important in certain respects.[34]

Besides completing questionnaires, participants can also be asked to prepare written comments on the programme; to go through checklists; or compile work diaries that record their activities over a specific period of time.[35]

Finally there are published or custom-built tests of attitude, personality and achievement. Such tests enjoy no privileged status within the study. Test scores cannot be considered in isolation;[36] they form merely one section of the data profile. Interest lies not so much in relating different test scores, but in accounting for them using the study's findings as a whole.

Documentary and background information

Innovations do not arise unheralded. They are preceded by committee minutes, funding proposals, architectural plans and consultants' reports. Also other primary sources are obtainable: e.g. non-confidential data from registrars' offices; autobiographical and eye-witness accounts of the innovation; tape recordings of meetings; and examples of students' assignments.

The assembly of such information can serve a useful function. It can provide an historical perspective of how the innovation was regarded by different people before the evaluation began. The data may also indicate areas for inquiry (e.g. how representative were the students taking part?); may point to topics for intensive discussion (e.g. why were certain major features of the original proposal later abandoned?); or may expose aspects of the innovation that would otherwise be missed (e.g. why were subject requirements not fulfilled?).[37]

34   In an unpublished questionnaire study at MIT, non-response was found to be the best predictor of student drop-out.

35   M. Parlett (1967). 'Classroom and beyond: a study of a sophomore physics section at MIT'. MIT: Education Research Center.

36   ' . . . Educators should continue to be apprehensive about evaluating teaching on the basis of performance testing alone. They should know how difficult it is to represent educational goals with statements of objectives. They should know how costly it is to provide suitable criterion testing. [And] They should know that the commonsense interpretation of these results is frequently wrong. . . .' R. E. Stake, *op. cit.*

37   These examples are drawn from an illuminative evaluation study of two innovative freshman programmes at MIT (The Unified Science Study Program, and the Experimental Study Group). Each offered a full-time alternative to the traditional first year programme. (M. Parlett (1972). 'A study of two experimental programs at MIT'. Report to the Committee on Educational Policy, MIT, Cambridge, Mass.

Problems and possibilities of illuminative evaluation

First encounters with the radically different perspective of illuminative evaluation prompt a number of important questions.

(a) Concern over the 'subjective' nature of the approach is usually foremost. Can 'personal interpretation' be scientific? Is not collection, analysis and reporting of data, sceptics ask, entirely at the discretion of the researchers themselves?

Behind such questions lies a basic but erroneous assumption: that forms of research exist which are immune to prejudice, experimenter bias and human error. This is not so. Any research study requires skilled human judgements and is thus vulnerable.[38] Even in evaluation studies that handle automatically processed numerical data, judgement is necessary at every stage: in the choice of samples; in the construction or selection of tests; in deciding conditions of administration; in selecting the mode of statistical treatment (e.g. whether or not to use factor analysis); in the relative weight given to different results; and, particularly, in the selection and presentation of findings in reports.

Nevertheless, the extensive use of open-ended techniques, progressive focusing and qualitative data in illuminative evaluation still raises the possibility of gross partiality on the part of the investigator. A number of precautionary tactics are possible. During the investigation different techniques can be used to cross-check the most important findings; open-ended material can be coded and checked by outside researchers; consultants to the evaluation can be charged with challenging preliminary interpretations and playing devil's advocate; and members of the research team can be commissioned to develop their own interpretations.[39] At the report stage, in addition to the findings, critical research processes can also be documented: theoretical principles and methodological ground rules can be discussed and made explicit; criteria for selecting or rejecting areas of investigation can be spelled out; and evidence can be presented in such a way that others can judge its quality.

Even with such precautions, the subjective element remains. It is inevitable. When the investigator abandons the agricultural-botany paradigm his role is necessarily redefined. The use of interpretative human insight and skills is, indeed, encouraged rather than discouraged. The illuminative evaluator thus joins a diverse group of specialists (e.g. psychiatrists, social anthropologists and historians), by whom this is taken for granted. In each of these fields the research worker has to weigh and sift a complex array of human evidence and draw conclusions from it.

38 For a general discussion of this problem area see R. Rosenthal (1966). *Experimenter Effects in Behavioral Research.* New York: Appleton-Century-Crofts.
39 The added possibility of research 'in tandem' with different investigators working in semi-isolation and pooling their findings at the end is currently being examined with respect to a proposed British evaluation involving the authors.

A further issue also focuses on the position of the investigator. Does not his presence have an effect on the conduct and progress of the innovatory scheme he is studying? Certainly it does; indeed, any form of data collection creates disturbance. Illuminative evaluators recognise this and attempt to be unobtrusive without being secretive; to be supportive without being collusive; and to be non-doctrinaire without appearing unsympathetic.

This leads to an important point: that research workers in this area need not only technical and intellectual capability, but also interpersonal skills. They seek cooperation but cannot demand it. There may be times when they encounter nervousness and even hostility. They are likely to be observing certain individuals at critical times in their lives (e.g. students about to leave, or instructors with a high personal investment in the innovation). The researchers need tact and a sense of responsibility similar to that pertaining in the medical profession. They seek and are given private opinions, often in confidence. They are likely to hear, in the course of their study, a great deal about personalities and institutional politics that others might be inquisitive to know. There are especially difficult decisions to make at the report stage: though full reporting is necessary, it is essential to safeguard the individual's privacy.

Such problems, confronting many research workers in the human sciences, are exacerbated in the case of close-up, intensive studies of the type outlined here. The price of achieving the richer, more informative data of illuminative evaluation is the greatly increased attention that must be paid to the evaluator's professional standards and behaviour. Though there can be no fixed rules, there are certain guidelines for the illuminative evaluator. For instance, to retain the viability and integrity of his research position and the trust of the participants in the programme, the investigator needs, from the outset, to clarify his role; to be open about the aims of his study; and to ensure that there is no misunderstanding or ambiguity about who, for example, will receive the report.[40]

(b) Besides concern with the investigator's special position, illuminative evaluation also prompts questions concerning the scope of the investigation. Is illuminative evaluation confined to small-scale innovations? Can it be applied to innovations that are being widely implemented? Detailed studies of specific learning milieux may be insightful and valid, but are the results and analyses generalisable to other situations? Is it possible to move from the particular to the universal?

Despite its basis in the close-up study of individual learning milieux, illuminative evaluation can also be applied on a wider scale. Suppose an

---

40 He must also not be a 'snooper' nor become an 'institutionalised voyeur' in succumbing to his private research interests. He should also avoid the dangers of 'going native' or getting caught up in political intrigues. For an early but still relevant discussion of these problems, see various papers in R. N. Adams & J. J. Preiss (eds.) (1960). *Human Organization Research*. Homewood, Illinois: Dorsey Press.

innovatory programme had been adopted by many different schools. At the beginning of the evaluation a small sample of schools could be selected for intensive study. As the study progressed, and as it focused on selected salient issues arising in the different learning milieux, the number of schools studied could be expanded. The new investigations, now more selective, could be pursued more speedily, with concentration more on noting similarities and differences between situations, than on full documentation of each learning milieu.[41] Finally, with this further information assimilated, short visits, or even—in the last resort—mailed questionnaires could be used for the remainder of the institutions.

The full progression from small sample studies to larger scale inquiries is often necessary only in widely applied programmes. But there is another way in which perceptive and rigorous study of specific situations can yield more generally applicable insights with either large or small-scale investigations. Learning milieux, despite their diversity, share many characteristics. Instruction is constrained by similar conventions, subject divisions and degrees of student involvement. Teachers encounter parallel sets of problems. Students' learning, participation, study habits and examination techniques are found to follow common lines; and innovations, as such, face habitual difficulties and provoke familiar reactions. There is a wide range of overlapping social and behavioural phenomena that accompany teaching, learning and innovating. This is widely acknowledged. However, few of these phenomena have been pinpointed, adequately described or defined accurately. Illuminative evaluation aims to contribute to this process. There is a need for abstracted summaries, for shared terminology and for insightful concepts. These can serve as aids to communication and facilitate theory-building. They have been conspicuously absent from most research in education. Yet, without this conceptual equipment, the universals of teaching will be cyclically discovered, described, forgotten, rediscovered and described again.

Decision-making, evaluation and illumination

The principal purpose of evaluation studies is to contribute to decision-making.[42] There are at least three separate but related groups of decision-makers to whom the evaluator addresses his report: (i) the programme's participants; (ii) the programme's sponsors, supervisory committee or educational board; (iii) interested outsiders (such as other researchers, curriculum planners, etc.).

41 At the same time it is necessary to remain extremely flexible and to be open to new issues that arise in the later stages of a study.

42 In practice, motives for commissioning evaluations are often mixed. Some 'evaluations' may be used to delay troublesome decisions or to window-dress a policy already formulated. Exceptionally they may be instigated simply to satisfy a funding agency's demands.

Each group or constituency will look to the report for help in making different decisions. The participants, for example, will be anxious to correct deficiencies, make improvements and establish future priorities. The sponsors and board members will be concerned with pedagogic issues but will also want to know about the innovation's costs, use of resources and outside reputation. The outsiders will read the report to decide whether or not the scheme has 'worked', or to see whether it could be applied or adapted to their own situations.

Clearly, if the evaluator is to acknowledge the interests of all these groups, he cannot, even if requested, provide a simple 'yes' or 'no' on the innovation's future. A decision based on one group's evaluative criteria would, almost certainly, be disputed by other groups with different priorities. A 'mastery of fundamentals' for one group is for another a 'stifling of creativity'. The investigator does not make decisions. Indeed, in these terms he cannot — except as a representative or agent of one of the interest groups.[43]

Illuminative evaluation thus concentrates on the information-gathering rather than the decision-making component of evaluation. The task is to provide a comprehensive understanding of the complex reality (or realities) surrounding the programme: in short to 'illuminate'. In his report, therefore, the evaluator aims to sharpen discussion, disentangle complexities, isolate the significant from the trivial and to raise the level of sophistication of debate.

Summary

When an innovation ceases to be an abstract concept or plan, and becomes part of the teaching and learning in a school or college, it assumes a different form altogether. The theatre provides an analogy: to know whether a play 'works' one has to look not only at the manuscript but also at the performance; that is, at the interpretation of the play by the director and actors. It is this that is registered by the audience and appraised by the critics. Similarly, it is not an instructional system as such but its translation and enactment by teachers and students, that is of concern to the evaluator and other interested parties. There is no play that is 'director-proof'. Equally, there is no innovation that is 'teacher-proof' or 'student-proof'.

If this is acknowledged, it becomes imperative to study an innovation through the medium of its performance and to adopt a research style and methodology that is appropriate.

This involves the investigator leaving his office and computer print-out to spend substantial periods in the field. The crucial figures in the working

43 If the evaluator allows his study to be defined in this way — orientated towards one constituency only — he accepts the more limited role and quite different tasks of the 'service' researcher.

of an innovation — learners and teachers — become his chief preoccupation. The evaluator concentrates on 'process' within the learning milieu, rather than on 'outcomes' derived from a specification of the instructional system.[44] Observation, linked with discussion and background inquiry, enable him to develop an informed account of the innovation in operation.

Ideally, the output of his research will be regarded as useful, intelligible and revealing by those involved in the enterprise itself. Further, by addressing key educational issues it can also be seen as a recognisable reality by others outside the innovation. If the report is seen merely as an arcane or irrelevant addition to a research literature already ignored by practising educators, clearly the evaluator will have failed.

In attempting to document the teacher-student interactions, intellectual habits, institutional constraints etc., that characterise classroom life, the investigator contributes to a field that has received only minimal attention from social scientists.[45] Until recently, perceptive accounts of learning milieux have, more often than not, been found in 'travellers' tales'[46] or 'non-fiction' novels[47] rather than in educational research reports. The investigator has, therefore, not only short-term goals, but also the long-term goal of contributing to a developing and urgently-required new field of study.

This approach does not cure all ills: no single approach could. Certainly, no simplified instant solutions to perennial educational questions will be delivered by such studies. Indeed, by discarding a spurious 'technological' simplification of reality, and by acknowledging the complexity of educational process, the illuminative evaluator is likely to increase rather than lessen the sense of uncertainty in education. On the other hand, unless studies such as these are vigorously pursued there is little hope of ever moving beyond helpless indecision or doctrinaire assertion in the conduct of instructional affairs.

44   An agricultural-botany evaluator is rather like a critic who reviews a production on the basis of the script and applause-meter readings, having missed the performance.

45   This paper has focused on the evaluation of innovatory programmes. There is an obvious need (not always acknowledged) for comparable studies to be made of traditional teaching. Illuminative evaluation need not be confined to innovation.

46   E.g., J. Holt (1964). *How Children Fail*. New York: Dell.

47   E.g., J. Herndon (1965). *The Way It Spozed to Be*. New York: Simon & Schuster.

Section 2
The objectives model revisited

Introduction

Ah, Love! could thou and I with Fate conspire
To grasp this sorry Scheme of Things entire,
Would we not shatter it to bits and then
Re-mould it nearer to the Heart's Desire.[1]

Evaluation entails a view of society. People differ about evaluation because they differ about what society is, what it can be and what it ought to be. Much of the debate about evaluation is ideology disguised as technology. This section of the book introduces the reader to one very powerful model of evaluation which provided the first and most enduring set of procedures in what is now regarded as a specialist field. To treat this model as an abstraction divorced from its cultural bedding would be to deny the reader a perspective which merits consideration.

There are many possible ways of seeking improvement in the quality and effectiveness of what goes on in schools. The most widely advocated proposes the following sequence of steps:

1   Secure agreement on the aims of the curriculum.

2   Express these aims as explicit learner behaviours or objectives.

3   Devise and provide experiences that seem likely to enable the learners to behave in the desired way.

4   Assess the congruence of pupil performance and objectives.

5   Vary the 'treatment' until behaviour matches objectives.

This process of systematic curriculum development is widely known as the 'objectives model', and the evaluation activity encompassed within it is known more variously as the 'traditional', 'classical', 'output' or 'orthodox' approach. This section provides an indication of its development over forty years since Ralph Tyler launched the prototype in the early 1930s. The model is significant for two reasons. The first is its immense influence on the curriculum reform movement, particularly in the United States of America. In the 1960s, with the influx of massive Federal finance for curriculum improvement, the objectives model came into its own. Federal policy-makers demanded of educational innovators that they both prespecified the intended performance gains and provided proof of 'pay-off'. The task of the evaluation in this 'performance contracting' was clearly defined as that of assessing the extent to which the pupils exposed

1   From *The Rubaiyat of Omar Khayyam* (Fitzgerald translation), The Riverside Press, Edinburgh, p. 89. First published in the United Kingdom in 1859.

25

to a new curriculum achieved its intended learning outcomes. Despite mounting criticisms of its engineering-type assumptions, the model has become influential in the planning of curriculum reform in this country, as the paper by Wiseman and Pidgeon, two of the doyens of British educational research, testifies.

The second reason is that all subsequent approaches to curriculum evaluation have either evolved or recoiled from Tyler's proposals. Two of the papers in this and the previous section were chosen because they exemplify such developments. Although it is doubtful whether the humanist Tyler would acknowledge either his paternity of Glaser's psycho-technology or his distance from Parlett and Hamilton, it is clear that they would have had to invent him if he had not existed.

The choice of Ralph Tyler to open the innings may seem arbitrary and perhaps even irritating to British readers who might prefer to see a line of development from the Revised Code of 1862, through Spencer, Galton and the measurement movement of the first half of the twentieth century. The recent harnessing of the objectives model to a political demand for educational accountability has directed attention to the precedent of 'payment by results' in Victorian England. The line of argument has elegance and plausibility, but no real force. The analogy between 'payment by results' and the objectives model of curriculum evaluation is superficial, ignoring as it does the true character of the Tylerian conception, and its relationship to the cultural tradition that nourished it. Let us turn briefly and speculatively to that, in the hope of illuminating the popularity of this approach in the United States and the difficulties and qualifications that have beset its attempted adoption in the United Kingdom.

An American dream

The inclination of some North Americans to perceive curriculum development as a technological problem of product specification and manufacture, is by itself unremarkable. Mechanistic analogies have a peculiar appeal for a people who see themselves as the raw materials of a vision which can be socially engineered. Their mainstream culture is essentially forward-looking, constructionist, optimistic and rational. Both the vision and the optimism are reflected in the assumption that goal-consensus in education, a prerequisite of social engineering, is a matter of clarification rather than reconciliation.

In contrast British culture in this respect is largely backward-looking, conservationist, complacent and distrustful of rationality. Pragmatic gardeners rather than scientific agronomists, we are not forging in our schools the new Briton, but rather providing discriminating transmission of a culture that has stood the test of time and will continue to do so, provided due attention is paid to points of adaptive growth. Goal-

consensus is neither ardently desired, nor determinedly pursued. Such pursuit would entail a confrontation of value-systems which have so far been contained within an all-embracing rhetoric of insubstantial slogans.

The theory and practice of 'traditional' evaluation is thus wedded to an American view of society, and an American faith in technology. Avowedly pluralist societies will find it difficult to use. Avowedly unified societies will use it, and find they are pluralist.

The reader may find these thumbnail analyses tendentious and inaccurate, and he may be right. But if he finds the perspective irrelevant, then this introduction will have failed in its purpose. Curriculum is a value-loaded area of cultural activity. It is something of an irony that its evaluators are commonly assumed to be value-free.

Behavioural objectives

In the literature of curriculum development and evaluation there has been no more powerful or pervasive idea than the 'behavioural objective'. It is the dominant concept in the field, and is the central construct of the model that Ralph Tyler devised and popularised. None of the subsequent development work centred on the model, such as Bloom (1956), Gagné (1967), Krathwohl, Bloom, Masia (1964), Mager (1962), Glaser (1963)[2] challenged its structure or its assumptions.

The classical exposition of the Tylerian paradigm remains Tyler's own monograph which he published in 1949, entitled Basic Principles of Curriculum and Instruction. *In this publication Tyler argued that the purposes of schooling could be stated as behavioural objectives and thus systematically pursued. The behavioural objective is defined as follows:*

One can define an objective with sufficient clarity if he can describe or illustrate the kind of behaviour the student is expected to acquire so that one could recognise such behaviour if he saw it. (pp. 59-60).

In the early chapters of the monograph Tyler considers the operations involved in choosing and formulating educational objectives and in selecting and organising learning experiences. He then goes on to consider the role and procedures of evaluation as the means of establishing intention attainment. It is this part of the monograph that is reproduced as the opening paper in this section.

2   B. Bloom (ed.) (1956). *Taxonomy of Educational Objectives, Handbook I: Cognitive Domain.* New York: Longmans, Green; R. Gagné (1967). 'Curriculum research and the promotion of learning'. In R. E. Stake (ed.), *Perspectives of Curriculum Evaluation.* AERA Monograph Series on Curriculum Evaluation, No. 1. Chicago: Rand McNally, pp. 19-38; D. Krathwohl, B. Bloom and B. Masia (1964). *Taxonomy of Educational Objectives, Handbook II: Affective Domain.* New York: David McKay; R. F. Mager (1962). *Preparing Objectives for Programmed Instruction.* San Francisco: Fearon; R. Glaser (1963). 'Instruction technology and the measurement of learning outcomes: some questions'. *American Psychologist,* **18**, pp. 519-21.

The approach to evaluation described here was first employed by Tyler and his associates on the staff of the Commission on the Relation of School and College (the famous eight-year study). During the following thirty years the influence of Tyler's ideas spread throughout the United States and it is still extensive. He is currently engaged in the National Assessment of Educational Progress, an objectives-based assessment programme supported by the United States Office of Education. This is the operationalisation of Tyler's plan for a data base for national educational policy-setting. It proceeds from the careful identification of subject-matter objectives to criterion-referenced testing based on critical task levels.

2.1 Ralph Tyler
Evaluating learning experiences

Basic notions regarding evaluation

The process of evaluation is essentially the process of determining to what extent the educational objectives are actually being realised by the programme of curriculum and instruction. However, since educational objectives are essentially changes in human beings, that is, the objectives aimed at are to produce certain desirable changes in the behaviour patterns of the student, then evaluation is the process for determining the degree to which these changes in behaviour are actually taking place.

This conception of evaluation has two important aspects. In the first place, it implies that evaluation must appraise the behaviour of students, since it is change in these behaviours which is sought in education. In the second place, it implies that evaluation must involve more than a single appraisal at any one time since to see whether change has taken place, it is necessary to make an appraisal at an early point and other appraisals at later points to identify changes that may be occurring. . . .

. . . it is not enough to have only two appraisals in making an educational evaluation, because some of the objectives aimed at may be acquired during an educational programme and then be rapidly dissipated or forgotten. In order to have some estimate of the permanence of the learning, it is necessary to have still another point of evaluation which is made sometime after the instruction has been completed. . . . In fact, so far as frequency of evaluation is concerned, much can be said for at least an annual appraisal carried on year after year as the children move through the school so that a continuing record of progress can be obtained and evidence accumulated to indicate whether desirable objectives are being realised and to indicate places where these changes are not actually taking place.

Since evaluation involves getting evidence about behaviour changes in the students, any valid evidence about behaviours that are desired as educational objectives provides an appropriate method of evaluation. This is important to recognise because many people think of evaluation as synonymous with the giving of paper and pencil tests. It is true that paper and pencil tests provide a practicable procedure for getting evidences

Source: R. W. Tyler (1949). 'Basic Principles of Curriculum and Instruction'. Chicago: University of Chicago Press, pp. 105-8, 111-13, 115-18, 120-21, 122.

about several kinds of student behaviour. For example, if one wishes to find out what knowledge students have, it may be easily gotten from paper and pencil tests if the students are able to express their ideas in writing, or can read and check off various items in a multiple response test or other similar tests. As another illustration, paper and pencil tests are useful devices to get at the ability of students to analyse and deal effectively with various types of verbal problems, with vocabulary, with reading, and a number of other types of skills and abilities easily expressed in verbal form. However, there are a great many other kinds of desired behaviours which represent educational objectives that are not easily appraised by paper and pencil devices. For example, such an objective as personal-social adjustment is more easily and validly appraised through observations of children under conditions in which social relations are involved. Observations are also useful devices to get at habits and certain kinds of operational skills. Another method which is useful in evaluation is the interview which may throw light upon changes taking place in attitudes, in interests, in appreciations and the like. Questionnaires sometimes serve to give evidence about interests, about attitudes and about other types of behaviour. The collection of actual products made by students is sometimes a useful way of getting evidence of behaviour. For example, the collection of themes students have written may serve to give some evidence of the writing ability of students, or the paintings students have made in an art class may serve to give evidence of skill and possibly interests in this area. Objects made in the shop or in the clothing construction course are additional illustrations of the collection of samples of products as an evaluation device. Even records made for other purposes sometimes provide evidence of types of behaviour or interest in terms of educational objectives. For example, books withdrawn from the library may provide some indication of reading interests. Menus checked in the cafeteria may provide some evidence of the eating habits of students. Health records may throw some light on health practices. These are all illustrations of the fact that there are many ways of getting evidence about behaviour changes and that when we think of evaluation we are not talking about any single or even any two or three particular appraisal methods. Any way of getting valid evidence about the kinds of behaviour represented by the educational object-ives of the school or college is an appropriate evaluation procedure. . . .

Evaluation procedures

The process of evaluation begins with the objectives of the educational programme. Since the purpose is to see how far these objectives are actually being realised, it is necessary to have evaluation procedures that will give evidence about each of the kinds of behaviour implied by each of the major educational objectives. If, for example, one of the objectives is to acquire important knowledge about contemporary social problems, then it is necessary that the evaluation give some evidence of the knowledge students are acquiring. If another is to develop methods of analysing social problems and appraising proposed solutions of them, then it is necessary that the evaluation procedures give us some evidence as to the skill of the student in analysing social problems and appraising suggested solutions to them. This means that the two-dimensional analysis which served as a basis for planning the learning experiences also serves as the basis for planning the evaluation procedures. The two-dimensional analysis of objectives thus serves as a set of specifications for evaluation. Each of the behavioural headings in the analysis indicates the kind of behaviour which should be appraised to see how far that kind of behaviour is developing; and each of the content headings of the analysis indicates the content to be sampled in connection with the behaviour appraisal. Thus, in the case of the objectives regarding knowledge about social problems, the two-dimensional analysis indicates that evaluation of knowledge must be made for the behaviour, and the content headings indicate what areas of knowledge should be sampled in order to have a satisfactory appraisal of the knowledge being acquired by the students in this field. Correspondingly, an objective, 'Developing Interests in Literature', would require an appraisal of developing interests in students for the behaviour aspect, and the content headings would indicate the areas in which interests might be expected to be developed and which should be sampled in order to see whether such interests are actually being developed. In this way a two-dimensional analysis of objectives becomes a guide to the evaluation of the curriculum.

It is, of course, assumed that these 'behavioural objectives' have been clearly defined by the curriculum worker. They should have been defined clearly so as to provide a concrete guide in the selection and planning of learning experiences. If they have not yet been clearly defined, it is absolutely essential that they be defined in order to make an evaluation since unless there is some clear conception of the sort of behaviour implied by the objectives, one has no way telling what kind of behaviour to look for in the students in order to see to what degree these objectives are being realised. This means that the process of evaluation may force persons who have not previously clarified their objectives to a further process of clarification. Definition of objectives, then, is an important step in evaluation.

The next step in evaluation procedure is to identify the situations which will give the student the chance to express the behaviour that is implied by the educational objectives. The only way that we can tell whether students have acquired given types of behaviour is to give them an opportunity to show this behaviour. This means that we must find situations which not only permit the expression of the behaviour but actually encourage or evoke this behaviour. We are then in a position to observe the degree to which the objectives are actually being realised. In some cases, it is easy to see the kinds of situations that give students the chance to express desired types of behaviour. We are accustomed to stimulating students to express ideas through questions and it is therefore possible in the question situation to evoke reactions of the students that involve knowledge and ability to deal with verbal materials. When we consider the whole range of desired objectives, we can see that the situations are not all of this type. If we are going to see how children are developing personal-social adjustment, we must use those situations which give children a chance to react to other children. This may mean looking for evidence about personal-social adjustment in the nursery school during those periods when children are playing and working together. It may mean that we shall look for evidences of interests in those situations where there is opportunity for free choice of activity. Students may, therefore, freely express their interests. If we want evidence of the student's ability to express himself orally, we must look in those situations which evoke oral expression. The principle is simple enough, that any evaluation situation is the kind of situation that gives an opportunity for the students to express the type of behaviour we are trying to appraise. Although the principle is simple, there are still many problems involved in finding situations that are sufficiently under control and permit the teacher or other evaluator to have access to them in order to see the types of behaviours the students are developing. In case some situations are difficult to handle, then one of the tasks of the specialist in evaluation is to try to find other simpler situations that will have a high correlation with the result obtained when the situation is used which directly evokes the kind of behaviour to be appraised. . . .

After deciding on certain situations used to get evidence about the behaviour of students, it is then necessary to devise a means of getting a record of the student's behaviour in this test situation. In the case of a written examination the student makes his own record in his writing. Hence, the problem of getting a record of his behaviour is not a serious one. On the other hand, a situation that gives nursery school children a chance to play and work together may be a good situation to provide evidence of personal-social adjustment but it is necessary to get some record of the children's reaction in this situation if there is to be opportunity to appraise this reaction after it has been made. This may involve making a detailed description of reaction by an observer, it may suggest the use of a motion picture or sound recording, it may suggest the use of an observer's check list by which he checks off particular types of behaviour that commonly appear or it may involve some other means of getting a satisfactory record of the children's reaction. This is a step that must be considered in connection with each test situation to be sure that the situation not only evokes the desired behaviour but that a record can be obtained which can be appraised later.

The next step in developing an evaluation instrument is to decide upon the terms or units that will be used to summarise or to appraise the record of behaviour obtained. This method of appraising the behaviour should, of course, parallel the implications of the objective itself. For example, if reading interests as an educational objective are to be defined as the development of increasingly broad and mature interests, it then becomes necessary to decide upon units by which a record of children's reading can be summarised to indicate breadth and to indicate maturity. Breadth may be indicated by a number which measures the different categories of reading material included in the youngster's reading for the year. . . . Correspondingly, if different reading levels can be classified under different levels of maturity, it becomes possible to summarise a reading record in terms of its average level of maturity and thus to provide a measure of that aspect of reading interest. This illustration has been chosen because it is very different from the problem as it is usually viewed by the person who reads and scores the test; and, yet, essentially all evaluation involves this problem, that is, the decision upon the characteristics that are to be appraised in the behaviour and the unit to be used in the measurement or summarisation of these characteristics. In the case of reading interests, the characteristics used were range and maturity so that the methods of summarisation provided a rating for range and maturity.

The problem is a similar one in summarising a typical objective type test. Suppose it is a measure of knowledge. The question then to be faced is: Will knowledge be summarised in terms of the number of different items in the sample which the student was able to remember properly, or is it better indicated by some classification of the items so as to indicate which topics he remembers best and which less well, or is there some other way by which the objective of knowledge can be most satisfactorily summarised or appraised in order to serve the purpose of evaluation? Every kind of human behaviour which is appraised for its part as an educational objective must be summarised or measured in some terms and the decision about these terms is an important problem in the development and use of evaluation instruments. . . .

The next step in the construction of an evaluation instrument is to determine how far these rating or summarising methods are objective, that is, to what degree two different persons, presumably competent, would be able to reach similar scores or summaries when they had an opportunity to score or summarise the same records of behaviour. If the scores or summaries vary markedly, depending upon who does the scoring or summarising, it is clearly a subjective kind of appraisal and requires improvement in its objectivity in order to be a more satisfactory means of appraising a human behaviour. . . .

Using the results of evaluation

Since every educational programme involves several objectives and since for almost every objective there will be several scores or descriptive terms used to summarise the behaviour of students in relation to this objective, it follows that the results obtained from evaluation instruments will not be a single score or a single descriptive term but an analysed profile or a comprehensive set of descriptive terms indicating the present student achievement. These scores or descriptive terms should, of course, be comparable to those used at a preceding date so that it is possible to indicate change taking place and one can then see whether or not educational progress is actually happening. . . .

It is not only desirable to analyse the results of an evaluation to indicate the various strengths and weaknesses, but it is also necessary to examine these data to suggest possible explanations or hypotheses about the reason for this particular pattern of strengths and weaknesses. . . .

When hypotheses have been suggested that might possibly explain the evaluation data, the next step is to check those hypotheses against the present available data, that is, against additional data that may be available, and to see whether the hypotheses are consistent with all the data then available. If they appear to be consistent with the available data, the next step is to modify the curriculum in the direction implied by the hypotheses and then to teach the material to see whether there is any actual improvement in student achievement when these modifications are made. . . .

The made-to-measure curriculum

Our second paper was published twenty-one years later. Glaser's 'Evaluation of instruction and changing educational models' is both a reiteration of Tyler's philosophy and a detailed treatment of the technological problems involved in its operationalisation. By the time this article appeared, two important aspects of the process had been fairly thoroughly reexamined. Firstly, the business of formulating objectives had been investigated by Bloom and his colleagues who, over a period of ten years, identified three domains of educational objectives — the cognitive, affective and psycho-motor, and produced for the first two of these exhaustive taxonomic classifications. Secondly, the appropriateness of norm-referenced testing to the evaluation of new curricula was challenged and a new orientation for educational measurers, towards the production of criterion-referenced tests, was pioneered by Glaser himself (1963).

Robert Glaser is the Director of the University of Pittsburgh's Learning Research and Development Centre, where Individually Prescribed Instruction (IPI), described by Oettinger as 'an experiment in reaching measurable universal goals through mass-produced processes with tailored application', was born. The Oakleaf Project, as it is known, is an effort to operationalise the model of instruction and evaluation which Glaser describes in his paper. In a large number of Pittsburgh high schools pupil progress in achieving programme objectives is individually tracked and monitored daily by teams of clerks in data-processing rooms, who receive information from teachers and teacher assistants, process it and return it to the classroom. The pupil passes from one curriculum unit to the next upon reaching a post-test mastery criterion of 85 per cent. The logistics of the operation are hair-raising, but susceptible to automation, which is now being considered. Although critics point to the Project's failure to take into account any factor in individual differences other than rate of learning, its restriction of recognised accomplishment to what is measurable, and its arbitrary assumption that an 85 per cent level of mastery is appropriate to all students and all subject matter, IPI claims that many students are performing two to four grade levels above the norms for their age. More than one thousand American school districts are now associated with this experiment. Although Tyler was not basically concerned with the individualisation of instruction, his work on the eight-year study became a major source of guidance for those, like Glaser, whose interests centred upon that aspiration. There is a poignant irony in the apparent continuity between Tyler and Glaser which should not be missed. When Tyler

35

evolved his model of evaluation in the 1930s, he was in part reacting against the tendency of the educational psychometrists of his day to concentrate narrowly on the assessment of very limited learning objectives. He wanted to acknowledge and assess a broader range of school purposes and outcomes. Glaser, on the other hand, insofar as he seems prepared to buy certainty at the expense of completeness, seems to be using Tyler's instrument to subvert his aspiration.

Glaser's thinking represents the intersection between a number of movements whose interrelationships had been somewhat obscure. His paper is an attempt to mesh the testing movement and curriculum development movement with programmed learning and individual instruction. Glaser's analysis and proposals constitute an excellent example of psycho-technology applied to the school. The mechanistic character of what is basically an engineering paradigm becomes clear. Tyler perceived schooling as a human act ruled by human judgement and necessarily susceptible to human frailty. Glaser is much closer to those who see in systems analysis and control the possibility of eliminating human error from the educational process.

2.2   Robert Glaser
Evaluation of instruction and changing educational models[1]

Social institutions, whether educational, medical, religious, economic or political, must constantly prove their effectiveness to ensure society's support. Acceptable proof of an institution's effectiveness depends largely upon the public attitude toward that institution, an attitude based both upon a respect for authority and tradition and a desire for demonstrated objective proof[2]. To some extent, the field of educational measurement and evaluation has developed in response to the requirement for objective proof of the effectiveness of the educational enterprise. Furthermore, the demand for evaluation is related to the growing alliance between educational practice and behavioural science and to the pressures that arise from the necessity to make competing social investments. These increasing pressures upon educators, in all parts of the field, to evaluate their activities are one aspect of a growing maturity of the profession and of the commitment of modern society to the belief that its educational problems can be met most effectively through development planned in conjunction with advancing knowledge. However, the main point I wish to make is that the form which evaluation procedures take is influenced by changes and advances in a given field.

It is reasonable for evaluation practices and procedures to change as the nature of education changes. This is not to imply that educational innovation can completely ignore current standards and procedures of evaluation — a concept that could lead to chaos — but change in educational practice should influence the need for evaluation and the form it takes. Suchman has pointed out that in the field of public health, evaluation techniques require change as the nature of disease changes. His discussion is pertinent to the theme of this paper. In recent years, acute communicable diseases have been displaced as major causes of death and disability by chronic degenerative diseases. The new diseases are not amenable to the traditional proven methods of environmental sanitation and immunisation. The degenerative disease programmes, unlike communicable disease programmes, cannot depend on either legislative fiat or mass immunisation drives but require a greater degree of voluntary public

1   Preparation of this chapter was supported under Contract No. Ponr-624(18) with the Personnel and Training Branch, Psychological Sciences Division, Office of Naval Research.

2   E. A. Suchman (1967). 'Principles and practice of evaluative research'. In J. T. Doby (ed.), *An Introduction to Social Research*. New York: Appleton-Century-Crofts, pp. 327-51.

Source: R. Glaser (1970). 'Evaluation of instruction and changing educational models'. In M. C. Wittrock and D. E. Wiley(eds), The Evaluation of Instruction Issues and Problems. New York: Holt, Rinehart and Winston, pp. 70-86.

co-operation and long-term programmes of prevention and treatment. Evaluation of the control of the new major diseases requires new objectives and the development of new criteria of effectiveness. A heart disease control programme, for example, in contrast to a smallpox or diphtheria control programme, cannot be evaluated solely in terms of decreasing mortality. Early detection and treatment become new objectives, replacing prevention; accomplishment is evaluated and measured in terms of such immediate goals as case finding and the continuity of medical care.

The objectives and evaluation practices of a field are influenced not only by changes in the nature of the field itself but also by changes in the organisation and operation of the field. For example, in public health, there is a trend toward broader responsibility for community health; and the dividing line between prevention and treatment is less distinct. Earlier public health services that concentrated on the poor and medically indigent now begin to encompass much larger segments of society. This broad emphasis enlarges the scope of a programme's planning, implementation and evaluation.

As the nature and organisation of the field change, so do the attitudes and behaviours of the public, who are both targets of the social enterprise and ultimate determiners of its support. In the early days of the public health movement, the need for environmental sanitation and compulsory immunisation did not require proof because the threats from disastrous epidemics were obvious. The feedback and consequences were relatively immediate. Today, the delayed effects of smoking or diet are much less immediate, and evaluation procedures require greater information and proof of the effectiveness of their measures. Today, motivation is a key problem in public health, and one of the primary conditions of motivation is the individual's belief in the effectiveness of the action he is being asked to undertake.

The field of public health provides an apt analogy to the situation that seems to be coming about in educational practice. Consider the three aspects mentioned above: the nature of the field, its organisation and expectations from its user and target groups. Several forces are changing the nature of educational practice, and of these I shall mention three. One is the increased focus on the cultivation of skill, understanding, and intellectual power in the basic disciplines. Witness the introduction of the massive curriculum development programmes in physics, mathematics, English, history and so forth. A second force is the growing conception that education does not have a fixed beginning or end point with neat packages of elementary, secondary and higher education. The stress is less upon third-grade arithmetic or freshman English and more upon the continuity from grade to grade and from age to age and upon a commitment to a transmission of the ability to teach people to teach themselves. The third force is that as we learn more about the psychological and technological foundations of education, the individualisation of instruction is being viewed less as an ideal and more as a practical enterprise.

Concurrent with the change in the nature of educational activities is the change in the structure, organisation and functioning of these activities and the agencies involved. The trend is toward larger schools, more pervasive educational philosophies and the integration of social classes in one educational environment. This larger organisation and integration de-emphasises local norms and introduces more widely accepted standards of accomplishment and competence. Coupled with this is the necessity for taking account of the increasing heterogeneity of a school by adapting to individual requirements. Another organisational factor that profoundly changes the nature of educational practice is the continued development of the educational profession and the accruing knowledge in the behavioural sciences.

There is a growing similarity between the public health field and education. Whereas the older diseases had immediately contingent effects that shaped the behaviour of the public, the consequences of the newer diseases are more delayed. Perhaps the educational field generally produces effects that have not had immediate consequences mandating immediate action. In this regard, evaluation procedures might provide more immediate feedback of educational outcomes.

A general instructional model

Since the nature of educational practice and its organisation influences evaluation procedures, it is necessary to present a model of educational practice that can be assumed to underlie any general discussion of the evaluation of instruction. The model I shall describe is one that I believe is likely to come about as a result of the trends I have indicated – the emphasis on cognitive development in the disciplines, the continuity of education over the span of life, the ability to know how to learn and to teach oneself and the adaptation of instruction to individual requirements. The accomplishment of these objectives suggests an instructional model with the following properties presented as a sequence of operations:

1   Outcomes of learning are specified in terms of the behavioural manifestations of competence and the conditions under which it is to be exercised. This is the platitudinous assertion of the fundamental necessity of describing the foreseeable outcomes of instruction in terms of certain measurable products and assessable student performance.

2   Detailed diagnosis is made of the initial state of a learner coming into a particular instructional situation. This careful workup of student performance characteristics relevant to the instruction at hand is necessary to pursue further education. Without the assessment of initial learner characteristics, carrying out an educational procedure is a presumption. It

is like prescribing medication for an illness without first describing the symptoms. In the early stages of a particular educational period, instructional procedures will adapt to the findings of the initial assessment, generally reflecting the accumulated performance capabilities resulting from the long-term behaviour history and activity of the learner. The history that is specifically measured is relevant to the next immediate educational step that is to be taken.

3   This immediate instructional step consists of educational alternatives adaptive to the classifications resulting from the initial student educational profiles. These alternative instructional procedures will be selectively assigned to the student or made available to him for his selection.

4   As the student learns, his performance will be monitored and continuously assessed at longer or shorter intervals appropriate to what is being taught. In early skill learning, assessment is quite continuous. Later on, as competence grows, problems grow larger; as the student becomes increasingly self-sustaining, assessment occurs more infrequently. This monitoring serves several purposes: providing a basis for knowledge of results and appropriate reinforcement contingencies to the learner and a basis for adaptation to learner demands. This learning history accumulated in the course of instruction is called 'short-term history' and, together with information from the long-term history, provides information for assignment of the next instructional unit. The short-term history also provides information about the effectiveness of the instructional material itself.

5   Instruction and learning proceed in a kind of servomechanism, cybernetic fashion, tracking the performance and selections of the student. Assessment and performance are interlinked, one determining the nature and requirement for the other. Instruction proceeds as a function of the relationship among measures of student performance, available instructional alternatives, and learning criteria that are chosen to be optimised. The question of which criteria are to be optimised becomes critical. Is it retention, transfer, the magnitude of difference between pre- and post-test scores, motivation to continue learning including the ability to do so with minimal instructional guidance, or is it all of these? If tracking of the instructional process permits instruction to become precise enough, then a good job can be done to optimise some gains and minimise others unless the presence of the latter gains is desired, expressed and assessed. The outcomes of learning measured at any point in instruction are referenced to and evaluated in terms of competence criteria and the values to be optimised; provision is always made for the ability of humans to surpass expectations.

6   Inherent in the system's design is its capability for improving itself. Perhaps a major defect in the implementation of educational innovations, especially in the area of individualisation, has been the lack of the

cumulative attainment of knowledge—on the basis of which the next innovation is better than the one that preceded it.

Given that the changing trends in education will lead to an instructional model somewhat like that just described, the main question to which this paper is addressed is: 'What are the implications for the nature of evaluation procedures?' I shall examine this question by some elaboration of each of the points just listed.

The specification of learning outcomes

In a system designed to maximise the attainment of certain objectives, the specification of learning outcomes in terms of observable student performance determines how the instructional components are used. Vague specification of desired outcomes leaves little concrete information for the evaluator about what to look for and what to help the system strive to attain. However, interaction between specification of outcomes and instructional procedure provides the basis for redefining objectives. The need for constant revision of objectives is as inherent in the system as is the initial need for defining them. There is a sustained process of clarifying goals, working toward them, evaluating progress, re-examining the objectives, modifying instructional procedures and clarifying the objectives in the light of evaluated experience. This process should indicate the inadequacies and omissions in a curriculum. The fear of many educators that detailed specification of objectives limits them to simple behaviours only—those which can be forced into measurable and observable terms—is an incorrect notion if one thinks of them as amendable approximations to our ideals. If complex reasoning and open-endedness are desirable aspects of human behaviour, then they need to be recognised and assessable goals. Overly general objectives may force us to settle for what can be easily expressed and measured.

A helpful distinction can be made between the evaluation of procedure and the evaluation of accomplishment. It is possible to evaluate a procedure, such as a difficult surgical operation, and to show that it is being done properly; it is another matter to evaluate its beneficial result. Evaluation of technique may be meaningless without evaluation of its effect, although it is often necessary to show that a new procedure in educational research in the schools is indeed being carried out appropriately. When one neglects the evaluation of technique and moves directly to the evaluation of accomplishment, the effective implementation of the procedure is assumed. One moves from procedural objectives to accomplishment objectives at many points in an instructional sequence. Attaining a procedural objective represents progress toward the accomplishment objective. Even though the two interact and accomplishment objectives are initially established, evaluation designed for the development of an operating instructional system should work from the evaluation of technique to the evaluation of accomplishment objectives, not the other way around as often seems to be the case. In succinct terms, it is necessary to make sure that the independent variable is in effect before measuring the dependent variable. Of course, in developmental or formative evaluation, assessment of each may suggest changes in the other.

A final point with respect to the specification of objectives relates to the distinction between criterion-referenced and norm-referenced measurement. The measurement of learning outcomes involves the assessment of criterion behaviour; implicit in this process is the determination of the characteristics of student performance with respect to specified standards. It can be assumed that regardless of the way a subject matter is structured, some existing hierarchy of sub-objectives indicates that certain performances must be attained as a basis for learning subsequent performance. An individual's competence level falls at some point on this hierarchy of increasing subject-matter competence. The degree to which the individual's measured performance resembles the desired performance at any specified competence level is assessed by referencing his performance to the criterion by some criterion-referenced measure. Criterion levels can be established at any point in instruction where it is necessary to obtain information concerning the adequacy of the learner's performance. The specific behaviours identified at each level of proficiency describe the tasks a student is capable of performing when he achieves this level of knowledge. Performance measured in this way provides explicit information concerning what the individual can and cannot do. Such criterion-referenced measures indicate the content of his behaviour and the correspondence between his performance and the continuum of educational objectives. Measures that assess learner performance in terms of such criterion-referenced standards thus provide information about the competence of a student, independently of reference to the performance of others. In contrast to this procedure, as has been pointed out by Glaser[3], the general practice in education is to measure achievement by norm referencing rather than by criterion referencing. Norm-referenced measures evaluate the learner's performance in terms of a comparison with the performance of others. Such measures need provide little or no information about the degree of competence exhibited by tested behaviours; they tell that one student is more or less proficient than the other but do not tell how proficient either of them is with respect to the desired learning outcomes. Evaluation in terms of criterion-referenced measures requires that we specify at least minimum levels of performance that the student is expected to attain or that he needs to attain in order to go on to the next step in an instructional sequence.

3 R. Glaser (1963). 'Instructional technology and the measurement of learning outcomes'. *American Psychologist*, 18, pp. 519-21.

Diagnosis of initial state (entering behaviour)

The second item in the description of the model refers to the measurement and diagnosis of the initial state or entering behaviour with which the learner comes into an instructional situation. Here we appear to be entering the domain of much of the work in the general field of psychological testing and evaluation. It seems obvious, however, that in order to follow through with the model I describe, we must go in the direction pointed to by Cronbach,[4] and by Cronbach and Gleser[5], that is, to depart from the standard practices of test theory based upon the basic data of correlations between tests and static criterion variables, and to move toward decision-making procedures based upon the relationships between entering behaviour and instructionally manipulated variables. The ultimate purpose of testing in this context is to arrive at decisions with respect to assignment to the instructional treatments defined by these instructional variables.

Evaluation of initial entering behaviour involves measuring the products of the long-term history of the learner, which includes what we generally have called aptitudes. These aptitudes have attained importance as fundamental characteristics in the measurement of human behaviour because they are useful in predicting long-range criteria such as school and college success. However, the model I describe demands that an additional task for measures of initial behaviour be the prediction of very immediate success, that is, success in immediate learning. It can be postulated that if the criteria for aptitude test validation had been immediate learning success rather than some long-range criteria, the nature of today's generally accepted aptitude batteries would be quite different. This postulation seems likely since factorial studies of the changing composition of abilities over the course of learning[6] show different abilities involved at the beginning and end of the course of learning. Thus, while it is useful to forecast over the long range, our instructional model also requires measures that are closely related to more immediate learning criteria, that is, success in initial instructional steps. Current types of measured aptitude may be limited in that they are operationally designed to predict over the long period, given reasonably non-adaptive forms of educational treatment.

Aptitude tests or general psychometric reference tests resulting from factor analyses of aptitude tests would not be expected to correlate very highly with individual differences in learning and thereby would not be useful for the placement of individuals in alternate instructional treat-

4   L. J. Cronbach (1957). 'The two disciplines of scientific psychology'. *American Psychologist*, **12**, pp. 671-84.

5   L. J. Cronbach & G. C. Gleser (1965). *Psychological Tests and Personnel Decisions*. Urbana, Ill.: University of Illinois Press.

6   E. A. Fleishman (1965). 'The description and prediction of perceptual-motor skill learning'. In R. Glaser (ed.), *Training Research and Education*. New York: John Wiley & Sons, Inc., pp. 137-76.

ments. As Jensen[7] has pointed out, the predictive power of tests like the Primary Mental Abilities test is due to the fact that they sample learned behaviour and therefore reflect something about the rate of learning in a given environment. They also measure the acquisition of broad verbal or symbolic capabilities (mediational systems), which play an important role in enabling an individual to generalise and solve problems. However, such standard psychometrically developed tests, as a result of the way in which they have been validated and evaluated, are more closely related to the products of learning that they predict, such as ability in school subjects, than they are to the kinds of variables generally dealt with in the learning laboratory; these are the variables relevant to instructional manipulation and educational alternatives. Evidence for this lack of utility of general psychometric measures with respect to instructional decisions comes from the line of studies dealing with correlations between psychometric variables and learning measures that was begun in 1946 by Woodrow's classic article.[8] Woodrow showed data from laboratory and classroom experiments that indicated that the correlations between intelligence measures and ability to learn, in the sense of ability to improve with practice, were generally insignificant and often close to zero. More recently, this work has been followed up by Gulliksen and his students, for example, Stake[9] and Duncanson[10]; but the results obtained are not clear-cut, and Woodrow's basic point has not been clearly disclaimed.

It seems that approximately five categories of entering behaviour would require measurement for instructional decision-making[11]: (a) the extent to which the individual has already learned the behaviour to be acquired in instruction, that is, previously attained achievement in the skills and knowledge to be taught, (b) the extent to which the individual possesses the prerequisites for learning the behaviour to be acquired, for example, knowing how to add before learning to multiply, (c) learning set variables, that consist of acquired ways of learning that facilitate or interfere with new learning procedures under certain instructional conditions, for example, prior success when acting impulsively or being cautious and reflective, (d) specific ability to make discriminations necessary in subsequent instruction, for example, musical aptitude or spatial visualisation, and (e) general mediating abilities as measured by general tests of verbal or symbolic intelligence.

7 A. R. Jensen (1967). 'Varieties of individual differences in learning'. In R. Gagné (ed.), *Learning and Individual Differences*. Columbus, Ohio: Charles E. Merrill Books, Inc., pp. 117-35.

8 H. A. Woodrow (1946). 'The ability to learn'. *Psychological Review*, 53, pp. 147-58.

9 R. E. Stake (1961). 'Learning parameters, aptitudes and achievements'. *Psychometric Monographs*, No. 9.

10 J. P. Duncanson (1964). *Intelligence and the Ability to Learn*. Princeton, N.J.: Educational Testing Service.

11 R. M. W. Travers (1963). *Essentials of Learning: An Overview for Students of Education*. New York: Crowell-Collier and Macmillan, Inc.

Instructional alternatives

On the basis of the initial measurement, instructional alternatives are available to the student. But what are these instructional alternatives, where do they come from and how are they developed? In other words, on what basis do different instructional treatments differ so as to be adaptive to individual requirements? This is a significant problem fundamental to psychologically-based instructional design but which, in this paper emphasising evaluation, can only be mentioned. Some alternatives seem easy to implement, such as adapting to the student's present level of accomplishment, his mastery of prerequisites, the speed at which he learns including the amount of practice he requires and his ability to learn independent of highly structured situations. Adaptation to treatments differing in these respects, which are shown to be related to measured aspects of entering behaviour, might be able to provide a significant beginning for effective adaptation to individual differences. However, in designing instructional alternatives, it is difficult to know how to use other variables that come out of learning theory (such as requirements for reinforcement, distribution of practice, the use of mediation and coding mechanisms, and stimulus and modality variables, for example, verbal, spatial, auditory, and visual presentation); and more needs to be known about their interaction with individual differences.

If one assumes that measures of entering behaviour and instructional treatments are both available, then at our present state of knowledge, empirical work must take place to determine those measures most efficient for assigning individuals to treatment classes. The task is to determine those measures that have the highest discriminating potential for allocating between treatments and then determine their intercorrelations so that they can be combined in some way and all of them need not be used. This task seems to be a reasonably typical mutivariate problem. As a result of the initial diagnostic or placement decision, the universe or sample of students involved is reduced to subsets, allocable to the various available instructional treatments. These initial decisions will be corrected by further assignments as learning proceeds so that the allocation procedure becomes a multistage decision process which defines an individualised instructional path.

Continuous assessment

The next item in the model indicates that as a student proceeds to learn, his performance will be monitored, and at appropriate intervals, measures of this performance will be summarised and indexed. In contrast to the long-term history used for initial placement, the measures obtained in learning are called the short-term history, even though prolonged use of the model may fuse the two items to some extent. Here again, the problem of what instructional alternatives are made available is of major concern. Of equal importance are the kinds of measures to be obtained in the course of learning.

The kinds of measures of learning progress one usually obtains, and on which instructional decisions are made, consist of test-score information that measures the frequency of correct responses, errors in relation to some performance standard and the speed of performance. Less frequently, measures of transfer and generalisation are specifically employed. Perhaps, to some extent, this is done when one selects a set of test items that are derived from the same universe of subject-matter content but are not the same sample as was used in initial learning.

Of special interest in the assessment of short-term history are measures that are being suggested by experimental work on learning; these are measures that can be obtained in the course of learning and may be predictive of future learning requirements. Two examples may give the flavour of this. One comes from the work of Zeaman and House[12] on a theory of discrimination learning accounting for the performance of retarded children learning to solve two-choice visual discrimination problems, such as may be involved in letter or numeral discrimination. The theory postulates a chain of two responses for problem solution: the first, paying attention to the relevant stimulus dimensions, and the second, the correct selection of the positive cue of the relevant dimensions. They ask whether individual differences in empirical learning curves are attributable to differences in the speed of acquisition or to some underlying process such as attention. The data they obtain show wide individual differences in learning curves, with higher IQ subjects doing better than the lower; however, the important differences in the curves between the brighter and duller subjects is not the slope of the curve, that is, the rate of learning, but the length of the initial plateau. Thus, it is not the rate of improvement, once it starts, that distinguishes bright and dull, but how long it takes for improvement to begin. The length of time for improvement to begin is considered an attentional variable and suggests, at least with respect to the concerns of this paper, that the measurement of plateau length rather than rate of improvement is a sensitive measure of discrimination learning.

The second example is a study performed in my own laboratory by Wilson Judd[13] on paired-associate learning. The interest here was on response latency, that is, the interval between the onset of a stimulus and the occurrence of a response, as an index of learning. Hull, in his theory and experimental work, strongly suggested latency as a measure of habit

12   D. Zeaman & B. J. House (1967). 'The relation of IQ and learning'. In R. Gagné (ed.), *Learning and Individual Differences*. Columbus, Ohio: Charles E. Merrill Books, Inc., pp. 192-212.

13   W. A. Judd & R. Glaser (1969). 'Response latency as a function of training method, information level, acquisition and overlearning'. *Journal of Educational Psychology Monograph*, 60 (Part 2).

strength. Our study investigated changes in the latency measure over the course of learning, from initial learning through a criterion of nearly perfect performance, and then through overlearning. Throughout this course, frequency of correct response increased to criterion and then continued at asymptote through overlearning. In contrast, latency showed no change and remained constant as correct response probability increased from chance to near 1.0; however, during the overlearning period, while response probability remained constant, latency showed a significant and sustained decrease, presumably related to the consolidation of learning during the overlearning period. The suggestion from this work is that the latency measure, as a short-term learning history variable, seems to detect aspects of learning not detectable from response frequency and may be related to and predictive of future retention. With the talk about the possibility of computer-assisted instruction, latency measures would be easy to obtain and be available for instructional decision-making.

The work of Jensen on individual differences in learning variables is also relevant here. His factor analyses of learning tasks of the kind used in the learning laboratory showed interesting results. For example, two types of learning that on the surface look very much alike, serial learning and paired-associate learning, were not found to be significantly inter-correlated, even when the stimulus materials were the same in both tasks. In addition there was little transfer between the two tasks. On the other hand, serial learning was found to have much in common with memory span. Jensen also found that in serial learning, individual differences in original learning are not highly correlated with individual differences in subsequent learning. The reliability of measures of learning variables for individual difference work posed problems for Jensen. This raises the point that the psychometrics of learning measures poses itself as a new evaluation task.

Adaptation and optimisation

The fifth item in the instructional model indicates that reassessment of behaviour during learning and instructional assignment are interlinked in a series of adaptive stages. Two points are appropriate here. First, information about learning relevant to this kind of instructional model should come primarily from the interaction effects generally neglected in studies of learning. As Cronbach and Gleser have pointed out, the learning experimentalist assumes a fixed population and hunts for the treatment with the highest average and least variability. The correlational psychologist has, by and large, assumed a fixed treatment and hunted for aptitude that maximises the slope of the function relating outcome to measured aptitude. The present instructional model assumes that there are strong interactions between individual measurements and treatment variables; and unless one treatment is clearly the best for everyone, as may rarely be the case, then treatments or instructional alternatives should be differentiated in a way to maximise their interaction with performance variables. If this assumption is correct, then individual performance measures that have high interactions with learning variables and their associated instructional alternatives are of greater importance than measures that do not show these interactions. This forces us to break out the error term in learning experiments so that the subject by independent-variable interaction can be evaluated. When this interaction is shown to be negligible, the learning variable can then be used in instruction without correcting its values with respect to individual differences. It seems that the model I have described will require major experimental research to determine the extent to which instructional treatments need to be qualified by individual difference interactions. The search for such interactions has been a major effort in the field of medical diagnosis and treatment and seems to be so in education[14].

Second, the continuous pattern of assessment and instructional prescription, and assessment and instructional prescription again, can be represented as a multistage decision process where decisions are made sequentially, and decisions made early in the process affect decisions made subsequently. The task of instruction is to prescribe the most effective sequence. Problems of this kind in other fields, such as electrical engineering, economics and operations research, have been tackled by mathematical procedures applied to optimisation problems. Essentially, optimisation procedures involve a method of making decisions by choosing a quantitative measure of effectiveness and determining the best solution according to this criterion with appropriate constraints. A quantitative model is then developed into which values can be placed to indicate the outcome that is produced when various values are introduced.

An article by Groen and Atkinson[15] has pointed out that the kind of instructional model I have described is set up for this kind of analysis. There is a multistage process that can be considered as a discrete N-stage process. At any given time, the state of the system, that is, the learner, can be characterised. This state, which is probably multivariate and described by a state vector, is determined by a decision which also may be multivariate; the state is transformed into the new updated state. The process consists of N successive stages where at each of the $N-1$ stages a decision is made. The last stage, the end of a lesson unit, is a terminal stage where no decision is made other than whether the terminal criteria have been attained. The optimisation problem of major concern in this process is finding a decision procedure for deciding which instructional alternatives to present at each stage, given the instructional alternatives

14 A. Lubin (1961). 'The interpretation of significant interaction'. *Educational and Psychological Measurement*, **21**, pp. 807-17.
15 G. J. Groen & R. C. Atkinson (1966). 'Models for optimizing the learning process'. *Psychological Bulletin*, **66**, pp. 309-20.

available, the set of possible student responses to the previous lesson unit and specification of the criteria to be optimised at the terminal stage. This decision procedure defines an instructional strategy and is determined by the functional relationship between (a) long- and short-range history and (b) student performance at each stage and at the terminal stage.

Groen and Atkinson point out that one way to find an optimal strategy is to enumerate every path of the decision tree generated by the multistage process. Obviously, this can be improved upon by the use of adequate learning models that can reduce the number of possible paths that can be considered. In order to reduce these paths still further, Bellman[16], and Bellman and Dreyfus[17], refer to dynamic programming procedures as useful for discovering optimal strategies and hence for providing a set of techniques for reducing the portion of the tree that must be searched. I am intrigued by this and suggest that it is an interesting approach for evaluation theory to consider, although some initial experimentation has not been overwhelmingly successful and, perhaps, slightly discouraging.

In order to carry out such an approach, we need only to do two trivial things: first, obtain quantitative knowledge of how the system variables interact, and second, obtain agreed measures of system effectiveness. Upon the completion of these two simple steps requiring, respectively, knowledge and value judgement, optimisation procedures can be carried out. It has been shown that relative to the total effort needed to achieve a rational decision, the optimisation procedure itself often requires little work when the first two steps are properly done[18]. We are thrown back to the tasks we have always known that we must confront: (a) knowledge and description of the instructional process and (b) the development of evaluation measures.

In the first task the question is what kinds of experimental tactics and learning theory are most useful for discovering individual-difference-learning-variable relationships required to develop an instructional system. Fortunately, there is a growing commitment in learning theory to the individual case — recognised but not incorporated to any extent by Hull, certainly urged upon us by Skinner and associates, and well recognised in the recent information-processing computer simulation models of human behaviour. There seems little doubt that one major test of the adequacy of competing learning theories will be the extent to which they incorporate individual differences.

The second task refers to the fact that in the educational model described, criterion measures and what is to be optimised become critical.

16   R. Bellman (1957). *Dynamic Programming*. Princeton, N.J.: Princeton University Press.
17   R. Bellman & S. E. Dreyfus (1962). *Applied Dynamic Programming*. Princeton, N.J.: Princeton University Press.
18   D. J. Wild & C. S. Beightler (1967). *Foundations of Optimization*. Englewood Cliffs, N.J.: Prentice-Hall, Inc.

If tracking the instructional process permits instruction to become precise enough, a good job can be done to maximise some gains and minimise others but some criteria may be minimised inadvertently unless the presence of the latter are desired, expressed and assessed. In this regard, it seems almost inescapable that we abandon only norm-referenced measurement and develop more fully criterion-referenced measures, measures that assess performance on a continuum of competence and growth in the area under consideration. In addition, serious attempts must be made to measure what has been heretofore so difficult; such aspects as transfer of knowledge to new situations, problem-solving and self-direction — those aspects of learning and knowledge that are basic to an individual's capability for continuous growth and development.

Evolutionary operation

The final item in my model refers to the capability of an instructional system to gather information and accumulate knowledge from which it can improve its own functioning and come closer to its expressed goals. I think the current notion of 'formative' evaluation inherent in programmed instruction and presently being discussed more generally in curriculum evaluation is a major step along these lines[19]. The industrial concept of 'evolutionary operation' is relevant here[20]. The underlying rationale of this concept states it is seldom efficient to run an industrial process to produce a product alone; the process should produce the product plus information about how to improve it.

In closing the remarks in this paper, I can think of nothing better than to quote the end of Cronbach's 1963 article entitled 'Evaluation for Course Improvement'. He writes:

Old habits of thought and long-established techniques are poor guides to the evaluation required for course improvement. Traditionally, educational measurement has been chiefly concerned with producing fair and precise scores for comparing individuals. Educational experimentation has been concerned with comparing score averages of competing courses. But course evaluation calls for description of outcomes. This description should be made on the broadest possible scale, even at the sacrifice of superficial fairness and precision.

Course evaluation should ascertain what changes a course produces and should identify aspects of the course that need revision.

. . . Evaluation is a fundamental part of curriculum development, not an appendage. Its job is to collect facts the course developer can and will use to do a better job, and facts from which a deeper understanding of the educational process will emerge.

19 L. J. Cronbach (1963). 'Evaluation for course improvement'. *Teachers College Record*, **64**, pp. 672-83.

20 G. E. P. Box (1957). 'Evolutionary operation: a method for increasing industrial productivity'. *Applied Statistics*, **6**, pp. 81-101.

Conclusion

I have stated the thesis that changing educational practices require changes in our theories and techniques of evaluation. In a general model of an emerging instructional process, I have itemised six educational practices and suggested the considerations for evaluation and measurement that each raises. They are the following:

1   With respect to the specification of learning outcomes, the following are required: (a) behavioural definition of goals, evaluating progress toward these goals, and clarifying these goals in the light of evaluated experience, (b) prior evaluation of educational procedures, insuring they are in effect before assessing educational accomplishment, and (c) development of techniques for criterion-referenced measurement.

2   For the diagnosis of initial state, what is required is determination of long-term individual differences that are related to adaptive educational alternatives.

3   For the design of instructional alternatives, a key task is to determine measures that have the highest discriminating potential for allocating between instructional treatments.

4   For continuous assessment, discovery of measurements of ongoing learning that facilitate prediction of the next instructional step is required.

5   For adaptation and optimisation, the instructional model requires: (a) the detailed analysis of individual-difference by instructional-treatment interactions and (b) the development of procedures like the optimising methods so far used in fields other than education.

6   For evolutionary operation, we require a systematic theory or model of instruction into which accumulated knowledge can be placed and then empirically tested and improved.

Defending the model

The critical debate about the objectives model began in the early 1960s and was boosted by the attack on the uses of the concept in evaluation published by Myron Atkin in 1963 (see Section 3). James Popham, director of the Instructional Objectives Exchange at the University of California, Los Angeles, and a leading propagandist of the objectives model, was soon at the forefront of a public discussion which is still going on today. The following article of his is included at this point because it portrays, in an engaging style, some of the flavour of the argument, and a number of the issues which were contended. Popham takes the role of attorney for the defence of the model, and reviews historically some landmarks in the development of his stance from 1960 to 1970.

2.3   W. James Popham
Must all objectives be behavioural?

Considerable insight can be gained about ancient man by inspecting the residual artifacts associated with his normal activities. A competent archaeologist, given a handful of potsherds and stone tools, can derive amazingly sound inferences regarding a preliterate society's life style, physical appearance, etc. During recent months I have been probing my own thinking regarding instructional objectives, and have found archaeological tactics useful. Specifically, I have been examining my personal artifacts, collected during the past decade, which are particularly relevant to the question of whether instructional objectives should be stated in behavioural, i.e. measurable, terms. By sharing with the reader these artifacts and the inferences I derived from them, a judgement can be made regarding the adequacy of my archaeologically-derived insights, and the merits of my current answer to the question, 'Must all objectives be behavioural?'

Date: Winter, 1960.

Artifact: Several used practice sheets from an early field test version of Robert Mager's classic book on instructional objectives.

Inference: These yellowed relics recall a time when I was on the faculty at San Francisco State College and Bob Mager, who lived nearby, was trying out preliminary versions of his self-instruction booklet, *Preparing Objectives for Programmed Instruction,* in my classes. For me, this was a period both of curiosity regarding the merits of measurable objectives and of increasing belief that such objectives could be useful in instruction. Having been reared during teacher education and graduate school days on a diet of grossly general objectives such as the 'Seven Cardinal Principles of Secondary Education' ('Worthy use of lesson time'), I was fascinated with what seemed to be a powerful way of clarifying a teacher's instructional intentions. Enough of gunky generalities. Precision was around the corner.

Date: Fall, 1962.

Artifact: A blue and gold bumper sticker which reads HELP STAMP OUT NON-BEHAVIORAL OBJECTIVES!

Source: W. James Popham (1972). 'Must all objectives be behavioral?', Educational Leadership, **29**, *No. 7.*

Inference: Upon joining the UCLA faculty, I had these bumper stickers printed (in UCLA colours) to distribute to my students, friends and selected enemies. This artifact probably reflects the zenith of my zeal for behavioural objectives, the religious ardour of any recent convert being a well-established phenomenon. If students asked 'Can I use non-behavioural objectives in my teaching?' I would respond 'Certainly, but they won't be helpful.' If I found a colleague using non-behavioural objectives for his own classes, I sneered disdainfully. Since I was a new, non-tenured faculty member, the degree to which my sneer was visible depended heavily on the academic rank of the colleague in question, full professors receiving only a mild upper-lip quiver.

Date: Fall, 1964.

Artifact: A two-tone bumper sticker which reads HELP STAMP OUT NON-BEHAVIORAL OBJECTIVES.

Inference: There are two important differences between this relic and the 1962 artifact. First, and unimportantly, there is the colour difference. This was attributable to the fact that at the same time I had exhausted the supply of blue and gold stickers I bought a green Volkswagen. I wanted a colour-compatible bumper sticker. But second, and more critical, note that in this new bumper sticker *there is no exclamation point*! I can recall asking the printer to delete it from the new version, primarily to reflect my increasingly moderate stance.

Date: Spring, 1966.

Artifact: A heavily marked copy of an AERA paper by Elliot Eisner entitled 'Educational objectives: help or hindrance?'

Inference: This paper was given by Elliot at an annual meeting of the American Educational Research Association. It represented the first time I had heard someone systematically attack the glories of behavioural objectives. I was aghast. I hadn't met Elliot previously and can recall standing up in the crowded meeting room after he read his paper and saying, 'I have never before heard a paper with which I was in total disagreement with every point made; fortunately, this is such a paper.' For me, it was an enthralling emotional experience. This artifact marked the beginning of my combative period.

Date: Spring, 1966.

Artifact: A handwritten first draft copy of a paper I wrote entitled, 'Probing the validity of arguments against behavioural objectives'.

Inference: It doesn't take a sophisticated analyst, archaeological or psychological, to infer from the title which side I was taking in what was emerging as a debate between proponents of behavioural objectives and 'those other villains'. An inspection of the contents of the paper reveals a pretty hard-line rejection of any criticism of behavioural objectives.

The emergence of critics had galvanised my support of measurable objectives as a technique for educational improvement — which, if not quite panaceatic, were almost that praiseworthy.

Date: Summer, 1966.

Artifact: An apparently unused white T-shirt with red block letters reading 'Help Stamp Out Non-behavioral Objectives'. This T-shirt had been given to me by several graduate students who were aware of my opposition to non-measurable objectives and also of my fondness for the Southern California beaches. They pointed out that since one could secure a sunburn through the white cloth, but not the red letters, I could wear the shirt on the beach for several sunny weekends, then remove it and be a 'living symbol of support for behavioral objectives!' The fact that the shirt appears to be unused suggests either a mellowing of my position or, probably, cowardice.

Date: Fall, 1966.

Artifact: A badly scratched filmstrip entitled *Educational Objectives*.

Inference: Preparation of this filmstrip marked the peak of my evangelical period. I continued to encounter scores of educators who hadn't even heard of a measurable instructional objective, much less were actively using them. So I developed a filmstrip-tape programme to spread the word. The half-hour programme was revised nine times before being released and was able to reliably accomplish its own objectives. Perhaps in part because it[1] has been so widely used, I now regret the choice of the expression 'behavioural objective' which is employed throughout the programme. Although for many people the term 'behavioural' connotes some sort of mechanistic approach to instruction, such an approach is not necessarily associated with this conception of an instructional objective. Undoubtedly the choice of a phrase such as 'performance objective' or 'operational objective' would have been preferable. As one surveys the general message conveyed in the filmstrip-tape programme, it is almost exclusively an advocacy of measurable goals and a castigation of non-behavioural goals 'because we really can't tell what such nebulous statements mean.'

Date: Spring, 1968.

Artifact: The original typescript of a colloquy destined to appear in the AERA monograph, *Instructional Objectives*.

Inference: A hard-liner begins to soften. This typescript was based on a February 1968 conversation between Elliot Eisner (the originator of the Spring 1966 artifact), Louise Tyler, Howard Sullivan and myself. We had each prepared separate chapters for an AERA monograph on the topic of instructional objectives and subsequently met one long evening

1   Distributed by Vimcet Associates, Inc., PO Box 24714, Los Angeles, California 90024, USA.

in a Chicago hotel room to conduct tape-recorded discussions of each of the chapters. These recordings were subsequently transcribed, edited and later appeared in the monograph published by Rand McNally in 1969. I had become better acquainted with Elliot since our first meeting in 1966. Nevertheless, on that February evening I expected him to be a recalcitrant opponent of measurable goals. He wasn't. He was quite reasonable. A skilled archaeologist analysing the transcript of the conversation wouldn't be able to tell that I was thinking, 'Elliot has some good points.' But I was.

Date: Fall, 1968.

Artifact: A handwritten proposal for the establishment of the Instructional Objectives Exchange.

Inference: Tired of hearing teachers complain they were too busy to write out measurable objectives for their instruction, it seemed that we might reasonably expect them to be selectors, not generators, of precise goals. Hence, while returning from an administrators' workshop in Fresno, I decided to try to set up an operation analogous to an 'objectives bank' so that educators could draw out collections of behavioural objectives, then select those which were appropriate for their local instructional situations. The Instructional Objectives Exchange was established as a project of the UCLA Center for the Study of Evaluation later that year and is now operating as a non-profit educational corporation (Box 24095 Los Angeles, California 90024, USA.). While the vast majority of objectives currently distributed by the Exchange are behaviourally stated, there are a number of general, non-behavioural goals which are used as descriptors of large groups of more specified objectives.

Date: Winter, 1970.

Artifact: A two-tone blue bumper sticker which reads HELP STAMP OUT SOME NON-BEHAVIORAL OBJECTIVES!

Inference: The floodgates may have been opened. The addition of the term 'some' to the sticker indicates a putty-like softening of the former hard-liner. The reintroduction of an exclamation mark (with its already demonstrated capability of being deleted) may foreshadow even more softening in the future. In reality, when I distribute the current bumper stickers it gives me an opportunity to describe my current thinking on the question of whether instructional objectives should be measured. A brief description of that position follows.

The current stance

It is probably unnecessary for one to observe that ten years of experience with a certain point of view had led to improvements. Nonetheless, I'm

going to assert that my current ideas regarding the necessity of opera-
tionality in objectives seem a great deal more defensible than my zealous
exclusivism of the early sixties.

My advocacy of measurable goals has not been altered one whit. Insofar
as an instructional objective is stated with sufficient clarity that we can
measure whether it has been achieved, then clear instruction and
evaluation benefits arise. Because some of our most important educational
goals are particularly elusive, we should invest greater resources in devising
sophisticated measurement tactics to assess such currently unmeasurable
outcomes. During recent months at the Instructional Objectives Exchange
we have been constructing measurement devices to get at such educational
outcomes as students' attitudes toward learning, tolerance toward minority
groups, self concept, judgement and attitudes toward drug use. These
objectives and measures aren't all that polished yet, but they're better than
we had a few years ago.

There are many promising measurement avenues which American
educators haven't yet travelled with sufficient verve, that is, financial
support. For example, a number of important advances have recently
been made in use of physiological indicators such as the pupil-dilation of
one's eyes to serve as a reliable index of interest. We cannot be satisfied
with the conventional testing approaches we've lived with for years. New,
unobtrusive and exotic assessment schemes must be developed. Thus,
point one in my current position is that we must continue to pursue
measurable objectives, for our ultimate aim should still be to employ
instructional objectives which permit us to tell whether they have been
accomplished.

However, there are some important goals, which we have for our
children, which are *currently* unassessable. To the extent that such goals
are extremely meritorious, they are *worth the risk* of our pursuing them
even if we can't reliably discern whether they have been accomplished.
High gain goals warrant high risk instructional strategies. Let's use an
illustration. Suppose our aim is to have children acquire a certain
attitudinal predisposition which will be manifest, by definition, only after
they become adults. Now our best hope for assessment is to isolate
predictor behaviours which are currently measurable and use these as
proxies for the long-term goals. This is a defensible plan, if we can isolate
proxy behaviours in which we can be confident. But since we've really just
begun to get very sophisticated and circumventious in our measurement
approaches, there are long-range goals for which we presently can't find
suitable proxies. Accordingly, I believe that a reasonable proportion of an
instructor's goals, if they are of sufficient import, can be of a non-
behavioural nature.

The magnitude of the proportion is, of course, at issue. It seems that in
some content-laden classes the proportions of non-measurable goals might
be very small. In other courses, e.g. the humanities and aesthetics, the

proportions might be much larger. What troubles one about ever voicing this 'permit some non-measurable goals' point of view is that too many teachers may employ it as an excuse for business as usual, and today's business as usual in American education is unacceptable. The *over-whelming* proportion of objectives pursued by our teachers are unmeasurable, hence of little utility. It may well be that the chief deterrent to improved educational quality is that our teachers have no way of telling how well they're doing. Measurable goals permit defensible quality judgements. Non-measurable goals don't. Thus, to endorse the inclusion of a proportion of non-measurable objectives for instructional planning is not to endorse the *status quo* in our educational system regarding the use of instructional goals. Too few teachers employ a sufficiently large proportion of measurable objectives to be able to discern whether the bulk of the instructional efforts are satisfactory. This situation must be altered.

'Must all objectives be behavioural?' The answer is *no*. 'Should most objectives be behavioural?' The answer is *yes*. It will demand far greater ingenuity and effort to produce an educational world compatible with the second answer than with the first. Hopefully, in eons to come some archaeologist of the future will unearth our present society's educational artifacts and discern that our answers and the resulting actions were correct.

Curriculum evaluation in Britain: the return of the Mayflower

In 1965 the newly-formed Schools Council set up a Working Party on Curriculum Evaluation which included in its membership Douglas Pidgeon and the late Stephen Wiseman. Wiseman was Director and Pidgeon Deputy Director of the National Foundation for Educational Research (NFER), the leading educational research organisation in Britain. Although the Council declined to publish the report when it was submitted in 1967, the review undertaken then led in 1970 to the publication by NFER of a monograph by Wiseman and Pidgeon entitled Curriculum Evaluation, *from which we reproduce extracts from Chapter 5 called 'Project Evaluation'.*

At the time of writing, the authors were fully aware of the growing army of critics who were beginning to lay siege to the objectives model, and pay considered attention to some of the major issues in the debate. Their conclusion is nevertheless clear, and their recommendation firm: 'Only by the evaluation of aim-achievement can we ensure that curricula remain flexible, and responsive to new demands and changing circumstances'.

The statement is significant. This was the first British publication in the new field, and it carried with it all the authority of the NFER and the long tradition of expertise in educational assessment which that organisation embodied. It constituted an endorsement by the British research establishment of the Tylerian prescription for curriculum evaluation.

2.4 Stephen Wiseman and Douglas Pidgeon Project evaluation

Over the past few years we have witnessed a rapidly growing activity in curriculum development and reform, spearheaded by the efforts of the Nuffield Foundation and massively extended by the Schools Council. This work attempts to assess the present state of curriculum evaluation in this developmental period and to consider some of the problems raised. Many of these arise from the complexity of projects, demanding co-operation between developers, evaluators and teachers involved in the field trials.

The classical approach to curriculum development is deceptively simple. It consists of three stages:

1   Definition of aims in behavioural terms.

2   The selection and invention of learning situations designed to achieve these aims.

3   The design and development of assessment methods to measure the degree of success in achieving these aims.

Experience of current projects — large and small, national and local, expensive and shoe-string — suggests that the major share of effort, energy and activity is concentrated on Stage 2. And furthermore, this tends (but by no means exclusively) to focus on the development of materials rather than on 'learning situations'. The distinction is important: as we have said earlier, for the achievement of certain aims, *method* is far more important than *content* (e.g. the understanding of scientific method, as opposed to knowledge; the achievement of important higher-order aims in history, which is presumably largely independent of the period studied).

The development enthusiast

The emphasis in Stage 2 in understandable. The curriculum reformer is always an enthusiast, with a keen sense of urgency and a strong motivation to get on with the job and produce the goods. And so he dives headlong into the production of materials, since he himself knows (or believes he knows) where he wants to go. The formulation of precise and detailed aims in behavioural terms is a slow and difficult process seen by him as prescribed by impractical theoreticians with little appreciation of the

Source: S. Wiseman and D. Pidgeon (1972). Curriculum Evaluation. *Windsor:* NFER, *pp. 77-83, 84-5, 86-7, 88, 90-1.*

expertise and flair of the subject-matter expert (himself), who should not be hampered by having to engage in this frustrating and unnecessary preliminary stage. Stage 3, too, is given little thought or emphasis, since the enthusiast is convinced from the outset that his new curriculum is bound to be successful, designed as it is to rectify the shortcomings of the old one. And so his time and energy are devoted to Stage 2, the meat in the sandwich: Stages 1 and 3 are merely trimmings, to which some lip-service must be paid and some rapid and superficial activities devoted, in order to give the project a spurious air of 'scientific' respectability. Such a course of action, in which little conviction—and less money—is given to Stages 1 and 3 is the primrose path to yet another educational cul-de-sac.

This description of the curriculum reform enthusiast is, of course, exaggerated. But it contains within it a point of view which is certainly attributable to many workers in the field. Quite apart from this analysis of bad practice arising from sound intentions, however, there are many teachers who are suspicious of, or openly antagonistic to, the 'classical' approach to curriculum reform, and it is necessary to consider some of the reasons for such attitudes.

Behavioural aims

Resistance to the formulation of behavioural aims is only to be expected in a profession which, by tradition and by training, has long become used to working to implicit rather than explicit goals. We are asking for a radical revision in habits of thought and action—always difficult of achievement. The definition of aims in precise terms demands hard thinking, and the human animal tends to avoid this whenever possible. It demands wide reading—first to survey, and then to judge, the aims put forward by other thinkers in the particular subject field—and patient discussion and concept-sharpening argument with contemporary practitioners. All this is time-consuming, demanding work: how much more comfortable we can be if it can be side-stepped.

But there are other objections of a more deep-seated nature. Aims formulated in *behavioural* terms, many suspect, will be incomplete: some goals are incapable of description in such a way. How true is this? Certainly it *is* true if 'behavioural' is defined too narrowly. It is essential that this definition is *not* used in such a way that it encompasses merely changes in the level of knowledge and skill of the pupils. Indeed, a great deal of the movement for curriculum reform has been inspired by deep dissatisfaction with existing syllabuses and curricula just because they are seen as demanding little more than the ingestion of facts and their parrot-like regurgitation. Changes in the affective sphere, in attitudes and interests, must, as has already been emphasised, be included here. If it is still believed that certain essential or desirable aims cannot be described in terms of pupils' behaviour (using this in the widest sense) then one must ask how realistic such aims are. It usually means that not enough thought has been devoted to their formulation in precise and detailed terms.

Another problem associated with the definition-of-aim approach is more intractable. Among the educational aims which are listed as the expected outcomes of new curricula are nearly always found some which are characterised as *long-term*. Frequently those are among the most important in the eyes of the teachers, and they often include effects which are hoped for some years later — which, for secondary school pupils, means after they have left school. How often, in reading autobiographies, do we find comment about the way in which the influence of a particular teacher has had effect on crucial decisions made by the adult many years later? Consider the long-term aims implicit in moral education or, to take a more homely example, domestic economy. Can any evaluation be complete without considering these? And yet their assessment and measurement is almost impossible, practically speaking. We have considerable sympathy for those teachers, working in particular curriculum areas, who reject evaluation in the practical, short-term form, on the grounds that it can be only partial, and therefore, perhaps, wholly misleading. While accepting the validity of their doubts, however, we would reject their conclusions. We believe that partial evaluation is better than no evaluation. And if the *majority* of the stated aims of any school programme were claimed to be long-term and inaccessible to evaluation, leaving only a few minor and relatively unimportant effects to be expected during the pupils' school life, we must confess that we would have the deepest suspicions of the validity of the particular curriculum. Teachers, parents and pupils have the right to expect immediate relevancy, and for this to be assessable. To discount such matters in favour of long-term goals — some of which might well prove to be pie-in-the-sky for the majority of pupils — is neither responsible nor wise.

Three stages in action

We have described the classical methodology in three stages, and these, logically, are placed in temporal order. Aims come first; planning of learning experiences follows; and we end with evaluation. But it is quite unrealistic to expect this logical order to be followed strictly in practice: a great deal of overlap must be expected and, indeed, deliberately planned for. In a truly effective development programme, all three activities will be found going on at the same time, each interacting with and moderating the other two. How this happens may become clearer if we consider who should be responsible for the various elements in the programme.

It is usually assumed that the job of producing the behavioural objectives belongs to the subject specialist, the curriculum developer. In the United States—with a rather longer experience in this field than we have in Britain—this view is usually taken, with the assumption that the educational psychologist or measurement expert responsible for the evaluation phase has the function of sitting in judgement on the aims produced and pronouncing on their adequacy. Some American writers, however[1,2], disagree with this, and place the responsibility for the formulation of aims on the evaluator. We believe that the best results will be produced if it is accepted as a joint responsibility. The evaluator cannot do it alone because he is—usually—insufficiently knowledgeable about and experienced in the subject area. The developer cannot do it alone because he is—usually—inexperienced in this novel task, and unpractised in the kind of analysis necessary to produce usable behavioural objectives. The developer needs the help of the evaluator in refining his basic aims and in breaking them down into discrete elements and measurable outcomes. Only by discussion, argument, interplay and disagreement can implicit and global aims be clarified into behavioural objectives. Questions from the evaluator such as 'What do you mean by . . . ?' 'How does this differ from . . . ?' 'Do you expect pupils to be able to . . . ?' 'Is . . . the kind of teaching you mean?' can all help the clarifying process. But best of all is the deliberate overlap between Stages 1 and 3. Right from the start of the exercise the evaluator should begin to assemble the 'measurement pool'. By this is meant the collection of questions, test items, rating scales, opinion lists, and so forth, to form the beginning of the evaluation instruments. These now become elements for discussion between developer and evaluator, and essential validity-checks on the reality of their agreement on aims. Not uncommonly it will be found that, having reached apparent agreement on a particular behavioural objective, the developer reacts to the evaluator's draft questions covering this objective by: 'Good heavens, *no*! This is not at all what I am after'. Back to the drawing board for both of them. This build-up of the measurement pool thus plays an invaluable part in the process by providing an essential check on the adequacy of the objectives. It also forces the developer to look much more closely not only at his aims, but also at his development materials. It is far easier for a geography teacher, or a history teacher, to look at a test question and say 'Yes, this is just what I want' or 'No, this is barking up the wrong tree', than to sit down in isolation and try to frame his own behavioural objectives.

The existence of the pool will also have its impact on Stage 2, by forcing the regular reappraisal of the behavioural objectives in the light of the developmental activities. Aims will be re-examined, modified and added to as development proceeds. And the changing pool exists as a constant

1   M. Scriven (1967). 'The methodology of evaluation'. In: R. W. Tyler, R. M. Gagné and M. Scriven, *Perspectives of Curriculum Evaluation*. AERA Monograph Series on Curriculum Evaluation, No. 1. Chicago: Rand McNally.
2   R. E. Stake (1967). 'The countenance of educational evaluation'. *Teachers College Record*, **68**, p. 7.

reminder to the developers of the objectives of the exercise. The pool will also be used as a source for the construction of progress tests during the development phase: it becomes the *operational version* of the behavioural objectives. Scriven makes the useful suggestion that midway, say, through the development phase it would be valuable to use outside judges to review the cohesiveness of objectives, materials and proposed measurements. This, he suggests, may present gross divergencies between *espoused*, *implicit* and *tested-for* goals. If this is done, we suggest that the priority qualities of such judges are intelligence, experience, judgement and common sense (probably in reverse order).

The measurement stage

Resistance to curriculum evaluation is far from uncommon among teachers, and — naturally enough — the measurement stage forms the major focus of hostility, suspicion, disagreement and misunderstanding.

The reasons for holding such opinions are easy to understand in view of past history, and it is difficult to deny them some degree of validity. Educational measurement in Britain has been unduly restricted in scope, concerning itself almost entirely with the measurement of attainment in the basic subjects. Many of the tests constructed for this purpose have — in the eyes of perceptive teachers — concentrated far too heavily on measuring the retention of factual information, and ignored the more subtle and more valuable products of good teaching. The stress laid on reliability and validity by the test constructors and the research workers, leading to an emphasis on multiple choice questions at the expense of those demanding creative answers, reinforces the suspicion that accuracy of measurement is regarded as more important than educational relevance, and that many psychometrists are cheerfully prepared to throw out the baby with the bath water. Over the past twenty-five years the only opportunity offered for the wide-scale application of technically sophisticated and professionally orientated methods of educational measurement has been the notorious 11-plus examination. Most teachers think of educational measurement and evaluation in terms of 11-plus tests, tests which are — deliberately — narrow in scope and restricted in coverage, and which carry with them (regrettably and quite unfairly) a large proportion of the obloquy now associated with the policy and ethos of selective education. Such tests are wholly inappropriate for use in curriculum evaluation, designed as they are to discriminate between pupils rather than to measure the degree of achievement of curricular aims. Nor can the curriculum evaluator confine his activities to the use of only cognitive tests in limited areas: the measurement of content mastery is the least demanding of his problems. Fortunately he has within his armoury a wide variety of measurement devices and techniques, and to imagine that his activities will be confined to objective tests of factual knowledge is a wholly mistaken view. As we have emphasised earlier, he will inevitably be involved in the construction and use of measures of attitude and interest, since many of the most important objectives of the teacher fall within this area. Nor can he afford to eschew measurement techniques of a more subjective nature, accepting some loss of precision in the interests of cogency, thus incorporating observation, judgement and personal assessment as valid measures of pupil behaviour and reaction. . . .

Measurement techniques

Curriculum evaluation cannot be content with conventional methods of test construction. These have been developed and refined in the pursuit of very different aims and objectives. The orthodox psychometrist starts from the assumption that the individuals for whom his measurements are designed vary demonstrably in their level of knowledge or skill, their possession of this, that or the other trait, their proficiency in various tasks. The techniques of item-writing and item-analysis which he employs are specifically designed to maximise these differences and to differentiate individuals as sharply as possible. His aim is to lay bare the *norm*, or average performance, and to identify each individual's performance in terms of difference—upwards or downwards—from the norm. His success is judged in terms of the amount of variability he can produce among his subjects—but such variability must be 'real' and not just the product of random errors of measurement. Hence the emphasis on reliability. The tests he produces are *norm-referenced*.

For the curriculum evaluator such an orientation is patently irrelevant. His interest lies not in some hypothetical norm about which the pupils are spread as widely as possible, but in an entirely different question. Having laid down a particular and clearly-defined aim, his concern is to discover how many pupils have reached it. The aim is the criterion: his questions or items will be designed to sample various aspects of this criterion, and his measurement objective is to discover the level of mastery of the pupils. The tests he produces are *criterion-referenced*. . . .

Analysis

Once we have produced our evaluation instruments, criterion-referenced, we are then faced with the problems of evaluating the results. The logic is simple, having adumbrated our aims in behavioural terms, and having constructed measurement instruments to assess whether the aims have been achieved, the test results provide us with the evidence. But difficult problems remain. . . .

Summative evaluation

The emphasis . . . has been on formative evaluation, the ongoing process during the course of curriculum development, since this we see as the current major need, and one in which teachers themselves are likely to find involvement. But perhaps we may profitably take a brief look at summative evaluation: the evaluation of completed, published curriculum programmes. . . .

The concept of the 'best buy' in educational processes is largely illusory. If curriculum A achieves most success with objectives 1, 3, 5 and 7; curriculum B with objectives 2, 4, 6 and 8, then what? The potential user must judge for himself his aim-priorities, choosing in the light of his own philosophy and his own imperatives. He is faced with a professional value-judgement, the responsibility for which cannot be shrugged off on to the shoulders of an unknown evaluator. Notice, too, that this judgement cannot only be based on successful aim-achievements of the curricula: scrutiny must also be made of the areas of comparative failure, since there may be an overriding lower threshold. As has been queried earlier, if a modern maths programme produced high levels of concept mastery, and good attitudes and motivations, can it be endorsed if, at the same time, the kids can't add, subtract, multiply and divide?

Conclusion

The purpose . . . has been to argue the case for evaluation as an essential and integral part of the whole process of curriculum reform and curriculum development. We have tried to show how the classroom teacher can gain an extra degree of freedom by re-orientating his thinking in terms of aim-achievement, and endeavoured to indicate how this may be done. We have suggested a rationale for the ongoing and summative evaluation of larger curriculum projects, and have indicated some of the difficulties which face both developers and evaluators in this process. Further experience and deeper analysis are likely to reveal even greater difficulties—but we would argue that these *must* be faced and overcome if we are to achieve greater precision and greater effectiveness in educating our children.

Curriculum reform as a large-scale, organised and structured process is relatively new to us in Britain. A promising start has been made, and with the activities of the Schools Council, centrally, and the growing number of teachers' centres, regionally, the educational scene has undergone a radical change. We believe, however, that the essential evaluation element in the curriculum development process is in danger of being neglected, or being given merely a token level of priority. If this is not remedied, the new syllabuses and programmes will become chains around our teachers just as heavy and frustrating as the old ones they replaced. Only by the evaluation of aim-achievement can we ensure that curricula remain flexible, and responsive to new demands and changing circumstances. Evaluation is not a superficial decoration to be applied once the curriculum structure has been erected: it must be built in from the start, forming an essential element in the architect's plans and constantly influencing the work of the bricklayers, the carpenters and the plasterers. . . .

Section 3
Five advocates of change

Introduction

There are a number of ways of monitoring changes within the history of ideas. One approach is through individual people. It was discovered recently that the history of a complex and politically amorphous institution like the Schools Council could not be written without an acknowledged personal dimension—the private vision and public inspiration of Derek Morrell. But to adopt this focus is not to deny others. A personalised account can never be the whole story, and there are the attendant dangers of over-personalisation suggesting that individual people are more important than issues.

Despite these qualifications a large part of this reader has been set aside to consider the contributions to evaluation theory and practice of five key figures. The five people selected as 'tracers' come from a variety of different disciplines and backgrounds and bring different experiences to our central problem area—alternative ways of evaluating educational programmes. The choice was a difficult one. The following are featured:

1 J. Myron Atkin, Professor of Science Education and Dean of the College of Education, University of Illinois, Urbana-Champaign.

2 Elliot Eisner, Professor of Education and Art at Stanford University.

3 Lawrence Stenhouse, Director of the Centre for Applied Research in Education, University of East Anglia, Norwich.

4 Michael Scriven, Professor of Philosophy, University of California, Berkeley.

5 Robert Stake, Center for Instructional Research and Curriculum Evaluation, University of Illinois, Urbana-Champaign.

Each has in his own way proved a pivotal influence, causing change as well as reflecting it. Each contributor, too, has exhibited intellectual shifts and development over time. There are changes of emphasis, changes of style and changes of tone. It is also necessary to acknowledge another difficulty: a summarising interpretative account of somebody's contribution to a field of inquiry is to some extent itself an exercise in judgement. There is no certainty that we see others as they would wish to be seen, or indeed see themselves.

Another arguable assertion may need to be taken into account: the heightened influence of innovative individuals is perhaps the mark of an early phase in the development of an academic field. This is the phase in which intellectual entrepreneurship and the making of power-bids are normal and unremarkable. The reader needs a sense of expanding and

71

contracting opportunities as well as a sense of intellectual debate. One man's bandwagon is another man's hearse.

The variation in tone and style of the selected papers is particularly interesting. The Popham paper featured in Section 2 is witty and contentious but also an implicit statement about the shared assumptions of the emerging evaluation community. Popham is self-consciously the objectives man adopting the spritely tone of the illuminators. Significantly, both Scriven and Stake are currently also quite capable of producing the occasional 'spoof' paper. Indeed one of the puzzling questions going the rounds in the evaluation community (and by no means getting a consistent answer) is whether Scriven's 'Goal-free evaluation' is not itself in part a spoof paper. Some of the uncertainty of tone evidenced in our selection of papers represents the fruits of another tendency in the evaluation community, towards 'soft' or 'limited circulation' papers. There is a real difference between producing definitive statements for publication and 'setting speculative snares' for insiders on your private mailing list, or members of a particular conference.

Within these papers, too, can be traced the emergence of some of the key issues summarised in the Parlett and Hamilton paper, 'Evaluation as illumination'. What analogies are available to those thinking about curriculum evaluation? What kinds of data are eligible for collection? Whose purposes is the exercise intended to serve? What is the role of judgement in an evaluation report? How ought such reports to be written?

Each author is introduced briefly in order to exhume the issues underlying our selection. The desired range over time and issues has been maintained at the expense of abridging rather sharply some of the papers. Our hope is that this has been done in a way that will not embarrass the individual authors.

Myron Atkin

Myron Atkin was one of the first to articulate the growing doubts felt about the conventional wisdom of curriculum evaluation. Atkin's critique of the behavioural objectives approach to curriculum evaluation becomes visibly less tentative as his views find increasing echoes elsewhere. It is interesting that Myron Atkin questioned the 'scientific' approach to curriculum design explicity from his position as a science educator. This may lead us to question the easy assumption that scientists in education respond more favourably to the apparent rigour and elegance of the operationalist's position than their colleagues within the creative arts. It is for this reason instructive to compare the arguments advanced by Atkin with those put forward by Elliot Eisner.

Myron Atkin's interest in evaluation grew out of his position as Co-Director of the Illinois Elementary School Science Project. The evaluation of a curriculum development project raises issues that jostle uneasily with the dominant objectives model. We saw that the Parlett and Hamilton paper linked the search for a new methodology quite explicitly with the demands of innovation and curriculum development. Not least, although Michael Scriven was yet to popularise the distinction, curriculum development poses problems of formative *as well as* summative *judgements. How can a curriculum development team handle problems related to the need to improve course content?*

Atkin's 1963 paper, 'Some evaluation problems in a course content improvement project', takes this problem as its starting point. The paper had a seminal effect. Not surprisingly, the most immediately favourable response came from the curriculum developers rather than from the educational researchers. Looking back on this paper one is immediately struck by the slight nervousness of tone. There is no pretext of being 'authoritative', merely the suggestion that 'inadequate attention' has previously been paid to certain broad problems in the area of curriculum development. The bite, however, comes in Atkin's choice of metaphors. For the first time, the objectives model and the entire apparatus of behavioural specification are taken off their pedestal as modus operandi *for responsible curriculum development. The panacea is debunked as an 'ingrained rubric'.*

Several years later Myron Atkin returns to metaphor and analogy in 'Research styles in science education' [1967-8]. This paper examines alternative models for educational research. Atkin develops the argument that there is a need for educational investigation placing greater reliance on an intuitive and aesthetic dimension for making decisions. Such research is likely to be research in natural settings. It is seen as 'high risk' and needs to be underwritten by 'senior scholars'.

This pairing of high risk with high status personnel exemplifies the developing social and political conservatism that underlies Atkin's writing. He finds attractive a cautious approach to educational change, and values both social consensus and traditional academic values. Atkin's subsequent career has taken him increasingly towards high-level policy-making and its impact on the classroom. Alternative evaluations do not in Atkin's view exist to articulate ambiguities or explore rich ironies, but to facilitate widely-discussed cautious change. It is a deeply conservative concept. Paradoxically, the logical concomitant of this view is to see the engineering model not as traditional but as potentially and dangerously radical.

The most widely quoted of Atkin's papers, and his fullest critique of the 'behavioural objectives' approach is 'Behavioural objectives in curriculum design: a cautionary note'. This first appeared in 'soft' form for an AERA meeting, and later appeared in the May 1968 issue of The Science Teacher. *The tone of the paper is self-assured, perhaps reflecting the increasing acceptability of Atkin's ideas to his specialised audience. He tells us that at his University of Illinois campus, bumper stickers appeared [as they did elsewhere, very widely] urging one to STAMP OUT NON-BEHAVIORAL OBJECTIVES. Popham also found these artifacts interesting.*

Finally in 'Curriculum design: the central development group and the local teacher' [1970], Myron Atkin returns to the inadequacies of the analogies underlying existing models of curriculum evaluation and argues for an approach to curriculum development and evaluation that begins as well as ends at the level of student and teacher. We reproduce extracts from this paper under the title 'Locus for decision-making'.

3.1 Myron Atkin
Evaluation for content improvement

It is not the purpose here to deprecate the standards that have come to be accepted for educational evaluation. Few would deny their usefulness for many educational purposes. Rather it is the contention here that inadequate attention has been given to certain evaluation problems in the broad area of curriculum development, particularly in a period of radical modification of course content such as we see today in mathematics and science, and that a few of the problems are only dimly recognised.

Specialists in evaluation may detect traces of pre-knowledge bias in what follows. The paper makes no pretext of being authoritative. However, certain evaluational rubrics seem deeply ingrained in educational practice and if a small body of researchers is challenging some of the older guidelines, their influence is not yet broad enough to have had an appreciable impact on curriculum evaluation.

It is hoped that some of the evaluation problems can be delineated in this paper, and they will be outlined in the context of a single course improvement activity, the University of Illinois Elementary-School Science Project. This Project, which received its initial support from the National Science Foundation in September 1960, has had as its major purpose from the inception the production of astronomy materials for children — materials that are sound astronomically, that reflect the structure of the subject as it is viewed by astronomers of stature, and that can be handled by teachers and children in actual classrooms. Thus, the Project reflects a trend characteristic of several of the current mathematics and science curriculum activities: a delineation of content is required that reveals a potent hierarchy of conceptual schemes, a few ideas with considerable intellectual mileage that help the learner understand in the most economical manner possible a given discipline as it is perceived by its senior practitioners. . . .

But it is in the intermediate stages of curriculum development that evaluation problems are most obvious. It is a fact, and to this writer a fortunate one, that prime movers in the large high school curriculum projects have moved ahead with a certain brashness in suggesting curriculum modifications. They have insisted on working on a new curriculum and its implementation in its entirety and immediately, often recognising but choosing to postpone some tough evaluational questions

Source: J. Myron Atkin (1963). 'Some evaluation problems in a course content improvement project'. Journal of Research in Science Teaching, 1, *pp. 129-32. The extracts reproduced here are taken from pp. 129, 130, 131, 132.*

rather than to accept a reductionist approach and work primarily on the more readily solvable subsidiary problems. The scientists and mathematicians in these projects seem to have had few doubts about their ability to recognise valid curriculum materials and effective teaching. However, few curriculum developers schooled primarily in elementary and secondary education feel confident enough about their own taste to place strong reliance on rather 'unsystematic' attempts at evaluation once feasible materials have been produced. There exists a pronounced expectation for the accumulation of objective evidence to ascertain the success of the materials in achieving specified aims.

The comprehension of content *per se* by the children represents one type of evaluation problem. Generally, curriculum developers are aware of a range of possible outcomes other than recall of specific information, e.g. application, comprehension of major principles. Test makers, among others, have made ingenious attempts to construct methods of measuring a multitude of content outcomes.

A major evaluation difficulty relates to the assessment of certain outcomes that may not be specific to a particular course but the outgrowth, hopefully, of many courses. Most of those engaged in science curriculum development consider the materials they produce to influence children's attitudes about science and scientists — in addition to extending understanding of certain concepts that reflect the structure of the discipline. Further, it is the hope of some that new curriculum materials will lead to a comprehension of certain broad scientific ideas — randomness, symmetry, arbitrariness, proportionality, successive approximation, reference frame, discreteness — that are tangential to the sequence of conceptual schemes within a given discipline. Few evaluation specialists seem to have directed attention to such broad questions; yet the total effect of a sequence of courses over a number of years seems to be a rather crucial educational outcome.

Still another difficulty lies in the fact that those engaged in curriculum development are exhorted to assess learning in terms of readily observable and measurable behavioural change in the students. . . .

The curriculum developer is urged, *at the start,* to formulate clear statements of anticipated behaviours. The possibility that such behaviours may be identified *later* in a new curriculum activity seems like too slipshod a procedure to certain evaluators. Of possibly greater significance is the fact that too early a statement of objectives may obscure potentially significant outcomes that do not become apparent until later because they are seldom anticipated. This statement, of course, applies to negative outcomes as well as positive ones. Scientists, as a rule, are not particularly articulate about listing the objectives of a course of study with which they are pleased. They sense the appropriateness of the course; when they enumerate their reasons, they can be expected to overlook a few of the most significant ones.

Evaluation activity in the University of Illinois Elementary-School Science Project has centred around more readily ascertainable information such as the following:

1   To what extent do children comprehend the content of the astronomy materials? . . .

2   To what extent does our delineation of content reflect a major and potent sequence of astronomical ideas? . . .

3   What modifications in approach are suggested by teachers? . . .

It is universally accepted that evaluation should be central to course improvement. But only when evaluation is seen as facilitating rather than limiting function will it be utilised more effectively by curriculum developers. To achieve this end, a flexible approach to the role of evaluation must be fostered by evaluation specialists themselves; there must be a willingness to question some of the conventional wisdom that has been accepted for decades, possibly with little analysis of the appropriateness today of the basic assumptions.

3.2 Myron Atkin
Research styles

Let me take a stab at identifying a major reason for the fact that educational research seems to have had little impact on the classroom — especially if we consider 'research' apart from 'development'. The models of educational research currently in vogue are rooted in 'scientific' approaches — inquiry modes that are based strongly on empirical, hypothesis-testing techniques. The overwhelming number of investigators using this model are either psychologists or individuals influenced primarily by psychology or another behavioural science. Doctoral programmes at my own institution, and I imagine at yours, stress behavioural science techniques almost to the exclusion of any other in the preparation of educational researchers. As a direct result of this research bias, we usually find that problems in education that are investigated turn out to be either trivial, or they bear little relevance to classroom practice.

The triviality often results from the strong reliance in much psychological experimentation on 'hard' measures of behavioural change. Inasmuch as we have not yet learned to assess behaviourally some of the most important educational changes for which we strive, the sophisticated research models that are used often manipulate insignificant variables. The researchers keep refining their procedures, largely but not exclusively statistical procedures, seemingly unaware of where the crucial problems lie. An elaborate research methodology was evolved around the investigation of inconsequential events. . . .

Activity in a classroom is complex and subtle. Any one of the traditional perspectives from which investigators have viewed the educational process has been extremely narrow in relation to that process. It may be true that these perspectives that have been used from the behavioural sciences are all that we have had. Perhaps it is best to work with what is available. However, the end result has been a view so simplified, or so segmented, as to have little relation to the total educational process.

For the moment, let us call teaching a craft to enable the construction of an analogy, an analogy with the craft of metallurgy. For centuries, and continuing today, skilled craftsmen have been making metals. They have learned to add a little of this substance and a little of that, then heat the batch for a certain length of time until it reaches a certain colour, then let

Source: J. Myron Atkin (1967-8). 'Research styles in science education'. Journal of Research in Science Teaching, 5, pp. 338-45. The extracts reproduced here are taken from pp. 339-41, 342, 343, 344, 345.

it cool at a certain rate. The craft has been continually developed through the centuries, apprentices learning from masters. Meanwhile 'scientific' approaches to metallurgy have not succeeded in fully explaining all that the master craftsman does. Physicists and chemists who study metallurgy recognise that the craftsman uses certain processes that scientists do not yet understand. Scientists study the metallurgists at work in the hope that this analysis will give them clues to better understand physics or chemistry. . . .

Isn't it possible that teaching is at least as complex as metallurgy? The theories of psychologists, anthropologists and sociologists — taken singly — do not permit us to deduce an educational programme any more than a physicist's theories lead directly to fabrication of new metals. It doesn't seem unreasonable to follow the route of metallurgy. Let's see how superb craftsmen operate, in this case teachers in the classroom. We might then learn more about the behavioural sciences.

A second model has been developed for educational research within recent years to supplement the model drawn from the behavioural sciences. . . . I am referring to the engineering model for educational research and development. . . . The engineering model is found under labels like 'systems analysis', 'operations analysis', 'planning-programming budgeting systems', and 'cost-benefit approaches'. . . .

I understand that when a spaceship is to be designed one of the first steps entails the delineation of performance specifications. There first must be general agreement about what the ship is expected to do. The next job is to prepare the designs and engage a manufacturer who will most economically achieve the objective.

On the surface this seems a most appealing model for educational research and development activities. First, identify the performance objectives toward which the system should be aimed. Then design the system such that these objectives will be achieved economically. In the application of this model to the field of education, equate 'performance objectives' with 'pupil behaviours'. . . .

I have written elsewhere and at greater length about the shortcomings of this approach in the design of curriculum. Let me mention here only that early specification of behavioural objectives builds in a bias against identification of worthwhile outcomes that aren't apparent until the curriculum has been in use for some time. . . .

I have puzzled long over possible reasons why the engineering model has been adopted so uncritically by the educational community, but it is doubtful that any of my speculation has been productive. It would be unkind perhaps to jump to a conclusion that educational researchers are using the style broadly solely because that is where the federal government is placing its money. . . .

The model of educational research I am proposing here, and that may have considerable promise for influence on practice, places classroom analysis and developmental work at the core. It is possible to obtain agreement from a wide range of individuals that given innovations are tasteful and effective. On this point, chemists, biologists, educationists, novelists, psychologists, anthropologists, lawyers, philosophers, administrators and historians will usually agree. An effective teacher is generally recognised as such. A job of the educational researcher is to begin examining the work of effective teachers, teachers working intelligently with appealing content, in an attempt to validate generalisations that may be made about the elements which make the teaching strong. I believe that a promising beginning may result if individuals from various disciplines, such as those listed above, immerse themselves in classrooms for a relatively long period of time and attempt to generate conversations across their special fields to describe the classroom activities and validate the quality of the judgements being made. I am suggesting a direct onslaught on the total educational picture as a substitute for the fragmentary approach that presently characterises most educational research. Research undertaken in such a context has a strong likelihood for major and broad impact on the schools. . . .

All of this suggests that there is a need for educational investigation which places greater reliance on an intuitive and aesthetic dimension for making decisions than we have become familiar with in the educational research literature of the last few decades. Of course, in ordinary discussion about education, conducted by professionals or non-professionals, the aesthetic and anecdotal elements usually are strong. People frequently talk about teachers who make the subject 'alive,' about the 'verve' characteristic of some teacher's approach, about the 'satisfactions' children get through doing certain types of investigation, about the superb timing that a specific second-grade teacher displays in teaching of reading. But in currently acceptable styles of educational research and development, it is usually deemed 'unscientific' to talk in such language. There is a continuing pressure for hard measures of educational change, a pressure and tradition that derives from the sources already described. . . .

Because of the variety of talents required to do educational research in naturalistic settings, I think that universities will continue to be at the centre of such activities. We don't find the necessary mix of philosophers, historians, novelists, chemists, journalists and anthropologists in the public schools, or anywhere else. . . .

In short, my view of a productive style of educational research still places strong reliance on individuals from the traditional academic disciplines as well as on educationists. These people are supplemented by writers of fiction, by journalists, perhaps by playwrights. All of them are encouraged to focus on classroom events. I don't think we have enough trials that exemplify this style of educational research to have yet made me pessimistic about the outcome. In fact, the few attempts in which I have engaged in such tentative explorations seem to me to have been productive. . . .

It should be reiterated also that this research style, in order to work, requires the talents of senior scholars in the various disciplines. Junior men are prone to operate within the closely defined boundaries of the field in which they have been recently trained. It seems that the only people who can afford professionally to go beyond the boundaries of their own formal education are individuals who have already earned a reputation for scholarship within the field as the field is conventionally conceived. I don't think that this phenomenological approach to educational research stands a chance unless we can enlist the aid of well-established academicians. . . .

It is possible that my plea for research in naturalistic settings, my plea for putting aside our psychologically based and engineering models for a time, my plea for phenomenological approaches, my plea for the involvement of a broad array of academicians who will focus on classroom events — it is possible that all of these pleas have relatively little merit. But it is *more* likely that they have some merit though not as much as I might claim for them — yet they will not be tried broadly because it is difficult to create an appropriate atmosphere at a university that will foster such a research style. . . . It will remain for some imaginative university to create a setting for a research style of this type. Where it will happen, I am not sure. But it will be at a place where relatively high-risk ventures are encouraged if they have the support of productive people. . . .

3.3   Myron Atkin
'STAMP OUT NON-BEHAVIORAL OBJECTIVES'

In certain influential circles, anyone who confesses to reservations about
the use of behaviourally stated objectives for curriculum planning runs the
risk of being labelled as the type of individual who would attack the
virtues of motherhood. Bumper stickers have appeared at my own
institution, and probably at yours, reading, STAMP OUT NON-
BEHAVIORAL OBJECTIVES. I trust that the person who prepared the
stickers had humour as his primary aim; nevertheless, the crusade for
specificity of educational outcome has become intense and evangelical.
The worthiness of this particular approach has come to be accepted as
self-evident by ardent proponents, proponents who sometimes sound like
the true believers who cluster about a new social or religious movement.

Behavioural objectives enthusiasts are warmly endorsed and embraced
by the systems and operations analysis advocates, most educational
technologists, the cost-benefit economists, the planning-programming
budgeting system stylists, and many others. In fact, the behavioural
objectives people are now near the centre of curriculum decision-making.
Make no mistake; they have replaced the academicians and the general
curriculum theorists — especially in the new electronically based education
industries and in governmental planning agencies. The engineering model
for educational research and development represents a forceful tide today.
Those who have a few doubts about the effects of the tide had better be
prepared to be considered uninitiated and naive, if not slightly addlepated
and antiquarian. . . .

A situation is created in the newer curriculum design procedures based
on behaviourally stated objectives in which scholars who do not talk a
behavioural-change language are expected to describe their goals at a time
when the intricate intellectual subtleties of their work may not be clear,
even in the disciplinary language with which they are familiar. At the
other end, the educational evaluator, the behavioural specifier, typically
has very little understanding of the curriculum that is being designed —
understanding with respect to the new view of the subject field that it
affords. It is too much to expect that the behavioural analyst, or anyone
else, recognise the shadings of meaning in various evolving economic

Source: J. Myron Atkin (May 1968). 'Behavioral objectives in curriculum design: a
cautionary note'. The Science Teacher, 35, No. 5, pp. 27-30. The extracts reproduced here are taken from pp. 27, 29-30.

theories, the complex applications of the intricacies of wave motion, or the richness of nuance reflected in a Stravinsky composition. . . .

A key educational task, and a task that is well handled by the effective teacher, is that of relating educational goals to the situation at hand — as well as relating the situation at hand to educational goals. It is impractical to pursue all goals thoroughly. And it does make a difference *when* you try to teach something. Considerable educational potential is lost when certain concepts are taught didactically. Let's assume that some third-grade teacher considers it important to develop concepts related to sportsmanship. It would be a rather naive teacher who decided that she would undertake this task at 1.40 p.m. on Friday of next week. The experienced teacher has always realised that learnings related to such an area must be stressed in an appropriate context, and the context often cannot be planned.

Perhaps there is no problem in accepting this view with respect to a concept like sportsmanship, but I submit that a similar case can be made for a range of crucial cognitive outcomes that are basic to various subject-matter fields. I use science for my examples because I know more about this field than about others. But equilibrium, successive approximation, symmetry, entropy and conservation are pervasive ideas with a broad range of application. These ideas are taught with the richest meaning only when they are emphasised repeatedly in appropriate and varied contexts. Many of these contexts arise in classroom situations that are unplanned, but that have powerful potential. It is detrimental to learning not to capitalise on the opportune moments for effectively teaching one idea or another. Riveting the teacher's attention to a few behavioural goals provides him with blinders that may limit his range. Directing him to hundreds of goals leads to confusing, mechanical pedagogic style and loss of spontaneity.

A final point to be made in this paper relates to values, and it deals with a primary flaw in the consumption of much educational research. It is difficult to resist the assumption that those attributes which we can measure are the elements which we consider most important. . . . What the educational community poorly realises at the moment is that behavioural goals may or may not be worthwhile. They are articulated from among the vast library of goals because they are stated relatively easily. Again, let's not assume that what we can presently measure necessarily represents our most important activity. . . .

The issues here represent a few of the basic questions that seem crucial enough to be examined in an open forum that admits the possibility of fresh perspectives. Too much of the debate related to the use of behavioural objectives has been conducted in an argumentative style that characterises discussions of fundamental religious views among adherents who are poorly informed. . . .

3.4 Myron Atkin
Locus for decision-making

One of the primary dilemmas in curriculum design is the question of the locus for decision-making. It can be argued, on the one hand, that no education takes place except at the level of the individual. The manner in which almost all educational systems are organised provides for students to meet in classes within schools under the tutelage of teachers. The events that transpire in this setting are the only events of significance; therefore all attempts at change must begin as well as end at the level of student and teacher. . . .

. . . in all countries pressures for centralisation of educational authority seem to be growing. Many of our most pressing problems are seen as resolvable only by strong, nationwide policy formulation. It is indeed the conclusion of some observers that the progressive centralisation of authority within the various countries is the most profound and basic social change in the western world during the last century. . . .

Permit me to sketch salient characteristics of a few results of centralisation of educational power in today's world. It is no surprise, probably, that in a highly industrialised society there is a tendency to use industrial models for any activity, even the implementation of social policy. It is necessary only to perceive educational services as 'products' to begin examining production models when drawing plans for new programmes in the schools. Mass production to highly detailed specifications with appropriate quality control is the goal of the factory. An increasing number of educational planners see the same aim for the school. Certain skills are to be mass-produced. Mass-production requires sophisticated pre-specification. And quality control is necessary if educators are to be responsible. . . .

If certain characteristics of the child are the 'product' of the educational system, exactly what are those characteristics in terms of performance? What must the child be able to do? What are the constraints in the 'production process'? What are some of the acceptable costs? Once this

Source: J. Myron Atkin (1970). 'Curriculum design: the central development group and the local teacher', prepared for the Institut für die Pädagogik der Naturwissenschaften Invitational Symposium, Kiel, West Germany, 14 October 1970. First published in IPN Symposium 1970 über Forschung und Entwicklung naturwissenschaftlicher Curricula, Institut für die Pädagogik der Naturwissenschaften an der Christian-Albrechts-Universitat, Kiel, 1971, pp. 35-43. We reprint extracts only.

framework for conceptualising the problem of educational change is established, the ground work is set for the behavioural engineers, those individuals who quite consciously apply the industrial model to social problems. The analogy between school and factory is then firmly established, and in a surprisingly explicit fashion. . . .

In this production-line model of education, the emphasis is on the replicable and the highly quantifiable, the readily describable and the unambiguous.

The debilitating limitations of the behavioural approach to curriculum design have been enunciated now in several places. And inasmuch as I personally have written on the subject,[1] I will not detail here the inattentiveness of the model to the tangential, to the private outcome, to the long-term effect, to the relatively subtle. But of perhaps greater significance, the engineering model is being called into sharp question today within the engineering field itself, and for many of the same reasons. . . .

The critics of the production-line model for schooling are learning to dismiss the rhetoric of 'individuality' that the behavioural engineers employ. There are claims in many new programmes about provision within various curriculum efforts for the individual student. But examination usually reveals that the so-called individualisation has all been predetermined! Thus a child may progress along any of fifteen pathways, but each of the pathways is elaborately detailed in advance!

It has so far been the posture of most curriculum development groups of which I have knowledge to utilise the 'linear' approach as a method of implementing a particular viewpoint with respect to curriculum. And, as indicated, the model is being criticised by students who feel some revulsion for the overall system. But today the model is being rejected also by teachers who are asserting increasingly their own prerogatives in all educational matters, including formulation of curriculum. It is the case that in the United States many of the new contracts that are being developed between unionised teachers and boards of education provide for an increased role for the local teacher in the determination of curriculum. Thus legal documents are being drafted at an increasing rate that put the power as well as the authority for curriculum determination right at the level of the classroom.

Thus political realities are adding to the problems of the theoretical weakness of the behavioural models for curriculum development, and it seems even clearer that alternatives must be examined. . . .

1 'Behavioral objectives in curriculum design: a cautionary note'. *The Science Teacher*, **35**, No. 5, 1968, pp. 27-30.

Elliot Eisner

Elliot Eisner's contribution towards developing new paradigms of curriculum evaluation has been the least surprising, given his background. Coming to curriculum theory as an art educator, he soon found that the field did not match up to his expectations. Although he entered the dispute flamboyantly with the provocatively-titled paper 'Educational objectives: help or hindrance?', a careful reading of Eisner would place his major shift in position much later. Only 'Emerging models for educational evaluation' and 'Applying educational connoisseurship and criticism to educational settings' are thoroughly radical in the terms of the central thesis of this reader. This is because Eisner's earlier work, concerned with the mismatch between the purposes of art education and the rhetoric of intent advocated by the 'behavioural objectives' model, did not question the dominant paradigm that sought to limit the 'countenance' of curriculum evaluation to the sum of student outcomes.

The earlier Eisner papers, featured here in our first three extracts, consequently exhibit two thrusts. The first is to elaborate a general critique of the objectives approach as it was then conventionally propounded. The second is to argue for the more open-ended so-called 'expressive' objectives. In appropriate circumstances those better reflect the actual intentions of the educator.

The general critique developed along now-familiar lines: that certain outcomes are complex, or unpredictable, or both; that in some subjects it is legitimate for the end-result to surprise the teacher and the student; that one should avoid confusing the application of a standard with the passing of a judgement, and that in some domains there is an absence of easy rules by which judgements can be reduced to standards.

The positive contribution arising out of this critique is found in 'Instructional and expressive educational objectives: their formulation and use in curriculum'. The problem of determining how educational objectives should be stated or used becomes not simply a question of technique, but a question of value. Once again we encounter an approach to the problems of curriculum evaluation in terms of identifying and teasing out underlying metaphors [here industrial, behaviouristic or biological]. In this respect Eisner is strongly reminiscent of Atkin.

The most significant single published paper for our present purposes, however, is 'Emerging models for educational evaluation', extracted here under the title 'Implications for evaluation'. Interestingly Eisner's 'expres-

sive objectives' were seen as the outcomes *of encounters, rather than as the encounters themselves. Eisner himself sternly warns us against blurring this distinction in an 'Epilogue' to 'Instructional and expressive educational objectives: their formulation and use in curriculum'. The implications for curriculum evaluation appear at this stage no more formidable than the assertion that pupils' work of art (i.e. their responses to the expressive objectives that gave rise to the activity) should be evaluated using the familiar techniques of art criticism. 'Emerging models for educational evaluation' appears at first to be working within this assumption: there is an early section dealing with 'images of types of outcome'.*

Soon, however, this becomes of much wider importance as the cuckoo grows too big for the nest. Eisner suggests that much that goes on in schools can be illuminated by the tools of criticism, and that the 'techniques of art criticism' model may become, by analogy, in its 'full-blown' form a way of evaluating the complex encounters and processes of teaching and learning. This shift in emphasis towards an interpretation of classroom situations *is quite explicit: 'a situation's expressive and underlying qualities are also candidates for description and interpretation'. This could lead to evaluation reports reading like film reviews. A number of reports in Section 5, like David Jenkins' account of the Integrated Studies lesson at Hardacre Secondary School, have this flavour.*

Eisner is currently developing the idea of criticism in a way that makes it dependent upon 'connoisseurship', the art of appreciation which the criticism 'discloses'. Our final extract is taken from 'Applying educational connoisseurship and criticism to educational settings'. It exhibits a tension between the private aestheticism of the connoisseur and the public role of the critic. The latter must convey some flavour within his account of the quality of the perceived event, perhaps employing 'a form of artistry replete with metaphor, contrast, redundancy and emphasis that captures some aspect of the quality and character of educational life'. Such artistry could take the form of 'thick description'.

Even seminal thinkers may have gaps in particular areas. Eisner has little to say on the various audiences for evaluation reports or on problems of presentation or display. Yet it is in these directions that his arguments ultimately take us. An illuminating contrast is with Robert Stake who chooses, in a paper called 'To evaluate an arts program', [extracted here as 'Responsive evaluation'], the expressive arts as the most apt area of the curriculum about which to make his most elaborate statement on 'responsive' evaluation. Eisner's 'disclosed connoisseurship' has some affinity with Stake's 'portrayal', although Stake's interest in making evaluation reports accessible to diverse audiences takes him away from the implicit elitism built into a 'high-culture' notion like connoisseurship.

3.5 Elliot Eisner
Educational objectives: help or hindrance?

As I view the situation, there are several limitations to theory in curriculum regarding the functions educational objectives are to perform. These limitations I would like to identify.

Educational objectives are typically derived from curriculum theory, which assumes that it is possible to predict with a fair degree of accuracy what the outcomes of instruction will be. In a general way this is possible. If you set about teaching a student algebra, there is no reason to assume he will learn to construct sonnets instead.

Yet the outcomes of instruction are far more numerous and complex for educational objectives to encompass. . . . The teacher uses the moment in a situation that is better described as kaleidoscopic than stable. In the very process of teaching and discussing, unexpected opportunities emerge for making a valuable point, for demonstrating an interesting idea and for teaching a significant concept. The first point I wish to make, therefore, is that the dynamic and complex process of instruction yields outcomes far too numerous to be specified in behavioural and content terms in advance.

A second limitation of theory concerning educational objectives is its failure to recognise the constraints various subject matters place upon objectives. The point here is brief. In some subject areas, such as mathematics, languages and the sciences, it is possible to specify with great precision the particular operation or behaviour the student is to perform after instruction. In other subject areas, especially the arts, such specification is frequently not possible, and when possible may not be desirable. . . . In the arts and in subject matters where, for example, novel or creative responses are desired, the particular behaviours to be developed cannot easily be identified. Here curriculum and instruction should yield behaviours and products which are unpredictable. The end achieved ought to be something of a surprise both to teacher and pupil. While it could be argued that one might formulate an educational objective which specified novelty, originality or creativeness as the desired outcome, the particular referents for these terms cannot be specified in advance; one must judge after the fact whether the product produced or the behaviour displayed belongs in the 'novel' class. This is a much different procedure than is determining whether or not a particular word

Source: E. W. Eisner (1967). 'Educational objectives: help or hindrance?', School Review, **75**, No. 3, pp. 250-60. *The extracts reproduced here are taken from pp. 253-6.*

has been spelled correctly or a specified performance, that is, jumping a three-foot hurdle, has been attained. . . .

The third point I wish to make deals with the belief that objectives stated in behavioural and content terms can be used as criteria by which to measure the outcomes of curriculum and instruction. Educational objectives provide, it is argued, the standard against which achievement is to be measured. Both taxonomies are built upon this assumption since their primary function is to demonstrate how objectives can be used to frame test items appropriate for evaluation. The assumption that objectives can be used as standards by which to measure achievement fails, I think, to distinguish adequately between the application of a standard and the making of a judgement. . . . By virtue of socially-defined rules of grammar (syntax and logic, for example) it is possible to quantitatively compare and measure error in discursive or mathematical statement. Some fields of activity, especially those which are qualitative in character, have no comparable rules and hence are less amenable to quantitative assessment. It is here that evaluation must be made, not primarily by applying a socially-defined standard, but by making a human qualitative judgement. . . .

3.6 Elliot Eisner
Establishing a direction

What curriculum theorists have tended to neglect is the difference between defining an objective and establishing a direction. . . .

To establish a direction for inquiry, dialogue or discussion is to identify a theme and to examine it as it unfolds through the process of inquiry. The particular form of behaviour or content learned might differ enormously for different students. The ends achieved are not preconceived but reflected upon in retrospect rather than in prospect. This, I believe, is what most teachers do in the process of curriculum development and what I suspect most of those reading this article do. . . .

When educational ends are directed toward open objectives, the form and content of the pupil's behaviour are identified and assessed after the educational activity concludes. The differences between open and closed concepts and open and closed objectives have not received much attention in the development of curriculum theory. . . .

Source: E. W. Eisner (1967). 'A response to my critics' School Review, **75**, No. 3, *pp. 277-82. The extracts reproduced here are taken from p. 279.*

3.7 Elliot Eisner
Instructional and expressive objectives

The formulation of educational means is never a neutral act. The tools employed and the metaphors used to describe education lead to actions which are not without consequences with respect to value. Many of the metaphors used to describe the importance and function of educational objectives have been associated with conceptions of education which I believe are alien to the educational values held by many of those who teach. These metaphors are not new: they have been with educators for some time and it will be fruitful, I believe, to compare some of the arguments and metaphors used today with conceptions of education developed within the past fifty years.

It seems to me that three metaphors can be used to characterise dominant views about the nature of education—at least as it has been conceived and carried on in American schools. These metaphors are *industrial, behaviouristic* and *biological.*

The industrial metaphor was perhaps most influential in education during the first and second decades of this century, a period in which the efficiency movement emerged. This movement . . . adopted and adapted industrial methods—especially time-and-motion study—to improve the educational process and make it more efficient. Under pressure from local boards of education and the muckraking magazines of the early twentieth century, school administrators tried to protect their positions and to reduce their vulnerability to public criticism by employing methods developed by Francis Taylor in industry in order to improve the efficiency of the school. . . .

To bring about this metamorphosis in the schools certain tasks had to be accomplished. First and foremost, quantitative and qualitative standards had to be formulated for judging the educational product. Second, time-and-motion studies had to be made to identify the most efficient means. Third, nothing that could be routinised and prescribed was to be left to the judgement of the worker since his decisions might lead to inefficiency and error. Fourth, the quality of the product was to be judged not by the workers in the school but by the consumers of the product—in

Source: E. W. Eisner (1969). 'Instructional and expressive educational objectives: their formulation and use in curriculum' and 'Epilogue'. In W. James Popham (ed.), Instructional Objectives, *AERA Monograph Series on Curriculum Evaluation, No. 3. Chicago: Rand McNally, pp. 1-18, 130-2. The extracts reproduced here are taken from pp. 3, 4-5, 6-7, 8, 14, 15-16, 17, 130.*

this case, society. Fifth, the tasks were to be divided into manageable units so that they could be taught and evaluated at every step along the production line. With these prescriptions for practice, prescriptions taken from industrial management, emerged metaphors through which education was viewed.

These metaphors, like the means, were industrial in character. The school was seen as a *plant*. The *superintendent* directed the operation of the plant. The teachers were engaged in a job of *engineering*, and the pupils were the *raw material* to be processed in the plant according to the demands of the *consumers*. Furthermore, the product was to be judged at regular intervals along the production line using *quality control standards* which were to be quantified to reduce the likelihood of error. *Product specifications* were to be prescribed before the raw material was processed. In this way efficiency, measured primarily with respect to cost, could be determined. . . .

Before comparing the educational assumptions embedded in the industrial metaphor with some of the assumptions and positions regarding educational objectives argued in the literature today, I should like to pass on to the second metaphor through which education has been viewed.

The behaviouristic metaphor had its birth with efforts to construct a science of education and psychology. At the same time that school administrators were embracing the principles of scientific management in an effort to make schools more efficient, Thorndike, Watson, Judd and Bobbitt were trying to construct and employ scientific methods useful for the study and conduct of education. One part of the task, if it was to be accomplished at all, was to relinquish the heritage of a psychology that did not lend itself to scientific verification. Intra-psychic events, thoughts and mental states couched in romantic language saturated with surplus meaning had to give way to careful, quantifiable descriptions of human behaviour. The poetic and insightful language of a William James had to give way to the objective precision of a John Watson, if psychology was to become a science. . . .

The significance of these views about the nature of science of psychology and education cannot in my opinion be overemphasised. If what education is after is a change in behaviour — something that you can bring about and then observe — there is little use talking about the development of fugitive forms of non-empirical thought. If educational objectives are to be meaningful, they must be anchored in sense data and the type of data with which education is concerned is that of human behaviour. . . .

A third metaphor that can be used to characterise educational thought and practice during the twentieth century is biological in character. . . . According to Dewey, man is an organism which lives not only in but through an environment. For Dewey and for those who followed his lead the child was not simply a matter to be moulded but an individual who brings with him needs, potentialities and experiences with which to transact with the environment. What was important educationally for Dewey was for the child to obtain increasing, intelligent control in planning his own education. To do this, to become a master of his own educational journey, required a teacher sympathetic to the child's background and talents. Educational experience was to be differentiated to suit the characteristics of a changing child; the cultivation of idiosyncracy was a dominant concern. . . .

What I am arguing is that the problem of determining how educational objectives should be stated or used is not simply a question of technique but a question of value. The differences between individuals regarding the nature and the use of educational objectives spring from differences in their conceptions of education; under the rug of technique lies an image of man. . . .

As an institution responsible for the transmission of culture, the school is concerned with enabling students to acquire those intellectual codes and skills which will make it possible for them to profit from the contributions of those who have gone before. To accomplish this task an array of socially-defined skills must be learned — reading, writing and arithmetic are some examples of coding systems that are basic to further inquiry into human culture.

While school programmes attempt to enable children to acquire these skills, to learn to employ the tools necessary for using cultural products, schools are also concerned with enabling children to make a contribution to that culture by providing opportunities for the individual to construe his own interpretation to the material he encounters or constructs. A simple repetition of the past is the surest path to cultural *rigor mortis*.

Given these dual concerns — helping children to become skilled in the use of cultural tools already available and helping them to modify and expand these tools so that the culture remains viable — it seems to me appropriate to differentiate between two types of educational objectives which can be formulated in curriculum planning. The first type is familiar to most readers and is called an *instructional objective*; the second I have called an *expressive objective*. . . .

Expressive objectives differ considerably from instructional objectives. An expressive objective does not specify the behaviour the student is to acquire after having engaged in one or more learning activities. An expressive objective describes an educational encounter: it identifies a situation in which children are to work, a problem with which they are to cope, a task in which they are to engage; but it does not specify what they are to learn from that encounter, situation, problem or task. An expressive objective provides both the teacher and the student with an invitation to explore, defer or focus on issues that are of peculiar interest or import to the inquirer. An expressive objective is evocative rather than prescriptive.

The expressive objective is intended to serve as a theme around which skills and understandings learned earlier can be brought to bear, but through which those skills and understandings can be expanded, elaborated and made idiosyncratic. With an expressive objective what is desired is not homogeneity of response among students but diversity. In the expressive context the teacher hopes to provide a situation in which meanings become personalised and in which children produce products, both theoretical and qualitative, that are as diverse as themselves. Consequently the evaluative task in this situation is not one of applying a common standard to the products produced but one of reflecting upon what has been produced in order to reveal its uniqueness and significance. In the expressive context, the product is likely to be as much of a surprise to the maker as it is for the teacher who encounters it. . . .

I believe that the most sophisticated modes of intellectual work — those, for example, undertaken in the studio, the research laboratory and the graduate seminar — most frequently employ expressive rather than instructional objectives. In the doctoral seminar, for example, a theme will be identified around which both teacher and students can interact in an effort to cope more adequately with the problems related to the theme. In such situations educational outcomes are appraised after they emerge. . . .

Epilogue

'Expressive objectives' is a new concept and needs clarification. In my paper I described expressive objectives in terms of encounters that students were to have in an educational setting. This was done in order to provide some type of description of the expressive objective. But I see now what I didn't anticipate at the time I wrote the paper, that describing expressive objectives this way tends to confuse them with learning activities. There is enough confusion in the field of curriculum without my contributing more. . . .

3.8   Elliot Eisner
Implications for evaluation

As I thought about instructional and expressive objectives, it occurred to me that neither of these types adequately fits the kind of tasks given to designers, architects, engineers and commercial artists. Product designers, for example, work for a client who generally has a problem — a specific problem — that he wants the designer to solve. He might say to the designer, 'I need a device that can be marketed for under fifty cents, which can be made on a vacuum press and which ladies can use to carry cosmetics.' The problem that the designer has is to take the specifications that are provided by the client, specifications which define function but which do not provide a solution, and to invent an image that provides a solution within the parameters set by the client. In such a situation, the problem is highly delineated but the range of potential solutions is, in principle, infinite. Furthermore, there is generally little difficulty in determining the success of the solution. In this Type III objective — I do not have an appropriate name for it yet — the designer, or architect or engineer must bring his imaginative resources to bear upon a highly specific problem but one that makes possible a wide variety of solutions. . . .

A second idea that I would like to discuss deals with an image of the types of outcomes that it seems reasonable to assume are the products of teaching. As you well know, the dominant, if not exclusive, orientation toward evaluating the effects of instruction is one which is aimed at determining the extent to which objectives are attained. Objectives in turn are usually couched within some subject-matter field, especially when it comes to the evaluation of academic achievement. Such a vision or model of evaluation fails, I believe, to attend to other, perhaps equally important, consequences of instruction. For example, it is part of educational lore that a teacher not only teaches a subject matter, he also teaches himself. Those of us who have had the good fortune to have studied under great teachers know this in acute terms, but even lesser teachers teach themselves. How teachers attack a problem, what their standards of excellence are, their sense of excitement or boredom when they encounter a new idea, their expectations for deportment, their

Source: E. W. Eisner (1972). 'Emerging models for educational evaluation', School Review, *1971-2,* **80**, *pp. 573-90. The extracts reproduced here are taken from pp. 581, 583-4, 585-6, 587. The footnote in the extract has been renumbered.*

tolerance for ambiguity, their need for precision: these are all teachable characteristics that teachers inevitably convey to students during the course of their work. These effects one might call teacher-specific outcomes. Outcomes dealing with subject-matter achievement are content-specific. . . .

Finally, I want to suggest a set of methods that I consider promising as a complement to the quantitative procedures now used so widely for educational evaluation. That set is the procedures and techniques of art criticism. The criticism of art is the use of methods designed to heighten one's perception of the qualities that constitute the work. The end of criticism, as Dewey observed, is the re-education of the perception of the work of art.[1] To achieve this end, the critic must bring two kinds of skills to his work. First, he must have developed highly refined visual sensibilities; that is, he must be able to see the elements that constitute a whole and their interplay. Second, he must be capable of rendering his perceptions into a language that makes it possible for others less perceptive than he to see qualities and aspects of the work that they would otherwise overlook. The critic, like a good teacher or book, directs attention to the subtle, he points out and articulates, he vivifies perception. . . .

Much of what goes on in schools can be illuminated by the tools of criticism. As a generic method, criticism is especially suited to articulating the unique and the personalistic outcomes that are so highly prized by those who complain of the school's impersonality. The reason criticism is so suited is because it does not depend upon the conventional application of class concepts for description and because it does not restrict itself to the primary surface of a situation; the secondary surface, that is, the situation's expressive and underlying qualities, is also a candidate for description and interpretation. Such a mode of evaluation has not, as far as I know, been employed in its full-blown form (although one of my students is using such a method to examine teaching as an art form). There are in the literature examples that approximate such an approach to evaluation. . . .

---

1   John Dewey (1934). *Art As Experience*. New York: Minton, Balch & Co., p. 324.

3.9   Elliot Eisner
Thick description

Thick description aims at describing the meaning or significance of behaviour as it occurs in a cultural network saturated with meaning. For example, a behavioural description of an eyelid closing on the left eye at the rate of two closures per second could be described in just that way. But a thick description of such behaviours within the context of a cultural subsystem could be described as a wink. The meaning of a wink, especially if the person at the other end is someone of the opposite sex, is entirely different from a description of eyelid closures at the rate of two closures per second. To fail to recognise the difference in the critical description of behaviour is the same as neglecting the iconography used in works of visual art. The splash in the ocean in Breughel's painting, *The Fall of Icarus*, can be critically described only if one knows the story of Icarus. Once aware of the story, the significance of the painting and the meaning of the splash become clear.

The point here is that criticism requires for its successful execution an understanding of the context, the symbols, the rules and the traditions in which an object or event participates. In educational criticism it requires an understanding of the range of educational styles possible in teaching, in organising classrooms and schools, in using curriculum materials and in providing educational activities. The educational critic employs an awareness of these possibilities to recognise the extent to which what he encounters participates in them and the extent to which it departs from them. His vision of pedagogical virtue in each of these realms and others functions as a touchstone for the critical description of what he sees.

Although thick description is a part of educational criticism, it does not by itself complete it. Educational criticism aims not only at revealing from an intellectual point of view the meanings and conventions made and broken that might occur in a classroom, but also aims at using language in a way so vivid that it enables the reader to participate vicariously in the quality of life that characterises the events being described. It is in this sense that educational criticism is itself an art form. It provides a form of understanding through the cues it uses, cues whose referents are live people acting in real contexts that penetrate the affective quality of their transactions.

Source: E. W. Eisner (1975). 'Applying educational connoisseurship and criticism to educational settings'. Paper in second draft form, published here for the first time. The extracts reproduced here are taken from pp. 20-22.

The ability to use language this way might account for the popularity of some of the so-called romantic criticism aimed at chastising American public schools. Lay people as well as professional educators are able to enter into the life of schooling through descriptions that are emotionally evocative and hence 'understand' aspects of educational life that slip through F ratios, 't' tests and the like.

It is instructive to note that the type of connoisseurship and particularly the type of criticism I am describing do not have a firm or well-developed tradition in schools of education. Such traditions do of course exist in highly sophisticated forms in literature, drama, the visual arts, poetry and music. And cinematography, the art form of the twentieth century, is rapidly developing a tradition of criticism. The study of education in this country has evolved from different roots; those of social science. To do research in education has meant to do scientific work. To have evidence regarding educational practice has meant to have scientific evidence. Those whose interests and aptitudes for studying educational phenomena veered toward the humanistic or artistic modes of conception and expression have, unfortunately, too often been thought of as woolly-headed, impressionistic romantics. Educational connoisseurship and critic-ism have not been encouraged. An ounce of data, it seems, has been worth a pound of insight.

Lawrence Stenhouse

One person likely to be missed out of a historical account of the development of alternative evaluation strategies is Lawrence Stenhouse. This is mainly because his view of curriculum evaluation is tangential to the one held by the evaluation community, whether 'traditional' or 'illuminative'. For Stenhouse, curriculum development is a particular kind of action research. Consequently he has progressively departed from the more traditional notion that a curriculum project allows teachers to test a programme of study, perhaps in a manner akin to consumer research. Stenhouse is at present Director of the Centre for Applied Research in Education at the University of East Anglia. He is perhaps most widely known for his work as Director of the Schools Council/Nuffield Humanities Curriculum Project.

The Humanities Curriculum Project was set up as part of the Raising of the School Leaving Age programme to help older pupils to 'develop an understanding of social situations and human acts and of the controversial value issues which they raise'.[1] Two of the major premises advanced by the Project get close to its essence. One was that teachers should submit their teaching in controversial areas to the criterion of neutrality. Another required that classroom discussion (the core activity) should aim to protect divergence of view rather than attempt to achieve consensus.

The extracts we feature here divide sharply into two groups—each arranged in historical sequence. In the first four we trace the development of Stenhouse's views on curriculum research in and beyond the Humanities Curriculum Project. The last two are from theoretical statements of a more general nature.

The first extract, 'Controversial value-issues in the classroom', explores the rationale behind the Humanities Curriculum Project. It is, if you like, the Authorised Version at the time of the Fourth International Curriculum Conference in Washington DC. It discusses 'three possible strategies' for handling value-issues in classroom discussion. The third strategy is the one that was adopted by the Project. This strategy suggests that the way to protect pupils from teacher bias while at the same time advancing their understanding is through the teacher's 'procedural neutrality'. It is worth noting in passing how the Project sees its task. Quite explicitly it 'devises a method of teaching' which forms the basis of a new 'professional ethic'. At

1 L. Stenhouse (1973). 'The Humanities Curriculum Project'. In H. J. Butcher and H. B. Pont (eds.), *Educational Research in Britain 3*. London: University of London Press, pp. 153-4.

this stage the other 'possible alternatives', barely articulated, are all but summarily dismissed. The (first alternative) teacher hoping to transmit an unchallenged value-position on controversial issues will be defeated by the impracticalities of the task, or become involved in systematic hypocrisy. The (second alternative) teacher claiming freedom to give his own sincerely-held viewpoint will leave himself open to a charge of using the classroom as a platform for these views. We are left with the impression that the Humanities Curriculum Project strategy is the only starter in a one-horse race.

Stenhouse was at this time making the astonishing claim that it was possible to examine objectively and dispassionately the effects of trying out in classrooms ideas which just happened to be his own. *The paradoxical quality of this position was later acknowledged by Stenhouse himself: 'This involves us in a paradox from the outset. Those who take part in research need to be driven by curiosity about the possible development of ideas in which they believe'.[2] He has defended this position in private with a further paradoxical assertion—that the* only *ideas human beings are able to examine objectively are their own.*

Our second extract, 'Aspirations into possibilities', articulates a shift in Stenhouse's account of the Humanities Curriculum Project. This may [in Winston Churchill's phrase] exemplify the many-sidedness of truth, rather than diversity of testimony, but as the shift has been insufficiently acknowledged we hesitate to go in for crude assertion. There is a wider issue here that requires us to proceed with proper caution. Lawrence Stenhouse does not lend himself to easy summary and is unusually difficult to 'anthologise'. He has a marked tendency towards highly complex and subtle argument and a taste for paradox which he himself only half acknowledges. This makes him an easy person to misrepresent.

What, then, is the substance of the shift? In 'Aspirations into possibilities' there is no interest in producing a rationale for the new professional ethic. Instead the concern is with a diametrically opposed problem: how can the claims of research and development be met without projects finding themselves in the business of making prescriptions? There are two ways out of the trap and [again characteristically] Stenhouse suggests both of them. The first is to pair curriculum projects so that they explore 'the consequences of contradictory premises advocated in educational debate'. This notion, in spite of superficial similarities, has little in common with the 'three possible strategies' of our first extract. The second way out of the trap of making recommendations is to emphasise the 'research' element, to concentrate attention on the building of new knowledge. The developer becomes the 'researcher', adhering to the canons of social science research [e.g. testing hypotheses about the effects of alternative strategies] or generating insights from case studies. 'Aspira-

2 Stenhouse (1973), p. 150.

tions into possibilities' outlines a six-stage procedure for such action research. Interestingly, Stenhouse sees only two of these as concerning the 'evaluation unit'. The two are 'case studies of experimental schools' and 'monitoring the effects of the dissemination'. Excluded, critically, are testing the logical consistency of the strategy and judging its feasibility in experimental schools. This could be read as an early indication of Stenhouse's growing hostility to curriculum evaluation, both as conventionally propounded and as represented in this reader. The emphasis on case studies is of particular interest to the illuminative evaluators, who share Stenhouse's paradoxical view that field study data are strong data which are difficult to organise, while test data are weak data susceptible to organisation.

If we are right in asserting that the central dilemma for the Humanities Curriculum Project was its need to reconcile its public image — as provider and upholder of a new professional ethic — with its evolving ideology of curriculum research, then the resulting ambivalence ought to have been visible in the trial schools. [They say that to look at the most distant stars is to perceive the universe as it was many million light years ago.] Certainly there was an embarrassing period towards the end of the Project during which time the trial schools, pursuing the categorical imperatives of neutral chairmanship, appeared more righteous than the scribes and pharisees at the centre, increasingly mindful of the canons of social science research.

In 'Aspirations into possibilities', too, it is not the Project's task to 'devise'. Curriculum development, even when it becomes in Stenhouse's sense 'curriculum research', exists to make aspirations into possibilities. Because in a pluralistic society aspirations are 'sectional', a project should tackle those aspirations which are shared by 'a substantial number of teachers and educationists'.

The 'paired project' idea is soon to be taken up and developed further, as will be seen from our next two extracts, 'Research into teaching about race relations' and 'Parallel studies'. Although the Humanities Curriculum Project articulated a single strategy, based on procedural neutrality, a follow-up project in the area of teaching race relations is exploring three strategies, one of them virtually identical to the [Humanities Curriculum Project] strategy. One would be forgiven for supposing this, if a three-horse race, at least to have a clear favourite. But no. The project team feel that they have 'no vested interest in that [Humanities Curriculum Project] strategy in this context'.[3] *Leaving aside the implication that the strategy in its previous context was one in which the researchers had a vested interest, one is immediately struck by the fact that the alternative strategies are not being set up competitively. That is, they are not being*

3 Not that there is anything unusual about research going hand in hand with 'vested interests'. The methodological and ethical problems of participant observation are well-documented, and lie precisely in this area. They are not likely to take the illuminative evaluator by surprise.

judged against each other but each within its own terms. ['The object of the exercise is not to test alternatives.'] This is because the major purpose of the exercise is to feed teacher judgement rather than propose a curriculum for teachers to judge. Such 'situational morality' of curriculum research echoes the concern of the illuminative evaluators to exhume the assumptions of teachers operating in authentic situations. We notice also that two broad fields within curriculum evaluation appear to be formally excluded. There can be no comparative evaluation if the strategies are not seen as alternatives. There can be no formative evaluation if there is no course to improve. In the Humanities Curriculum Project it was the Project team who aspired to being researchers as well as developers. Now it is the teacher who must combine the role of teacher with the role of researcher. The responsibility for managing Stenhouse's self-imposed ambiguity has moved on.

What one is saying is that the Humanities Curriculum Project is capable of interpretation, not too fancifully, as a projection of Stenhouse's equivocal intellectual style, and that the subsequent turns in the argument represent, more than is openly acknowledged, benchmarks in a personal intellectual history. The Humanities Curriculum Project curriculum was not only controversial, it was in a real sense about controversy, which was elevated into a criterion for determining its content areas. Although the Humanities Curriculum Project's 'procedural neutrality' could lead to well-articulated differences of viewpoint in classrooms, Stenhouse himself appears oddly attached emotionally to the notion of agreement. Increasingly he views curriculum problems as centring on attempts to define the common ground shared by groups of teachers. But even this development was not without attendant ironies. At the same time as Stenhouse's public image was in danger of becoming narrowly tied up with the recessive neutrality of the Humanities Curriculum Project chairman, his writings about curriculum design were exhibiting a taste for argument and passion. It was around this time that the Project began to be called, impersonally and cryptically, the 'HCP'. It had previously been referred to, almost universally, as 'the Stenhouse project'. This tribute to the Stenhouse charisma was quite unique in British curriculum projects and echoes a point we made earlier, that the 'personalisation' of innovation often marks the early stages of an emerging field. A related irony is that somebody whose influence has been so seminal should claim so consistently that his position has frequently been misrepresented or misunderstood. At times Stenhouse can seem a chess player lost in a world of draughts or even remind one of the final scenes in Dr Faustus *where, cornered by the fiends, the hero falls back on medieval disputation.*

The last two extracts are from more general theoretical statements. 'Some limitations of the use of objectives' is a major theoretical paper. It shows clearly that Stenhouse's ideas about curriculum evaluation arise directly out of his novel approach to curriculum design. The paper proved influential in Britain to curriculum developers struggling to free themselves from the straitjacket of the objectives model. Stenhouse was our earliest apologist, well in advance of the fashion, for an approach to curriculum design that allowed a drastic rewording of Popham's famous bumper sticker to read HELP STAMP OUT BEHAVIORAL OBJECTIVES. Now that the arguments of the limitations paper are widely known, and have even to some extent entered the conventional wisdom of the field, it is surprising to note in retrospect the self-assurance and conviction with which the ideas are presented. Although at the time of writing our final paper, 'Defining the curriculum problem', Stenhouse was able to talk of the security of tradition, we should not forget that in Britain at least Stenhouse was for quite a time a lone voice, struggling to establish the taste by which he could be enjoyed.

3.10   Lawrence Stenhouse
Controversial value-issues in the classroom

Given that we are working in the area of controversial issues and attempting to achieve understanding, there appear to be three possible strategies which can be employed in the school.

One might argue that the school should attempt to transmit an agreed position adopted as a matter of policy. This fails in practical political terms because it is impossible to obtain the agreement of parents or policy-makers on the huge range of issues involved. Moreover, even if it were possible to lay down an agreed line, the teachers would still disagree among themselves, and the schools would find themselves involved in an organised and systematic hypocrisy which would make them extremely vulnerable to the criticism of pupils. This approach is also unacceptable in terms of our aim, since it cannot possibly further the understanding of a controversial issue to pretend that it is not in fact controversial.

A second possibility is that each teacher should be free to give his own sincerely-held point of view. But the inescapable authority position of the teacher must in this case leave him open to the charge of using the classroom as a platform for his views. In the face of such criticism, the profession would have committed itself to defending the teacher who advocated pacifism to the children of regular army soldiers or who advocated premarital sexual intercourse in the face of parental disapproval. This position seems scarcely tenable in practice, though attractive at first view. In theory it might be possible to get around the difficulty by ensuring that only teachers whose opinions were relatively conformist were given appointments. Questions about a teacher's political, religious and moral beliefs and practices would then become appropriate at interviews. This is unacceptable to the teaching profession, certainly in Britain. Our experience in classrooms suggests that the authority position of the teacher is much stronger than most teachers realise, and that it is almost insuperably difficult for him to put forward his own points of view without implying that controversial issues can be settled on the basis of the authority of others.

Source: L. Stenhouse (1970). 'Controversial value-issues in the classroom'. In W. G. Carr (ed.), Values and the Curriculum. *Report of the Fourth International Curriculum Conference. Washington DC: National Educational Association Center for the Study of Instruction (CSI), pp. 103-15. The extracts reproduced here are taken from pp. 105-6, 108-9, 114-15. The footnote has been renumbered.*

The third strategy, and the one adopted by the [Humanities Curriculum] project, is to attempt to devise a method of teaching which should within itself guarantee that the teacher is doing all he can to protect pupils from his own bias, while advancing their understanding. This involves the teacher in a procedural neutrality in handling controversial issues which could be the basis of a professional ethic for dealing with controversy in the classroom.

It was on this basis that we designed our curriculum experiment. Of course, I have not been able to outline the position fully here, nor have I time to describe at length and defend our strategy and its premises. . . .

We adopted a research plan based upon the specification of a procedure of teaching which should embody the values implied in the aim in a form which could be realised in the classroom. This means that the changes which we specify are not changes in terminal student behaviour but in the criteria to which teachers work in the classroom. These changes are defined by enunciating certain principles of procedure or criteria of criticism which are expressions of the aim. They are, if you like, specifications of a form of process. Some might be tempted to call them 'process objectives', though that phrase does not seem to me a helpful one.

The difficulty in designing an effective curriculum experiment which does not use behavioural objectives might be expected to be most acute in the field of evaluation. Our evaluation officer, Barry MacDonald, who is present at this Conference, has devised an evaluation strategy based on the premise that the main function of curriculum evaluation is to inform decision-makers. This enables him to bring in the questions which decision-makers do in fact ask of us in order to assist him in selecting what effects to measure. Questions can be gathered from our funding agencies, from educational administrators, from parents, and from teachers.

I believe that this experimental approach to curriculum design and evaluation has considerable potential and, in certain situations, marked advantages over the approach through objectives as a way of translating a value position which has been stated as a general aim into a practical teaching strategy. . . .

However, there are basic assumptions in our work which represent a value position, which would not be affected by our results.

First, we assume that an educator has a responsibility to choose curriculum content—the broad agenda of education—on the value judgement that certain activities, experiences, or forms of knowledge are worthwhile in themselves, and he has to make clear the grounds on which he believes them worthwhile.

Second, we assume that the educational process must embody certain basic values such as rationality, respect for persons, acceptance of consistent criteria and so forth. To call a process 'education' is to assert that it embodies certain values as principles of procedure.

Third, that certainly in the face of controversial issues, and probably in a much wider field than that, a democracy has a value commitment which should be represented in its educational procedures.

This commitment has been well expressed by Griffin. 'Societies are democratic in the degree to which they refrain from setting limits upon matters that may be thought about. It is a corollary that such societies place their faith in knowledge and actively promote occasions for doubt on the ground that doubt is the beginning of all knowledge'.[1]

In a democracy, ethical, political and social values must always be held open to question and discussion. To say this is not to express indifference to the values people hold. On the contrary. If you want to know what value problems most concern a dictatorship, you look for the area where it is most intent on indoctrination. If you want to know what values most concern a democracy, you look for the areas where it is most concerned to stimulate discussion. And it is the strength of education in a democracy that discussion rests upon firmer and more defensible educational values than does indoctrination.

1   Summary of Griffin's position in Lawrence E. Metcalf (1963). 'Research on teaching the social studies', pp. 934-5. In N. L. Gage (ed.), *Handbook of Research on Teaching*. Chicago: Rand McNally.

3.11 Lawrence Stenhouse
Aspirations into possibilities

Curriculum research exists to make aspirations into practical possibilities and the aspirations should be those of a substantial number of teachers and educationists. Since education is an area of debate, however, these aspirations will inevitably be those of one section or party in this debate. In a decentralised system such as ours, the function of curriculum research is to make alternatives practicable.

Any one research, however, can probably only explore one alternative. Ideally, perhaps, curriculum projects should be paired, each of the pair exploring the consequences of contradictory premises advocated in educational debate. This is seldom possible. Failing this, the best safeguard is to attempt to assimilate curriculum research to the generally accepted canons of social science research. This means an attempt to make work in curriculum speculative rather than evangelical and cumulative rather than *ad hoc*. This is a position difficult to hold for two reasons. First, curriculum is so much a branch of policy that it is difficult consistently to avoid moving from the speculative to the evangelical, especially in the face of a public which expects advocacy and sees the renunciation of the evangelical as a flight from responsibility. Second, the field is so underdeveloped that it is difficult to hold to social science canons: because there is no integrated and developed theory of curriculum innovation, hypotheses have to be derived from case study in an effort to build theory rather than being deduced from theory and used to test it. Moreover, action research can never be undividedly orientated towards theory. Such difficulties are not overcome by failing to face them.

The following procedure was adopted [by the Humanities Curriculum Project]:

1 Select a cogent general educational policy statement in the curricular field in question.

2 By relating its logical implications to the realities of the classroom, produce the outline of a teaching strategy consistent with the aim and feasible in practice.

3 Attempt to develop the strategy, testing its logical consistency in discussion and its feasibility in experimental schools.

4 Make case studies of experimental schools to generate hypotheses

Source: L. Stenhouse (1973). 'The Humanities Curriculum Project'. In H. J. Butcher and H. B. Pont (eds.). Educational Research in Britain 3. *London: University of London Press, pp. 149-67. The extract reproduced here is taken from pp. 150-51.*

regarding the problems and effects to be expected in implementing the curriculum in a wider range of schools.

5   Use this case-study experience to design dissemination procedures which will attempt to meet the anticipated problems.

6   Monitor the effects in dissemination both by case study and by measurement.

1, 2, 3 and 5 were the concern of the Project; 4 and 6 of the evaluation unit. . . .

3.12 Lawrence Stenhouse
Research into teaching about race relations

The [Humanities Curriculum] project prepared for publication a collection of teaching materials on race relations similar to those on its other themes. As it turned out, the programme committee of the Schools Council, after considerable deliberation and for complex reasons, vetoed the publication of these materials.

Further research was not abandoned, however. Support was attracted from the Social Science Research Council and the Gulbenkian Foundation for a project on 'The Problems and Effects of Teaching about Race Relations'. One of the Humanities Project team (L. Stenhouse) and one of the Evaluation team (G. K. Verma) passed on to this project.

It is probably necessary at this point to make clear the position taken up as a result of the experience of the Humanities Project and its evaluation.

First, there seemed reason to believe that some positive effects, modest though they might be, might accrue from six weeks' to one term's teaching to adolescents in the area of race relations, and further that much might be learned about the problems of teaching about race relations in the context of such teaching. This is not to deny that there is a need for a much more thoroughgoing programme of education for a multi-racial society. But it does question a position put to the project by the Institute of Race Relations (1973),[1] namely that:

Race relations should not be taught or discussed as a separate subject without the foundation for informed discussion first being established through the school curriculum as a whole, from the earliest stage at infant school onwards.

To take this position would be to sanction a policy of do-nothing on the part of secondary school teachers; and there is no basis in research for such a sanction. On the contrary, we believe that an experimental approach to the problem with adolescents is not only justified in itself, but is also likely to stimulate reflection about needs farther down the school.

Second, the Humanities Project strategy does not stand or fall on the case of race relations. We feel that we have no vested interest in that strategy in this context. More, our hypothesis is that a variety of different

1 This paper was used in our conference for teachers.

Source: L. Stenhouse (1975). 'Problems of research in teaching about race relations'. In G. K. Verma and C. Bagley (eds.), Race and Education Across Cultures. *London: Heinemann Educational Books, pp. 305-21. The extracts reproduced here are taken from pp. 308, 309-10, 311, 313-14.*

109

strategies will be found useful in a variety of different contexts, though in view of the research evidence we do feel some reserve about authoritarian approaches to teaching in this area.

Third, experience in the field of curriculum suggests to us that the contextual variables in the school and its environment are so important that there can be no basis for general recommendations. Each school will have to assess its own problems and evolve its own policy. A research on problems and effects of teaching about race relations should concentrate on collecting the data which schools will need to support them in exercising their own judgement. . . .

Three groups of schools are taking part in the present project. Fourteen schools are following Strategy A, sixteen are following Strategy B and ten are following Strategy C (Drama). Teachers from each strategy came together for a strategy-based conference before embarking on the teaching.

The first group to meet were the Strategy B schools. Their problem was to find some consensus within which they could work together. In the end the consensus was embodied in a conference paper. It is not possible to quote this in full here, and the result may be to make the statement appear more abstract than it is. Here are the aim, some agreed principles of procedure and a definition of the role of the teacher.

Aim
To educate for the elimination of racial tensions and ill-feeling within our society—which is and will be multi-racial—by undermining prejudice, by developing respect for varied traditions and by encouraging mutual understanding, reasonableness and justice.

Principles of Procedure
1   We should help pupils become aware of their own attitudes.
2   We should assist pupils to detect bias and the motives behind this.
3   We should help pupils become aware of the emotional content in racial tension or conflict.
4   We should make clear the historical and social factors which help explain the presence of racial/ethnic groups in society.
5   We should help pupils to see that many problems which appear to stem from racial causes may be predominantly social.
6   We need to help pupils to see the possibility of organising for change.

Role of the Teacher
The teacher should be an example of a person critical of prejudiced attitudes and opinions held by himself and by society at large and trying to achieve some degree of mutual understanding and respect between identifiably different human groups.

Two points of importance need to be made about this position. First, the teachers we recruited on to Strategy B were not prepared to take an authoritarian line or even to assume that they were not prejudiced while their pupils were. They saw prejudice as a social problem in which everyone is involved. Whether this rather open posture of the teachers who joined the project is typical of committed teachers we have no means of knowing. It is possible that the project was generally associated with non-authoritarian views and attracted teachers who were inclined in that direction, but it should be noted that in most cases schools were selected by local authorities. If the project were a laboratory experiment it might be argued that it would have been more fruitful to have an authoritarian Strategy B but curriculum experiment does not allow us to override teacher judgement for the sake of experimental neatness or to pursue policies which do not appear to offer promise of success (in the view of the research workers and teachers involved).

Second . . . the Strategy B specification has an ethical base. It represents an ambitious aspiration whose pedagogical implications would take time to work out. It must be regarded more as an expression of intention than as an empirical specification. Accordingly, we must expect a good deal of diversity in Strategy B schools. This means that the process and the results in each school must be studied separately. . . .

I would conclude that within the experiment comparisons of the effectiveness of Strategy B with other strategies are invalid. This is an important point. The natural but naive assumption might be that an experiment of this sort is directed to testing the strategies against one another. As I shall explain more fully below, it is not.

Strategy A is relatively straightforward since it derives from the Humanities Project. The aim is *to develop an understanding in the area of race relations of social situations and human acts and of the controversial value-issues which they raise.* The hope is that this will lead to better race relations. The teacher submits his teaching to the criterion of neutrality, and can draw on the techniques and insights provided by the work of the Humanities Project.

Strategy C is concerned with teaching about race relations through drama. The potential of such an approach is obvious. The schools will be working mainly through situational improvised drama. The main divergence within the group concerns the issue of whether to approach racial situations directly or within the context of a study of human relations. . . .

So much for the action. What of the research? . . .

Teacher participation in research is a key factor. Our starting point for this position is twofold: the logistic problem of covering the large number of schools and our working within a tradition (in the Centre) which is concerned for teacher participation in research as a basis for the betterment of teaching.

However, Wild, who carries within the present project the main responsibility for the development of field study strategies, is now adumbrating an approach in which teacher participation is more intrinsic to the study.

Originally he suggested in a paper addressed to the project conference of teachers the following conditions for teacher participation in research:

1   Research should be located in the reality of the particular school and the particular classroom.
2   The research roles of the teacher and of the project team member should complement one another.
3   The development and maintenance of a common language is a prerequisite.
4   The role of the teacher as a researcher must relate closely to the role of the teacher as teacher. . . .

Since the design departs from the common models in curriculum development, it is helpful to outline the *classical* approach in order to point the contrast.

In curriculum development, a curriculum or programme is developed as a tentative proposal or recommendation. The proposal may be flexible but it has an identity. It may, in American usage, be *adopted* by a school. Teachers may say, 'We are doing the Humanities Project'; or, 'We are doing Nuffield Science'. The development is commonly evaluated, traditionally in terms of its success in achieving its objectives.

Experience in the research aspects of the Humanities Project and in its unorthodox evaluation . . . threw into relief the possibility of yields in terms of insights into teaching and the climate of schools and the problems of innovation. For those who took part in it, both research and development personnel and teachers, it constituted a learning experience. It got problems clearer and exposed their ramifications, and it suggested strategies through which to tackle problems rather than specifying solutions.

This suggested the possibility of the explicit use of curriculum as an experimental probe, the aim being to capture understanding which could feed teacher judgement rather than to propose a curriculum for teachers to judge. If you come out of the laboratory into the school, what is an experimental procedure? The answer can be a curriculum.

Such an approach depends on the acceptance of a Popperian view that no curriculum policy can be *right first time*. On the contrary, progress depends on the gradual improvement of practice by the elimination of errors and failures and the accumulation of insights. . . .

3.13 Lawrence Stenhouse
Parallel studies

Evaluation is concerned with the explication of the relation between a curriculum, the contextual variables in the school and the teaching situation, psychological factors in pupils and teachers and the effects obtained. It attempts to evaluate the relationship between the curriculum (the content-methods bundle) as a (relatively) controlled variable, and the uncontrolled variables in the individual settings in which the curriculum is implemented. Evaluation is not, in short, product-testing. . . .

In the evaluation of the Humanities Project the basic model was that of a testing programme designed to confirm or deny teacher judgements about the potential effects of the project and, interacting with this, a case-study approach in the schools, whose object was to go some way to defining the variables which accounted for the variance in the tests.

Some light was thrown on the interrelation of variables by correlations within the testing programme, but the design was limited in this respect.

The SSRC Project provides the first case I know of where two (or three) curricula can be studied in parallel. Moreover, it is a rare example of a curriculum research, rather than a curriculum development. No proposal is made to publish teaching materials, though a proposal contingent on the research results has now been submitted to the Gulbenkian Foundation.

Thus the project offers prospects of a major breakthrough in experimental design in curriculum. Where the model has been: develop a curriculum as a proposal and attach an evaluation, the model in this case is, develop x curricula in a research context in order to understand the complex of variables (and hence in policy the complex of considerations) which have to be taken into account in planning a (race teaching) curriculum in any given context.

I am at present beginning a series of papers exploring the implications of this design for curriculum research, but it will take some time to work out the full implications. . . .

For the moment, it is enough to make it clear that these considerations of research design are at stake, and for me of primary importance. I do not mean by this that I am less interested in improving race relations

Source: L. Stenhouse (*1973*). SSRC Project: Problems and Effects of Teaching about Race Relations. Working Paper No. 1. The Design of the Project. *Internal project working paper, published here for the first time. The extracts reproduced here are taken from pp. 3-4.*

through the schools, but rather convinced that a main means to doing this is good experimental design.

In the light of the above it will be clear that the object of the exercise is not to test alternatives, but to use multiple strategies in order to discover as much as possible about 'the problems and effects of teaching race relations to adolescents', and to communicate what we learn to schools planning work in this curricular area. . . .

3.14   Lawrence Stenhouse
Some limitations of the use of objectives

1   Behavioural objectives in curriculum design:
the classic model

Unfortunately, the objectives model has been advanced dogmatically, and this has placed pressure on those who wish to work along alternative lines. In part, the pressure in America has come from funding agencies, which are able by the use of the objectives model to operate an oversimplified but comforting payment-by-results system in making curriculum research and development allocations. The dogma is, however, not confined to this setting; and in Europe too the objectives model is often advanced naively and yet confidently, even assertively. For example:

Realistic planning of any curriculum involves the direct and careful consideration of three closely interrelated categories of elements. First there are the educational objectives (A) which are being aimed at. These are the developments we wish to see in our pupils: qualities of mind, attitudes, values, skills, dispositions, as well as the acquisition of a great deal of knowledge. Secondly, there is the content or the matter (B) employed in the curriculum as a means to these objectives. By this I mean the plays of Shakespeare to be studied, the historical period that is selected and its particular aspects, the range of problems of a practical kind connected with the house or home, etc. Thirdly, there are the activities and the methods (C) that are employed to achieve the objectives. These nowadays include not merely the traditional methods of chalk and talk, but the more informal methods of model-making, visiting, library and group work, and those methods made possible by technological advance, use of television, teaching machines, etc.
    As I understand it, rational curriculum planning consists of developing and tailoring a course under B and C to achieve A, the planning of content and methods to achieve the objectives. It is as simple and straightforward as that.[1]

In this paper I propose to argue that it is by no means as simple and straightforward as that.

1   P. H. Hirst (1963). 'The Curriculum'. *Western European Education*, 1, i, 31-48, (p. 31.)

Source: L. Stenhouse (1970). 'Some limitations of the use of objectives in curriculum research and planning'. In S. J. Eggleston (ed.), Paedogogica Europaea VI, 1970/71. Braunschweig: L. C. G. Malmberg N.V./Georg Wester-mann, pp. 73-83. The extracts reproduced here are taken from pp. 73-5, 76-7, 78-9, 80-1, 82. The footnotes have been renumbered.

2   The objectives model and the problem of instrumentality of content

One of the problems of the objectives model is well brought out in the statement of Hirst above. He writes of 'the content or matter employed in the curriculum as a means to these objectives.' It appears that the objectives model reduces content in education to an instrumental role. This position appears to have serious weaknesses.

If we look back over the history of thinking about the curriculum, we find that curriculum has sometimes been specified in terms of terminal behaviours (objectives), as in 'the education of the courtier' — where 'courtier' implies an ideal of man analysable in terms of behaviour — and has sometimes been specified in terms of content, as in 'the biology of simple organisms' or *Hamlet*. There are objections to a model of curriculum which cuts off the second of these traditions of specification.

Let us take as an example one suggested both by Hirst and by me. He cites as content, 'the plays of Shakespeare to be studied', and I have mentioned *Hamlet*. What are the problems of seeing a work of art — here a play — as a means to pre-specified objectives couched in terms of specified changes in students?

We might argue that the aim is 'to know — or to understand — the play.' Then, if the play could be analysed into knowledge and understandings or interpretations, the capacity to recall or demonstrate these would be the behaviour required of the student. I am doubtful if it is possible to reduce a work of art to a specification of this kind, and others would appear to doubt with me. Northrop Frye, for example: 'From this point of view *poetry* is something to be explained, and the notion that any kind of commentary will ever explain any kind of poetry is of course vulgar. Even if there is a hidden meaning, a poem which contains no more than what an explanation of that meaning can translate should have been written in the form of the explanation in the first place.'[2] In short, if content — the play — were analysed into specified items of sub-content to be mastered by the students, then we should simply have an *explanation* in Frye's sense. The content of a work of art cannot be reduced to students' behaviours. . . .

It does seem that alternative models to that based on objectives could perhaps help in such situations.

Let us accept that education is concerned with disciplined activity in some broad sense. Then we may distinguish two forms of disciplined action, action disciplined by preconceived goals and action disciplined by form or by principles of procedure. Thus, to set out to learn eight guitar chords is to embark on a course of action disciplined by the consciousness of a specific goal. On the other hand, to write a sonnet is to hammer out a part-formed intention in the framework of a form. And to embark on a

2   Northrop Frye (1947). *Fearful Symmetry. A Study of William Blake*. Princeton, New Jersey: Princeton University Press, p. 9.

philosophical argument is to work in the light of principles of procedure rather than of a preconceived goal.

It would appear that a form or principles model could be used in curriculum research and planning. Thus, one could start from a specification of content, say lyric poetry or moral philosophy, and then attempt to design a method which would be consonant with a defined view of the nature and educational worth of lyric poetry or moral philosophy. One would rely on the consonance between content and method to provide the teacher with a vehicle through which an area of experience or knowledge could be explored appropriately. One could also sharpen and define the criteria by which students' work might be judged.

This is really to say that if you define the content of a philosophy course, define what constitutes a philosophically acceptable teaching procedure and articulate standards by which students' work is to be judged, you may be planning rationally without using objectives.

This may be a particularly useful strategy in the arts and in the advanced stages of study on the academic disciplines because it allows of students themselves having objectives, and suggests that the teacher can accept a range of objectives rather than one, while still being able to exclude some objectives as wholly inappropriate or misconceived.

A discipline of knowledge or a disciplined art form can in this way be faced squarely without being translated into student behaviours. I believe this is what discipline of content is about. It places knowledge at the disposal of the student, given that he learn its standards and principles, rather than trapping him in objectives conceived by his teacher.

I am arguing then that one of the main functional advantages of the disciplines of knowledge and of the arts is to allow us to specify content, rather than objectives, in curriculum, the content being so structured and infused with criteria that, given good teaching, student learnings can be treated as outcomes, rather than made the subject of pre-specifications. Disciplines allow us to specify input rather than output in the educational process. This is fairer to the needs of individual students because, relative to objectives, disciplined content is liberating to the individual. . . .

3   The objectives model and the problem of simplification

Rational curriculum planning must take account of the realities of class-room situations. It is not enough to be logical. And there are two crucial practical problems; achieving a degree of value consensus as a basis for action,[3] and interpreting that consensus into educational practice.

3   Robert Emans defines this need for consensus. 'Before values can be considered as focal points for educational objectives suitable for any large numbers of students, they have to become the values of a large, influential segment of the population.' (p. 331). See R. Emans (1966). 'A proposed conceptual framework for curriculum development'. *Journal of Educational Research,* **59**, pp. 327-32. In decentralised systems, consensus needs to be achieved at school level at the least.

Now, the basic weakness of the objectives approach in any area where these are significant problems is that it attempts to tackle both at once and tends to fail in practice without adequately adding to our knowledge. It rests upon two assumptions: 1, that teachers who assent to lists of objectives agree in their values; and 2, that teachers who profess objectives will be able to operationalise them in the classroom. Because an objective professes both to embody value and to interpret it in terms of student behaviour, it is assumed that it is a ready means of interpreting values in practice.

But when we look at practice, we find, as Rubin observes, that objectives are inadequate as definitions of value positions. Their analytic nature, far from clarifying and defining value divergence, appears to make it possible to mask such divergence. Teachers interpret objectives differently and synthesise them in different ways, according them differing hierarchical status. Of course, objectives *may* clarify problems of value consensus, but it seems clear that they frequently provide a conceptual framework which serves as a medium through which to rationalise incoherence of values. Groups of teachers who claim to have agreed on their objectives often demonstrate in the classroom that their agreement was illusory.

The second practical assumption of the objectives approach constitutes a still more important weakness. Teachers who profess objectives cannot easily realise them in intelligent classroom procedures. Hirst writes: 'Rational curriculum planning consists of developing and tailoring a course . . ., the planning of content and methods to achieve the objectives.' In many cases intelligent and experienced people seem unable to do this adequately, despite Hirst's assertion that it is simple.

A *course*, which involves — as it must — a relatively flexible mix of content and methods, exists primarily in the mind of the teacher. The crucial problem seems to be to write a course specification which communicates even grossly similar things to a number of different teachers. A central concern of any curriculum planner must be to communicate through a specification. . . .

The lesson is, I think, that curricular schemes need to be realised in a number of classrooms, closely studied, and turned into meaningful specifications. The language of these specifications will draw on concepts of proven worth in empirically based theory. As Myron Atkin argues, we need to adopt a strategy which 'places classroom analysis and developmental work at the core'. The securest foundation for curriculum planning is grounded theory. . . .

4   J. Myron Atkin (1967-8). 'Research styles in science education', *Journal of Research in Science Teaching*, 5, p. 343.

4   Objectives Versus hypotheses in curriculum research and development

In mounting curriculum research and development, we shall in general — particularly since many of the rewards of the objectives model have already been reaped — do better to deal in hypotheses concerning effects than in objectives. To attach the value-laden tag, *objectives,* to some of our hypotheses is an odd and usually unproductive scientific procedure.

The normal procedure in experimental curricular innovation would, we might expect, be derived from the social sciences. Either from past experience or from exploratory case studies or from theory, where this is sufficiently developed, hypotheses may be generated regarding the possible range of effects of a given curriculum specification and their variation in relation to the web of contextual variables in schools. From these hypotheses some would be selected as crucial and tested.

There is a simplification involved here in the selection of hypotheses for testing, but it is much more open to critical examination than the specification of objectives, since untested hypotheses will naturally be listed. By contrast, the use of objectives as a master concept will tend towards the selection of hypotheses in the light of one's hopes.

Thus, Bloom writes: 'The categories of the affective-domain structure are developed to handle primarily positive values rather than aversions, fears, and dislikes. This is because this is the way in which educational objectives are generally stated, and the *Taxonomy* is a framework for classifying these objectives.'[5]

In an experimental setting, there is a strong case for thinking in terms of a taxonomy (including a pathology) of educational effects rather than of objectives, if we are to prevent our perceptions from being blinkered by our intentions. It is important not to underemphasise undesirable effects, cost effects (e.g. the loss in manipulative skill which we may pay for increasing understanding of mathematical concepts) and important side effects (e.g. rise in level of aspiration or IQ).

A curriculum planner or developer should be able to tell us much more than whether he has achieved objectives. Indeed, in many cases objectives may be measured for him in the examination system, while he himself needs to concentrate far more on aspects which will not be measured in this way. Thus a curriculum worker or a teacher may often be most interested in exploring some of the aspects of a curriculum in practice which puzzle or surprise. Hypotheses are needed here. . . .

I am really arguing that there is no substitute for an understanding of the ways in which curriculum and methods are likely to impact upon students and of the complex of variables that make the settings of

5   Benjamin S. Bloom, in David R. Krathwohl, B. S. Bloom & B. B. Masia (1964). *Taxonomy of Educational Objectives: II Affective Domain.* New York: Longmans Green, p. viii.

individual schools. And once we face that, the objectives approach, which at first looks like a short cut to effective action, becomes an impediment to the development of less simplistic research designs.

And if workers in curriculum research and development are going to find the language of objectives naive, then curriculum planners must face the developed research frameworks they evolve as the raw material of planning. . . .

5   Rational curriculum planning

Realistic planning of any curriculum involves the direct and careful consideration of alternative curricular offerings which have been shown to have some likelihood of realisation in practice. In order that the planner should have the best possible basis on which to make his decisions, he needs to examine carefully the work of teachers and of curriculum research workers or developers who have described or devised curricula. These workers need accordingly to attempt:

1   To define the value positions embodied in the curriculum specification or specifications. A possible strategy is to define the value position taken at each major choice point encountered in the design of the specification. This exposes the values to the decision-maker, and allows the experimenter to regard the values as variables (most often held constant, though not necessarily so).

2   To specify a curriculum in terms of content, materials and method, to spell out what kinds of classroom activity it stands for and to define the most critical observations which reveal whether the specification is or is not being met in any given classroom.

3   To indicate necessary training procedures for teachers, and estimate their importance for realisation of the specification.

4   To define the contextual variables in schools, school systems and out-of school environment which make it likely or unlikely that the specification will be realised in practice.

5   To list, and so far as is practicable to test, hypotheses regarding the effects of successfully realising the specification and perhaps of failing to realise it in circumstances which are likely to arise in practice. The selection of hypotheses for testing should be made on two grounds, to help the decision-maker (developmental grounds) and because of significance for theory building (research grounds).

6   To attempt to relate differential effects to differential contextual variables of the kind noticed in 4 above.

Rational curriculum planning consists in the exercise of cautious judgement in making inevitably precarious decisions as one attempts to achieve some sort of coordinated curriculum in the presence of so many variables and uncertainties. It will usually be important to try to offer a balanced combination of worthwhile experiences likely to serve the needs of students with differing purposes.

Planners might aim to break the hypothesis: 'The effects of any curriculum differ in important ways from those expected by planners, experimenters and teachers.' . . .

3.15 Lawrence Stenhouse
Defining the curriculum problem

Notionally the essence of curriculum might be located in the relation of my own ideas as a teacher to the reality of my classroom: 'the true blueprint is in the minds and hearts of the teachers'.[1] But the plural here is important. Except for empirical micro-studies of the classroom, the private curriculum of the individual teacher is not of central interest. What is of practical importance in curriculum work is the public curriculum or curricula, that is, curricula that can be held to be in some sense and to some extent publicly accessible to 'the minds and hearts' of many teachers.

Thus, a curriculum may be said to be an attempt to define the common ground shared by those teachers who follow it. Although it may sometimes be useful to think of it as the offering to pupils, we must always bear in mind that any similarity between the offering in one classroom and another, in one school and another must begin in the like-mindedness of teachers. Most commonly this like-mindedness is a matter of tradition. . . .

A new curriculum will never be secure until it accumulates around it a tradition. The strain of a uniformly selfconscious and thoughtful approach to curriculum is in the long run intolerable. No doubt self-critical analysis is always desirable, but not analysis of everything. New curricula, too, however much the idealist may regret it, must develop comfortable, easy and anxiety-free habits — though not be captured by them.

A new curriculum expresses ideas in terms of practice and disciplines practice by ideas. It is, I would maintain, the best way of dealing in educational ideas. . . .

1 Harold Spears (1950). *The High School for Today*, New York: American Book Company. p. 27. Quoted in Edmund C. Short and George D. Marconnit (1968). *Contemporary Thought on Public School Curriculum*. Dubuque, Iowa: Wm. C. Brown.

Source: L. Stenhouse (1972). 'Defining the curriculum problem'. Paper published here for the first time. The extracts reproduced here are taken from pp. 2-3, 4.

Michael Scriven

Amongst those who have written on the theory of curriculum evaluation, Michael Scriven is a central, although to some extent an enigmatic, figure. Central because his 'Methodology of evaluation' paper, from which we include extracts, was such an intellectual tour de force *that much of the subsequent thinking stood on its shoulders. Enigmatic because just when we thought we could 'place' Scriven, he shifted his emphasis abruptly.*

We feature seven papers by Scriven, which divide neatly into two groups. Having pride of place is the 'Methodology of evaluation' paper, which was written in 1967. It is followed by six products of a later period (1971-2) in which Scriven was considering a number of issues relating to the elaboration in detail of a single controversial evaluation style which he called 'goal-free evaluation'. Not that there is much hint in the earlier paper of the goal-free revolution to come. Indeed, a critique of goal-free evaluation might refer Scriven back to his own pronouncements about goals in the 'Methodology' paper, where Scriven commits himself to the proposition that:

evaluation is itself a methodological activity which is essentially similar whether we are trying to evaluate coffee machines or teaching machines, plans for a house or plans for a curriculum. The activity consists simply in the gathering and combining of performance data with a weighted set of goal scales to yield either comparative or numerical ratings, and in the justification of (a) *the data-gathering instruments,* (b) *the weightings, and* (c) *the selection of goals.*

The most interesting section of the 'Methodology' paper, from the point of view of illuminative evaluation, is the section on process studies (interpretative descriptions of what actually goes on in classrooms). These are seen as lying outside the mainstream of evaluation, which is typically concerned with judgements of merit and worth. Nevertheless, Scriven acknowledges that some evaluations of a situation will take the form of 'an analytical description of the process . . . indeed an 'interpretation'.

The first of the later papers we feature is 'Intended and unintended effects — why distinguish?' This comes from 'Prose and cons about goal-free evaluation' (sic). The thrust behind goal-free evaluation is the view that an evaluator needs to study a programme's effects, intended or unintended, and that contact with the programme-builder's rhetoric of intent can only be contaminating. This shift appears so major that in the language of the geophysicists who chart reversals in geological time of the direction of the earth's magnetic field it could almost be called 'reverse polarity'. In 'Prose and cons about goal-free evaluation', Scriven himself is able to cite a number of methodological analogies. There is the 'intentional fallacy' in aesthetics (which makes legitimate a literary criticism not dependent upon an author's intentions); 'double blind' designs in research (blind in terms of the subject and experimenter's knowledge of who is getting what treatment); and situational ethics (which considers whether the morality of an act is determined by its motivation or its consequences).

This whole notion of methodological analogy is an engaging one to the illuminative evaluator, and is taken up in our next extract. Scriven's own list of 'contrasts and analogies' offering insight to evaluators is found in 'Current evaluation problems' (from 'Current problems: philosophy and practice of evaluation'). It includes administration, counselling, bridge bidding, teaching, technical writing, criticising legal arguments and decision-making.

If goal-free evaluation took the evaluation world by surprise, some of it must be chalked up to style. This is particularly true of the paper called 'Goal-free evaluation'. The tone is teasing and at times witty. The paper begins with a morality play in which an outraged client argues with an unbelievably smug and unrepentant goal-free evaluator. The American audience for the paper has been surprisingly prepared to miss the allegorical element, some expressing puzzlement that the new wave of evaluators should contemplate approaching a client so truculently. Perhaps it is a measure of Michael Scriven's stature that he was able to legitimise a novelty and almost single-handed force people to take it into account. But the amusing excesses   of goal-free evaluation, at least as expressed by Scriven's argumentative goal-free evaluator, leave open the question about how firmly the tongue is lodged in the cheek. It would be a mistake to misread the seriousness of intention behind 'Goal-free evaluation', and our next extract, 'Legitimate and illegitimate cases of evaluating the treatment rather than the effects'. This in spite of the fact that a conference paper promised by Scriven on 'data-free evaluation' turned out to be a Popham-inspired hoax, itself an example of the 'ideological softening-up' attributed to Popham in the extracts from 'Goal-free behavioural objectives' which we have renamed 'Ideological softening-up'.

Finally, in 'Goal Lib' the goal-free evaluation movement has acquired a fashionable title as well as a manifesto. Although school is not a pill, to be evaluated on its effects alone, Scriven believes that in a forced choice one would not be able to abandon an evaluation based on 'outcomes'. So perhaps goal-free evaluation is best seen as a valid alternative tradition. Whatever it is, it isn't an excuse for the evaluator to substitute his goals.

As put forward by Michael Scriven, GFE is not merely any evaluation freed from consideration of programme goals. It is associated with the use of Scriven's own 'lethal' checklist. Scriven's Product Checklist has thirteen checkpoints, on a five point scale 0-4. The checklist is 'lethal' because

Scriven conceives it in terms not of desiderata, *but* necessitata. *Scriven claims that his checkpoints have an* a priori *rationale so that 'a straight-forward argument can be constructed that failure to meet any one of the checkpoints immediately leaves open serious doubts that the product is simply not of good quality.'*

A consistent thread throughout Michael Scriven's work is his belief in the evaluator as judge. In this respect Scriven can be contrasted with Robert Stake. Stake takes a relativistic view of evaluation pronouncements: there are a number of truths and the evaluator presents versions as they are perceived by the various parties who define the problems under study. Scriven, however, believes that an educational programme has a truth impact that is not a function of the people who look at it. This is supported philosophically by his interest in logic, ethics and pragmatism.

3.16   Michael Scriven
The methodology of evaluation

Introduction

Current conceptions of the evaluation of educational instruments (e.g. new curricula, programmed texts, inductive methods, individual teachers) are still inadequate both philosophically and practically. This paper attempts to exhibit and reduce some of the deficiencies. Intellectual progress is possible only because newcomers can stand on the shoulders of giants. This feat is often confused with treading on their toes, particularly but not only by the newcomer. . . .

Goals of evaluation versus roles of evaluation: formative and summative evaluation

The function of evaluation may be thought of in two ways. At the methodological level, we may talk of the goals of evaluation; in a particular sociological or pedagogical context we may further distinguish several possible *roles* of evaluation.

In the abstract, we may say that evaluation attempts to answer certain *types of question* about certain *entities*. The entities are the various educational 'instruments' (processes, personnel, procedures, programmes, etc.). The types of question include questions of the form: *How well* does this instrument perform (with respect to such-and-such criteria)? Does it perform *better* than this other instrument? *What* does this instrument do (i.e. what variables from the group in which we are interested are significantly affected by its application)? Is the use of this instrument *worth* what it's costing? Evaluation is itself a methodological activity which is essentially similar whether we are trying to evaluate coffee machines or teaching machines, plans for a house or plans for a curriculum. The activity consists simply in the gathering and combining of performance data with a weighted set of goal scales to yield either comparative or numerical ratings, and in the justification of (*a*) the data-gathering instruments, (*b*) the weightings, and (*c*) the selection of goals.

Source: M. Scriven (1967). 'The methodology of evaluation'. In R. Tyler, R. Gagné and M. Scriven, Perspectives of Curriculum Evaluation. *AERA Monograph Series on Curriculum Evaluation, No. 1. Chicago: Rand McNally, pp. 39-83. The extracts reproduced here are taken from pp. 39, 40-41, 42-3, 49-51. The footnote has been renumbered.*

But the *role* which evaluation has in a particular educational context may be enormously various; it may form part of a teacher-training activity, of the process of curriculum development, of a field experiment connected with the improvement of learning theory, of an investigation preliminary to a decision about purchase or rejection of materials; it may be a data-gathering activity for supporting a request for tax increases or research support, or a preliminary to the reward or punishment of people as in an executive training programme, a prison or a classroom. Failure to make this rather obvious distinction between the roles and goals of evaluation, not necessarily in this terminology, is one of the factors that has led to the dilution of the process of evaluation to the point where it can no longer serve as a basis for answering the questions which are its goal. This dilution has sacrificed goals to roles. One can be against evaluation only if one can show that it is improper to seek an answer to questions about the merit of educational instruments, which would involve showing that there are *no* legitimate activities (roles) in which these questions can be raised, an extraordinary claim. Obviously the fact that evaluation is sometimes given an inappropriate role hardly justifies the conclusion that we *never* need to know the answers to the goal questions. Anxiety about 'evaluation', especially among teachers or students, is all too frequently an illicitly generalised response originating in legitimate objections to a situation in which an evaluation was given a role quite beyond its reliability or comprehensiveness. . . .

One of the reasons for the tolerance or indeed encouragement of the confusion between roles and goals is the well-meaning attempt to allay the anxiety on the part of teachers that the word 'evaluation' precipitates. By stressing the constructive part evaluation may play in non-threatening activities (roles) we slur over the fact that its goals always include the estimation of merit, worth, value, etc., which all too clearly contribute in another role to decisions about promotion and rejection of personnel and courses. But we cannot afford to tackle anxiety about evaluation by ignoring its importance and confusing its presentation; the loss in efficiency is too great. . . . it may even be true that 'the greatest service evaluation can perform is to identify aspects of the course where revision is desirable' (Cronbach, p. 236),[1] though it is not clear how one would establish this, but it is certainly also true that there are other extremely important evaluation services which must be done for almost any given curriculum project or other educational innovation. And there are many contexts in which calling in an evaluator to perform a final evaluation of the project or person is an act of proper recognition of responsibility to the person, product or taxpayers. It therefore seems a little excessive to refer to this as simply 'a menial role', as Cronbach does. It is obviously a great

---

1 'Evaluation for course improvement,' *Teachers' College Record,* **64**, No. 8, 1963. Reprinted in R. Heath (ed.) (1964). *New Curricula.* New York: Harper & Row, pp. 231-248; references in this paper are to the latter version.

service if this kind of terminal, overall or 'outcome' evaluation can demonstrate that a very expensive textbook (etc.) is not significantly better than the competition, or that it is enormously better than any competitor. In more general terms it may be possible to demonstrate that a certain type of approach to (for example) mathematics is not yielding significantly better pupil performance on any dimension that mathematicians or vocational users are prepared to regard as important. This would certainly save a great deal of expenditure of time and money and constitute a valuable contribution to educational development, as would the converse, favourable, result. Thus there seem to be a number of qualifications that would have to be made before one could accept a statement asserting the greater importance of formative evaluation by comparison with summative. ('Evaluation, used to improve the course while it is still fluid, contributes more to improvement of education than evaluation used to appraise a product already placed on the market.'—Cronbach, p. 236.) Fortunately we do not have to make this choice. Educational projects, particularly curricular ones, clearly must attempt to make best use of evaluation in both these roles. As a matter of terminology, I think that novel terms are worthwhile here, to avoid inappropriate connotations, and I propose to use the terms 'formative' and 'summative' to qualify evaluation in these roles. . . .

Evaluation studies versus process studies

In the course of clarifying the concept of evaluation it is important not to simplify it. Although the *typical* goals of evaluation require judgements of merit and worth, when somebody is asked to evaluate a situation or the impact of certain kinds of materials on the market, then what is being called for is an analytical description of the process, usually with respect to certain possible causal connections, indeed an *interpretation*. . . . In this sense it is not inappropriate to regard some kinds of process investigation as evaluation. But the range of process research only overlaps with and is neither subsumed by nor equivalent to that of evaluation. We may conveniently distinguish three types of process research, as the term is used by Cronbach and others.

1   The non-inferential study of what actually goes on in the classroom. Perhaps this has the most direct claim to being called a study of the process of teaching (learning, etc.). We might for example be interested in the proportion of the class period during which the teacher talks, the amount of time that the students spend in homework for a class, the proportion of the dialogue devoted to explaining, defining, opining, etc. . . . The great problem about work like this is to show that it is worth doing, in *any* sense. *Some* pure research is idle research. . . .

2   The second kind of process research involves the investigation of casual claims ('dynamic hypotheses') about the process. Here we are interested in such questions as whether an increase of time spent on class discussions of the goals of a curriculum at the expense of time spent on training drills leads to improved comprehension in (*a*) algebra, (*b*) geography, etc. This kind of investigation is essentially a miniature limited-scope 'new instrument' project. Another kind looks for the answer to such questions as: Is the formation of subgroup allegiance and identification with the teacher facilitated by strong emphasis on pupil-teacher dialogue? The feature of this subgroup of process hypotheses that distinguishes them from evaluation hypotheses is that the dependent variables either are ones which would not figure among the set of criteria we would use in a summative evaluation study (though we might think of them as important because of their relevance to improved teaching techniques) or they are only a subgroup of such summative criteria; and in either case no attempt is made to justify any correlative assignments of merit.

Process hypotheses of this second kind are in general about as difficult to substantiate as any 'outcome' hypothesis, i.e. summative evaluation. Indeed they are sometimes harder to substantiate because they may require identifying the effects of only one of several independent variables that are present, and it is extremely hard—though usually not impossible—to apply ordinary matching techniques to take care of the others. The advantage of some summative evaluation investigation is that it is concerned with evaluating the effects of a whole teacher–curriculum package and has no need to identify the specific agent responsible for the overall improvement or deterioration. That advantage lapses when we are concerned to identify the variance due to the curriculum as opposed to the teacher.

3   Formulative evaluation. This kind of research is often called process research, but it is of course simply outcome evaluation of an intermediate stage in the development of the teaching instrument. The distinction between this and the first kind of dynamic hypothesis mentioned above is twofold. There is a distinction of role: the role of formative evaluation is to discover deficiencies and successes in the intermediate versions of a new curriculum; the role of dynamic hypothesis investigation is *sui generis:* it is to provide the answer to an important question about the mechanism of teaching. And there is a distinction in the extent to which it matters whether the criteria used are an adequate analysis of the proper goals of the curriculum. The dynamic hypothesis study has no obligation to this; the formative evaluation does. But the two types of study are not always sharply distinct. They both play an important role in good curriculum research. . . .

3.17   Michael Scriven
Intended and unintended effects — why distinguish?

It seemed very natural to start off the evaluation form with a rating of goals of the project and to go on with a rating of the effectiveness in meeting them, costs, etc. By the sixth draft of the form another item had become very prominent, namely side-effects. Naturally, these had also to be rated, and in one case a product finished up in the Top Ten in spite of zero results with respect to its intended outcomes because it did so well on an unanticipated effect.

Reflecting on this experience later, I became increasingly uneasy about the separation of goals and side-effects. After all, we weren't there to evaluate goals as such — that would be an important part of an evaluation of a *proposal*, but not (I began to think) of a *product*. All that should be concerning us, surely, was determining exactly what effects this product had (or most likely had), and evaluating those, whether or not they were intended.

In fact, it was obvious that the rhetoric of the original proposal which had led to a particular product was frequently put forward as if it somehow constituted supporting evidence for the excellence of the product. This rhetoric was often couched in terms of the 'in' phrases of five-year-old educational fads, sometimes given a swift updating with references to the current jargons or lists of educational priorities. That is, the rhetoric of intent was being used as a substitute for evidence of success. Was it affecting us? It would be hard to prove it didn't. And it contributed nothing, since we were not supposed to be rewarding good intentions.

Furthermore, the whole *language* of 'side-effect' or 'secondary effect' or even 'unanticipated effect' (the terms were then used as approximate synonyms) tended to be a put-down of what might well be the crucial achievement, especially in terms of new priorities. Worse, it tended to make one look less hard for such effects in the data and to demand less evidence about them — which is extremely unsatisfactory with respect to the many potentially very harmful side-effects that have turned up over the years.

It seemed to me, in short, that consideration and evaluation of goals was an unnecessary but also a possibly contaminating step. I began to work on an alternative approach — simply, the evaluation of *actual* effects

Source: M. Scriven (1972). 'Prose and cons about goal-free evaluation'. Evaluation Comment: The Journal of Educational Evaluation, 3, No. 4, pp. 1-4. The extract reproduced here is taken from p. 1.

against (typically) a profile of *demonstrated* needs in this region of education. (This is close to what Consumers' Union actually does.) I call this Goal-Free Evaluation (GFE). . . .

3.18   Michael Scriven
Current evaluation problems

1   (The 'role-conflict' problem). The in-house evaluator must, to be effective, relate well to the 'producer' (e.g. a writing or R & D team). In particular, he should be succeeding in getting improvements made in the products as a result of his suggestions. Thus they become in part 'his' products; and over the course of several years, quite markedly so. On the other hand, we would never accept an evaluation by a co-author of his own materials as meeting even the minimal methodological standards for objectivity. How can one avoid this 'contamination' of formative evaluators? (Suggestions include: rotation between projects, auxiliary external evaluation committee visits, etc.)

2   (The 'censorship' problem). If a client commissions an evaluation and doesn't like it, he can — as things are now — effectively gag it. When the client is a state agency and the dislike is based on fear of political repercussions adversely affecting the agency's budget, this may be a serious disservice to the taxpayer. What strategies could assist with this? (Possibilities include encouraging . . . publication of 'censored' passages or reports, plus rebuttals or replies.) . . .

3   In considering the nature of evaluation, and the problems of training evaluators, can any insights be obtained by contrasts and analogies with other practices/skills which, like evaluation, do not consist in the application of an elaborate theory; for example, administration, counselling, bridge bidding, teaching, technical writing, criticising legal arguments, decision-making? To what extent is evaluation unique in the sense that *it* is presupposed by all these activities but not *vice versa*? . . .

4   (*a*) In what sense is the evaluator a 'change-agent' and to the extent that he is, if any, what can be extracted from change-agent theory that would be useful in training evaluators and for practising evaluators? (*b*) A more general concern is the extent to which the evaluator is or should self-consciously be a *moral* agent and the extent to which his knowledge of moral theory and analytical procedures should therefore be greater than one can expect for every citizen.

5   What consequences emerge from the preceding reflections for notoriously tricky evaluation tasks such as the evaluation of aesthetic education, creativity, moral education, affective education, complete

Source: M. Scriven (1971). 'Curriculum problems: philosophy and practice of evaluation', a paper produced for ETS Product Evaluation Pool, Draft VII (private circulation). The extracts reproduced here are taken from pp. 2, 4-5.

school systems . . . research proposals that are competing with dissemination proposals . . . student work and worth (grading and IQ scores, for example), performance contracting, products with a higher apparent *potential* but lower actual performance than others? . . .

3.19 Michael Scriven
Goal-free evaluation

In the summative context

Suppose the client is an agency which wishes to get independent evaluation of a project done under contract. To illustrate the radical approach to which the title refers, consider the goal-free evaluator at his first interview with the client.

Client. Well, we're very glad you were able to take this on for us. We consider this programme in reading for the disadvantaged to be one of the most important we have ever funded. I expect you'd like to get together with the project staff as soon as possible — the director is here now — and of course, there's quite a collection of documents covering the background of the project that you'll need. We've assembled a set of these for you to take back with you tonight.

G. F. Evaluator. Thanks, but I think I'll pass on meeting the staff and on the materials. I *will* have my secretary get in touch with the director soon, though, if you can give me the phone numbers.

Client. You mean you're planning to see them *later*? But you've got so little time — we thought that bringing the director in would really speed things up. Maybe you'd *better* see him — I'm afraid he'll be pretty upset about making the trip for nothing. Besides, he's understandably nervous about the whole evaluation. I think his team is worried that you won't really appreciate their approach unless you spend a good deal of time with them.

Evaluator. Unfortunately, I can't *both* evaluate their achievements with reasonable objectivity and also go through a lengthy indoctrination session with them.

Client. Well, surely you want to know what they are trying to do — what's distinctive about their approach?

Evaluator. I already know more than I need to know about their goals — teaching reading to disadvantaged youngsters, right?

Client. But that's so vague — why, they developed their own instruments, and a *very* detailed curriculum. You can't cut yourself off from *that*! Otherwise, you'll finish up criticising them for failing to do what they never tried to do. I can't let you do that. In fact, I'm getting a little

Source: M. Scriven (1971). 'Goal-free evaluation, Part I', 11-71 NIE 2A, and 'Goal-free evaluation, Part II', 11-71 NIE 2B. The extracts reproduced here are taken from Part I, pp. 1-6, and from Part II, pp. 2-3.

nervous about letting you go any further with the whole thing. Aren't you going to see them *at all*? You're proposing to evaluate a three million dollar project without even *looking* at it?

Evaluator. As far as possible, yes. Of course, I'm handicapped by being brought in so late and under a tight deadline, so I may have to make some compromises. On the general issue, I think you're suffering from some misconception about evaluation. You're used to the rather cosy relationship which often — in my view — contaminates the objectivity of the evaluator. **You should think about the evaluation of drugs by the double-blind approach . . .**

Client. But even there, the evaluator has to know the intended effect of the drug in order to set up the tests. In the educational field, it's much harder to pin down goals and that's where you'll *have* to get together with the developers.

Evaluator. The drug evaluator and the educational evaluator do not even have to know the *direction* of the intended effect, stated in very general terms, let alone the intended *extent* of success. It's the evaluator's job to *find out* what effects the drug has, and to assess them. If (s)he is told in which direction to look, that's a handy hint but it's potentially prejudicial. One of the evaluator's most useful contributions may be to reconceptualise the effects, rather than regurgitating the experimenter's conception of them.

Client. This is too far-out altogether. What are you suggesting the evaluator do — test for effects on every possible variable? He can't do that.

Evaluator. Oh, but he has to do that *anyway*. I'm not adding to his burden. How do you suppose he picks up side-effects? Asks the experimenter for a list? That *would* be cosy. It's the evaluator's job to look out for effects the experimenter (or producer, etc.) *did not expect or notice*. The so-called 'side effects', whether good or bad, often wholly determine the outcome of the evaluation. It's absolutely irrelevant to the evaluator whether these are 'side' or 'main' effects; that language refers to the *intentions* of the producer and the evaluator isn't evaluating intentions but *achievements*. In fact, it's risky to hear even general descriptions of the intentions, because it focuses your attention away from the 'side-effects' and tends to make you overlook or down-weight them.

Client. You still haven't answered the *practical* question. You can't test for all possible effects. So this posture is absurd. It's much more useful to tell the producer how well he's achieved what he set out to achieve.

Evaluator. The producer undoubtedly set out to do something really worthwhile in education. That's the really significant formulation of his goals and it's to that formulation the evaluator must address himself. There's also a highly particularised description of the goals — or there should be — and the producer may need some technical help in deciding whether he got there, but that certainly isn't what *you*, as the dispenser of taxpayer's funds, need to know. You need to know if the money was wasted or well-spent, etc.

Client. Look, I already *had* advice on the goals. That's what my advisory panel tells me when it recommends which proposal to fund. What I'm paying *you* for is to judge success, not legitimacy of the direction of effort.

Evaluator. Unfortunately for that way of dividing the pie, your panel can't tell what *configuration* of actual effects would result, and that's what I'm here to assess. Moreover, your panel is just part of the whole process that led to this product. They're not immune to criticism, nor are you, and nor is the producer. (And nor am I.) Right now, you have — with assistance — produced something, and I am going to try to determine whether it has any merit. When I've produced my evaluation, you can switch roles and evaluate *it* — or get someone else to do so. But it's neither possible nor proper for an evaluator to get by without assessing the *merits* of what has been done, not just its consonance with what someone else thought was meritorious. It isn't proper because it's passing the buck, dodging the — or one of the — issue(s). It isn't possible because (it's almost certain that) no one else *has* laid down the merits of what has *actually* happened. It's very unlikely, you'll agree, that the producer has achieved exactly the original goals, without shortfall, overrun or side-effects. So — unless you want to abrogate the contract we just signed — you really have to face the fact that I shall be passing on the *merits* of whatever has been done — as well as determining exactly what that is.

Client. I'm thinking of at least getting someone else in to do it too — someone with a less peculiar notion of evaluation.

Evaluator. I certainly hope you do. There's very little evidence about the interjudge reliability of evaluators. I would of course cooperate fully in any such arrangement by refraining from any communication whatsoever with the other evaluator.

Client. I'm beginning to get the feeling you get paid rather well for speaking to no one. Will you kindly explain how you're going to check on all variables? Or are you going to take advantage of the fact that I have told you it's a reading programme — I'm beginning to feel that I let slip some classified information. What's your idea of an ideal evaluation situation — one where you don't know what you're evaluating?

Evaluator. In evaluation, blind is beautiful. Remember that Justice herself is blind, and good medical research is double-blind. The educational evaluator is severely handicapped by the impossibility of double-blind conditions in most educational contexts. But (s)he must still work very hard at keeping out prejudicial information. You can't do an evaluation without knowing what it is you're supposed to evaluate — the treatment — but you do not need or want to know what it's supposed to do. You've already told me too much in that direction. I still need to know some things about the nature of the treatment itself, and I'll find those out from looking at it and perhaps occasionally from the director, via my secretary, who can filter out surplus data on intentions, etc., before relaying it to me. That data on the treatment is what cuts the problem down to size; I have the knowledge about probable or possible effects of treatments like that, from the research literature, that enables me to avoid the necessity for examining *all* possible variants.

Client. Given the weakness of research in this area, aren't you still pretty vulnerable to missing an unprecedented effect?

Evaluator. Somewhat, but I have a series of procedures for picking these up, from participant observation to teacher interview to sampling from a list of educational variables. I don't doubt I slip up, too; but I'm willing to bet I miss less than anyone sloshing through the swamp towards goal-achievement. I really think you should hire someone else to do it independently, and see if I'm right about that.

Client. We really don't have the budget for it . . . maybe you *can* do something your way. But I don't know how I'm going to reassure the project staff. This is going to seem a very alien, threatening kind of approach to them, I'm afraid.

Evaluator. People that feel threatened by referees who won't accept their hospitality don't understand about impartiality. This isn't support for the enemy, it's neutrality. I don't want to penalise them for failing to reach over-ambitious goals. I want to give them credit for doing something worthwhile in getting halfway to those goals. I don't want to restrict them to credit for their announced contracts. Educators often do more good in unexpected directions than the intended ones. My approach preserves their chances in those directions. In my experience, interviews with project staff are excessively concerned with explanations of shortfall. But shortfall has no significance for me at all. It has some for you, because it's a measure of the reliability of the projections they make in the future. If I were evaluating them as a production team, I'd look at that as part of the track record. But right now I'm evaluating their product – a reading programme. And it may be the best in the world even if it's only half as good as they intended. No, I'm not working in a way that's prejudiced against them.

Client. I'm still haunted by a feeling this is an unrealistic approach. For example, how the devil would I ever know who to get as an evaluator except in terms of goal-loaded descriptions? I got you – in fact, I invited you on the phone – to handle a 'reading programme for disadvantaged kids' which is goal-loaded. I couldn't even have worked out whether you'd had any experience in this area except by using that description. Do you think evaluators should be *universal* geniuses? How can they avoid goal-laden language in describing themselves?

Evaluator. There's nothing wrong with classifying evaluators by their *past* performance. You only risk contamination when you tell them what you want them to do *this* time, using the goals of *this* project as you do so. There's nothing unrealistic about the alternative, any more than there is about cutting names off scientific papers when you, as an editor, send them out to be refereed. You could perfectly well have asked me if I was free to take on an evaluation task in an area of previous experience—a particularly important one, you could have added—requiring, as it seemed to you, about so much time and with so much fees involved. I could have made a tentative acceptance and then come in to look into details, as I did today.

Client. *What* details can you look at?

Evaluator. Sample materials, or descriptions by an observer of the process, availability of controls, time constraints, etc. What I found today made it clear you simply wanted the best that could be done in a very limited time, and I took it on that basis—details later. Of course, it probably won't answer some of the crucial evaluation questions, but to do that you should have brought someone in at the beginning. Your best plan would have been to send me reasonably typical materials and tell me how long the treatment runs. That would have let me form my own tentative framework. But no evaluator gets perfect conditions. The trouble is that the loss is not his, its the consumer's. And that means he's usually not very motivated to preserve his objectivity. It's more fun to be on friendly terms with the project people. . . .

In the formative context

The goal-free evaluator (GFE) is a hunter out on his own and he goes over the ground very carefully, looking for signs of any kind of game, setting speculative snares when in doubt. The goals man has been given a map which supposedly shows the main game trails; it's hard for him to work quite so hard in the rest of the jungle.

The GFE can work in the formative role as well as in the summative— but he will not be doing what most formative evaluators do. He will not be spending much of his time helping the project staff convert their plans into behavioural objectives. He will not be advising them on probable mismatch between their abstract goals and some implicit commitments of their materials. He will not be constructing biserial correlation matrices for item analysis on their quizzes. He will simply get a look at the materials plus procedures (or descriptions of what they will be like) and a deadline by which time he must get evaluative feedback into the rewrite/replan process. Then he'll go out and set up his snares, developing special instruments and setting up controls if he is granted the resources and time. . . .

3.20   Michael Scriven
Legitimate and illegitimate cases of evaluating the treatment rather than the effects

Although almost all classroom transaction analysis is irrelevant to evaluation, there are two types of exception. The first concerns the morality of the process and the second its enjoyability. Injustice or cruelty in the classroom is not, in general, readily detectable by its delayed effects, any more than it is in prisons, police stations or mobs: but we abhor it just the same — or should. A liberal utilitarian may feel sure that the long-term effects of injustice in the classroom (or school) far outweigh, in their ultimate consequences for society, anything else that transpires there. But even he will agree that our instruments for detecting those effects are imprecise and slow-acting. The more conservative moralist may entirely reject considerations of effects and simply argue that teacher-student interactions are part of the moral domain and must exhibit respect for the rights and duties of each. In either case, the evaluative task requires some examination of classroom process. . . .

If school were a pill, taken in an instant, it would be appropriate — moral considerations apart — to evaluate it on its effects alone. But school goes on for a long time by any standards, and almost interminably by youthful standards. Consequently one must recognise the necessity for regarding the consequences of giving the treatment as including the consequence of lengthy incarceration within the system. That is often a heavy cost, as seen by the child, and I believe the most striking residue of paternalism in evaluation is the failure to include it in most studies, e.g. of Headstart. If students had a better time during the treatment, even if (as Larry Kohlberg once put it) they just cried less, that's *something* to be said for it, learning *residues* apart. . . .

Source: M. Scriven (1971). 'Legitimate and illegitimate cases of evaluating the treatment rather than the effects', 11-71 NIE 2C. The extracts reproduced here are taken from pp. 1, 2.

3.21   Michael Scriven
Ideological softening-up

In a recent paper ['Must all objectives be behavioral?', October 1971] Jim Popham, the internationally famous comedian and licensed midwife for birth of behavioural objectives [Instructional Objectives Exchange, Box 24095, Los Angeles, California 90024] has traced his own ideological softening-up. He now concedes that, in some areas, our deficiencies in instrumentation may justify using non-behavioural objectives because they are all we have for some very important goals of education, especially long-range ones. Should we make that concession; or less; or more; or others? . . .

Straying from the *usual* behavioural objectives path in several directions *is* sometimes defensible — but not in the direction Popham favours. For the governing slogans include . . . 'A bird in the hand is worth two in the bush'. Which, being interpreted, does not mean 'any scrawny little sparrow is worth several fat turkeys in this bush which I have just surrounded with my forces', but 'one plump chicken is worth a covey of quail in *that* bush, on the horizon'. In short, if there isn't something worthwhile you definitely can teach effectively in *this* subject, there certainly is in another subject. There just aren't any long-term goals which can't be approached by intrinsically useful steps *or* displaced by equally valuable goals which *can* be thus approached. The alternative seems to me to stem from too leisurely a conception of the educational task which I view as a desperate race against time, difficulty and the press of needs. I can see we *may* have to allow 'non-behavioural objectives' in the direction of holistic abstract intrinsic criteria, but not that we're reduced to whistling in the dark. As Popham says (ibid., p. 8), of his latest position; 'The floodgates may have been opened' by it. . . .

Source: M. Scriven (1971). 'Goal-free behavioral objectives', 11-71 NIE 2D. The extracts reproduced here are taken from pp. 1-2, 3-4.

3.22 Michael Scriven
Goal Lib (the GFE's manifesto)

There's no way to do responsible *planning and production* without goals/objectives/measures/tests, but planning is simply a means to an achievement, whereas evaluation is the determination of the merit of what's achieved. Doing the latter doesn't necessitate following the same route as the former, *unless* you want to evaluate the planning and management performance. Of course, you have to evaluate achievement against *something* (at least you do on my view of evaluation . . .), but the best basis is the very same one that the producer used in deciding what to produce, namely, the needs of the target population. There's no reason why his/her judgement of the best way to combine those needs and his/her capacity/resources into worthwhile production should be immune to evaluation. Important errors are made at that point, and new evidence often turns up to put that judgement in a new light now, though it was well-justified at the time. The GBEr [Goal Based Evaluator] can't look at this, because (s)he accepts the goals as the ultimate criterion. The GFEr doesn't look at this, because (s)he's not interested in *where* the failings came in, only in *whether* they were any. (The former is a task for a *management* evaluation as such.) But the GFEr takes the same line of thought one stage further. Having seen that the producer cannot argue that his goals are beyond criticism, and that one would criticise them against the needs to which they are supposed to be responsive, the GFEr sees that (s)he can bypass the producer's formulation of goals because the crucial question is *not* what the producer intended to do, but what *was* actually achieved.

It is quite attractive to the producer to use either GBE or 'management evaluation' because the first completely finesses any consideration of errors in the selection of goals, and the second relativises the selection of goals to the data available at the time of the decision. The GFEr uses *current* needs data, casts no aspersions on management with regard to the original selection of goals (since (s)he knows neither the goals nor the data on which they were based) and goes straight into judgements of congruence between achievements and needs, against costs and alternatives. The advantages of bypassing goals are numerous and perhaps worth listing. (See below.) But it's perfectly true that it's *sometimes much harder* to do evaluation against needs rather than goals. Needs data is sometimes hard

Source: M. Scriven (1972). 'Goal Lib (the GFE's manifesto)', NIE 3A.

to get and 'needs' analysis involves some evaluation in itself. (Needs, unlike wants, are dimensions of mismatch between actual and required or *ideal*.) But, contrary to the suggestions of several respondents, it is quite false to say that the GFEr simply substitutes his/her own goals for those of the producer. One might as well say that any evaluator only substitutes his/her own value judgements for those of the producer. The GFEr must be able to *support* any claims about needs against which the evaluation is made. If there is support for those claims and for the logic of the evaluation, then we have an evaluation which may have absolutely no reference to the goals of the evaluator at all. The evaluator's goals may be doing good evaluation, or filling the political need for documented criticism of current social studies curricula.

But at least the GFEr *does* get liberated from some of the problems which his or her colleagues do face with regard to goals. We can sum these up in a list of difficulties for the GBEr—towards the end, one begins to see that (s)he has to do much of what the GFEr does, and didn't need the rest, and is handicapped in doing what *does* need to be done by having heard and seen too much.

1   Specifying goals at all.

2   Resolving the dilemma between accepting the ones the producer allegedly supports (but which are obviously almost irrelevant to the project) and reconstructing ones from the actual practice (in which case there's too little mismatch between goals and performance to enable GBE to give a realistic perspective).

3   Deciding between goals that conflict because (*a*) drawn up or interpreted by different persons/groups; (*b*) inconsistently formulated by one person; (*c*) based on different factual assumptions.

4   Handling over- and under-achievement of goals.

5   Identifying 'side-effects'.

6   Avoiding perceptual distortion of the magnitude of the main effects.

7   Handling offsets of desirable effects (intended or not) by undesirable ones (intended or not).

8   (For Enlightened GBErs only.) Judging the goals.

Finally, it's worth remembering that the GFEr isn't going to miss the *main* aims of the project, since (s)he looks at the student materials, the classroom process and the raw scores of the staff testing programme. If (s)he doesn't notice the project's main goals as achievements, they are going to be pretty minor—usually. Sometimes (s)he *will* miss them. But usually there'll be some pretty interesting compensating observations. The GFE approach is better at some things than GBE, perhaps better overall, but ideally should only be part of an evaluation approach.

Robert Stake

In turns droll, dense, cryptic, analytical or provocative, Robert Stake repays careful reading. He is basically an evaluation theorist and as such there is no final judgement to be squeezed out of his T-City evaluation report, featured in Section 5, the style of which is extremely compressed, enigmatic, frequently throwaway. Stake writes like he talks, with a personal openness that belies a rather private person. There is an abiding sense of compression, and occasional disconcerting silences between the words.

Robert Stake's major contribution to the theory of curriculum evaluation is perhaps 'The countenance of educational evaluation'. This takes another look at the framing assumptions that control the perceived scope of evaluation. For an art in which practice had begun to relate awkwardly to comprehensive theoretical overviews, it offered a more complete framework. The 'Countenance' paper offers a data matrix, suggesting that the evaluator needs to concern himself with three kinds of data, antecedent data (having prior existence), transactional data (dynamic, relating to encounters or engagements) and outcome data (widened to include impact, wear and tear, etc., as well as achievements). But Stake's natural interest is not towards 'overviews'. He tends towards tangling with particular issues which become recurrent themes in his writing.

One of the issues taken up in the 'Countenance' paper is the role of judgement in evaluation reports. Stake's position is quite explicitly different from Scriven's. Stake sees the evaluator as processing judgments more than rendering them. His approach is nearer to what MacDonald calls in Section 4 a 'democratic' style, refusing to set up the evaluator as a person uniquely qualified to offer criticism or endorsement.

In the same paper it emerges that in considering the goals of a programme Stake does not confine his attention to those pre-specified before its implementation. Neither does he accept any stated goals as the only legitimate basis on which to evaluate. To do so would be to accept the 'preordinate objectives' model. Stake does not deny that goals can form a basis for generating tests to determine whether a curriculum measures up to its own aspirations, but he also sees goal statements as data to be brought within an interpretative description of the programme as it evolves over time. The evaluator has no obligation to help programme-builders with formulating behavioural objectives, although he may be interested in authentic statements of intent. There is no reason, in principle, why these should not be taxonomic, mechanistic, humanistic, scriptural or whatever.

Another thread running through Stake's papers is the formative-summative distinction. The distinction as usually put forward is about time-scales; that a formative evaluation takes place during the development of a programme, a summative evaluation at its conclusion. This gave rise to the beguiling metaphor that formative evaluation is an equivalent of military intelligence, summative evaluation akin to military history. But there was also implicit a distinction of role. Scriven's 'Methodology' paper discussed the different roles that an evaluation seems likely to play at different points in time.

In the paper 'Formative and summative evaluation' Stake approaches the formative-summative distinction differently, dismissing the 'temporal' aspect as trivial. Stake's starting point is that the real value of the distinction is only apparent when we subordinate the idea of time to the idea that there are multiple audiences for evaluation reports. Although Myron Atkin attacked the behavioural objectives paradigm precisely because it made poor formative methodology, Stake urges formative evaluators to attempt generalisations about underlying regularities in the area of the curriculum development, and summative evaluators to portray programmes in a way that does justice to their uniqueness and their setting. This isn't as paradoxical as it sounds. It is during the life of a project that the enduring academic issues are tackled and only later that questions about a programme's style and setting predominate, particularly for an audience of would-be adopters. Whether one prefers Stake's sense of audience to Scriven's sense of time is to some extent a matter of taste. Some of Stake's military historians are present on the battlefield. Some of his spies write retrospective biographies.

'Comments and conjectures: the seeds of doubt', although selfconsciously enigmatic, is a beautifully balanced internal dialogue. However, it has been considered by some as overpersonal in tone and its inflated language taken as part of Stake's bid for the hair-shirt of the prophet. A striking contrast is with Scriven's shrill and self-righteous goal-free evaluator who wags his argumentative finger at a .client. 'The seeds of doubt' is a personal statement about choices for clothing the truth. It ends typically with a twin paradox: measurement is itself an activity that can be 'weighed' qualitatively; measurements, even when we arrive at them, are not established certainties but new seeds of doubt. There are times when it is useful to recall that Stake was a fellow in psychometric measurement at Princeton.

'The seven principal cardinals of educational evaluation' is a spoof paper. It was given at the 1972 AERA conference accompanied by off-beat examples [it's not a see-through blouse if nobody is looking]. But we know of few single-page handouts that put the main issues more succinctly.

In 'An approach to the evaluation of instructional programmes [Programme portrayal v analysis]', from which we reproduce several extracts under the heading 'Description versus analysis', Stake sets up another antithesis, this time between description and analysis in evaluation reports. He urges a greater interest in portrayal [description], even at the expense of focus. He has a sharper sense than most theorists that the illuminative paradigm is purchased at a price.

Preoccupation with the role of the evaluator vis à vis his separate audiences leads Stake to coin and elaborate the concept 'responsive evaluation' in the paper 'To evaluate an arts programme' [from which we reproduce extracts under the heading 'Responsive evaluation']. Responsive evaluation is 'responsive' to the questions of non-specialist audiences. It is consequently democratic, avoiding jargon and having a preference for 'natural' communication. It is focused on activities rather than intentions, and offers interpretations and descriptions. It is issue-centred, using issues as a way in to the understanding of complex phenomena. However, 'responsive evaluation' was seen by some as a preference for style over content. Scriven commented, rather waspishly, that it was responsive to everything except data.

3.23 Robert Stake
The countenance of educational evaluation

Dissatisfaction with the formal approach is not without cause. Few highly relevant, readable research studies can be found. The professional journals are not disposed to publish evaluation studies. Behavioural data are costly, and often do not provide the answers. Too many accreditation-type visitation teams lack special training or even experience in evaluation. Many checklists are ambiguous; some focus too much attention on the physical attributes of a school. Psychometric tests have been developed primarily to differentiate among students at the same point in training rather than to assess the effect of instruction on acquisition of skill and understanding. Today's educator may rely little on formal evaluation because its answers have seldom been answers to questions *he* is asking.

Potential contributions of formal evaluation

The educator's disdain of formal evaluation is due also to his sensitivity to criticism — and his *is* a critical clientele. It is not uncommon for him to draw before him such curtains as 'national norm comparisons', 'innovation phase' and 'academic freedom' to avoid exposure through evaluation. The 'politics' of evaluation is an interesting issue in itself, but it is not the issue here. The issue here is the *potential* contribution to education of formal evaluation. Today, educators fail to perceive what formal evaluation could do for them. They should be imploring measurement specialists to develop a methodology that reflects the fullness, the complexity and the importance of their programmes. They are not. What one finds when he examines formal evaluation activities in education today is too little effort to spell out antecedent conditions and classroom transactions (a few of which visitation teams do record) and too little effort to couple them with the various outcomes (a few of which are portrayed by conventional test scores). Little attempt has been made to measure the match between what an educator intends to do and what he does do. The traditional concern of educational-measurement specialists for reliability of individual-student scores and predictive validity, thoroughly and competently stated in the American Council on Education's 1950 edition of *Educational Measure-*

Source: R. E. Stake (1967). 'The countenance of educational evaluation'. Teachers College Record, 68, No. 7, pp. 523-40. The extracts reproduced here are taken from pp. 524-36. The footnotes have been renumbered.

ment[1] is a questionable resource. For evaluation of curricula, attention to individual differences among students should give way to attention to the contingencies among background conditions, classroom activities and scholastic outcomes.

This paper is not about what should be measured or how to measure. It is background for developing an evaluation plan. What and how are decided later. My orientation here is around educational programmes rather than educational products. I presume that the value of a product depends on its programme of use. The evaluation of a programme includes the evaluation of its materials.

The countenance of educational evaluation appears to be changing. On the pages that follow, I will indicate what the countenance can, and perhaps, should be. My attempt here is to introduce a conceptualisation of evaluation orientated to the complex and dynamic nature of education, one which gives proper attention to the diverse purposes and judgements of the practitioner. . . .

The purposes and procedures of educational evaluation will vary from instance to instance. What is quite appropriate for one school may be less appropriate for another. Standardised achievement tests here but not there. A great concern for expense there but not over there. How do evaluation purposes and procedures vary? What are the basic characteristics of evaluation activities? They are identified in these pages as the evaluation acts, the data sources, the congruence and contingencies, the standards and the uses of evaluation. The first distinction to be made will be between description and judgement in evaluation. The countenance of evaluation beheld by the educator is not the same one beheld by the specialist in evaluation. The specialist sees himself as a 'describer,' one who describes aptitudes and environments and accomplishments. The teacher and school administrator, on the other hand, expect an evaluator to grade something or someone as to merit. Moreover, they expect that he will judge things against external standards, on criteria perhaps little related to the local school's resources and goals.

Neither sees evaluation broadly enough. *Both* description and judgement are essential—in fact, they are the two basic acts of evaluation. Any individual evaluator may attempt to refrain from judging or from collecting the judgements of others. Any individual evaluator may seek only to bring to light the worth of the programme. But their evaluations are incomplete. To be fully understood, the educational programme must be fully described and fully judged.

Towards full description

The specialist in evaluation seems to be increasing his emphasis on fullness

1   E. F. Lindquist (ed.) (1951). *Educational Measurement*. Washington D.C.: American Council on Education.

of description. For many years he evaluated primarily by measuring student progress toward academic objectives. . . . To the traditional description of pupil achievement, we add the description of instruction and the description of relationships between them. Like the instructional researcher, the evaluator—as so defined—seeks generalisations about educational practices. Many curriculum project evaluators are adopting this definition of evaluation.

The role of judgement

Description is one thing, judgement is another. Most evaluation specialists have chosen not to judge. But Michael Scriven, in his recent 'Methodology of evaluation'[2] has charged evaluators with responsibility for passing upon the merit of an educational practice. (Note that he has urged the evaluator to do what the educator has expected the evaluator to be doing.) Scriven's position is that there is no evaluation until judgement has been passed, and by his reckoning the evaluator is best qualified to judge.

By being well experienced and by becoming well-informed in the case at hand in matters of research and educational practice the evaluator does become at least partially qualified to judge. But is it wise for him to accept this responsibility? Even now when few evaluators expect to judge, educators are reluctant to initiate a formal evaluation. If evaluators were *more* frequently identified with the passing of judgement, with the discrimination among poorer and better programmes, and with the awarding of support and censure, their access to data would probably diminish. Evaluators collaborate with other social scientists and behavioural research workers. Those who do not want to judge deplore the acceptance of such responsibility by their associates. They believe that in the eyes of many practitioners, social science and behavioural research will become more suspect than it already is.

Many evaluators feel that they are not capable of perceiving, as they think a judge should, the unidimensional *value* of alternative program-mes. . . . Who should judge? The answer comes easily to Scriven partly because he expects little interaction between treatment and learner, i.e. what works best for one learner will work best for others, at least within broad categories. He also expects that where the local good is at odds with the common good, the local good can be shown to be detrimental to the common good, to the end that the doctrine of local option is invalidated. According to Scriven the evaluator must judge.

Whether or not evaluation specialists will accept Scriven's challenge remains to be seen. In any case, it is likely that judgements will become an increasing part of the evaluation report. Evaluators will seek out and

2 M. Scriven (1967). 'The methodology of evaluation.' In R. Tyler, R. Gagné and M. Scriven, *Perspectives of Curriculum Evaluation*. AERA Monograph Series on Curriculum Evaluation, No. 1. Chicago: Rand McNally, pp. 39-83.

record the opinions of persons of special qualification. These opinions, though subjective, can be very useful and can be gathered objectively, independently of the solicitor's opinions. A responsibility for processing judgements is much more acceptable to the evaluation specialist than one for rendering judgements himself. . . .

Data matrices

In order to evaluate, an educator will gather together certain data. The data are likely to be from several quite different sources, gathered in several quite different ways. Whether the immediate purpose is description or judgement, three bodies of information should be tapped. In the evaluation report it can be helpful to distinguish between *antecedent, transaction* and *outcome* data.

An antecedent is any condition existing prior to teaching and learning which may relate to outcomes. The status of a student prior to his lesson, e.g. his aptitude, previous experience, interest and willingness, is a complex antecedent. The programmed-instruction specialist calls some antecedents 'entry behaviours'. The state-accrediting agency emphasises the investment of community resources. All of these are examples of the antecedents which an evaluator will describe. Transactions are the countless encounters of students with teacher, student with student, author with reader, parent with counsellor — the succession of engagements which comprise the process of education. Examples are the presentation of a film, a class discussion, the working of a homework problem, an explanation on the margin of a term paper and the administration of a test. Smith and Meux studied such transactions in detail and have provided an 18-category classification system.[3] One very visible emphasis on a particular class of transactions was the National Defense Education Act support of audio-visual media.

Transactions are dynamic whereas antecedents and outcomes are relatively static. The boundaries between them are not clear, e.g. during a transaction we can identify certain outcomes which are feedback antecedents for subsequent learning. These boundaries do not need to be distinct. The categories should be used to stimulate rather than to subdivide our data collection.

Traditionally, most attention in formal evaluation has been given to outcomes — outcomes such as the abilities, achievements, attitudes and aspirations of students resulting from an educational experience. . . .

Antecedents, transactions and outcomes, the elements of evaluation statements, are shown in Figure 1 to have a place in both description and judgement. To fill in these matrices the evaluator will collect judgements (e.g. of community prejudice, of problem-solving styles and of teacher

3 B. Othanel Smith and M. O. Meux, (*A Study of the Logic of Teaching*. Urbana: Bureau of Educational Research. University of Illinois. Undated).

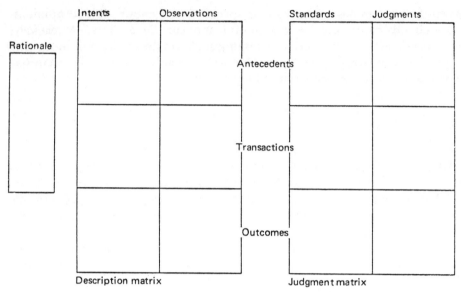

Figure 1   A layout of statements and data to be collected by the evaluator of an educational programme

personality) as well as descriptions. In Figure 1 it is also indicated that judgemental statements are classified either as general standards of quality or as judgements specific to the given programme. Descriptive data are classified as intents and observations. The evaluator can organise his data-gathering to conform to the format shown in Figure 1.

The evaluator can prepare a record of what educators intend, of what observers perceive, of what patrons generally expect and of what judges value the immediate programme to be. The record may treat antecedents, transactions and outcomes separately within the four classes identified as *Intents, Observations, Standards* and *Judgements*, as in Figure 1. . . . Next I would like to consider the description data matrix in detail.

Goals and intents

For many years instructional technologists, test specialists and others have pleaded for more explicit statement of educational goals. I consider 'goals', 'objectives' and 'intents' to be synonymous. I use the category title *Intents* because many educators now equate 'goals' and 'objectives' with 'intended student outcomes.' In this paper Intents includes the planned-for environmental conditions, the planned-for demonstrations, planned-for coverage of certain subject matter, etc., as well as the planned-for student behaviour. To be included in this three-cell column are effects which are desired, those which are hoped for, those which are anticipated and even those which are feared. This class of data includes goals and plans that others have, especially the students. (It should be noted that it is not the educator's privilege to rule out the study of a variable by saying, 'that is not one of our objectives'. The evaluator should include both the variable and the negation.) The resulting collection of *Intents* is a priority listing of all that may happen.

The fact that many educators now equate 'goals' with 'intended student outcomes' is to the credit of the behaviourists, particularly the advocates of programmed instruction. . . .

The educational evaluator should not list goals only in terms of anticipated student behaviour. To *evaluate* an educational programme, we must examine what teaching, as well as what learning, is intended. (Many antecedent conditions and teaching transactions can be worded behaviouristically, if desired.) How intentions are worded is not a criterion for inclusion. Intents can be the global goals of the Educational Policies Commission or the detailed goals of the programmer.[4] Taxonomic, mechanistic, humanistic, even scriptural — any mixture of goal statements are acceptable as part of the evaluation picture. Many a contemporary evaluator expects trouble when he sets out to record the educator's objectives. Early in the work he urged the educator to declare his objectives so that outcome-testing devices could be built. He finds the educator either reluctant or unable to verbalise objectives. With diligence, if not with pleasure, the evaluator assists with what he presumes to be the educator's job: writing behavioural goals. His presumption is wrong. As Scriven has said, the responsibility for describing curricular objectives is the responsibility of the evaluator. He is the one who is experienced with the language of behaviours, traits and habits. . . .

It is necessary for him to continue to ask the educator for statements of intent. He should augment the replies by asking, 'Is this another way of saying it?' or 'Is this an instance?' It is not wrong for an evaluator to teach a willing educator about behavioural objectives — they may facilitate the work. It is wrong for him to insist that every educator should use them. Obtaining authentic statements of intent is a new challenge for the evaluator. The methodology remains to be developed. Let us now shift attention to the second column of the data cells.

Observational choice

Most of the descriptive data cited early in the previous section are classified as *Observations*. In Figure 1 when he described surroundings and events and the subsequent consequences, the evaluator[5] is telling of

4   R. F. Mager (1962). *Preparing Objectives for Programmed Instruction*. San Francisco: Fearon Publishers.

5   Here and elsewhere in this paper, for simplicity of presentation, the evaluator and the educator are referred to as two different persons. The educator will often be his own evaluator or a member of the evaluation team.

his observations. Sometimes the evaluator observes these characteristics in a direct and personal way. Sometimes he uses instruments. His instruments include inventory schedules, biographical data sheets, interview routines, check lists, opinionnaires and all kinds of psychometric tests. The experienced evaluator gives special attention to the measurement of student outcomes, but he does not fail to observe the other outcomes, nor the antecedent conditions and instructional transactions. . . .

An evaluation is not complete without a statement of the rationale of the programme. It needs to be considered separately, as indicated in Figure 1. Every programme has its rationale, though often it is only implicit. The rationale indicates the philosophic background and basic purposes of the programme. Its importance to evaluation has been indicated by Berlak.[6] The rationale should provide one basis for evaluating intents. The evaluator asks himself or other judges whether the plan developed by the educator constitutes a logical step in the implementation of the basic purposes. The rationale also is of value in choosing the reference groups, e.g. merchants, mathematicians and mathematics educators, which later are to pass judgement on various aspects of the programme. . . .

Contingency and congruence

For any one educational programme there are two principal ways of processing descriptive evaluation data: finding the contingencies among antecedents, transactions and outcomes and finding the congruence between intents and observations. The processing of judgements follows a different model. The first two main columns of the data matrix in Figure 1 contain the descriptive data. The format for processing these data is represented in Figure 2. The data for a curriculum are *congruent* if what was intended actually happens. To be fully congruent the intended antecedents, transactions and outcomes would have to come to pass. (This seldom happens—and often should not.) Within one row of the data matrix the evaluator should be able to compare the cells containing intents and observations, to note the discrepancies and to describe the amount of congruence for that row. (Congruence of outcomes has been emphasised in the evaluation model proposed by Taylor and Maguire.) Congruence does not indicate that outcomes are reliable or valid, but that what was intended did occur. . . .

Lesson planning and curriculum revision through the years has been built upon faith in certain contingencies. Day to day, the master teacher arranges his presentation and selects his input materials to fit his

6   Harold Berlak. Comments recorded in Irving Morrisett (ed.) (1966). *Concepts and Structure in the New Social Science Curricula*. Lafayette, Indiana: Social Science Education Consortium, Purdue University, pp. 88-9.

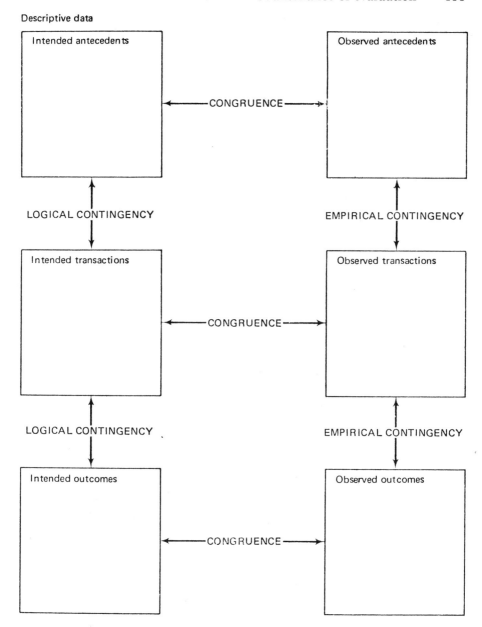

Descriptive data

Figure 2   A representation of the processing of descriptive data

instructional goals. For him the contingencies, in the main, are logical, intuitive and supported by a history of satisfactions and endorsements. Even the master teacher, and certainly less-experienced teachers need to bring their intuited contingencies under the scrutiny of appropriate juries.

As a first step in evaluation it is important just to record them. A film on floodwaters may be scheduled (intended transaction) to expose students to a background to conservation legislation (intended outcome). Of those who know both subject matter and pedagogy, we ask, 'Is there a logical connection between this event and this purpose?' If so, a logical contingency exists between these two intents. The record should show it. Whenever intents are evaluated the contingency criterion is one of logic. To test the logic of an educational contingency the evaluators rely on previous experience, perhaps on research experience, with similar observables. No immediate observation of these variables, however, is necessary to test the strength of the contingencies among intents.

Evaluation of observation contingencies depend on empirical evidence. To say, 'this arithmetic class progressed rapidly because the teacher was somewhat but not too sophisticated in mathematics' demands empirical data, either from within the evaluation or from the research literature.[7] The usual evaluation of a single programme will not alone provide the data necessary for contingency statements. Here too, then, previous experience with similar observables is a basic qualification of the evaluator. The contingencies and congruences identified by evaluators are subject to judgement by experts and participants just as more unitary descriptive data are. The importance of non-congruence will vary with different viewpoints. The school superintendent and the school counsellor may disagree as to the importance of a cancellation of the scheduled lessons on sex hygiene in the health class. As an example of judging contingencies, the degree to which teacher morale is contingent on the length of the school day may be deemed cause enough to abandon an early morning class by one judge and not another. Perceptions of importance of congruence and contingency deserve the evaluator's careful attention.

Standards and judgements

. . . There is little knowledge anywhere today of the quality of a student's education. School grades are based on the private criteria and standards of the individual teacher. Most 'standardised' test scores tell where an examinee performing 'psychometrically useful' tasks stands with regard to a reference group, rather than the level of competence at which he performs essential scholastic tasks. Although most teachers are competent to teach their subject matter and to spot learning difficulties, few have the ability to *describe* a student's command over his intellectual environment. Neither school grades nor standardised test scores nor the candid opinions of teachers are very informative as to the excellence of students.

7   See H. Bassham (1962). 'Teacher understanding and pupil efficiency in mathematics: a study of relationship'. *Arithmetic Teacher,* **9,** pp. 383-7.

Even when measurements are effectively interpreted, evaluation is complicated by a multiplicity of standards. Standards vary from student to student, from instructor to instructor, and from reference group to reference group. This is not wrong. In a healthy society, different parties have different standards. Part of the responsibility of evaluation is to make known which standards are held by whom. . . .

While a curriculum is being developed and disseminated, even the major classes of criteria vary. In their analysis of nationwide assimilation of new educational programmes, Clark and Guba[8] identified eight stages of change through which new programmes go. For each stage they identified special criteria (each with its own standards) on which the programme should be evaluated before it advances to another stage. Each of their criteria deserves elaboration, but here it is merely noted that there are quite different criteria at each successive curriculum-development stage.

Informal evaluation tends to leave criteria unspecified. Formal evaluation is more specific. But it seems the more careful the evaluation, the fewer the criteria; and the more carefully the criteria are specified, the less the concern given to standards of acceptability. It is a great misfortune that the best trained evaluators have been looking at education with a microscope rather than with a panoramic view finder.

There is no clear picture of what any school or any curriculum project is accomplishing today partly because the methodology of processing judgements is inadequate. . . .

8   David L. Clark and Egon G. Guba, (1965). 'An examination of potential change roles in education.' Columbus, Ohio: Ohio State University, (mimeo).

3.24   Robert Stake
Formative and summative evaluation

Because attention is being drawn to these two names, it seems reasonable to give them meaning that will indicate differences in the way the evaluation will be carried out. I would substitute the 'utility' distinction for the 'temporal' distinction. I would have us emphasise the difference between the responsibility for forming programmes and the responsibility for being acquainted with a programme in its (summative) totality. People within the programme carry both responsibilities. People more remote are more easily identified with one responsibility or the other. So it may help our definition-building to speak of those more remote audiences of an evaluation report.

Let me use a genealogical metaphor. For any person of interest we can attend to his pedigree and we can attend to his offspring. We can identify his ancestors and we can identify his descendents. With an instructional programme—one classroom or nationwide—we can attend to those who have directly or indirectly contributed to its creation and we can attend to those who—knowingly or unknowingly—are its heirs. . . .

Here are some terms that roughly characterise the information the two groups ask for:

Programme developers request:
relatively molecular analyses,
cause-seeking studies,
broader experience,
ways of ignoring local effects.

Programme clients request:
relatively molar analyses,
descriptive information,
efficiency statements,
emphasis on local effects.

The formative-evaluation study should be more 'experimental', sacrificing effectiveness of the immediate treatment in order to attain more generalisable findings. The summative-evaluation design should be more like the plan for a TV documentary, sacrificing controls and standardisation in order to accommodate to the uniqueness of the programme and its setting. Each design should be attuned to its own audience. The key distinction, as I see it, between formative and summative evaluation should rest on the distinction between information as a basis for generalisation and information as a basis for specification.

It is clear that people on both sides of the programme look for both generalisations and specifications. The distinction is a matter of emphasis.

Source: R. E. Stake. 'Formative and summative evaluation'. Paper published here for the first time.

156

The creators and abstractors are relatively more interested in the pervasive relationships between teaching and learning. The local citizens are more interested in details of teaching-and-learning accruing to this particular programme. . . .

A third group of people, those most directly responsible for the operation of the programme, i.e. teachers and administrators, will have an interest in both summative and formative evaluation. They need to know about how to put new programmes together and they need to know what the present programmes are. (Most of them are not inclined to value the information from formal studies over their own immediate perceptions, but their own perceptions can be classified as formative or summative.)

In addition to these two kinds of evaluation, they need something I will call operative evaluation. Operative evaluation is perhaps some blend of formative and summative evaluation, but I will differentiate it just now because the information needs of the two audiences identified earlier are not adequate here. Operative evaluation is for monitoring, trouble-shooting, crisis-managing, the alleviation of problems that arise, the making of decisions with least-hurtful compromises. This sort of evaluation is aimed neither at generalisation nor understanding of specific programmes. It is not orientated to the goals and objectives of the programme — it is aimed at recognising catastrophe, potential and realised; it is aimed at identifying choice points, the alternatives available, and the implication of each alternative. Dan Stufflebeam's CIPP model (1971) comes the closest of anything I know, but his approach is — like most others — orientated to piety and perfection more than to cancer and arson. (Attention to objectives takes your mind off your problem rather than helping you come to grips with it.)

3.25 Robert Stake
The seeds of doubt

. . . I wonder if there is an answer to the question 'Why do I continue to be a measurements man?'

I am not a man of change so part of the answer is 'inertia'. But I am a man of purpose, and I see that the long-range purposes usually given for educational measurement are seldom achieved. For example, sophisticated use of test results is not prominent in contemporary education even though in-service instruction in test use has been prominent in this country for forty years. Worse than that, our formal measurements are not directly useful in the solution of most important educational problems.

But I have known this for a long time. 'Why do I continue to be a measurements man?'

The answer I usually hear — it is an answer I have believed until recently — is that measurement leads to analysis. Analysis leads to rational thinking. We measure in order 'to tell it like it really is.' When we know how it really is, then we can consider the alternatives and their implication and make the rational choice. Good choices will increase our control over our destinies or postpone our succumbing to them.

For myself and my fellow men I want a freedom of choice, a chance to control our destinies. Science, technology and measurement are the instruments of choice — so that answer goes.

I am increasingly less persuaded by that answer. I do not see people becoming more rational even when their measurements are better. I do not see people increasingly in control of their destinies. Just the opposite. I see them more isolated from control and feeling much more alienated by the increasing demands and constraints of commerce, transportation, war, protests and government.

People do not see our data as key to the solution of their problems. My measurements are praised often by my colleagues, seldom by my clients. Will that change?

Science and technology seem to be contributing less to our enlightenment, more to our alienation. Sometimes the man in the street tells me point-blank that he doesn't want any more of my coefficients. But I say that he still guesses that the potential misuse of my information outweighs

Source: R. E. Stake (1972). 'Comments and conjectures: the seeds of doubt'. The Educational Forum, *January 1972, pp. 271-2. The extract reproduced here is taken from pp. 271-2. The material is used by permission of Kappa Delta Pi, an Honor Society in Education.*

the potential good use. For the present he may be right. But my productive life is half over. Will he soon fear my measurements less?

But the problem runs even further. What am I measuring? I have lost the sense that there is any 'the way it is'. *What is* only seems to be. That I can measure more accurately and reliably and verifiably does not mean that I am measuring *what is*. In fact, by de-emphasising temporal impressions, clinical judgements—those personal determinants of the world—I am withdrawing from the challenge of measuring *what is*. What they see and feel is *what is*.

My measurements are not the first approximations to truth; they are choices I make as to how to clothe the truth. It is another case of the Emperor's clothes—with the minor switch that it is the Emperor who is invisible and it is only the clothes that are seen.

Have my measurements no more purpose than to stimulate my fellow specialists and to delude all others? I think so. There *is* a purpose. It is a purpose seldom recognised, seldom honoured. I think measurements help counter that onrush of the Great Simplification.

Philosophers and technologists are colleagues in the Great Simplification. Only observations stand in their way. Data occasionally support an idea, often not; never do they confirm an idea. Sometimes they, simplifiers, use research data to argue a point. But the principal effect of research—as we see it today in education—is to deny the validity of the hypothesis. Measurements always say, 'No, it is not quite like that.' Measurements are new seeds of doubt.

The world needs advocates; the world needs sceptics. I see a world that scrunches its sceptics and counter-advocates, glorifies its advocates, each in his time. One truth, one set of values, one perspective is honoured over others.

I see measurements as vital to this world, not because they tell us what is truth but because they keep the other sides of truth alive.

3.26   Robert Stake
The seven principal cardinals of educational evaluation

Parity[1] Evaluation is a declaration of the worth of something. There are many dimensions of merit and shortcoming to anything. Standards for judging worth may be explicit or implicit.

Ubiquity[2] Evaluation is a partner to all endeavour. Little is judged by 'cold facts' or by 'passion' alone. The most sophisticated evaluation is that done by individual persons — mature, some ways rational, some ways intuitive. *They* are the models for evaluators to contemplate.

Diversity[3] Every aspect of an educational programme holds at least as many truths as there are viewers. Each sees value in a different light. The evaluator has no cause to force a consensus, but certainly to show the distribution of perceptions.

Utility[4] Evaluation studies should be a service rather than a research function, to provide needed assistance and useful information to a clientele or audience. These studies may or may not be attentive to the aims and concerns of those developing or operating the programme.

Redundancy[5] Understanding comes with repeated encounter. Something worth knowing needs to be looked at from several points of view. Even in the greatest ambiguity, that of substance emerges on repeated probing.

Ambiguity[6] Evaluators strive for specificity, at the price of validity. They should: avoid oversimplification; compromise with ambiguity. There is no comfort in accurate measurement of the irrelevant.

Generalisability[7] To know the reach, and failing grasp, of covariation is the researcher's lot. Not necessarily the evaluator's. The evaluator knows that the act of specification, experimental design, randomisation or formal measurement (mechanisms for increasing generalisation) reacts with a programme, and makes it other than it would have been. The client may hold generalisability not worth the cost and the intrusion.

1   'The value of X is set by people; not by Y nor by any other covariate.'
2   'Birds do it. Bees do it. Even educated fleas do it.'
3   'It's not a see-through blouse if no one's looking.'
4   'Remind them to aim earthward before firing the retrorockets.'
5   'A rose is a rose is a rose is more than a rose is a rose.'
6   'A name is to hang one on.'
7   'So I should think that all white whales are bad?'

Source: R. E. Stake (1972). 'The seven principal cardinals of educational evaluation'. Handout for presentation by Robert Stake, AERA Annual Meeting, Chicago, 1972.

160

3.27 Robert Stake
Description versus analysis

The evaluator of an instructional programme is faced with a description *vs* analysis dilemma. His design and final report can emphasise what he can measure most effectively, given his modest resources—or his design and final report can reflect the nature of the programme, with fidelity to the many important perceptions and expectations of it. Both cannot prevail. What the evaluator has to say cannot be both a sharp analysis of high-priority achievement *and* a broad and accurate reflection of the programme's complex transactions. One message crowds out the other.

I am saying something more than 'You can't feature both product and process in the evaluation study.' I am saying, 'Any focus on the analysis of product *or* process distorts the picture as to what the instruction is.' Which is more important: to tell of some very special things about the programme or to provide the most veridical portrayal of the programme?

I am today going to advocate the latter, the emphasis on portrayal, at the expense of focus. I do not mean this to be an emphasis on descriptive data rather than judgemental; both kinds of data are needed both places—in veridical-portrayal evaluations and in sharp-focus evaluations. I do not mean this to be an emphasis on summative rather than formative evaluation; in either case the same dilemma appears. I acknowledge that any study that emphasises a particular issue, or a particular decision, or a particular goal, or two or three issues or goals, at the great diminution of all others, might be a most appropriate research or evaluation effort—but it should not be passed off as an evaluation *of the programme.* . . .

Consensus is one of the great simplifiers. Theory is another. Statistical processes are simplifiers. Test scores are simple representations of the complex. These simplifiers help us by reducing the phenomena to something within our power of comprehension. But they mislead us by saying that education is much less than it really is. We work day by day with the simplifications—the statements of objectives, the central tendencies, the criterion tests—and we become transfixed by them, losing our awareness of the fundamental activities of teaching and learning. We do it to ourselves and we do it to our audiences. Evaluators should be helping

Source: R. E. Stake (1972). 'An approach to the evaluation of instructional programs (program portrayal vs. analysis)', a paper delivered at the AERA Annual Meeting in Chicago, 4 April 1972, pp. 1-4. The extracts reproduced here are taken from pp. 1, 3-4.

people keep in touch with the reality of instruction, but our scrapbooks are full of enlargements of enlargements. . . .

It is difficult for many clients to perceive the scope and movement of the programme. The programme director's perspective is partially obscured; the outsider's is evanescent. They need to see more, to share more in the experience. If the programme glows, the evaluation should reflect some of it. If the programme wobbles, the tremor should pass through the evaluation report. The first duty of the evaluator should be to offer the client a comprehensive portrayal of the programme.

The client may want something else. OK. He may want more than portrayal. He may want something other than portrayal. OK. He may want a concentrated examination of the pursuit of a few objectives. He may want a study of the causes of success or failure, or a study of transportability, or a study of the efficiency of the programme. If he has the resources, he should get what he wants. But he should not be encouraged to pursue those costly and sometimes elusive phantoms if what he needs is a substantive portrayal of his instructional programme.

It's a tough choice: focus or portrayal. The evaluator has to help figure out which will be more useful. Many of us are biased in favour of focus. I vote for portrayal.

Think for a moment what a book review has become in *The Sunday Times:* an opportunity for the reviewer to get something off his chest, a chance to pamper a pet idea, with at most a tenuous connection to the book reviewed. Are programme evaluation studies connected to programmes by more than a tenuous shoestring? Are they little more than the exploiting of an instructional researcher's hunch or a psychometrician's fascination? We owe people more than that.

3.28 Robert Stake
Responsive evaluation

An educational evaluation is *responsive evaluation* (1) if it orients more directly to programme activities than to programme intents, (2) if it responds to audience requirements for information and (3) if the different value-perspectives present are referred to in reporting the success and failure of the programme. In these three separate ways an evaluation plan can be responsive.

To do a responsive evaluation, the evaluator conceives of a plan of observations and negotiations. He arranges for various persons to observe the programme. With their help he prepares brief narratives, portrayals, product displays, graphs, etc. He finds out what is of value to his audiences. He gathers expressions of worth from various individuals whose points of view differ. Of course, he checks the quality of his records. He gets programme personnel to react to the accuracy of his portrayals. He gets authority figures to react to the importance of various findings. He gets audience members to react to the relevance of his findings. He does much of this informally — iterating and keeping a record of action and reaction. He chooses media accessible to his audiences to increase the likelihood and fidelity of communication. He might prepare a final written report, he might not — depending on what he and his clients have agreed on. . . .

Instead of objectives, or hypotheses as 'advanced organisers' for an evaluation study, I prefer *issues.* I think the word 'issues' better reflects a sense of complexity, immediacy and valuing. After getting acquainted with a programme, partly by talking with students, parents, taxpayers, programme sponsors, and programme staff, the evaluator acknowledges certain issues or problems or potential problems. These issues are a structure for continuing discussions with clients, staff and audiences. These issues are a structure for the data-gathering plan. The systematic observations to be made, the interviews and tests to be given, if any, should be those that contribute to understanding or resolving the issues identified. . . .

One of the principal reasons for backing away from the preordinate approach to evaluation is to improve communication with audiences. The conventional style of research-reporting is a 'clearly explicit' way of

Source: R. E. Stake. 'To evaluate an arts program'. To appear in a forthcoming issue of the Journal of Aesthetic Education. *The preparation of this paper was supported by the JDR 3rd Fund.*

communicating. In a typical research project characteristics (i.e. descriptors, traits) are identified and relationships among them are sought. Individuals are observed, found to differ, and distributions of scores are displayed. Covariations of various kinds are analysed and interpreted. From a report of such analytic inquiry it is very hard, often impossible, for a reader to know 'what the programme was like.' If he is supposed to learn 'what the programme was like,' the evaluation report should be different from the conventional research report.

The responsive approach is an attempt to respond to the natural ways in which people assimilate information and arrive at understanding. *Direct* personal experience is an efficient, comprehensive and satisfying way of creating understanding,[1] but a way not usually available to our audiences. The best substitute for direct experience probably is *vicarious experience* — increasingly better when the evaluator uses attending and conceptualising styles similar to those which members of the audience use. Such styles are not likely to be those of the specialist in measurement or theoretically-minded social scientist. Vicarious experience often will be conceptualised in terms of persons, places and events.

We need a reporting procedure for facilitating vicarious experience. And it is available. Among the better evangelists, anthropologists and dramatists are those who have developed the art of storytelling. We need to portray complexity. We need to convey holistic impression, the mood, even the mystery of the experience. The programme staff or people in the community may be 'uncertain'. The audiences should feel that uncertainty. More ambiguity rather than less may be needed in our reports. Oversimplification obfuscates. . . .

The responsive evaluator prepares portrayals. Some will be short, featuring perhaps a five-minute 'script,' a log or scrapbook. A longer portrayal may require several media: narratives, maps and graphs, exhibits, taped conversations, photographs, even audience role-playing. . . .

---

1 Direct experience does not always lead to clear perception or valid understanding. The analyst believes that separate examination of the components leads to better understanding. The experimentalist believes in examination of a controlled, simplified experience. But these examinations are just as susceptible to misunderstanding and faulty generalisation as direct experience. The bias of direct or vicarious experience is reduced as repeated observations and diverse points of view are attained.

Section 4
Alternative methodology

Introduction

This section builds upon the methodological overview in the Parlett and Hamilton paper 'Evaluation as illumination' [*see Section 1*]. *There is some difficulty, however, in giving a purely methodological account of alternative evaluation. This is partly, as Parlett and Hamilton point out, because such evaluation activity is not premised on the existence of a standard methodological package. It is not only eclectic, but adaptive and responsive to the particular learning milieu in which the evaluator is working. The eclecticism is hardly surprising, and may be compared to the use of multiple sources of data in social-area analysis, or the deliberately broad perspectives employed in family casework. The methodological ragbag is more of a problem, as research methodology is an area in which it is reasonable to expect a low tolerance of imprecision. Insofar as there is a loose general research strategy behind illuminative evaluation, it arises from the many intellectual traditions which encourage wholistic descriptions and explanations of human acts. These substantive traditions provide an intellectual basis for constructing an interpretative account of an educational programme interacting with its social context. The aim is to unravel its day-to-day realities.*

Methodology in a loosely-defined area is also to some extent personal to the researcher. Or at least he is at liberty to put his own signature on it. The five 'advocates of change' featured in Section 3 exhibit only a family resemblance. Their positions on many issues, including methodological issues, are quite disparate.

Like other sections of the reader, this section also considers ways of doing evaluation. But its central concern is more narrowly methodological. It is tentative and exploratory, as befits the present state of the art. Any authenticity it can claim arises from its emphasis on evaluators themselves reflecting on the diversity of the practices they employ. All of the authors presented below sense themselves to be investigators in an ill-defined, or imperfectly understood, area. One reassuring sign is that illuminative evaluators tend to adopt a low profile, to reflect a taste for self-doubt. Evaluators, whether working within a psychometric or social anthropology paradigm, need to repudiate any notion of themselves as new mandarins, an expert class laying tacit claims to extensive or even magical powers of divination, clairvoyance or prediction. Indeed several investigators have seen the subversion of this idea as an important part of their work. At every stage, from research proposal to final postscript, they are at pains to stress the limited and partial nature of their endeavour.

167

Alternative methodology has its own situational morality. Methods of investigation and reportage are typically 'made to measure' and responsive to the particular programme under review. This situational adjustment was less possible when the evaluator paid homage to the subtly-authoritarian ingrained rubrics of behavioural research. The resulting situation is a complex one: not only do evaluators differ from one another, but they may well change the ground-rules of their professional work to accord with the circumstances of a particular study.

While there are general principles or standard procedures embedded in other fields [for example, the principle of confidentiality in medicine] that could form the beginning of an evaluators' professional code, there are still enormous areas of uncertainty where each evaluator is on his own. What are appropriate styles of reporting in one study may not be in another, given different problems, time-scales or audiences. What is an unacceptable invasion of privacy in one investigation is a probing, useful and popular analysis in another. What is a totally unwarranted abuse of evaluative privilege in one instance is a highly acceptable and necessary intervention in another. One evaluator is in the forefront of the quest for 'unobtrusive measures', another sees himself as a 'change agent' in the situation under study.

There are, of course, intellectual traditions outside education that the new-style illuminative evaluators can draw upon: participant observation in sociology, ethnographic fieldwork in social anthropology, literary criticism, film documentary, historical research, law and clinical psychiatry. But even psychotherapists differ greatly in terms of the intimacy they allow with patients, and participant observers frequently exhibit all the dilemmas and contradictions of marginal man, forced to live in the interstices between conflicting cultures.

*When Parlett and Hamilton spoke of an evaluation stemming from a social anthropology paradigm, there was no proposal, of course, that the evaluator proceed exactly as if he were an anthropologist on location. The paradigm only provides a general framework, a research philosophy. The chief connection with social anthropology is the emphasis on interpreting, on building up explanatory models of particular systems, on discovering patterns of coherence and interconnectedness that usually go unnoticed. In the case of ethnographic fieldwork the investigator literally lives with the community he is studying. His investigation is extremely wide-ranging: he collects data with a variety of techniques, e.g. observations, films, conversations and the study of written records. His aim is to understand and portray the cultural setting he is in. He works by building up an overall picture, model or schema that is constantly modified and expanded as he acquires new information. He seeks to comprehend relationships, e.g. between beliefs and practices, and between organisational patterns and customary responses of individuals. The end product of his 'research' is not a set of findings, as such, nor an undigested assembly of facts and figures, * *but an interpretation of a highly complex system. But given the unlikelihood that the evaluator can transcend his marginal status and become a fully participating member of the educational community under study, it is more likely that evaluation methodology will be either a weakened version of ethnographic fieldwork or aspire to the imaginative syntheses of the creative artist. Participant observation covers anything from full to fringe membership. Fringe members have all the methodological problems of the 'lurker'. Role-conflicts are virtually unavoidable. The participant observer in an educational setting is not infrequently placed under some obligation to teach, and may have to produce appropriate 'gestures of competence' and go in for impression-management.*

Also, as Colin Bell has pointed out,[1] *not only is data collected by participant observation often used as* illustration *rather than* proof, *but the social position of the observer determines what he is likely to see. This led Bell to formalise the roles available to the research worker, in order to provide a framework for some of the ethical decisions in participant observation:*

Firstly, social systems, institutions, organisations and groups can be characterised by their degree of 'openness', by which is meant ease of access for the research worker. Communities in this country are more open than universities, universities than firms, firms than prisons and so on. 'Openness' is a relative concept but may for these purposes be dichotomised as 'open' and 'closed'. Secondly the research worker can make the choice as to whether he will work openly and overtly or secretly and covertly. This again is not in reality a true dichotomy but will vary between social situations. Combining these two dichotomies, however, gives a useful classification of styles and types of participant observation:

		SYSTEM	
		OPEN	*CLOSED*
	OVERT	*1*	*2*
ROLE	*COVERT*	*3*	*4*

The three stages that participant observation passes through, of entry, of maintaining a position and of exit, vary with the four styles. Overt entry into an open system involves publicity, into a closed system sponsorship; covert entry into an open system involves stealth, into a closed system guile.[2]

It must not be thought, however, that the 'precedents' or the 'supportive traditions' somehow exist in a fixed or settled way. There are many canonical inspirations, few canonical texts. Even a classic statement like Howard Becker's 'Problems of inference and proof in participant

---

1 Colin Bell (1969). 'A note on participant observation'. *Sociology*, **3**, No. 3, September 1969, pp. 417-18.

2 Bell, *op. cit.* p. 417.

observation',[3] *may be welcomed only selectively by an illuminative evaluator. He is likely to agree that it is all 'something more than merely immersing oneself in data and having insights', but Becker's strictures concerning the credibility of informers may speak to his condition more directly than Becker's contention that interpretative accounts are dealing with 'implicitly-numerical quasi-statistics'. Indeed, Becker quotes with approval Lazarsfeld and Barton's dictum that the logical structure of quantitative research should at least be kept in mind to give warnings and directions to the qualitative observer. This proposition is less than self-evident to the illuminative evaluator. Levine suggests a different method for testing the inferences that are derived from natural field situations, clinical studies and programmes where the variables are completely embedded in the social context. His methodological analogy begins with the advocacy—adversary model in which there are claims and counter-claims, arguments and counter-arguments.*[4] *This again raises the problem of the locus of decision-making. Investigators should not make decisions, but instead should help policy-makers to do so, by throwing light on the implications of different policies, by challenging stereotyped thinking and by communicating their specialised knowledge and insight.*

Yet another difficulty concerns the duration of the evaluative effort. If the evaluation is to be both formative and democratic, it must feed any discussions undertaken prior to the taking of educational decisions. Thus the researcher needs to report before the passage of time changes the situation under review. For example, Howard Becker's Making the Grade *was published in 1968, but the fieldwork, which began in 1955, was completed in 1961.*[5] *Too little is known about the methodological problems of 'condensed' or 'hit-and-run' fieldwork. The circumstances are such that the pressure of deadlines typically disallows the free-ranging pursuit of individual interest. Some of the implications of these limitations are discussed in the Barry MacDonald/Rob Walker paper, 'Case-study and the social philosophy of educational research' [reprinted below]. The emphasis on* audiences, *too, may take one intellectually in the direction of the decision theorists. Their abiding concern is the problem of choice under conditions of uncertainty, often in practical social policy fields like medicine, management and education.*

Canonical inspirations

Certain writers, as we have said, can be identified as having a seminal influence on the development of illuminative evaluation. A number of

3 Howard Becker (1958). 'Problems of inference and proof in participant observation', *American Sociological Review,* **23**, pp. 652-60.

4 See Robert Stake and Craig Gjerde's *An evaluation of T-City* in Section 5, which explicitly includes an advocate's report and an adversary's report.

5 Howard Becker, Blanche Geer and Everett Hughes (1968). *Making the Grade: The Academic Side of College Life.* New York: John Wiley.

these are being rediscovered and restored to their rightful place. They are seen in retrospect as having kept alive a 'latent tradition'. Two such writers are Waller and Wright Mills.

We turn first to Willard Waller. Within the field of education, Willard Waller's The Sociology of Teaching *[1932] rapidly became lost beneath fallout from the postwar explosion in large-scale survey research. Only recently, following a 1961 reprinting, has its value become more widely recognised. Waller belongs theoretically to the Chicago School, a group of sociologists working at the University of Chicago who between them produced a superabundance of studies that focused on small-scale, real-life settings. Eventually, however, this concern with the dynamics of social and interpersonal behaviour fell out of favour. It went underground, to form part of a 'latent tradition' overshadowed by more extensively-funded and theoretically-respectable survey-type research. Waller's starting point is that school is a social world 'compact with meaning'. He distrusts statistical methods, believing that the understanding of human life will be as much advanced by the direct study of social phenomena as by the study of numerical symbols abstracted from these phenomena. Willard Waller's technique is closer to that of the novelist:*

In some instances we shall apply ourselves to the description of social behaviour in the manner of the cultural anthropologist, attempting to equal him in detachment and devotion to detail. In others, where fidelity to the inwardness of social behaviour is desired, we shall not hesitate to borrow the technique or the materials of the realistic novelist. Otherwise we shall rely upon such descriptions and analyses of the group life of the schools as we may be able to work out for ourselves or to find in the literature, and for our understanding of this group life in its individual aspects we shall have recourse to life histories, case records, diaries, letters, and other personal documents. In our analysis of this material we shall be guided by such scientific concepts from the various fields of psychology, psychiatry, and sociology as seem to be clearly relevant, neither dragging any interpretation in by the heels nor failing to cross academic boundary lines in search of usable interpretations.[6]

The work of C. Wright Mills, like that of Waller, has also been the subject of a recent revival. During his lifetime Wright Mills expended much of his energy on projects considered suspect by other academics. Expansive in both his personal and intellectual style, Wright Mills nevertheless took some delight in the marginality of his position. He was frequently found in intellectual controversy or espousing unpopular causes. He was intellectually and temperamentally attracted to debunking and de-mystifying as authentic endeavours. In an appendix to The Sociological Imagination *[1959] Wright Mills highlights two apparently contradictory research processes relevant to alternative evaluation. On the one hand he argues that social science is the practice of a craft; on the*

6   Willard Waller (1961). *The Sociology of Teaching.* New York: Russell & Russell, p. 2.

other he makes a powerful plea for the free deployment of novel insight. The craft is learned in conversation with experienced practitioners, through a period of intellectual apprenticeship.

It is much better . . . to have one account by a working student of how he is going about his work than a dozen 'codifications of procedure' by specialists who as often as not have never done much work of consequence. Only by conversations in which experienced thinkers exchange information about their actual ways of working can a useful sense of method and theory be imparted to the beginning student.[7]

Novel insight, however, derives from the sociological imagination:

The sociological imagination, I remind you, in considerable part consists of the capacity to shift from one perspective to another, and in the process to build up an adequate view of a total society and of its components. It is this imagination, of course, that sets off the social scientist from the mere technician. Adequate technicians can be trained in a few years. The sociological imagination can also be cultivated; certainly it seldom occurs without a great deal of often routine work. Yet there is an unexpected quality about it, perhaps because its essence is the combination of ideas that no one expected were combinable — say, a mess of ideas from German philosophy and British economics. There is a playfulness of mind at the back of such combining as well as a truly fierce drive to make sense of the world, which the technician as such usually lacks. Perhaps he is too well trained, too precisely trained. Since one can be trained only in what is already known, training sometimes incapacitates one from learning new ways; it makes one rebel against what is bound to be at first loose and even sloppy. But you must cling to such vague images and notions, if they are yours, and you must work them out. For it is in such forms that original ideas, if any, almost always first appear.[8]

Taken together, these propositions may appear in opposition. For Wright Mills, however, they are closely linked. In each case he is tilting at the established position of research. By describing social science as a craft he contends that it is not an esoteric endeavour but, typically, a much more down to earth process; one that is governed by day-to-day practical reasoning. Secondly, by emphasising the relevance of a 'sociological imagination' Wright Mills is at pains to point out that social science [if not all science] is much more than the mere execution of a methodology. This is particularly important since evaluation research can rarely afford to offer its clients totally unambiguous, repeatable and conclusive findings.

The first extract featured in this section comes from Philip Jackson's Life in Classrooms [1968]. It was written more than thirty years after Waller's The Sociology of Teaching, but has a similar sense of what is important. Although trained as a behavioural psychologist, Jackson has gradually moved away from mental testing and personality assessment.

7 C. Wright Mills (1959). *The Sociological Imagination*. New York: Oxford University Press, p. 195.
8 Wright Mills (1959), pp. 211-12.

Currently he is Chairman of the Education Department at the University of Chicago. Jackson's general interest in classroom life grew from a chance encounter at the Centre for Advanced Study in the Behavioural Sciences [Palo Alto, California]. Jackson found himself among a group of ethnologists whose speciality was the study of animal behaviour in natural settings. This turned his attention towards the possibility of similar analyses being conducted in schools. Life in Classrooms *was the major outcome of that interest. The book has two major themes. The first is that research into classroom life should 'move up close to the phenomena of the teacher's world'. The second is the now familiar one that engineering models are an inadequate basis for discussing the realities of teaching. Although strictly speaking Jackson was investigating rather than evaluating, his research methodology fits the illuminative model. We note particularly the attention he pays to the 'institutional matrix in which students and teachers are embedded', and his general advocacy of ethnographic methods.*

4.1 Philip Jackson
Life in classrooms

People who are interested in the application of learning theory or the engineering point of view to teaching practice often have as their goal the transformation of teaching from something crudely resembling an art to something crudely resembling a science. But there is no good evidence to suggest that such a transformation is either possible or desirable. An equally reasonable goal, and one more in keeping with the views expressed here, is to seek an understanding of the teaching process as it is commonly performed before making an effort to change it. As we learn more about what goes on in these densely populated hives of educational activity it may turn out that we will seek to preserve, rather than to transform, whatever amount of artistry is contained in the teacher's work.

The goal of discovering what really goes on in classrooms is certainly not new, even though it could hardly be called the dominant concern of today's educational researchers. Much is already known about how to set out in pursuit of such a goal and we also have a fair idea of some of the sights to be encountered along the way. It may be gratuitous, therefore, to end . . . with either admonishment or advice concerning how future work might proceed. Yet a few such statements do seem in order, if only because the point of view represented here is still far from enjoying wide acceptance in most educational circles.

First, it almost goes without saying that in the future more researchers will spend more time observing in more classrooms, or at least poring over records of classroom events. There has already been a noticeable increase of observational studies in recent years and the trend looks as though it will continue.[1] Moreover, there is some evidence that classroom researchers are beginning to turn to disciplines other than psychology and educational measurement for their methods of analysing classroom phenomena.[2] The techniques of participant observation and anthropological field study are among those receiving greater attention from educational researchers.

But though much can likely be gained by increasing the number of participant observers in our schools, the growth in our understanding of

1   The work of Marie Hughes, B. O. Smith, Ned Flanders, Jacob Kounin, Arno Bellack, Edmund Amidon and Hilda Taba is representative of this trend.

2   The recent studies of Louis Smith, Bruch Biddle, and Jules Henry make use of some of these newer methodologies.

Source: P. W. Jackson (1968). Life in Classrooms. London: Holt, Rinehart and Winston, pp. 175-7.

what goes on in these environments need not be limited to the information contained in the field notes of professional teacher-watchers. In addition to participant observers it might be wise to foster the growth of observant participators in our schools—teachers, administrators, and perhaps even students, who have the capacity to step back from their own experiences, view them analytically, and talk about them articulately.[3] It is probable that only a few participants will ever be equipped, by either temperament or training, to do this job while continuing to perform their regular duties, but considering the size of our teaching population even one out of every ten thousand or so teachers would be sufficient to comprise a salient group of 'internal critics' of the teaching process.

It should be noted in passing that the descriptive terms derived from observational studies may provide a language of educational criticism that will be useful to insiders and outsiders alike. When teachers and researchers begin to talk the same language, as it were, the possible benefits that each may derive from listening to the other will be greatly increased. At present teachers in particular lack an effective set of descriptive terms for talking about what they do. As a result, they often must fall back on clichés and outworn slogans when called upon to describe their work. Perhaps such a state of affairs is inevitable. Perhaps by the time a set of critical terms has become common among teachers it has already hardened into clichés. But the need for a fresh and vibrant language with which to talk about educational affairs seems apparent.

Almost as important as observation *per se* is the requirement of keeping an open mind about what we see. Our ways of looking at the classroom should not be unnecessarily restricted by prior assumptions about what should be going on there, nor even, as we have seen, by the seemingly logical link between the abstract processes of teaching and learning. In short, we must be prepared and willing to give up many of our comfortable beliefs about what classroom life is all about.

Finally, as we look we must keep in mind the ubiquity of classroom phenomena in both time and space. Only as we remember that each classroom minute is one of millions of similar minutes experienced by millions of persons and by each person millions of times, are we led to look closely at the details of the events before us. Considered singly many aspects of classroom life look trivial. And, in a sense, they are. It is only when their cumulative occurrence is considered that the realisation of their full importance begins to emerge. Thus, in addition to looking at the dominant features of instructional interchanges and the overall design of the curriculum we must not fail to ponder, as we watch, the significance of things that come and go in a twinkling—things like a student's yawn or a teacher's frown. Such transitory events may contain more information about classroom life than might appear at first glance.

3   The recent writings of John Holt offer a striking example of the insights to be gained from articulate practitioners.

Case-studies

We now present two papers on case-studies. Both are concerned with a rationale for the use of case-studies in educational evaluation. Both, too, come from the same stable, and there is an obvious continuity and development of ideas between them. But they approach the central issues from different directions.

Helen Simons is examining the case-study as a means of documenting innovation. Read today it is the tone of the paper that occasions most surprise, being tentative almost to the point of timidity. But it was written in 1971, early in the life of the Humanities Curriculum Project school-based evaluation, at a time when the project was striving to explain and justify its novel evaluation strategies, a central feature of which was the careful documentation of individual schools. The assumption was that the vicissitudes of the project in individual trial schools were only explicable by reference to its full social context in the unique setting of particular schools. This assumption appeared to challenge one of the cherished illusions of the research, development and dissemination model of planned change. The R, D and D model encouraged those interested in educational innovation to attempt generalisations across schools. It saw a developmental project as directly analogous to consumer research; a single product is being tested. What Helen Simons is suggesting is not that an evaluation should switch to a pathological perspective when it needs to monitor the process of reinterpretation within the trial schools, but rather that the important truths are themselves embedded in 'authentic situations'.

In contrast, Barry MacDonald and Rob Walker begin with the anatomy of the case-study, whether encountered in educational research or evaluation. Their first concern is with its internal logic. True, they share with Helen Simons an interest in the ethical problems of the case-study, but whereas Simons is content to counsel cautious impartiality, MacDonald and Walker develop a deep and disturbing paradox. On the one hand they agree with Simons (and Stake in Section 3) that the evaluator will tend to process judgements rather than make them, acting as an honest broker or 'collector of definitions'. On the other hand they argue that the case-study is paradigmatically the province of the artist. Science and philosophy teach by precept, art by example. Somehow the illuminative evaluator may need at one and the same time to acknowledge a democratic role (collecting and marketing definitions of the programme under study) and an artistic style, not holding back from the imaginative

176

synthesis, and working in a manner not unlike that of the journalist, the novelist or the documentary film-maker.

The MacDonald and Walker paper was presented by Rob Walker to a conference of professional evaluators convened by the Schools Council at the West Midlands College of Education, Walsall, in September 1974. The model of case-studies it advocates is being developed for the Ford-sponsored SAFARI project. The acronym reflects the project's investigating brief (Success And Failure And Recent Innovation) but also manages to capture the all-important style of case-study inquiry.

4.2   Helen Simons
Case-studies of innovation

Teaching is a complex activity strongly influenced by the environment in which it takes place, but it is rarely studied in this light. Sociologists have been largely preoccupied with the allocation of pupils to secondary school, psychologists with individual learning. The need to widen the basis of educational research by adopting an anthropological approach to the study of schooling has been recognised,[1] but little has come of it. A similar situation obtains in the United States. Willower[2] has pointed to the relevance of field studies of schools but noted that few were available.

Part of the reason for this may lie with the dominant mode of evaluations employed by innovating projects. These are often too tied to the artificial conditions that are especially created in the schools to give the method or product a 'fair' chance of success. The results of such evaluations have limited relevance to the normal school situation. What we need to know is what happens to these projects, how and why they survive or fail in the rough and tumble of the schools once the external support systems that have initiated and promoted them are withdrawn.

Some help could be provided by case-studies of innovation in more normal conditions. The detailed study of instances of innovation could advance our understanding of how schools deal with change and thus inform all levels of curriculum decision-making. In particular such studies could help innovators prepare the defences of new curricula against institutional attacks.

The Evaluation Unit of the Humanities Curriculum Project has undertaken studies with this aim as part of the evaluation of the Project. In so doing we have encountered problems which constitute a further reason why so few studies of this kind have been reported. The case-studies we have been carrying out are designed to explore four basic propositions

---

1   For instance, see W. A. L. Blyth (1959). 'School groups and neighbourhood groups: a study in predictive sociometry.' A paper read to the Education Section of the Fourth World Congress of Sociology, Stresa.

2   Donald J. Willower. 'Schools as organisations: some illustrated strategies for educational research and practice.' A paper presented in the West Virginia University Social Science Colloquium Series, Morgantown, West Virginia, December 1967; and *Journal of Educational Administration*, October 1969.

Source: H. Simons (1971). 'Innovation and the case-study of schools'. Cambridge Journal of Education, 3, *pp. 118-24. The extracts reproduced here are taken from pp. 120-21, 122. The footnotes have been renumbered.*

which were formulated on the basis of early field-work. Barry MacDonald, Director of the Evaluation Unit, has outlined these propositions as follows.

1   Human action in educational institutions differs widely because of the number of variable influences that determine it.
2   The impact of an innovation is not a set of discrete effects but an organically related pattern of acts and consequences. To understand fully a single act one must locate it functionally within that pattern.
3   No two schools are sufficiently alike in their circumstances for prescriptions of curricular action to be able adequately to supplant the judgement of the people in them.
4   The goals and purposes of the programme developers are not necessarily shared by its users.[3]

If these propositions are sound we believe that the best way to advance the practice of innovation is to make available fully documented accounts of individual cases. The problem posed by such studies comes when one tries to reconcile their three indispensable characteristics. These are: firstly, they must be true, secondly, they must not omit relevant data, and finally, they must be publishable.

Fictions have low credibility and quite rightly, because our present grasp of the complex reality is far too tentative to permit accurate predictions of what might have been in hypothetical situations. The same is true of composites. Case-studies must not only be based on actual schools, they must report authentic situations. The second characteristic of such studies is just as important. Descriptive accounts of what took place in a given situation will provide needed information, but will do little to advance understanding unless there is, alongside such descriptions, sufficient interpretative data. If people are to make judgements about why an innovation took the course that it did in a particular school, they will need a great deal of contextual information. While it is true that much of the information required raises no problem in terms of publication, some significant areas will present certain difficulties. In order to interpret events in a school the reader needs to have information about the patterns of functional and affective relationships which constitute the organisational and social setting. . . .

This is a key problem in the development and publication of case-studies of schools. It will always be a problem, but it could be less of a problem than it is now if certain developments take place.

The first development concerns the way the case-studies are carried out and presented. Such studies must depart from the tradition of subjective impressionism that has caused educational researchers to shun them. The case-study must not only be authentic and detailed, as I have already suggested, it must also be rigorously accurate and impartial. The purpose

3   Barry MacDonald. 'Evaluation of the Humanities Project: a wholistic approach.' Paper presented to the Annual Meeting of the American Educational Research Association, New York 1971.

of the case-study is to make the experience of innovation accessible to public and professional judgement, and not to provide a vehicle for the biases or personal judgements of the evaluator. Case-study presentations should be basically *inconclusive* accounts of what happens in a particular school and should contain accurate reports of the judgements, convergent or divergent, of those involved in the events. Misinterpretation can be largely avoided by tape-recording all interviews and classroom trans-actions, and seeking the agreement of those involved to the fairness of the report. Of course there is no escaping the judgement of the evaluator in terms of what to include and what to leave out of the account, but if he is seen to be impartial and to be avoiding, by close consultation, 'rigging' the evidence, then the problems associated both with publication and with research 'respectability' will be significantly reduced. . . .

4.3 Barry MacDonald and Rob Walker Case-study and the social philosophy of educational research[1]

The methodological difficulties faced by curriculum evaluators who want to offer a comprehensive range of information about new programmes have drawn them to the case-study as a technique. Many of the quite legitimate questions that are put to evaluators, especially by teachers, cannot be answered by the experimental methods and numerical analyses that constitute the instrumental repertoire of conventional educational research. Such questions are directed at the experience of the participants, and at the nature and variety of transactions which characterise the learning milieu of the programme. There seems to be a need to find ways of portraying this experience and this milieu so that prospective users of new programmes can relate them to their own experience, circumstances, concerns and preferences. The case-study is one such way, and evaluators have been prominent among those who are beginning to advocate, and explore in practice, its fruitfulness in educational inquiry. The purpose of this brief paper is to examine the pedigree of the case-study as a research method, to draw attention to features of our educational system which pose problems for the conduct of case-study, and to suggest some guidelines for its use in education.

Case-study is the examination of an instance in action. The choice of the word 'instance' is significant in this definition, because it implies a goal of generalisation. We might say that case-study is that form of research where $n = 1$, only that would be misleading, because the case-study method lies outside the discourse of quantitative experimentalism that has dominated Anglo-American educational research.

It is difficult to account for the neglect of the case-study as a general method of educational science, especially in view of its significant role in the history of learning theory. An adequate explanation would need to embrace the following considerations: aspirations to the status of the natural sciences via the adoption of their alleged paradigm, bureaucratic demands for actuarial data susceptible to policy manipulation, genuine scepticism about the research value of the approach, and the late arrival on the educational scene of research practitioners with relevant skills.

1 Most of the points raised in this paper are treated more fully by Rob Walker in a longer SAFARI article entitled 'The conduct of educational case-study: ethics, theory and procedure'.

Source: Paper presented by Rob Walker to a conference of professional evaluators convened by the Schools Council at the West Midlands College of Education, Walsall, in September 1974.

But there is another reason for this neglect, one which has status implications, but which poses a dilemma for the aspiring educational scientist in a curious form. It has to do with the fact that the kind of case-studies which we believe education needs have characteristics which call for a fusion of the styles of the artist and the scientist. When Freud said, 'It still strikes me myself as strange that the case-histories I write should read like short stories and that, as one might say, they lack the serious stamp of science'[2] he caught the unease of the researcher who, disdaining the 'safety of numbers', discovers that his data is most effectively expressed in a mode which is generically associated with the artist.

Although this comes as a surprise to the scientist who adopts this approach, and generally a disconcerting one, it is a logical consequence of his field of vision. Case-study is the way of the artist, who achieves greatness when, though the portrayal of a single instance locked in time and circumstance, he communicates enduring truths about the human condition. For both scientist and artist, content and intent emerge in form. There have been periods in art, especially in the novel, when the artist has consciously aspired to 'scientific' generalisation. Writers of the French naturalist school, such as Zola, created characters to represent the social type, and blurred the lines between literal truth and special pleading by carefully researching the factual settings of their fictional puppets. The naturalists were part of an intellectual movement in French society which encompassed the sciences as well as the arts, a movement which had no parallel in this country. It is interesting to ponder, therefore, the significance of one school of British television dramatists whose preference for documentary style, accurate research and 'representative' heroes, owes nothing to the legacy of a native 'comic' tradition, and may constitute a take-over bid by them for an area neglected by the social scientist. Fusion, or confusion? If we are not simply to ignore this new 'pseudo-science', perhaps we might begin by examining carefully the case for the case-study, and elaborating some rules which could effectively discipline its use in educational research.

As a method of research, the case-study commands a respected place in the repertoire of theory builders from a wide range of disciplines; medicine, law, engineering, psychology and anthropology are examples. The case can generate a theory as well as test one; instance and abstraction go hand in hand in an iterative process of cumulative growth. The instance may be a patient with a particular ailment, a verdict, a bridge, a chimpanzee, or a whole community, but the dominant research aim is the same — to reveal properties of the class to which the instance belongs.

When we read Malinowski we get the impression that he is stating something of general importance. Yet how can this be? He is simply writing about the

2 S. Freud. 1953 Standard Edition, Vol. 2, p. 160. London: Hogarth Press and the Institute of Psychoanalysis.

Trobriand Islanders. Somehow he has so assimilated himself into the Trobriand situation that he is able to make the Trobriands a microcosm of the whole primitive world.[3]

Clearly representativeness is an important consideration. In fields where individual variation within a class appears to us to be limited, as in medical diagnosis or in the social anthropology of non-literate peoples, case-study is widely accepted as a valid basis of generalisation, and adopted with confidence. Psychopathology is an interesting area where the issue of cultural specificity continues to dog the theories Freud based on case-studies of the Viennese bourgeoisie. Nevertheless, the truth remains that, in a very important sense, we are all Freudians now.

Case-study methods are rarely spelled out in advance, except in the most general of terms, and apprenticeship is the usual means of induction into its techniques. In the social sciences, as in bank robberies, the method of attack is characteristically an opportunistic response to the observed nature of the case. The sociologist Whyte, looking back on his research plans for the study of Cornerville, remarks: 'It seems to me that the most impressive thing about them is their remoteness from the actual study I carried out'.[4] More experienced practitioners may deflect questions about method with some panache. Alan Beals, an anthropologist, writes, 'In 1952, on the way to India, I asked a distinguished British anthropologist the secret of his success in doing fieldwork. His response was, "Never accept free housing, and always carry a supply of marmalade" '.[5] But for those with less established reputations, doubt and unease are endemic. Thus Dollard: 'Many times during the conduct of the research and the arrangement of the material, I have had a bad conscience on the score of method. Should the researcher expect to be believed if he cannot hook his findings into the number system and present them in a manner conventional in the physical sciences?'[6] Dollard subsequently came under pressure from the experimentalists on methodological grounds, but though he applied himself lengthily to psychophysical methods thereafter, he still maintained that case-study method in the social sciences, must follow a different path. 'Not every nth person can be a friend'.[7]

Problems of case-studying social action

Despite Dollard's flight to numerical methods, it is a mistake to think that a major distinction between experimental and case-study research has lain

3 E. R. Leach (1962). *Rethinking Anthropology*. London: Athlone Press.
4 W. F. Whyte (1955) *Street Corner Society*. Chicago: University of Chicago Press.
5 A. Beals (1972). *Field Work in Eleven Cultures*, (ed. G. Spindler). New York: Holt, Rinehart and Winston.
6 J. Dollard (1940). *Caste and Class in a Southern Town*. New York: Harper.
7 J. Dollard, *op. cit.* (1957 edition).

in the area of quantification. In fact, the case-study worker is typically much more quantitative than is appreciated. Becker writes:

The observer, possessing many provisional problems, concepts and indicators . . . wishes to know which of these are worth pursuing as major foci of his study. He does this, in part, by discovering if the events that prompted their development are typical and widespread, and by seeing how these events are distributed among categories of people and organisational sub-units. *He reaches conclusions that are essentially quantitative,* using them to describe the organisation he is studying.[8]

Much more to the point is the fact that, whereas experimental method is conceptually asocial, the most important feature of case-study in the human sciences is that it is pursued via a social process and leads to a social product. Although this is, of course, true of all human research, in case-study the process is significantly more intimate, the product more directly consequential for those involved. A list of the problems which the case-study worker encounters includes therefore:
— Problems of the researcher becoming involved in the issues, events or situations under study.
— Problems over confidentiality of data.
— Problems stemming from competition from different interest groups for access to and control over the data.
— Problems concerning publication, such as the need to preserve anonymity of subjects.
— Problems arising from the audience being unable to distinguish data from the researcher's interpretation of the data.
And prior to these, although linked to them, there is the problem of how to gain access to the data. The investigator of social mechanisms is seldom free to follow Bacon's dictum for Natural Sciences, 'to put Nature to the question', or, as R. G. Collingwood put it in laying a similar duty upon his historical method, 'to compel Nature to answer'.[9] For the observational scientist there is no 'command performance'. He must find vantage points and roles within a web of human relationships without destroying the fabric. The delicacy and subtlety of his instruments is a precondition of their validity, especially in those situations where consciousness of the researcher's purposes evokes behavioural illusions designed to protect self-serving images. Educational situations are typically of this kind. Indeed, education is a field which is likely to raise in an acute form most of the problems endemic to case-study research. This being correct, we would argue that case-studies in education need to be conceived and conducted in new ways if they are to gain widespread acceptability.

8   Howard S. Becker (1971). *Sociological Work.* Harmondsworth: Allen Lane.
9   R. J. Collingwood (1946, 1961). *The Idea of History.* London: Oxford University Press.

The social philosophy of educational case-studies

Case-study research is used occasionally in education but mostly in an 'autocratic' mode. That is to say the problems listed in the previous section are perceived as 'technical' issues, irritating obstructions to the scientist's uncompromising pursuit of new knowledge. The study is typically conceived as a piece of 'pure' research directed to an audience of research professionals. The interpretations made are essentially the interpretations of the researcher. The responsibility for the final account is his alone. The researcher's right to control his work in these ways has not been seriously questioned. We believe it is time to question it now. The critical issues which emerge in this reappraisal can be posed quite simply:
— To whose needs and interests does the research respond?
— Who owns the data (the researcher, the subject, the sponsor)?
— Who has access to the data? (Who is excluded or denied?)
— What is the status of the researcher's interpretation of events, *vis-à-vis* the interpretations made by others? (Who decides who tells the truth?)
— What obligations does the researcher owe to his subjects, his sponsors, his fellow professionals, others?
— Who is the research for?
Research is primarily concerned with the creation, organisation and dissemination of knowledge. Conventionally, dissemination comes last in the order. In some definitions it is omitted altogether. We believe that the dissemination of new knowledge ought to be a prior, not a post, consideration in the planning and conduct of educational research. Knowledge is the basis on which many forms of power are legitimated, and, in the case of education, the medium through which power is exercised.

Case-study research in education takes the researcher into a complex set of politically sensitive relationships. In a related paper one of the authors classified evaluation studies under three ideal types on a political dimension. He called these types 'bureaucratic', 'autocratic' and 'democratic'. The principal question which determines this classification is 'Who controls the pursuit of new knowledge, and who has access to it?' One of the purposes behind this paper is to endorse specifically the 'democratic' approach as particularly appropriate in case-study research or evaluation activities using case-study techniques. Democratic evaluation is described as follows:

Democratic evaluation is an information service to the community about the characteristics of an educational programme. It recognises value pluralism and seeks to represent a range of interests in its issue formulation. The basic value is an informed citizenry, and the evaluator acts as broker in exchanges of information between differing groups. His techniques of data gathering and presentation must be accessible to non-specialist audiences. His main activity is the collection of definitions of, and reactions to, the programme. He offers confidentiality to informants and gives them control over his use of information. The report is non-recommendatory, and the evaluator has no concept of information misuse. The evaluator engages in periodic negotiation of his relationships with sponsors and programme participants. The criterion of success is the range of audiences served. The report aspires to 'best-seller' status. The key concepts of democratic evaluation are 'confidentiality', 'negotiation' and 'accessibility'. The key justificatory concept is the 'right to know'.[10]

We feel there is a need to develop case-study in education within this mode. Although the concepts and principles we will advance fall short of this 'ideal', they embody an approach that is sharply differentiated from past or current practice, an approach which rejects monopolistic concepts of control and access. These concepts and principles also take account of significant, but neglected, features of the educational system. In this concluding section of the paper, some of these features will be specified and related to characteristics of case-study before we present our recommendations.

1   Significant features of the educational system

(a) Happy alliances between theorist and practitioner in our system are rare: more often, the relationship is one of mutual mistrust punctuated by open antagonism. Between sub-groups of practitioners also, and perhaps particularly between teachers and managers, the unity of common purpose rests on almost religious observance of territorial boundaries. Practitioners can, however, generally rely on each other for support when faced with an external enemy, such as public criticism, whereas the theorist's behaviour in such circumstances is less predictable.

(b) Partly as a consequence of this, education has a highly developed and longstanding mythology which acts as a protective public image projected by its members. At all levels of the system what people *think* they are doing, what they *say* they are doing, what they *appear* to others to be doing, and what in fact they *are* doing, may be sources of considerable discrepancy. This is generally as true of children in class as it is of teachers, head teachers and administrators. Any research which threatens to reveal these discrepancies threatens to create dissonance, both personal and political.

(c) There is a tradition of freedom from scrutiny by outsiders in education (the inspectorial role being mainly benign and supportive).

(d) Educational institutions are hierarchical and competitive, for staff and for children. But, in our country, teachers, headmasters, inspectors and administrators all have similar professional qualifications, so the hierarchy

10   Barry MacDonald (1976). 'Evaluation and the control of education'. In D. Tawney (ed.) *Curriculum Evaluation Today: Trends and Implications*. Schools Council Research Studies. London: Macmillan Education. pp. 125-36.

of staff is based on experience and is consultative. Expertise cannot be claimed on extrinsic criteria and used as a basis for authority. This characteristic of the structure, allied to mythological aspects of the culture, creates an inherent need for secrecy that is all-pervasive. Case-study research may penetrate the secrecy and so threaten the carefully constructed claims which form the basis of authority.

(*e*) The educational enterprise continuously generates its own reflective languages. Since the process itself contains its own theoretical, analytical and descriptive constructs, this creates the potential for presenting case-studies within the language of those studied.

2   Related aspects of case-study

(*a*) Case-studies are public documents about individuals and events. They are identifiable at least to those involved and usually to wider audiences. They have consequences for the lives of those portrayed as well as for the reader.

(*b*) Educational case-studies are usually financed by people who have, directly or indirectly, power over those studied and portrayed.

(*c*) Case-study methods rely heavily on human instruments, about which only limited knowledge can be obtained and whose private expectations, desires and interests may bias the study in unanticipated and unacknowledged ways. Lack of rules for case-study leaves research opportunities open to both real and imagined abuse.

(*d*) Case-studies are always partial accounts, involving selection at every stage, from choosing cases for study to sampling events and instances, and to editing and presenting material. Educational case-studies are almost always conducted under constraints of time and resources and therefore reliability and validity pose considerable problems.

3   Proposed guidelines

(*a*) It seems to us feasible to contemplate a form of educational research that would be practice-based in a way research has not been previously. We see this as a form of research which responds actively to practitioners' definitions of situations, conceptual structures and language. Constrained by these the researcher would act as the representative of the various groups involved, exploring their hypotheses, using their language and conceptual structures, both as starting points and as a continuous reference. The aim would not be to create alternative realities for practitioners but to find ways of encouraging them to develop insight into their existing realities, and to understand the realities of other inhabitants.

(*b*) We have to think in terms of '*condensed field work*' in order to feed back information quickly enough to fit the time-scales of participants. This cuts us off from traditions of case-study work in the social sciences and draws us closer to other traditions in journalism, documentary film-making and the novel. These traditions have not systematically addressed the issues of reliability and validity which condensed field-work will raise in acute form. New criteria are needed.

(c) Proof is rarely obtainable in case-study research. Rather than setting proof as a primary goal, the case-study worker should aim to increase understanding of the variables, parameters and dynamics of the case under study. Cross-checking rather than consistency is the main strategy of validation. The case-study worker is guided in his research by the pursuit of discrepancy. It is implicit in the notion of case-study that there is no one true definition of the situation. In social situations, truth is multiple. The case-study worker is a collector of definitions. The collection is validated via a continuous process of negotiation with those involved. Wherever appropriate the case-study should contain the expressed reactions (unedited and unglossed) of the principal characters portrayed, to the report in its final draft form. The reliability of the study, i.e. the probability of its findings being confirmed by replication, seems likely to be significantly enhanced where such procedures are adopted.

(d) Confidentiality will become a critical aspect of procedure. Confidentiality should be accorded to informants for the term of the study and, thereafter, release of material for publication negotiated with them. The nature of case-study is such that participants can often only judge the consequences of release in retrospect and when the context of presentation is available. Offering blanket confidentiality affords the researcher faster access to relevant data and prevents the need for informants to continuously monitor what they say. This is especially critical in interview situations, for in the hands of a skilled interviewer most people are inexperienced and will reveal things they did not intend. Allowing retrospective control of editing and release of data to informants affords them some protection from the penetrative power of the research as well as allowing the researcher to check on misinterpretation or misunderstanding on his part.

This sharing of control over data with participants does mean that the researcher often has to face the fact that some of his finest data is lost, diluted or permanently consigned to the files. On the other hand his access to knowledge about what are sensitive issues to his informants may guide his research in significant and unexpected ways.

(e) Case-study methods lend themselves to a variety of means of presentation; written reports, audio-visual recordings, displays and exhibitions. Generally, these presentations should be devoid of indications of praise or blame from the point of view of the researcher. They should present contingency relationships only, leaving it to those studied and other audiences, to infer cause. They should attempt to be explicit about rationale and procedure, and the principles governing the selection and presentation of content.

(f) The data must be accessible to the judgement and understanding of all those whose interests may be influenced by its contents. If this is not to remain at the lipservice level, the researcher may have to explore relationships between himself and the artist.

Summary

We have presented a view of case-study research in education which has its primary focus on the political nature of relationships between the researcher and his subjects, sponsors, audiences and related groups. We have emphasised such questions as *who* has control over, or access to, data, and under what conditions and constraints should the researcher seek and present his findings. Our recommendations are derived from a particular socio-philosophical stance.

As we imagine and describe it, educational case-study has as yet no practitioners. We have attempted to describe a kind of research we feel ourselves working towards rather than one we have successfully accomplished.

The real prize is the prospect of developing techniques and procedures which can be used by schools and ancillary agencies. A specialist research profession will always be a poor substitute for a self-monitoring educational community.

Fieldwork and the generation of theory

Although 'the generation of theory' is a term strongly suggestive of a research rather than an evaluation perspective, there is a sense in which the illuminative evaluator, writing an interpretative description of a programme under study, is generating new knowledge. How this knowledge can be theoretically grounded (as well as merely insightful or useful) is one of the principal problems.

In the grey area between evaluation and research it is often necessary to ask questions about the role of the researcher–evaluator vis-à-vis the community or system being studied. We have already seen how a feedback or formative evaluation role forces methodological compromises in the direction of condensed fieldwork. Otherwise the evaluator will be supplying his military intelligence after the war is over.

The first paper we look at is by Steve Wilson and his colleagues at the Center for New Schools in Chicago, 'A review of the use of ethnographic techniques in educational research'.[1] Although the paper could have been written to articulate an alternative research methodology for education its interest in the present context is that Center for New Schools has developed an evaluation philosophy commensurate with its own desired and perceived role as an agent of change. Center for New Schools is committed to assisting (rather than simply monitoring) the processes of change.[2] This role is stated quite explicitly. Center for New Schools is a non-profit, tax-exempt organisation 'carrying out research, evaluation and technical assistance through long-term face-to-face contact with teachers, administrators, parents and students in specific schools and communities'. Their present position springs in part from dissatisfaction with existing provision for planned change. In another paper[3] Center for New Schools offers a damning critique of the research, development and dissemination model of planned change. They dismiss the model as mechanistic,[4]

1 Steve Wilson wrote a follow-up paper two months later (July 1974) relating these research techniques to the *evaluation* activities undertaken by Center for New Schools at New School, Cleveland Heights, Ohio: 'The use of ethnography in educational evaluation' (mimeo).

2 See Donald Moore *et al.* (1972). 'Strengthening alternative high schools'. *Harvard Educational Review*, **42**, No. 3, 315-50. The title reflects the political commitment of the Center for New Schools' evaluation activities.

3 'On-site technical assistance as a facilitator of educational change: a comparative study of five technical assistance groups' (mimeo.). Submitted by Center for New Schools to the Russell Sage Foundation, February 1974.

4 This suggests an interesting parallel with the behavioural objectives model, often associated with a research, development and dissemination design, which is also criticised for its implicitly mechanistic assumptions.

treating school systems as machines into which new parts can be installed: this makes it indifferent to the perspectives of practitioners and clients. It neglects two-way communication, refusing to see clients as resources for change. The model also confuses formal adoption of an innovation with its meaningful implementation. Finally research, development and dissemination processes are unlikely to employ appropriate media or methods for communicating insights to practitioners.

Center for New Schools sees itself as bringing the techniques of ethnographic research into the service of a formative evaluation strategy, a strategy in the hands of people who perceive themselves as change-agents in the situation being studied. Examples of the strategy as it was employed at Chicago's Metro High School are included in Section 5.

From the Center for New Schools' paper, we turn to the work of Louis Smith, who has also written interestingly and at length (either going solo or in collaboration with other authors) on similar problems of evaluation, ethnographic fieldwork and the generation of theory. Louis Smith echoes from a practitioner's viewpoint one of the assertions made by Stake, that evaluation activity may be stimulus *as well as* response. *Smith and his colleagues are interested in the kind of fieldwork that may generate rather than verify hypotheses. An interesting question is the extent to which the evaluator–researcher is able to do this and yet remain within the meaningful social world of the client as well as the intellectual world of the researcher. At the end of the day, how one breaks on this dilemma may be a useful rule-of-thumb way of determining whether the activity is best called 'evaluation' or 'research'.*

Like a number of the authors whose work appears above, Louis Smith began his academic career as a psychometrician. Later—when involved in teaching educational psychology—he gradually shifted his centre of research interest towards the teacher and the classroom. This was not a fortuitous move, but one that rose from tutoring post-experience teachers at Washington University, St Louis. The Complexities of an Urban Classroom *[1968]*[5] *was the first major outcome of this shift. For an entire school term Louis Smith sat in the classroom of one of his former students William Geoffrey and, between them, they generated the ideas to be found in that book. It was a major development in the theory of classroom research.*

When, following Federal initiatives, a Regional Educational Laboratory was set up in St Louis, Smith joined the staff part-time and began a series of year-long evaluation projects. Working usually with a colleague [often a research student] and a part-time secretary, Louis Smith has produced an annual crop of books, research monographs and papers. As a deliberate policy each evaluation report has included a substantial methodological appendix. Taken separately these show the gradual evolution of Louis

5   L. M. Smith and W. Geoffrey (1968). *The Complexities of an Urban Classroom*, New York: Holt, Rinehart and Winston.

Smith's ideas; taken together they are a formidable corpus of practical and theoretical insight. Few researchers [whether in evaluation or elsewhere] have written so extensively, openly and perceptively about the application of their craft.

The three extracts presented here [one of which was written with Paul Pohland, and another with Sally Schumacher] contain a number of recurrent themes. Throughout his work Louis Smith calls for the collection of detailed descriptive data, stresses the importance of cumulative research and highlights the importance of theory generation. At the same time he casts doubt on the existence of 'standard' methodological procedures.

Thus, while most of Louis Smith's studies are based on short-term, one-off investigations, they show a general and enduring concern with the overall development of evaluation research. As such, they speak forcefully to the long-term survival of the methods he advocates.

4.4 Center for New Schools
Ethnographic techniques in educational research

I Rationale

Ethnographic techniques are part of a research tradition that has been developed over many years by anthropologists and community-study sociologists. These researchers have found the methods useful for gathering certain important kinds of data, and some have even claimed that these anthropological techniques may gather information that is impossible to obtain by other methods. Social scientists within all traditions, however, can benefit from understanding the rationale underlying this methodology. It is based on two sets of hypotheses about human behaviour: (1) the naturalistic-ecological hypothesis and (2) the qualitative-phenomenological hypothesis. . . .

Naturalistic-ecological perspective

Many social scientists believe that human behaviour is significantly influenced by the settings in which it occurs. They, therefore, believe that it is essential to study psychological events in natural settings, and they claim that settings generate regularities in behaviour that often transcend differences among individuals. Over the years, extensive research has been conducted which demonstrates the importance of the influence of the setting and the often divergent findings which result when the same phenomenon is studied in the laboratory and in the field. . . . Ecological psychologists claim that if one hopes to generalise research findings to the everyday world where most human events occur, the research must be conducted in settings similar to those the researchers hope to generalise about.

    In what ways does the setting influence the people in it? Barker, in *Ecological Psychology* (1968) writes of forces generated both by the

Source: Center for New Schools (1974) 'A review of the use of ethnographic techniques in educational research' (mimeo). The extracts reproduced here are taken from pp. 3, 4-5, 6-9, 12-13, 14-16, 17, 18-19, 20-1, 22, 25. The original paper is lavishly supported by references to the literature which we have excluded because of pressure of space.

*   Steve Wilson had the major responsibility for writing the article in its present form with the assistance of Richard Johnson, Thomas Wilson, Emile Schepers, Donald Moore, Phyllis Wilson, Monica Ingram and Hazel Domangue.*

physical arrangements of the settings and by internalised notions of what is expected or allowed. The inability of classical learning theories to say very much that is meaningful about everyday classroom learning can be explained in part by the absence of these school/organisational forces in the research laboratories where the theories were discovered.

Significantly, a second tradition of social science has arrived independently at the same point of emphasising the importance of the internalised notions generated in settings. Sociologists studying organisations assert the importance of the traditions, roles, values and norms that are part of life in organisations. Much behaviour in organisations (including schools, of course) is influenced by the participants' awareness of these mental states and by pressures generated by others influenced by these states. . . .

The same kind of realisation about the importance of context for research has been arrived at in a third independent tradition of research. Social psychologists realised that their experiments were often picking up influences other than what they were focusing on. They then discovered that the experimental situation — for example, the questionnaire, the interview, the laboratory — was a unique setting of its own with its own dynamics and influences on behaviour.

Rosenthal and Rosnow in *Artifact in Behavioural Research* (1969) review the findings of extensive research undertaken to determine the nature of these influences. For instance, the role of being a research subject in social science research often includes the following influences on behaviour: a suspiciousness of the intent of the research, a sense of the behaviour that is either appropriate or expected, a special interpersonal relationship with the experimenter and a desire to be evaluated positively. All these forces can shape behaviour in a way that is extraneous to the focus of the research. A person filling out a questionnaire, responding to an interview or behaving in an experiment — even though he is trying to be genuine — may not be able to provide accurate information about his usual behaviour in real, complex settings. One area in which this shortcoming has been especially frustrating is attitude research. Consistently, people's responses on questionnaires and in interview have not provided adequate information about their observed actions. . . .

Many researchers will have no trouble accepting the preceding rationale. Observation is deeply ingrained in the American educational research tradition, and the only demand that the ecological hypothesis makes is that behaviour be studied in the field. The rest of standard technique is left intact — for example, deriving explicit *a priori* hypotheses, defining operational categories of observation, developing objective methods of data gathering and conducting appropriate statistical analyses. The next section discusses a part of the rationale behind anthropological techniques that challenge these processes.

Qualitative-phenomenological hypothesis

Much of American social science strives toward the natural-science model of objectivity. Phenomenology, a tradition of social science which has thrived in Europe but has been largely neglected in educational research in the United States, offers an alternative view of objectivity and methods appropriate for studying human behaviour. Those who work within this tradition assert that the social scientist *cannot understand human behaviour without understanding the framework within which the subjects interpret their thoughts, feelings and actions.* They point out that the natural science approach to objectivity requires the researcher to impose *a priori* limitation on the data, an act which makes it difficult to discover the perspectives of the subjects. . . .

The ramifications of this position are far-ranging: the traditional stance of objective outsider so favoured by social scientists and the usual research procedures are deemed inadequate for gathering information which takes these participant perspectives into account. Moreover, the customary deductive activities of framing hypotheses and defining categories *a priori* and of analysing within prespecified frameworks are seen as inappropriate. . . .

Typically, researchers try to find strategies which minimise the role of subjectivity. They try to standardise the interpretations which they (or anyone else) attribute to data perceived by their senses — for instance, by deriving a scheme for coding behaviours observed in a classroom. Theoretically, a coding scheme and a framework for interpreting observed behaviours can be developed and communicated such that anyone with exposure to the scheme and some training will interpret the behaviours in approximately the same way. This method is seen as guaranteeing objectivity.

The phenomenologist points out that the adoption of this particular framework for interpreting and coding behaviour is arbitrary. Any number of meaning systems could be selected. In fact, the most important frameworks to understand might be those of the subjects, rather than the researchers. The objective social scientist in standardising the interpretation may have destroyed some of the most valuable data he had. Severyn Bruyn has expressed this view:

The traditional empiricist considers himself (as a scientist) to be the primary source of knowledge, and trusts his own senses and logic more than he would trust that of his subjects. The participant observer, on the other hand, considers the interpretations of his subjects to have first importance. . . . By taking the role of his subjects he re-creates in his own imagination and experience the thoughts and feelings which are in the minds of those he studies.
(*The Human Perspective in Sociology,* 1966, p. 12)

To know merely that feelings, thoughts or actions exist is not enough without also knowing the framework within which these behaviours fit.

The social scientist must come to understand how all those who are involved interpret behaviour in addition to the way he as scientist interprets it from his 'objective outside' perspective. Moreover, since the subjects cannot always articulate their perspectives, the researcher must find ways to cultivate awareness of the latent meanings without becoming oversocialised and unaware as most participants may be. He must develop a dynamic tension between his subjective role of participant and his role of observer so that he is neither one entirely.

The necessity of abandoning traditional deductive processes such as *a priori* hypothesis generation follows as a consequence to this general approach to understanding human behaviour. Because the quantitative researcher is restricted within its own perspective, he risks being concerned about irrelevant variables. Glaser and Strauss describe a careful method by which social scientists can ground their theory and research in the reality they are studying:

The consequence (of the traditional approach) is often a forcing of data as well as a neglect of relevant concepts and hypotheses that may emerge. . . . Our approach, allowing substantive concepts and hypotheses to emerge first, on their own, enables the analyst to ascertain which, if any, existing formal theory may help him generate his substantive theories. He can then be more objective and less theoretically biased.
(*Discovery of Grounded Theory* 1967, p. 34)

No one, of course, enters a situation as a true *tabula rasa*. Language is itself a limiting factor which provides one set of conceptual tools, and screens out others. Similarly, the previous experiences of the scientist influence his observation and thought. In fact, traditional empirical scientific methods have sought to extrapolate along these lines by asking the researcher to be most explicit and rigorous in the formulation of the perspective underlying the research. There is room in the realms of research, however, for other more inductive approaches where the role of the preformed hypothesis and circumscribed data-gathering techniques are reduced to a minimum. . . .

II   Research process

Understanding the actual processes involved in this kind of research is as important as understanding the rationale. Ethnographic research is much like quantitative research in that it has a long tradition within which investigators have been working to refine and develop effective and appropriate research methods. . . .

Educational researchers who are unfamiliar with the anthropological research tradition often see this kind of research as synonymous with 'journalistic reporting' and 'anecdotal' or 'impressionistic' storytelling. Their expectation is that someone enters a setting, looks around for a time, talks to some people and writes up his impressions. They speculate that any person in the setting could produce the same insights by writing up their recollections. They do not see this as real research and fear a lack of objectivity. . . . For the sake of analysis, the ethnographic research process will be divided up into a series of issues: (A) Entry and establishment of researcher role, (B) Data-collection procedures, (C) Objectivity and (D) Analysis of data.

A. Entry and establishment of role

As explained in the rationale, ethnography is based on the assumption that what people say and do is consciously and unconsciously shaped by the social situation. The ethnographer is sensitive to the way he enters a setting and carefully establishes a role that facilitates collection of information. He must take decisions about how involved he will become in community activities . . . because he knows his activities will influence the ways people react to him. He monitors the way his entry into the community is initiated both officially and unofficially because he knows this will influence how people see him. . . . He tries not to be identified with any particular group in the setting. Moreover, throughout the study he monitors the views participants have of him . . .

Most importantly, the participants must come to trust and value the observer enough that they are willing to share intimate thoughts with him and answer his endless questions. . . . The outsider occasionally coming in and talking to people does not have this opportunity to systematically cultivate and monitor a role that facilitates collection of all kinds and levels of information. . . .

In every ethnographic study we have conducted in high schools, students have expressed their concern about the researcher's identity and role. In one alternative school, an assembly was held to introduce the observer and to answer questions about the research. One student asked from the audience, 'Are you a teacher or a student?' Later events demonstrated that this was an important concern. The observer tried to explain his unique status of belonging to no one group. This explanation was not fully accepted or understood at that time. During the next several weeks, the observer spent much energy establishing his role and finally was accepted as being in neither group, as illustrated by student willingness to discuss with him issues that were taboo in front of teachers.

B. Data collection

Also key in understanding ethnographic research is a realisation of what constitutes data and the customary methods of obtaining it. This kind of anthropological inquiry seeks to discover the meaning structures of the participants in whatever forms they are expressed. Hence, this research is multimodal and all of the following are relevant kinds of data:

1 Form and content of verbal interaction between participants
2 Form and content of verbal interaction with the researcher
3 Non-verbal behaviour
4 Patterns of action and non-action
5 Traces, archival records, artifacts, documents.

The essential tasks for the anthropological researcher are learning what data will be necessary to answer his questions and getting access to that information. The previous section illustrated how the researcher works on interpersonal access by becoming someone with whom participants are willing and eager to share information and reactions. Even as these problems are being solved, however, the ethnographer must constantly make decisions about where to be, what kind of data to collect and whom to talk to. Unlike prestructured research designs, the information that is gathered and the theories that emerge must be used to direct subsequent data collection. . . .

Also important is the choice of whom to talk to. The researcher becomes aware of various persons' roles in the community and the personal matrix through which they filter information. The methodological literature . . . is rich with discussions of the bases for making these decisions about who is an appropriate respondent or informant for various purposes. . . .

Much of the information gathered by participant observation is similar to that which can be gathered by other methods — for instance, systematic observation and structured interviewing. The participant observer has more latitude in that he is not limited to pre-specified places and times. He can interview and observe in many situations not usually available to other researchers. He also has an advantage in his ability to monitor the rapport he has built with interviewees and to gain access to confidential information. . . . The researcher shares the daily life with participants and systematically works to understand their feelings and reactions. . . . He also tries to take advantage of serendipity by being open to new information, but in a calculated fashion — for instance, seeking out places that are likely to present this new information. . . .

C. Objectivity

Because the qualitative researcher does not use familiar quantitative methods of standardising subjects' expression or researchers' observations, those not acquainted with participant observation fear that the data will be polluted with the observers' subjective bias. However, well-executed ethnographic research is as 'objective' as other kinds of research. To explain this assertion, we must refer back to the qualitative-phenomenological hypothesis about human behaviour discussed previously. Human actions have more meaning than just the concrete facts of who, what, where and when that an outsider can observe; they have more meanings than even the responses subjects could give when being introspective (for instance, in an interview or attitude scale marking). The ethnographer strives to uncover these meanings.

He uses the techniques we have described to be in touch with a wide range of participant experiences. He makes sure his sampling is representative . . . and that data is interpreted in terms of the situation where it was gathered. . . . In order to understand these hidden or unexpressed meanings, the researcher must learn to systematically empathise with the participants. He must synthesise the various experiences of participants to comprehend the subtleties of their actions, thoughts and feelings. Sometimes he uses his own reactions, which he has cultivated by undergoing the same experiences as participants, to understand the reactions of those he is studying. Use of these techniques may lead other scientists to fear subjectivity.

The assumption about human behaviours, that these meanings exist and that understanding them requires involvement in the participants' perspectives, calls for such techniques as empathy and non-standardised observation. There are, however, important differences between the subjectivity of the participants and that of the researcher, who is careful never to abandon himself to these perspectives. The discipline of the research tradition calls for him to constantly monitor and test his reactions. In addition to systematically taking the perspective of the subjects, he also views actions from the perspective of the outsider. Also, all the participants in a setting rarely share a monolithic perspective. By systematically seeking to understand actions from the different perspectives of various groups of participants, the researcher avoids getting caught in any one outlook. . . . He is able to view behaviour simultaneously from all perspectives. These tensions in point of view — between outsider and insider and between groups of insiders — keep the careful researcher from lapsing into the feared subjectivity. . . .

It is important to explain how this disciplined subjectivity is 'objective'. One operational definition of 'objectivity' in science is the assertion that any independent scientists viewing the same reality with the same techniques would gather similar data. The same claim could be made about participant observation if an important qualification is made. In discussing the qualitative hypothesis, we have explained that 'any' observer would *not* be expected to arrive at the same data because not every observer would know the various participant perspectives. If, however, the phrase 'any independent scientist using the same techniques' was interpreted to mean that each scientist took the pains we have described to become acquainted with the participant meanings, then 'objectivity' could be claimed. All scientists who applied this disciplined research method might indeed be expected to gather similar data.

D. Analysis of data

A final area that it is important to understand is how ethnographers analyse their data and develop theory. Some ethnographic research is very similar to traditional educational research in its deductive use and development of theory. Other kinds of ethnographic research, however, are much more inductive.

The anthropologist seeks to understand the meanings of the participants and hence seeks to be careful not to have his interpretations prematurely over-structured by theory or previous research. Furthermore, he is perhaps more ready than other kinds of researchers to accept the possible uniqueness of the various settings, groups, organisations, etc., that he studies.

Seeking theory grounded in the reality of participants does not mean a disregard for previous work. In fact, the researcher must become thoroughly acquainted with related research and theory so that he can use it whenever it is helpful for explaining events. Similarly, he contributes to development of knowledge by pointing out corroboration and contradiction of his findings with the findings of other researchers. Moreover, he uses previous research and theory to select the setting he is studying and to inform the initial focus of his information-gathering.

The development of grounded theory is not haphazard. The researcher constantly tests his emerging hypotheses against the reality he is observing daily. Unlike the usual prestructured research designs, participant observation includes a constant necessity for testing theory against real data. . . . Becker (in *Boys in White,* 1961) . . . points out that the search for *negative evidence* is another way that participant observers refine and test their theories. Because of his awareness of the setting, the researcher knows what situations are likely to provide discordant information. He enters these situations to confront this possibly negative evidence, probes to find out why the theory cannot account for what is observed and gradually develops his theory. It makes sense, then, to think of participant observation as a series of studies which follow each other daily and build on each other in a cybernetic fashion. . . .

III Summary

As this article has shown, the ethnographic researcher works systematically to gather data and develop theory, just as other researchers do. His methodology is rigorous and objective, not casual and impressionistic.

Ethnography is not a new fad; rather it is part of a long, respected research tradition that has remained outside the mainstream of educational research. Similarly, it is not a static tradition and researchers are constantly working to refine the methods. Educational research will be considerably enriched as qualitative and quantitative researchers learn to integrate their approaches.

4.5 Louis Smith and Paul Pohland Computer-assisted instruction fieldwork procedures

Persons engaged in qualitative research strategies disagree regarding the degree to which there should be *a* problem, *some* problem or *no* problem which initially guides the observer. Our position has come to be strongly in accord with Malinowski's 'foreshadowed problem' conception.[1] In June, before beginning systematic observation of the July teacher workshop, but after making preliminary arrangements regarding entry, we wrote the following three paragraphs indicating our initial definition of the problem.

During the 1968-69 school year, we will engage in intensive observation, description and conceptualisation of the Computer-Assisted Instruction programme. At the descriptive level, our intent is to gather careful, valid data regarding the day-to-day utilisation of CAI by pupils, teachers and schools. The mundane ways the equipment is used and its impact on the school will provide the data for the conceptualising and theorising. Hopefully, the research will result in a number of useful implications for teachers, administrators and researchers in education.

The foci for analysis can not be indicated finally at this stage; participant observational research does not lend itself to this kind of initial conceptual clarity. In this sense, it contrasts sharply with hypothesis-testing in more usual verificational research. Several tentative 'foreshadowed problems' from the Psychology of Teaching project do exist, however, and will guide the initial observations: firstly, the impact of CAI on teacher decision-making will be considered. In *The Complexities of an Urban Classroom*,[2] and later in *Teacher Plans and Classroom Interaction*,[3] we developed initial ideas which we hope to elaborate in the context of CAI. Secondly, dimensions of teacher–pupil relationships, e.g. teacher awareness, ringmastership, control, and so forth, were raised in the earlier monographs and will be built upon here. Thirdly, concepts of classroom social structure and process, e.g. pupil roles, activities and interactions, will be analysed in terms of the descriptive data from CAI classrooms. Fourthly, the personality and behaviour of children in the rural poverty setting of the Rural Highlands will

1 B. Malinowski (1922). *The Argonauts of the Western Pacific*. London: Routledge.

2 L. M. Smith & W. Geoffrey (1968). *The Complexities of an Urban Classroom*. New York: Holt, Rinehart and Winston.

3 L. M. Smith & J. A. M. Brock. *Teacher Plans and Classroom Interaction*. St. Ann, Mo.: CEMREL (in process).

Source: L. M. Smith and P. A. Pohland (1972). 'Education, technology and the rural highlands'. In Four Evaluation Examples: Anthropological, Economic, Narrative, and Portrayal, *AERA Monograph Series on Curriculum Evaluation, No. 7. Chicago: Rand McNally, pp. 5-54. The extract reproduced here is taken from pp. 38, 40. The footnotes have been renumbered.*

be compared and contrasted with that found in poor urban children who had come from rural areas and who had roots in similar settings.

The organisational and innovative aspects of CAI will be focused upon also. We think these are a most understudied aspect of a psychology of teaching and should contribute greatly to enhanced understanding of CAI. Specifically, we hope to build upon the kinds of analyses begun in *Anatomy of Educational Innovation.*[4] In that volume we were concerned with team teaching, non-gradedness, individualised instruction and so forth. CAI represents another important innovation. The problem of changes in school organisation wrought by innovative practices are largely unknown. Our attempt will be to focus on anticipated-unanticipated consequences.

The reader will note that the final product is only partially a result of the initial problem statement. The problem evolved as events in the real world played themselves out.[5] . . .

4   L. M. Smith & P. M. Keith (1971). *Anatomy of Educational Innovation.* New York: Wiley.

5   In training students for field work we now emphasise strongly the initial problem statement and the expected evolution and redefinition of the problem. Our experience with the 'no initial focus' stance is that many beginning field workers are left apprehensive and confused. In retrospect, we always had to write such statements because we were seeking funds or justifying our activities for our organisational superiors who needed such a statement in their files. We had not appreciated the latent function of such organisational demands for an initial clarity in the problem under study.

4.6 Louis Smith
Integrating participant observation into broader evaluation strategies[1]

At this point I want to shift from moderator to panellist and develop briefly an argument regarding the relationship of participant observation to more general research and evaluation strategies. Three alternatives seem plausible and reflect our efforts so far: (1) a general structural model, (2) a sequential model and (3) a case-study accumulation model.

A general structural model

My own thinking and use of participant observation had been initially as a general research strategy to approach complex naturalistic problems. Howard Russell, then at CEMREL, and I began talking about a 'three-legged' model of evaluation. The model sought to bring together three research strategies. (1) An experimental design with pre and post tests of achievement, control groups and inferential statistics. (2) A second strategy was the social survey with interviews and questionnaires, random sampling of programme-relevant individuals (teachers, parents and pupils), quantification and cross-tabulation of response. (3) The third 'leg' of the model was a participant observer study of the programme.

My colleague Paul Pohland and I engaged in the description and analysis of the mundane, day-to-day operation of the programme.[2] We have observed children at the teletypes, talked with teachers about the joys and tribulations and inquired into arithmetic instruction. As it turned out, the problems in keeping the programme running were severe. This

1 The research reported herein was supported in part by the Central Midwestern Regional Educational Laboratory, Inc. (CEMREL), a private non-profit corporation supported in part as a regional educational laboratory by funds from the United States Office of Education, Department of Health, Education and Welfare. The opinions expressed in this publication do not necessarily reflect the position or policy of the Office of Education, and no official endorsement by the Office of Education should be inferred.

We owe thanks to Ann Berlak, George Fairgrieve, John Good and Paul Pohland who pursued other problems, but whose ideas and points of view enlivened and facilitated the discussions.

2 L. M. Smith & P. A. Pohland (1969). 'Participant observation of the CAI program'. In H. Russell (ed.), *Evaluation of Computer-Assisted Instruction Program*. St Ann, Missouri: CEMREL. L. M. Smith & P. A. Pohland (1974). 'Education, technology and the rural highlands'. In *Four Evaluation Examples: Anthropological, Economic, Narrative and Portrayal*, AERA Monograph Series on Curriculum Evaluation, No. 7. Chicago: Rand McNally, pp. 5-54.

Source: L. M. Smith (1971). 'Participant observation and evaluation strategies'. A paper presented as part of a symposium Participant Observation and Curriculum: Research and Evaluation *AERA, New York, February 1971. The extract reproduced here is taken from pp. 2-6. The footnotes have been renumbered.*

moved us into a careful and serious consideration of the problems in putting highly sophisticated twenty-first century technology into an impoverished rural area of the nation. Our data analysis suggested issues in complex technical and social systems. The roots of the innovation problems were as varied and complex as congressional funding patterns (lateness, cuts, rerouting through the state department) and the mobilisation of five independent telephone companies to install lines and equipment. We think we have important data for understanding this kind of curriculum change.

The major point I would make is not that people have not used direct observation in curriculum development and evaluation, but that they have not exploited it as a major tool in the analysis. In a recent AERA curriculum evaluation monograph, Grobman[3] devotes several pages to what she calls 'visits'. Her introductory paragraph states:

No project can afford to omit classroom visits, and such visits can serve a variety of purposes. Visits can serve to verify other feedback or to put it in a more meaningful context. Teachers who are reluctant to write criticism or who find writing difficult may talk quite openly in a face-to-face encounter. Conversation with school officials, teachers, students and parents can elicit information that cannot be provided by questionnaires and may open up new avenues of thought not previously considered by the project. (p. 54)

In effect, we have taken seriously her doubts regarding the validity of responses people give. More basically though, we see the participant observer strand as an attempt to describe and conceptualise the nature of a very complex independent variable—the nature and utilisation of the new curriculum. Such a research strategy has a potency which we felt had not been utilised fully before.

As Russell[4] pointed out in the introductory chapter of the final report in the CAI evaluation, the combined analysis made a powerful summative analysis of the programme. The learning gains, the rise and fall of changing attitudes toward the programme, and the implementation of the programme by pupils, teachers, classes and organisations was clarified.

The sequential model

The sequential model attempts to cumulate efforts over time rather than concurrently in time. The major position we take is that the kind of field work we have been doing is important for the generation rather than the verification of hypotheses. To accomplish the latter, one moves to other research paradigms. For instance, in our intensive observational study of

3 Hulda Grobman (1968). *Evaluation Activities of Curriculum Projects: a Starting Point.* AERA Monograph Series on Curriculum Evaluation, No. 2. Chicago: Rand McNally.
4 H. Russell (ed.) (1969). *Evaluation of Computer-Assisted Instruction Program.* St Ann, Missouri: CEMREL.

an urban classroom[5] we utilised the concept of 'teacher awareness' to interpret some of our data. The concept was defined as:

a dimension of teacher behaviour in which the teacher knows information important in the group members' lives and indicates his knowledge to the group. (p. 470)

One of the explicit illustrations used to educe the concept was the teacher's teasing of an adolescent boy about his girlfriend and about the fact that he, the teacher, might have to move their seats. Besides the two adolescents, at least one audience pupil had an incredulous look on her face. A second illustration involved a pupil's seeming intention to 'fool' the teacher in getting an extra turn at a simple and pleasurable alphabetising task. The teacher caught her at the game and she responded with a sheepish grin and a return to her seatwork. We developed a number of hypotheses surrounding the phenomenon of teacher awareness.

Paul Kleine and I sought to explore the implications of the concept of teacher awareness.[6] In an intensive theoretical analysis of the concept of cognitive complexity as this has grown out of the Kelly tradition and cognitive differentiation from the Witkin tradition, Kleine[7] argued for the theoretical similarity of the ideas. Each is concerned with the degree of structure (differentiation or complexity) the individual possesses in his conceptual organisation of the environment. We predicted that these personality variables would correlate with teacher awareness and would be important antecedents of this part of the ongoing classroom situation. That is, the teachers with the more differentiated and complex cognitive structures would be more aware, more knowledgeable of the ongoing classroom social system. In our analysis we hypothesised also that teacher awareness, the knowledge of events in pupils' lives, leads to pupil esteem for the teacher. Pupil esteem refers to the generalised sentiment which the pupils hold for the teacher. For many years commentators have talked about pupil attitudes toward school, toward lessons and toward their teachers. Some investigators of attitude-learning and opinion-change have argued that prestige and esteem are important social psychological variables.

While the conception of teacher awareness began with several intriguing illustrative observations from our field study,[8] the translation we made for quantitative purposes proceeded as follows:

1   Each teacher rank ordered her pupils on three dimensions: popularity, arithmetic ability and psychomotor ability,

5   L. M. Smith & W. Geoffrey (1968). *The Complexities of an Urban Classroom*. New York: Holt, Rinehart and Winston.

6   L. M. Smith & Paul F. Kleine (1969). 'Teacher awareness: social cognition in the classroom', *School Review*, 77, 245-56.

7   P. Kleine (1968), *The Interrelation of Psychological and Cognitive Differentiation in Two Experimental Tasks in an Educational Setting*. Unpublished Ph.D. dissertation. Washington University.

8   L. M. Smith & W. Geoffrey (1968). *The Complexities of an Urban Classroom*. New York: Holt, Rinehart and Winston.

2   The pupils in each class filled out a best friends choice type sociometric questionnaire regarding their classmates. They took a short arithmetic achievement test. And they filled out a 'Guess who?' type sociometric perception questionnaire regarding psychomotor ability,

3   Correlations between teacher rankings and pupil measures were obtained for each classroom,

4   The correlation coefficients were converted to z scores and combined to form a single score of teacher awareness.

Methodologically, a sample of sixty-nine teachers and their classes was drawn from the CEMREL region (Tennessee, Kentucky, Missouri and Illinois). Some were from rural and small-town communities; others were suburban. The majority of teachers were female (fifty-eight). Their range of experience varied from one to forty-nine years and averaged sixteen years. All classes were at the fifth and sixth grade levels.

Among the results we found a significant correlation between cognitive complexity and teacher awareness and a significant correlation between teacher awareness and pupil esteem.[9]

However, my point is not theoretical but methodological. We have found the field study important for the generation of concepts, hypotheses and miniature theories. These ideas can then be operationalised, quantified and tested in broad-scale correlational analyses as we did with 'teacher awareness'. Hopefully, also, these ideas can be moved into even more rigorous experimental designs. Only after that kind of endeavour can one have confidence that the findings pertain to more than our one case. The sequential blending of the techniques seems to produce extra benefits.

Cumulating case studies

A third strategy of participant observation and curriculum evaluation is the one we are illustrating today; the cumulation of participant observation case studies. In general, the argument we have been making is that participant observation is especially fruitful for what Glaser and Strauss[10] have called the 'generation of grounded theory'. However, as one engages in multiple case studies, questions arise regarding the increasing credibility of hypotheses and models generated in one setting and now reappearing in second and third settings. In turn, we have been asking ourselves additional questions: (1) Must we always turn to the quantitative experimental model for verification? (2) Are there some problems that the laboratory cannot replicate — as Kounin suggests in his recent work on classroom management? (3) Are research skills different enough and idiosyncratic enough that specialisation of labour is a major issue? (4) Are enough persons doing enough work with any one technique to be especially facile with it? And so forth.

9   Correlational data have known and admitted limitations for cause-effect interpretations.
10   B. G. Glaser & A. L. Strauss (1967). *The Discovery of Grounded Theory: Strategies for Qualitative Research*. Chicago: Aldine.

Within the cumulative case study approach several sub-strategies seem to be viable: first, a sequential thrust of one classroom study, then another, then another — in effect, cumulating cases (descriptions, concepts hypotheses and models) in the same domain; second, a sequential thrust wherein one moves from classrooms to curricula to school organisation to community analysis. In effect, one maps enlarging and interlocking domains into more comprehensive theory. Third, and more illustrative of our efforts in today's symposium is the concurrent attack upon several parts of the same curriculum — for instance a concern for the curriculum writer's intentions compared and contrasted with the realities of the situation, a focus on the teacher's behaviour and the kind of thought processes generated by the curriculum, and reconceptualisation of a special technique — role-playing which is a major tactic in the curriculum. Such a concurrent 'triangulated' attack seems to have a further kind of analytical power.

Conclusion

In this symposium we are raising issues regarding participant observation as a research and evaluation strategy. Individually and collectively the members of this symposium have been actively involved in the approach and its problems and its relationships to other points of view. The three most general ways of integrating participation into more general research and evaluation models might be labelled (1) the general structural model, (2) the sequential model, (3) the case-study accumulation model. Each brings certain plusses as well as certain weaknesses. Each holds promise for making increasingly credible statements about important problems in curriculum and instruction.

4.7 Louis Smith and Sally Schumacher
Some further aspects of fieldwork methodology[1]

Introduction

One of the felicitous consequences of pursuing a particular methodological approach through a series of problems over a number of years is the creation of novel resolutions to the particular setting and issues under study. Another is the development of insights into the strengths and limits of the methodological *genre* one uses. Finally, one develops both more abstract generalisations of procedures and more differentiation of component structures. In short, a theory of methodology accrues. In several places: Chapter 1 and the Appendix of *The Complexities of an Urban Classroom* (1968), a series of footnotes in *Anatomy of Educational Innovation* (1971), a technical report entitled *Go, Bug, Go!: Methodological Issues in Classroom Observational Research* (1970), in an evaluation monograph chapter 'Education, technology and the Rural Highlands' (1972);[2] and several journal articles and unpublished AERA papers, we have chipped away at fieldwork methodology. We think we are heeding C. Wright Mills' (1959)[3] plea for intellectual craftsmanship.

A description of the procedures

At one time we spoke of our approach as involving 'standard participant observation procedures'. More careful analysis (Smith & Pohland, 1972),

1 The research reported herein was supported in part by the Central Midwestern Regional Educational Laboratory, Inc. (CEMREL), a private non-profit corporation supported in part as a regional educational laboratory by funds from the United States Office of Education, Department of Health, Education and Welfare. The opinions expressed in this publication do not necessarily reflect the position or policy of the Office of Education, and no official endorsement by the Office of Education should be inferred.

2 L. M. Smith & W. Geoffrey (1968). *The Complexities of an Urban Classroom*. New York: Holt, Rinehart and Winston; L. M. Smith & P. Keith (1971). *Anatomy of Educational Innovation*. New York: Wiley; L. M. Smith & J. A. M. Brock (1970). *Go, Bug, Go!: Methodological Issues in Classroom Observational Research*. Occasional Paper Series: No. 5. St. Ann, Missouri: CEMREL; L. M. Smith & P. A. Pohland (1974). 'Education, technology and the rural highlands'. In *Four Evaluation Examples: Anthropological, Economic, Narrative, and Portrayal*, AERA Monograph Series on Curriculum Evaluation, No. 7. Chicago: Rand McNally, pp. 5-54.

Source: L. M. Smith and S. Schumacher (1972). Extended Pilot Trials of the Aesthetic Education Program: A Qualitative Description, Analysis and Evaluation, Appendix I. St Ann, Missouri: *CEMREL. The extracts reproduced here are taken from pp. 167-8, 175-6, 177-8. The footnotes have been renumbered.*

suggested that that was a fiction.[4] Researchers using observational procedures vary markedly in their stress on description, quantification, generation of theory and verification of theory. In general we have tended to accent qualitative data, a strong descriptive narrative and the generation of theoretical interpretations. As we have worked in an 'evaluation' setting, we have tried to put the data, the descriptions and the interpretations next to sets of standards and develop evaluations.

A number of comments are in order, as we try to specify the procedures of this particular investigation. First, in chapter one we presented a verbatim copy of our agreements regarding this year's 'observational evaluation'. As seems to be true of all organisational agreements, this was a compromise among a number of issues. For example, we were much more disposed to work on what we have called the degree of implementation problem; others pushed for a more concentrated effort on pupil test results;[5] the final agreements were those presented earlier.

The time involved in the field is also difficult to describe. Each of us was employed half time by CEMREL during the year. In one sense that means we were on the project the equivalent of one full-time person for the year; we were around the Laboratory at least that much time. The time in Pennsylvania was obviously much less. We had intended for each of us to make one trip to Pennsylvania each month. Each trip would involve three days (one day/school) in the geographical area. Because of the package delivery delays and the illness of one of us (LMS), we observed less than intended. We spent approximately thirty-five man-days in Pennsylvania and averaged approximately four visits per school district. In addition we both attended all three workshops which involved another twelve days altogether. We attended the AEP's National Advisory Committee meeting and an AEP National Conference on teacher-training. In addition we were a part of the irregular visits of staff associates, visitors from various Pennsylvania organisations and planning groups. In July we participated in a three-day AEP staff retreat.

In general our role was 'non-interfering observers'. On a number of occasions we stepped out of this role. In the workshops we occasionally helped run discussion groups. In the classes we occasionally played the role of teacher's aides. With CEMREL personnel, and to a lesser degree with PDE personnel, we were colleagues in the struggle to make the project

4 The general traditions to which we would appeal include such scholars as B. Malinowski (1922). *The Argonauts of the Western Pacific*. London: Routledge; G. C. Homans (1950). *The Human Group*. New York: Harcourt Brace; H. S. Becker, *et al.* (1961). *Boys in White*. Chicago: University of Chicago Press; W. E. Whyte (1955). *Street Corner Society*. (Rev. ed.) Chicago.: University of Chicago Press; B. G. Glaser & A. L. Strauss (1967). *The Discovery of Grounded Theory: Strategies for Qualitative Research*. Chicago: Aldine; S. T. Bruyn (1966). *The Human Perspective in Sociology: the Methodology of Participant Observation*. Englewood Cliffs, NJ: Prentice-Hall.

5 We resisted this for several reasons, all of which are debatable: (1) a concern for the validity of available instruments; (2) the vagaries of first year trials in any innovation; (3) the difficulty in monitoring test administration from a distance of 1000 miles; (4) the dilution of the qualitative observational effort.

'go'. In several instances we were friends and colleagues of some years. The issue of 'feedback' involved us in a series of memos based on preliminary observations and analyses of the data. These involved us much more than usual in two way communication with programme staff. In general we found this very stimulating.

Our data involve several thousand pages of field notes and several file drawers of 'documents' — reports, pupil papers, tests and comments from teachers. As always in this type of inquiring, we feel inundated with 'the data'.

In terms of the 'independence - cooptation' continuum we were some-where in the middle. Neither of us had worked in AEP before this year. Our formal line responsibility was to the director of evaluation, as part of his summative evaluation group. A number of the programme staff became our good friends as we travelled the workshop circuit together and found far-reaching commonalities of interests, values and personalities. As we indicated elsewhere, the memos we instituted for feedback involved us in a variety of intense discussions regarding 'aesthetic experience', 'aes-thetic education', 'evaluator–developer' problems and conflict, the 'process of curriculum development' and so forth. At several public meetings (e.g. at the May Harrisburg meeting when negotiations for 1972-3 were undertaken) we reported our preliminary findings from our observa-tions. . . .

Some specific methodological and procedural issues

Ethnographers and coordinators

In the evaluation of large curriculum projects, or working in any organisational setting for that matter, there is a continuing problem of how the ethnographer as evaluator interrelates with other project staff. The notes contain part of the early development in our role as evaluator and the coordinator's role as coordinator.

I arrived in Pittsburg late yesterday evening after an interesting trip on the plane reading, thinking and making some notes. Those are recorded in the field notes proper. This morning the coordinator and I met for breakfast at 8.30 and we've had a delightful hour to hour and a half conversing about the nature of the programme etc. We are on our way to the School now. It seems like in kind of random fashion we said a number of things. First, we got a bit more squared away on the problems of the notes. As we talked about data she might collect, I went through some of our procedures on the portable dictating, the confidentiality of the notes, and the difficulty in not wanting them circulated, etc. In this regard she commented that she knew that I wasn't going to give them the notes way back when. At this point she sees that very clearly. While we didn't push it to conclusion I think the point I'm going to argue for is to have her send us as much of the public documents as possible and to have her keep her own notes as private as she likes. Later we can play off one set of notes vs. another as we do the memos, and the essays, and interpretations. In this sense we'll get an important validity check and at the same time retain some independence and privacy of our own work and not demand of them things that we won't contribute back. Hopefully at lunch I'll be able to work that out in more detail. (11/3).

Later in the day the notes continued:

We continued to get our working relationships squared away and straightened out. I've remained pleased with how that's going and the fact there seems to be little tension and little conflict between us. I have a strong feeling that she relates what happens in a very open sort of fashion and we talk about the problems as they arise and as they come up with very little moralising on either side. While we sat in the back of the room this morning (we were going over various papers) we talked about the possibility of Xeroxing and sharing a variety of public memos and data, for instance the sheet of comments that the teacher had written out about the pre-test. I contrasted this to the more personal notes and note books that each of us were keeping. The relationship here was that we would probably both be better off to keep those private so that we could put in what we wanted to put in without any screening and shielding. Later as we wrote memos and reports we could then kind of check each other's stuff out against each other's notes. This seems to be agreeable to her and seems to settle it in a reasonable way. As part of this discussion, we got to talking about the differences in the job and particularly around the problems she has just keeping up-to-date with the notes. She's finding that that's impossible to do. Only recently has she gotten a stenorette that she can operate portably. As we contrasted the inquiry role and the coordinating role the relative emphasis upon data and upon making the programme go became very apparent. Again I urged her to keep as much track of that as she could. But not to worry about it. Late in the day some of the same issues came up and we talked about the fact that I would be keeping records on the kinds of things she had told me, sort of secondhand observations and that I've appreciated talking about and hearing about all the things and knew that Sally would also. This came up in the context that she was kind of free-associating about what was going on. (11/3).

Overall, we were able to maintain a relative independence and definition of roles and also to pursue cooperatively joint visitations of most of the sites.

Memos in evaluation

Writing memos in an organisation is an ancient and not so honourable tradition. The paper which is generated often defies filing cabinet resources and time available for reading much less doing one's prescribed job. If everyone does it and if it floods the system, why raise it as a 'novel' methodological point? First, we hadn't done it before to any great degree and secondly, it seemed to have some major payoffs. This was our initial statement:

Traditionally, our use of participant observation has been in the role of 'outsiders', that is, observers who are around, who observe, who record, who describe and who analyse. Such non-interventionism has major assets in letting systems wend their own way, objectivity of evaluation, credibility of interpretations, anonymity to participants, and minimisation of cooptation of the research and evaluation personnel. The results have seemed useful and relevant to a variety of issues (see footnote 2). Such advantages should not be relinquished lightly, so it seems to me. However, a major limitation of this stance lies in feedback; the delay, the stress on general theoretical issues, and the difficulty in synchronising with other programme activities. In an effort to handle this dilemma and to achieve the two major evaluation purposes of this year, (1) the description and analysis of the first-year extended pilot trials and (2) the development of a five-year evaluation plan, I would like to propose a modification of our usual procedures. . . .

What I'm proposing, for a provisional trial, is the formalisation of the foreshadowed problems and the asides into brief memos for your consideration. On the positive side they should provide substantive issues for conversation and debate and hence enable us to see and understand the system better. On the negative side, they may become self-fulfilling prophecies and cause some loss in independence and objectivity. Further, their naiveté may undermine some of our credibility, but hopefully you'll bear with us in that regard. In a major sense, I hope it will culminate in the development of a long-run evaluation programme all of us will find as both livable and worthwhile.

The consequences have been multiple. We have been able to provide some feedback immediately. Preliminary theorising has been very helpful in later report writing. Many of the issues we raised proved to be discriminative stimuli for major discussions which provided us with references, insights and further data. The conversations led to extended and absorbing professional relationships. To a degree, we were probably coopted. . . .

Skimming the cream

. . . The situation was this. During our last week of data collection we had to make a brief presentation of results to the several parties of the larger project we were investigating; these individuals were making decisions regarding the form the project would take in the succeeding years. The tactic we adopted was a simple one. In a local coffee shop for a period of a couple of hours we asked ourselves 'What are the major things we have learned from our year in the field?' As we brainstormed these, with no reference to our file drawer of notes, interpretative asides, or summary interpretations (some of which were still untyped on tapes because of organisation resource problems) we gradually accumulated a list of ideas and findings. We pushed and pulled on these until they gradually fell into reasonable broader topics and differentiated outlines. Points of debate were joined and countered with images recalled from classroom observations and informal conversations (interviews) with children, teachers and supervisors. The most intriguing methodological question this raises is suggested by the 'skimming the cream' metaphor. In this simple procedure can the really significant rich items be obtained? Do the laboured procedures suggested by Becker *et al.* (1961) in the *Boys in White* analysis and by Glaser & Strauss (1967), in their constant comparative method yield more creative, more comprehensive, and more reliable theory and interpretations? At the moment our guess is that the differences in creative propositions is probably minimal. Some comprehensiveness is probably lost by 'cream-skimming'. The reliability of interpretation, or perhaps better, the confidence in the interpretation, probably drops off more sharply. For students of methodology this is obviously a testable empirical problem. . . .

The community context of evaluation

Finally we take a brief look at the political and community frameworks within which research and evaluation operate. Not only will illuminative evaluation be responsive to the idiosyncracies of particular programmes, it will also be sensitive to a number of framing concepts, including notions of appropriateness that govern the role of the evaluator vis-à-vis *the system under study. A number of underpinning assumptions, often implicitly political, will directly influence and constrain the methods employed. What is legitimised by one political ideology is often denied by another.*

The first extract, from Gordon Hoke, reflects the influence of Scriven's paper 'Current problems: philosophy and practice of evaluation'.[1] *It comes from the introduction to the evaluation report* Goodbye to Yesterday *which exhibits an evaluator-researcher selfconsciously 'thinking aloud' and unveiling what were his thought-processes faced with problems associated with the evaluator's need to achieve a community role. The reader is offered a guided tour through some of the subjective processes employed. The concern is to outline possibilities, weigh alternatives and develop appropriate strategies. Gordon Hoke is currently at the Center for Instructional Research and Curriculum Evaluation (CIRCE) at the University of Illinois, Urbana-Champaign. The research programme to which it relates is a study of the dynamics of social, political and economic change as they affect Effingham, a mid-west rural community. Hoke's openness helps to establish the credibility of his style of evaluation. The scenery, props and lighting are visible, so that the play is not presented as a mystery. Hoke's concern to establish appropriate channels of communication back to the Effingham community itself to some extent parallels Black and Geiser's 'peer research'. The guidelines for community involvement reflect Hoke's interest in the advocacy model.*

The second extract by Ernest House—also at CIRCE—is from a paper central to one of House's current concerns, to take a cool look at evaluation research from a politically realistic perspective. House is on record elsewhere that educational evaluation is increasingly likely to be political, used to allocate resources, cover up mistakes, build reputations and make money. Although House's overview of the 'unpleasant facts' of

1 Extracts from Scriven's paper are reproduced in Section 3 under the title 'Current evaluation problems'.

214

evaluation is much more wide-ranging than Hoke's, it is similar in intent. It deals with a number of issues that are often glossed over. The key point is put succinctly by House himself at the end of 'The conscience of educational evaluation':

So there it is—a thumbnail sketch of the problems of trying to determine the social worth of educational programmes: valuation, justification, persuasion; values, thought, action; morality, knowledge, power. New problems for education perhaps, but perennial problems for society.

House offers few conclusions. Yet his analysis is critically important for the future of evaluation research, particularly if evaluation is to remain sceptical of its own endeavour.

The third extract, by Sam Black and Ken Geiser, is from the Home Base School methodology report. Its main interest is its concept of 'peer' research; that is, evaluation research conducted by the participants in a project. The Home Base School was set up in 1971 as a public alternative to the existing school system in Watertown, Massachusetts. With student numbers around 100 it operated from 'home base' premises in the basement of the Armenian Cultural Center. When the school was being planned Sam Black was a post-graduate student in Urban Planning at MIT. As part of course requirements he began a participant observation study of the negotiations prior to the establishment of the school. When, eventually, the project received a degree of Federal Funding (a Title III grant) he was invited to become the evaluator. Reluctant to do the work singlehanded he enlisted the assistance of a fellow student, Ken Geiser. Between them they conducted the early evaluation studies. Both were highly committed to the idea of 'alternative' schooling.

In an earlier part of their report Black and Geiser discuss the problem of establishing a methodology suited to the dispersed nature of the Home Base School. Peer research grew out of two main difficulties: the inability of the evaluators to be everywhere at the same time; and the misunderstandings that arose when they presented feedback to the participants. In the second instance Black and Geiser found that while the evaluators had become extremely knowledgeable about the project, the participants had remained completely ignorant of the evaluator's aims, theory or methods. As a result two-way communication became difficult: the feedback loop had become twisted. Black and Geiser's subsequent efforts to form a knowledgeable evaluation culture among the participants fall directly in line with Philip Jackson's ideas on 'observant participators'. There is a shared concern to help participants step back from their experiences and perform their own assessments.

The final extract, from Barry MacDonald, is the most directly and uncomfortably political of the extracts featured. Although the political classification of evaluation studies that MacDonald advances could be seen *as an exercise in the construction of ideal types, the real world of evaluation activity frequently evidences alarming approximation to the taxonomy. One says alarming not because any of the ideal types possesses a definitional wickedness but because the underpinning assumptions of one type are frequently masked by the rhetoric of another. As the framing assumptions of the evaluation get winkled out, the evaluator himself is increasingly driven to occupy open ground. That in itself can be no bad thing.*

4.8 Gordon Hoke
Working guidelines

From the outset I tried to pattern my behaviour in Effingham along lines suggested by Art Gallaher, Jr.[1] This model, Gallaher submits,

defines the advocate's role as one concerned mainly with creating a climate conducive to acceptance; the view of the culture change is global. Acceptance is to be achieved, but the *processes of acceptance* are accorded signal importance. A basic premise underlying the role is that plans for the future grow out of the present and that often they must incorporate what has been established in the past. (Italics added)

Gallaher's description subsumes the two critical dimensions of my dual role in Effingham—i.e., the intent to act as an advocate of change within a particularly dynamic community context and to utilise evaluation of the results of that activity as a means of predicting future trends. The implicit assumptions in trying to fulfill such demands are cited by Michael Scriven.[2]

In what sense is the evaluator a 'change agent' and . . . what can be extracted from a change-agent theory that would be useful in training evaluators and for practising evaluators?
    A more general concern is the extent to which the evaluator is or should self-consciously be a *moral* agent and the extent to which his knowledge of moral theory and analytical procedures should therefore be greater than one can expect from every citizen.[3] (Italics in original)

1   Art Gallaher, Jr. (1964). 'The role of the advocate and directed change'. In W. C. Meierhenry (ed.), *Media and Educational Innovation*. Lincoln, Nebraska: University of Nebraska Press, pp. 33-40.
    2   Michael Scriven, 'Current problems in philosophy and practice of evaluation', June, 1971 (informal memo). Scriven's questions assume greater significance when the observer notes a comment that 'contemporary social science is increasingly giving adherence to an interventionist mode of thought. In economics, political science, anthropology, interventionist models are becoming dominant. . . . Lewis S. Feuer (1965). 'Causality in the social sciences'. In D. Lerner (ed.) *Cause and Effect*. New York: The Free Press, p. 191.
    3   This writer sees a close relationship between Scriven's concerns as expressed above, and the basic theme of *Pedagogy of the Oppressed*. For example, Freire writes: 'No pedagogy which is truly liberating can remain distant from the oppressed by treating them as unfortunates and by presenting for their emulation models from among the oppressors.' Paulo Freire (1970). *Pedagogy of the Oppressed*. New York: Herder and Herder, p. 39.

Source: G. Hoke (1972). Goodbye to Yesterday, *Center for Instructional Research and Curriculum Evaluation, University of Illinois. Our extracts are taken from the introduction to* Goodbye to Yesterday. *The footnotes have been renumbered.*

217

It is my belief that efforts to change the schools cannot be effective without vertical involvement of staff, students and administrators, on the one hand, and horizontal involvement encompassing elements of the community on the other hand. Schools are pivotal social institutions. Unless the enormity of their central place in modern society is grasped, there is real danger that both praise and criticism, problems and possibilities, will be misunderstood.[4] Hence, the necessity to view change in global terms.

4 'There was a time, after all, when education didn't matter so much to most people, but today, education is a key to power and influence in our society. Who controls it and who has access to it and how much of it, is a very, very important question, and anything that important is political. So I think we're going to see education more political in the years ahead, not less. . . . Politics is, after all, the highest art of democracy.' An excerpt from a series of statements by Norman D. Kurland regarding the Ocean Hill-Brownsville confrontation in New York City, 1968; as reported in Melvin I. Urofsky (ed.) (1970). *Why Teachers Strike: Teachers' Rights and Community Control.* Garden City, NY: Anchor Books, p. 68.

4.9   Ernest House
Context and justification

Philosophers of science have found it useful to distinguish between an idea's 'context of discovery' — the psychological background from which the idea arose — and its 'context of justification' — the publicly determined worth of the idea.[1] Even though we do not think in syllogisms or use formal logic, it is often desirable, perhaps necessary, to construct a logically idealised version of an idea so that it may be critically examined.

Analogously, in formal evaluation it may be useful to distinguish between the 'context of valuation' and the 'context of justification'. The 'context of valuation' involves the basic value slant derived from the genesis of the evaluation, and includes all those motivations, biases, values, attitudes and pressures from which the evaluation arose. The 'context of justification' involves our attempt to justify our findings. There are many means of justifying findings, but in formal educational evaluation it usually means using the logic and methodology of the social sciences (predominantly psychology) to collect and analyse data. In fact, Michael Scriven defines evaluation as a methodological activity which consists of gathering and combining performance data to yield ratings, and in justifying the data-collection procedures, the weighings of data and the goals themselves.[2] (Most operating definitions of evaluation set it down squarely within the 'context of justification.')

Such 'scientific' procedures do not *guarantee* that the findings are 'true', but they do promise that biases originating from the 'context of valuation' will be greatly reduced. Hence we get concepts like 'control group' and 'random sampling' which are commonsense attempts to eliminate one bias or another. It should be noted that in addition to the non-argumentative logic of science, argumentative forms of logic are available for justifying findings; for example, the methodology of our court system to which we entrust our property and our lives. This raises the possibility of other legitimate forms of justification. In the main, however, we rely on the institutionalised methods of science to exorcise the demons of subjectivity.

1   Israel Scheffler (1967). *Science and Subjectivity*. Indianapolis, Indiana: Bobbs-Merrill Co.
2   Michael Scriven (1967). 'The methodology of evaluation,' In R. W. Tyler, R. M. Gagné and M. Scriven, *Perspectives of Curriculum Evaluation*, AERA Monograph Series on Curriculum Evaluation, No 1. Chicago: Rand McNally, pp. 39-83.

Source: E. W. House (1972). 'The conscience of educational evaluation'. Teachers College Record, **73**, 405-14. *The extracts reproduced here are taken from pp. 409-11. The footnotes have been renumbered.*

Thus utilising scientific methodology in the 'context of justification' enables us to justify findings arising from the 'concept of evaluation'. But, as much as evaluators love to appear in white lab coats and tell their clients that this brand of individualised instruction will decrease tooth decay (and as much as it comforts clients to have them do so), life is not so simple. Many leading scientists tell us that even our scientific approaches are ultimately biased. After all, the communities of men who establish scientific canons are subject to the same pressures as the rest of us. In fact, there can be no value-free social research. All research must proceed from initial valuations of some kind. So if being 'objective' means being totally free from bias, there can be no 'objective' research. Try as we will, there is no escape from the 'context of valuation'.

Gunnar Myrdal, the Swedish social scientist, contends that it is not necessary for social research to meet the impossible condition of being value-free in order to be useful to us.[3] All that is important is that the scientist reveal the values on which his research is based. It is the hidden, unseen valuation which is damaging and which leads to opportunistically distorted research findings, for covert valuations allow us to pursue our base interests at the expense of proper justification. We trick ourselves as well as others.

Making valuations explicit demonstrates the evaluator's awareness of them, forces him to account for them and exposes them for what they are. Ideally one would use alternative sets of values to judge a programme. Resources are seldom available to do so. Practically one usually chooses one set of valuations and puts one's meagre resources into that. But one can try to see that the valuations are neither hidden nor arbitrary. They should be relevant and significant to the audiences involved. According to Myrdal, only in this way can the evaluation be as *fair* and *honest* as possible.

For example, when I began to evaluate the Illinois Gifted Program I was not a neutral observer. I was not about (nor is anyone likely) to invest much time and effort in a project about which I had no feelings. Early in the project it was suggested by several people that we set up a massive testing design using standardised achievement tests to measure the outcomes of the state programme. That was the 'normal' thing to do and in fact would have been done by a 'neutral' evaluator who was unwilling to spend much time. I knew in advance that the nature of achievement tests plus technical problems like regression effects would combine to show no significant difference in favour of gifted programmes.

Most importantly, by familiarity with the programme, I knew that increasing achievement was not the state's main intent, and that the major efforts of the programme had been to promote certain kinds of classroom achievements, namely higher thought processes and student involvement.

3   Gunnar Myrdal (1969). *Objectivity in Social Research*. New York: Random House.

So we looked into the area of environmental press measures and eventually developed an instrument to measure those factors. We measured the programme at perhaps its point of greatest strength — that's what I mean by being fair.

At the same time in the 'context of justification' we developed our instrument in a rigorous fashion and employed as good a sampling design as we were able. We in no way 'set-up' the gifted people. Where the programme did turn out badly we reported it. Through familiarity with the programme we also knew where the weakest points lay. We knew that many districts were taking state funds for the programme and doing absolutely nothing for the gifted. So we developed instruments to measure that too. That's what I mean by being honest.

We reported both favourable and unfavourable data to people in the programme, to people with control over the programme and to state legislators, saying that in our opinion the good outweighed the bad. . . .

4.10 Sam Black and Ken Geiser
Facilitating peer research

By early November, two currents inherent in the design of the methodology and a research bias converged to reorient the evaluation. First, as noted earlier, proper implementation of the process evaluation proved to require a tremendous time-commitment with only two people in the field. Second, the Work Statement and our own commitment drove us to seek out means of effective participation of the students and staff. Third, both of us as evaluators were extremely reluctant to set ourselves up as research experts. In fact, we did not feel expert, but even more significant, both of us were repelled by the growing professionalism of evaluation research and from past experience felt an aversion to social science research which institutionalised a wide gap between researcher and subject; that is, knower and known. We felt unable to fully understand the students we were coming to like so much if we permitted the abstract methodology to stand between us and them. Further . . . we felt that our evaluation could be greatly augmented by trying to understand the Home Base School experience through the 'eyes' of the students themselves. Therefore, we instituted a class in research methodology to teach a cadre of students (and a staff member) how to do their own research and as their interests dictated, invited them to begin participant-observation of the various groups we were interested in. Here we had what we dubbed 'peer research', students, that is subjects, and staff, doing their own observation, field notes, analysis and final explanation — following groups of which they were a part. In all we have six students and one staff member participating in this project and by all accounts we feel so far it is our most successful venture. First phase reports are now being prepared for an upcoming 'snap-shot' view of the school. It seems that research where properly supervised can be competently carried out and enjoyed by students upon themselves and others. Peer research can extend and reinforce a process of self-awareness among peers. . . .

Source: S. Black and K. Geiser (1971). The Watertown Home Base School Evaluation Methodology Report, Watertown, Mass. (mimeo). The extracts reproduced here are taken from pp. 1-3.

The report was supported by funds from Title III of the Elementary and Secondary Education Act (ESEA).

Implementing collaborative evaluation

. . . The Work Statement called for 'snap-shot' overviews and periodic interim feedback. This belied the controversy. Indeed we as evaluators were involved in the research because we believed in the Home Base School ideology and we wished to help the school grow, adapt and improve. In fact, because we found ourselves the ever-present audience for the developments of the school, we found ourselves in an excellent position to observe, objectify and comment on the alternative directions the school might take. If we were required to report on the problems of the school, we felt eager to direct reporting to solution-formation. Egon Guba has pointed out this same direction in criticising:

. . . an evaluation paradigm that emphasised control when invited interference is needed; that prevents attention to more than one problem at a time; . . . that provides only terminal data; and that renders impossible the crucial requirement for continuous adjustment and refinement, simply cannot be judged very useful by the practitioner.[1]

We have, therefore, begun an effort at what we call 'collaborative evaluation'. The idea here is to focus more attention upon the interface between the evaluation reporting and the policy-making function. Under this thinking it is not enough for the evaluators merely to dump weighty research findings upon the school community. Rather it is part of the evaluator's responsibilities to identify problem areas and present data in terms which easily lead to policy discussion and decision-making. . . .

1 Egon Guba (1969). 'Significant differences', *Educational Researcher,* **20,** No. 4, p. 4.

4.11   Barry MacDonald
A political classification of evaluation studies

After stating that the basic and utilitarian purpose of evaluation studies is to provide information for choice among alternatives, and that the choice is a subsequent activity not engaged in by the evaluators, Hemphill says: 'This fact might lead to the conclusion that an evaluation study could avoid questions of value and utility leaving them to the decision-maker, and thus not need to be distinguished from research, either basic or applied. The crux of the issue, however, is not *who* makes a decision about what alternatives or *what information* serves as the basis for a decision; rather, it is the *degree to which concern with value questions is part and parcel of the study.*'

A matter of 'degree' may not suggest a major distinction. It is necessary to be more explicit. Of course, values enter into research, in a number of ways. There are many people in this country who have resisted the conclusions of a great deal of educational research since the war, on the grounds of value bias inherent in problem selection and definition. This was notable in the response to research into educational opportunity, and seems likely to characterise the reception of current research in the field of multi-ethnic education. Other value judgements of the researcher are less perceptible and lie buried in his technology. The more esoteric the technology, the less likely are these values to be detected. Test and survey instruments are wrongly assumed to be value-free because of the deper-sonalised procedures of administration and analysis that govern their application. The position of the evaluator is quite distinct, and much more complex. The enterprise he is called upon to study is neither of his choosing nor under his control. He soon discovers, if he failed to assume it, that the issues of educational action and consequence he is required to elucidate are enacted in a socio-political theatre which infiltrates the enterprise at every stage. He finds he can make few assumptions about what has happened, what is happening or what is going to happen. He is faced with competing interest groups with divergent definitions of the situation and conflicting informational needs. If he has accepted narrowly stipulative terms of reference, he may find that his options have been pre-empted by contractual restraints that are subsequently difficult to justify. If, on the other hand, he has freedom of action, he faces acute problems. He has to decide which decision-makers he will serve, what information

Source: Written by Barry MacDonald for the Schools Council.

will be of most use, when it is needed and how it can be obtained. I am suggesting that the resolution of these issues commits the evaluator to a political stance, an attitude to the government of education. No such commitment is required of the researcher. He stands outside the political process, and values his detachment from it. The researcher is free to select his questions, and to seek answers to them. He will naturally select questions which are susceptible to the problem-solving techniques of his craft.

The relevance of this issue to my present thesis is easy to demonstrate. The political stance of the evaluator has consequences for his choice of techniques of information gathering and analysis.

A great deal of new knowledge is produced by researchers and evaluators by means of techniques and procedures which are difficult to understand. Conclusions are reached and judgements made by the few who are qualified to make them. Others accept or reject these conclusions according to the degree of respect they feel towards those who make them, or the degree to which the conclusions coincide with their beliefs and self-interests.

For many years now those concerned with the failure of the educational system to make full use of the results of educational research have pleaded the case for all teachers to be trained in the techniques of research. Perhaps some of that effort should have been expended in exploring techniques that more closely resemble the ways in which teachers normally make judgements, techniques that are more accessible to non-specialist decision-makers. The evaluator who sees his task as feeding the judgement of a range of non-specialist audiences faces the problem of devising such techniques, the problem of trying to respond to the ways of knowing that his audiences use. Such an effort is presently hampered by subjecting evaluators to a research critique which is divorced from considerations of socio-political consequence. Evaluators influence changing power relationships. Their work produces information which functions as a resource for the promotion of particular interests and values. Evaluators are committed to a political stance because they must choose between competing claims for this resource. The selection of roles, goals, audiences, issues and techniques by evaluators, provides clues to their political allegiances. I will describe three distinct types of evaluation study—bureaucratic, autocratic and democratic. The last of these will be the least familiar to students of evaluation. The field has been characterised by evaluation studies which fall into one or other of the first two types. The democratic evaluation study is an emerging model, not yet substantially realised, but one which embodies some recent theoretical and practical trends. It is, in part, a reaction to the dominance of the bureaucratic types of study currently associated with American programmes.

Bureaucratic evaluation

Bureaucratic evaluation is an unconditional service to those government agencies which have major control over the allocation of educational resources. The evaluator accepts the values of those who hold office, and offers information which will help them to accomplish their policy objectives. He acts as a management consultant, and his criterion of success is client satisfaction. His techniques of study must be credible to the policy-makers and not lay them open to public criticism. He has no independence, no control over the use that is made of his information and no court of appeal. The report is owned by the bureaucracy and lodged in its files. The key concepts of bureaucratic evaluation are 'service', 'utility' and 'efficiency'. Its key justificatory concept is 'the reality of power'.

Autocratic evaluation

Autocratic evaluation is a conditional service to those government agencies which have major control over the allocation of educational resources. It offers external validation of policy in exchange for compliance with its recommendations. Its values are derived from the evaluator's perception of the constitutional and moral obligations of the bureaucracy. He focuses upon issues of educational merit, and acts as expert adviser. His techniques of study must yield scientific proofs, because his power base is the academic research community. His contractual arrangements guarantee non-interference by the client, and he retains ownership of the study. His report is lodged in the files of the bureaucracy, but is also published in academic journals. If his recommendations are rejected, policy is not validated. His court of appeal is the research community, and higher levels in the bureaucracy. The key concepts of the autocratic evaluator are 'principle' and 'objectivity'. Its key justificatory concept is 'the responsibility of office'.

Democratic evaluation

Democratic evaluation is an information service to the community about the characteristics of an educational programme. It recognises value-pluralism and seeks to represent a range of interests in its issue-formulation. The basic value is an informed citizenry, and the evaluator acts as broker in exchanges of information between differing groups. His techniques of data-gathering and presentation must be accessible to non-specialist audiences. His main activity is the collection of definitions of, and reactions to, the programme. He offers confidentiality to informants and gives them control over his use of the information. The report is non-recommendatory, and the evaluator has no concept of information misuse. The evaluator engages in periodic negotiation of his relationships with sponsors and programme participants. The criterion of success is the range of audiences served. The report aspires to 'bestseller' status. The key concepts of democratic evaluation are 'confidentiality', 'negotiation' and 'accessibility'. The key justificatory concept is 'the right to know'.

Section 5
Alternative evaluation: the new paradigm in action

Introduction: the evaluator as private eye

In a book full of hopes, claims and innovative methodology, there is need for some evidence of results. What actually happens when the new thinking is applied? What types of studies are done, and how good are they? What do reports look like and are they useful to anyone? Are illuminative, interpretative, descriptive-analytic types of evaluation — when put into practice — more useful, more informative, more profound, than traditional forms?

Such questions are legitimate. To answer them properly, however, poses a medley of editorial problems. First, the number of non-traditional studies is not large. Definitive verdicts on the new paradigm in action would be premature. Second, to assess the total impact of a style of research itself requires further study. Research on research, throughout the social sciences, is woefully neglected.[1] Thus, while evaluation reports exist, case-histories of the studies themselves do not; nor do investigations of their aftermath. Third, space considerations do not permit even inclusion of complete evaluation studies, let alone any supporting evidence of their success or failure: that would be another whole book in itself.

These limitations prevent our 'validating by example' the foregoing claims of the new paradigm. We settle here on more modest goals, and select for examination some different styles and types of evaluation report. In short, we reproduce extracts from evaluations that embody the new paradigm. Parlett and Hamilton (see Section I) used 'paradigm' in T. S. Kuhn's sense — as an over-arching, widely accepted framework of 'givens' that lends structure and shape to an area, providing in tacit fashion the ground rules for inquiry and also the criteria for adjudicating quality of work done. The emergence of a new paradigm, according to Kuhn, is often linked to the definition of certain research studies, statements, and books as exemplary. It would be premature in a fast-evolving field to describe the following as authoritative exemplars; and certainly their authors would draw back from any such claim made on their behalf. They would rather — as we would — see the reports as examples rather than exemplars, samples of the new paradigm as it has been variously interpreted and applied.

There are obvious reasons for allocating a major section of the book to reports. First, while some readers thrive on a continuous diet of methodology and theory, others have a small appetite for the genre. They

1 One early exception is P. E. Hammond (1964). *Sociologists at Work*. New York: Basic Books.

231

want instead some concrete examples, short demonstrations to show the method and theory in action. The book would be almost wholly programmatic without the present section. A second reason is that, to our knowledge, no similar collection has ever been compiled. Evaluation reports in general are distressingly hard to get hold of: if not actually marked confidential they frequently circulate in small numbers privately or with restrictions imposed, regarded as of transitory and local interest only. As with many of the more theoretical papers about evaluation, they often remain in mimeograph form, and are thus technically 'unpublished'. Inaccessibility of material, of course, is one reason for the comparative isolation of evaluators working in the new paradigm. Even the writers of the evaluation reports that follow will almost certainly be reading a number of the other contributions for the first time. That there exists a family resemblance is the more remarkable.

However, there are other compelling reasons for including sample reports and, indeed, for according them appropriate status in the reader. The most visible outcome of an evaluation study is generally its report. Although MacDonald and Walker (see 4.3 above) speak of a 'variety of means of presentation; written reports, audio-visual recordings, displays and exhibitions', there have been few departures from the customary pattern of written documentation. Reports come in many shapes and sizes: brief memoranda for committees or programme organisers (as in Jenkins' report in this section); lengthy, descriptive historical accounts (as in House's study of PLATO); and collections of what amount to mini-reports on different themes, sometimes by different writers (e.g. in the 'display' report by Stake and Gjerde on T-City, also included). In terms of its effects upon programme policies, the written report may not always be the evaluation's most significant outcome. Sometimes the mere doing of a study, or even of its being commissioned, may have more far-reaching consequences. And, clearly, in more formative studies, procedures for interim feedback, advice, or suggestions, in verbal or possibly note form, may count more than a subsequent final report. But overall the typical way in which the illuminative evaluators still communicate to their audiences is by written word.

This allegiance to the report form is of interest. In an era of growing use of non-verbal media, of general profligacy of paper, and of 'nobody having time to read any more', it is surprising that alarm bells have not rung already. It is possible that the assiduously compiled and reasoned written report may rather rapidly go the way of the dodo. At present, though, there is no evidence of its demise or of any rapid preventative mutations. Yet the lengthy final report (and often they are lengthy) may be one of the chief obstacles to wide acceptance and rapid evolution of the new paradigm.

Although Section 4 did not include discussion specifically about the preparation and delivery of the eventual report, there were many pointers in its direction. A report comes at the end and reflects what has gone before. Its writing constitutes an integral part of the total methodology. Any suggestion that one first completes the study, then analyses the data, and finally sets about writing a report, is misleading. The stages are not insulated; there is a progression. This section therefore extends the preceding one on methodology. The continuity of the report-writing with the investigative stages of the work is even more evident with non-traditional evaluations. Here the data are often not numerical, awaiting conversion to verbal summary; rather they come already verbalised — as opinions, descriptions, stories, portrayals and considered statements of policy. Data processing involves dealing with this complex array of evidence. Interview notes or transcripts, summaries of test and question-naire results, observation reports, personal memoranda, historical sum-maries, extracts from documents, and so on, have all to be organised and collated, summarised and selected from for quotation. It means, in practice, that handling the data and imposing some form upon it naturally merges with the assembling of the first draft.

As with other areas of methodology, report-writing has its hazards. Arguably they are among the most perilous of all for illuminative evaluators. The first difficulty — encountered at one time or another by almost every evaluator — is 'data overload': the equivalent of stacks of computer printout is here the row of interview tapes or field notebooks in a stage of partial analysis. Overload is often not seen as a problem until the stage of writing-up. Indeed, up to that time, the less experienced evaluator sees the boxes of tapes as security symbols — evidence to self and others that effort has been expended. It is when a succinct summary is seen to be called for that the problem is recognised. Too late a recognition of this can put the report's appearance back by months or years and reduces its chance of impact. One soon learns that it is easier to collect data than to know what to do with them. Data overload can be responsible for producing the constipated writer or, a different breed, the one with verbal diarrhoea.

A second area of difficulty, already mentioned by MacDonald and Walker in the previous section, concerns confidentiality and the sharing of draft reports. Although many would subscribe to the ideals implicit in the term 'democratic evaluation', there are recurring difficulties. If preliminary drafts are widely circulated, they come to assume primary place: the final version, with all the amendments and changes now democratically decided upon, is of less interest. Everyone wants to read the first authoritative draft, nobody the 'watered-down' or 'with teeth pulled' final version. It is also worth noting that people who read first drafts may not read a later one.

Deciding on who should see the report in draft and whose comments should be taken into account are two tricky professional and political dilemmas facing the evaluators. But there are many others equally perplexing. How neutral should the evaluator try to be? How are failures reported without unduly damaging professional reputations? How is authenticity balanced against the need to maintain privacy through the process of rendering settings and persons anonymous? How exhaustive a detailing of what may amount to a semi-private world is justified by the evaluator's recognition of the public's right to know? Who 'owns' the data?

These questions come home to roost at the reporting stage with a vengeance. They cannot be considered in isolation, as mere technical matters to be looked up in a methodological text: they have to do with the personal professional stance and definition of the role of the evaluator in a particular evaluation context, and require sound judgement. The evaluator — even in the most democratic context — will often wield considerable power. There is no easy solution to the problem that some may abuse it. Evaluation studies involve, by definition, intervention in the affairs of others. They result in reports that become political documents. As long as evaluation is practised this is likely to be the case.

It is easy to see how the writing of the report has to be done with great care. Significant decisions may rest on the precise interpretation of what has been written. For instance, in Parlett's study of two experimental programmes at MIT (the last extract of the section), both the overseeing committee he was reporting to and the programme being studied, found 'ammunition' in the report for their respective positions in argument. In circumstances like these, close attention has to be given to the detailed wording of the report's potentially sensitive sections. A hastily written, sloppy, poorly argued statement can easily lead to severe unintended consequences for individuals or groups.

A third common difficulty for writers of evaluations in this style is to know how much 'raw' data or evidence to include. Should the report contain extended quotations and verbatim records, so that readers can themselves draw conclusions and weigh the evidence directly? Or should the evaluators summarise, condense and themselves do the main part of the interpreting? To some extent the issue is an academic one. It is, after all, clearly impossible in most studies to present all the data collected. And, on the other side, no evaluator is going to be convincing without at least some passing glimpse of the original data. Yet how much to report and with what degree of selectivity and specificity are very real problems. Highly numerical kinds of evaluations do not report all their data either, but there are easy means of summarising available, e.g. tables of mean values and variances. No such straightforward route can be followed by those dealing with the mostly qualitative, complex, diverse and often ambiguous material collected in the kinds of study that we sample here.

Given that at least some degree of ordering, weighting and selectivity is necessarily called for, there are related problems of letting readers know, for instance, what criteria are being used for acceptance and rejection.

*How much data were the assertions based upon? What, precisely, were the
circumstances of acquiring a particular group of crucial opinions? It is not
always possible to summarise such information simply and briefly, but
each evaluator should have an answer to such questions. Given the
importance of such items, are they all to be discussed? It raises the spectre
of every evaluation report containing its own lengthy methodological
treatise, with effort and writing time diverted from the main report to its
appendix on methods.*

*As with the other problem areas noted, there are no generally agreed
strategies to cope with this question. Each evaluator tends to develop and
justify an individual style of work. In the following series of studies, each
writer has been a selfconscious innovator. Each may have relatively
consistent standards of what constitutes, say, adequate documentation to
sustain an inference, but the standards are not the same from one
investigator to the next. It is not surprising: as noted before, we are
speaking of a family resemblance not an enclosed orthodoxy guided by a
tacit uniformity of practice.*

*Despite the family resemblance, what perhaps will strike the reader
most forcefully about the extracts that follow is the broad range of types of
report we include. Some of the variation may be attributed to different
evaluators achieving their own resolution to the problems discussed
above — their own sense of 'getting the balance right'. But there are other
reasons for the diversity, reasons which illuminate aspects of the new
paradigm in revealing ways.*

*One of the chief reasons for the diversity of reports selected is that while
certain general propositions may be widely agreed upon by the contributors, their detailed theoretical positions differ quite dramatically. One
basic issue, already hinted at, relates to whether the evaluator sees the
study as predominantly descriptive, analytic, an exercise in 'storytelling', a
contribution to the research literature, an attempt to clarify and explain
or — alternatively — as predominantly a detailed description. In Sections 3
and 4 there were clear indications of these discrepant orientations. Robert
Stake, for instance, seeks a 'comprehensive, substantive portrayal'. He
writes (Section 3.28): 'We need to portray complexity. We need to convey
holistic impression, the mood, even the mystery of the experience.'*

*Louis Smith, on the other hand, while probably not explicitly dis-
agreeing with Stake, is clearly concerned with the 'generation of concepts,
hypotheses, and miniature theories'. While Stake argues provocatively for
'more ambiguity rather than less in our reports', Smith seeks 'analytic
power'. He wants to 'skim the cream' and develop 'creative propositions'.
Some of the differences between Stake and Smith will be evident in their
reports that follow. The competition between the evaluator's desire to
mirror what he sees and, on the other hand, his wish to explain it or
account for it, is often acute: it is a tension that recurs throughout the
following section, within as well as between writers. To opt for the portrait*

or the mirror reflection is to want to capture the intimate flavour, the feeling of uniqueness, complexity and idiosyncrasy, a portion of life in its most 'real' form. To lean towards interpretation arises through wanting, at some level, to generalise or to seek patterns of invariance, to condense, to abstract, or to capture the essence of what is being studied. It is necessarily more selective. It is an attempt to encode — rather than increase — ambiguity. Smith acknowledges that preliminary theorising can lead to 'some loss of comprehensiveness' but it is 'helpful in later report-writing'. Stake comments briefly, 'over-simplification obfuscates'. Parlett and Hamilton argue for 'seeking general principles . . ., spotting patterns of cause and effect . . ., placing individual findings within a broader explanatory context'.

A closely related but not quite identical tension has to do with the degree to which the evaluator is deferential to his audience. Does he consider — or appear to consider — that the readership has an equal chance to develop its own theories and opinions? 'Responsive' and 'democratic' evaluation styles are ideologically committed to a high degree of 'audience participation'. Parlett and Hamilton, however, seem to place more emphasis on the need to 'raise the level of sophistication of debate' and Eisner goes even further: he thinks the evaluator, like the critic, 'must be capable of rendering his perceptions into a language that makes it possible for others less perceptive than he to see qualities and aspects of the work that they would otherwise overlook'. It would be foolish, by selecting single statements, to play up the differences too far: in practice positions are blurred. But these and other tensions do exist, and will be returned to in the separate introductions to the individual reports.

A second and more straightforward reason for observed variations between reports has to do with the specific commission and audience in each case. Each evaluation study is tailor-made. Indeed, one of the principal strengths of the new paradigm is its versatility. A diversity among reports is an inevitable and desirable consequence of the new approach. Instead of building evaluations around requirements of methodology, methods are built around problem definitions and contracts negotiated between evaluator and sponsor (or proposed audience). Studies are thus directed to specified groups and discuss questions, problems and policy issues germane to those groups. Administrators receiving a memo (as in the Center for New Schools studies reported here) require a different inquiry, report and 'evaluator stance' than a general audience, say, of the programme participants and interested outsiders that Stake and Gjerde and Smith and Schumacher seem to be writing for (see below). When there are — as is often the case — multiple or general audiences, it may permit the writer to include a greater variety of material, to have a little more reporting freedom, directing different groups to specific sections of the report.

Finally, of course, in considering the degree of variation of reports, one must remember that there are straightforward stylistic differences between writers. Evaluators, in the new paradigm, are not of a single stamp. They can display their individual distinctiveness, and they do. The degree to which they employ artistic flourish or deadpan prose, the lucidity or calculated ambiguity, the succinctness or verbosity is as much a reflection of personal style as it is a function of their evaluation contract.

Before turning to the examples we include here, there is one further point deserving of special note. Perhaps the greatest difficulty facing evaluators is to get people to read their reports. If we enter a single plea, it is for readability, brevity and interest. Given the overloaded lives of the majority of professional people, it is hopeless to expect the reading of tedious and long-winded reports. No evaluator can afford to ignore this. However apt and intelligent an evaluation report is, it will still have negligible impact if it remains unread.

The evaluator as private eye: shadow studies at Illinois Junior High

We begin with an evaluation study in miniature.[2] Terry Denny explains the genesis of the first reports featured as follows:

The three descriptions of a day at 'Illinois Junior High School' were written by a team of three observers who visited the school on a day in the spring of 1971. . . .

The three authors were invited by the staff of Illinois Junior High to conduct a 'shadow study' of the school day in the lives of three students. An attempt was made to match the observer's background to the student he was to observe and the school personnel.

At the conclusion of the day of the study the observer-authors gave an oral report to the faculty. They left the meeting with very little attempt having been made to interpret, defend or extend their remarks.

The faculty discussed the observers' reports for an hour after their departure and found them sufficiently stimulating to request a typescript for their use. These were the conditions and circumstances which brought these reports to papered life.[3]

Clearly it is debatable whether any of the shadow studies is an evaluation report at all. 'Three reflections' could be seen simply as a collection of informative memoranda, each summarising remarks made on a particular occasion. Certainly there is a brevity, a journalistic crispness, a lightness of tone that belies any notion of the professional ethnographer at work. But this is of no consequence. Our present purpose is not to draw rigid boundaries in defining what precisely is, and what is not, an

2   From Terry Denny, Clencie Cotton and Gary Storm (1971). 'Three reflections', CIRCE Working Paper No. 11. Each of the reflections was made in April 1971.
3   Taken from Terry Denny's foreword to 'Three reflections.'

illuminative evaluation. Rather we take an open exploratory stance, allowing a number of different reports to speak for themselves while, at the same time, acknowledging—and detailing here—their family resemblances. There are not only numerous alternative methodological features available for investigations within the new paradigm: there are also diverse investigative contracts or forms of relationship between observers and the observed. Some of these contracts may not be evaluations in any strictly orthodox sense. But, again, we see no point in arguing over this: we accept that there are numerous different types of systematic study of educational situations, events and issues, that are both useful and insightful. Some are manifestly evaluative, others less so. What is important, in our view, is not that studies conform or not to predetermined formats, but rather that it is made clear as to what each study purports to be: investigations should not misrepresent themselves. Here, for example, the significant feedback was immediate, and oral. *Equally there was nothing complex or eclectic about the methodology. Individual children were selected as 'tracers' within the school system and simply followed about. Each of the three 'reflections' suggests that the contract negotiated between observer and sponsor (in this case the staff of the school) was the simplest possible. The value of the reports was the discussion they stimulated: the study could comfortably run the risk of being extremely impressionistic. There was little investment in its success; it would not have been of great consequence if the results had appeared somewhat off-target.*

There are, however, even within these mini-reports, several significant themes of the social anthropology paradigm. There is, for instance, a quality of critical appraisal. The observation is interpretative, and goes beyond mere description, drawing inferences and paying attention to underlying pedagogical assumptions. It is also hooked into recurringly difficult educational value-questions. Furthermore, there is evidence of the outsider's sharpened perceptions of the more or less taken-for-granted world of the school. Finally, the attention is focused on detailed incidents in a way that suggests more widely-based phenomena.

Although it would be absurd to expect 'Three reflections' to carry a Louis Smith-style methodological appendix this does not mean that these brief reports are without methodological interest. The observers seek to be unobtrusive in the teeth of a difficult brief ('I followed a kid to the john and he used it and stared at himself in the mirror for a couple or three minutes');[4] they do not come across as opinionated or doctrinaire; they document how they went about making their observations and acknowledge the difficulties they encountered; and they manifestly seek to provide a type of feedback that is immediate, apt and low-key, but telling and significant. However, it is worth pointing out that in a shadow study, the shadow is the substance. Yet only the report labelled 'This' appears to remain within the self-imposed limits. Shadow studies, being based on

4   Denny, Cotton and Storm (1971), p. 6.

hit-and-run fieldwork, need especially to tackle the problem of relating any generalisation to observed events. The main interest is in how inferences can be made about the functioning of a whole school from the observation, even 'in context', of a single pupil. Indeed the 'After' report does not even mention the subject shadowed, and the 'My' report mentions him only in a single sentence. Consequently the conclusions reached by the 'This' report appear more firmly based and worthy of greater attention than the other two studies.

The three extracts differ therefore in tone, length and in how much descriptive information is provided. They present three separate inputs contributing to the portrayal of a single setting. As such, each derives benefit from being adjacent to the other two.

The following quotation from Terry Denny's foreword to the shadow studies should help in distinguishing the three accounts.

The three descriptions begin with the words 'After', 'This' and 'My' which will serve as titles of a sort.

'After' was written by a white doctoral candidate in educational philosophy who was himself a product of the school system. He grew up near the university and is deeply committed to exploring the creation of successful learning environments for adolescents.

'This' was written by an elementary education university professor, white, forty — the son of a high school graduate. He is interested in conducting evaluations that have worth to people other than the evaluators.

'My' was written by a black senior law student who held assistantships within the College of Education during his junior and senior law school years. He is chiefly concerned that minority programmes in schools be sensible to their intended constituents.

5.1 Terry Denny, Clencie Cotton and Gary Storm
Reflections on a day at Illinois Junior High

After

After a week's reflection, I do not think life at Illinois Junior High is as fundamentally different from junior high school life in the same city fourteen years ago as I had thought a week ago. The major difference seems to be that students who were once forced to be quiet and inactive (even though they were not paying attention or learning much) are now noisily engaged in social talk and physical interaction. True, classroom talk and action is much cruder and more openly abusive of adult authority than it was even 'in the halls' or 'on school grounds' in the 1950s but so is the talk and action of the culture as a whole. I am not sure these students are any more 'radical' vis-à-vis the culture at large than students ever have been. The major problem seems to be one of 'what do you do when hundreds of kids under one roof quite naturally express themselves in ways their young adult models are expressing themselves?'

The consequences of this kind of aggressive individual and social expressiveness for education in the traditional sense are difficult to assess. But one thing is eminently clear: traditional, hard-nosed, authoritarian approaches to keeping order and teaching (?) in the classroom are doomed to failure. There are too many sources of reinforcement encouraging students to reject such approaches to expect them to be able to succeed. It would seem that a shift away from teacher-centred, 'didactic' approaches to teaching toward environment-centred, discovery and problem-solving 'heuristic' approaches to teaching might be in order. An heuristic approach appears less 'repressive' to students—giving them greater opportunities to choose what and when to engage in various learning activities—but at the same time can be more structured than the present situation. If combined with examinations that can be taken whenever students feel they are ready for them (and which are required before they can advance to other learning activities), the heuristic approach to teaching might be very fruitful. (Note that in the heuristic approach the teacher becomes an 'arranger of interesting learning environments' and a resource person to students grappling with these environments.)

Source: T. Denny, C. Cotton and G. Storm (1971). 'Three reflections'. CIRCE Working Paper No. 11. The study was sponsored by the State Gifted Programme of the Office of the Superintendent of Public Instruction of Illinois. The extracts reproduced here are taken from pp. 1-4, 5, 6-9.

It also seems to me that a dose of 'socratics' would improve the educational milieu of Illinois Junior High. By socratics, I mean teacher-student interaction of a form that is concerned largely with the student's moral and personal development. The interaction need not always be one-to-one; symposia (in the Greek sense) involved a small group of students and teachers who were 'socratic' in the sense used here. Socratic relationships could help counteract the extreme disinterest for adults typical among today's students and *vice versa*. Topics discussed in teacher-student symposia might include such fundamental things as 'What is education really for?' 'What goals do students have for their immediate adolescent and later adult lives?' 'What role should school play in relation to these goals?', etc.

I was favourably impressed with the equalitarian spirit that pervaded the students at Illinois Junior High. I saw little 'racism' in evidence among students; in fact, I was amazed at how relaxed and casual the interaction between black and white students really was. There was much more racism expressed by teachers who tried to *isolate* blacks who were active and 'disruptive' of normal classroom activity and by teachers *who tried to ignore those who were passive but inattentive*. Socratics could be especially useful for the moral development of white teachers relative to black students.

The last comment I want to make is that I was very disappointed in the amount of classwide (i.e. social or 'public') discussion of exciting ideas — whether pertaining to the formal disciplines of maths, English, science, etc., or to more social, psychological or literary types of subject matter. It seemed that most assignments could be carried out individually and that very little discussion and group action (and growth) were fostered. I think it is especially bad when subjects in which personal values and interpretations play a large and valuable role (the arts, humanities, social studies) lack group analysis and opportunities for group discussion.

This

This is an impressionistic report of things I saw or think I saw, things I heard and did not hear, and the feelings that I guessed kids were having as well as the feelings that I knew I was having during my day in Illinois Junior High School. . . .

The first thing I observed about the neatly dressed, short-haired, smiling boy that I was going to follow was his talking first to a black girl and then to a black boy and subsequently to six other students all in the course of two or three minutes (about grades, assignments and the like). He offered comments easily about who was present yesterday and absent when the teacher asked a question while taking attendance.

The teacher's opening message — one that was to be repeated several times throughout the day by other teachers to this student — was filled with words about points, papers, schedules. It was not a highly pressured message and the students seemed to slide easily into chatting and individual and small group work or play. After getting the details of what was expected of him my student went to the library. I did not know it at the time but this was a key to his day and mine at Illinois Junior High.

The first thing I noticed in the library was two tables of black students only — (does this mean something?) — who were chatting unconcernedly, wiseacreing, engaging in social challenging. Next I noted several other students, all white, working independently, sex segregated, four girls here, six girls there, two boys there. I get the feeling that work is not necessarily a part of the expectations of being in the library. An event occurred that took me back a bit when a teacher confronted a male teacher, a male black teacher, in front of a group of black girls that were making some loud comments to one another. When he departed I heard the 'leader' of the group string out a few choice words about him when he was out of earshot. The other girls laughed and that was the end of that topic. I wondered at the time if this library was used as a bullpen for classroom problems or troublemakers. Whatever it is, it's not a dull place to be. I came to discover as the day wore on that the pace, tempo and atmosphere of the library changed from hour to hour and time to time and that it was not possible that day to select the atmosphere of any one hour as typical for the entire day.

During the first thirty minutes I noted twelve shifts from apparent work to open socialising on the part of the boy that I was observing. (I wonder what I mean when I talk with my college students about 'on task' behaviour?) Then with the beginning of the thirteenth segment he worked steadily for fifteen minutes, reading, taking notes interruptedly.

When the bell rang and students left for the next class, everything was up for grabs in the library and out. There was no quiet, hush-hush filing from the library to the hall. Should there be?

When I went to the second class I got the distinct feeling that work was acceptable here, and so was low-level horsing around, and so was quiet singing while you are working and so was quiet staring. I felt pretty good about that and after a little over an hour in the school I was thinking how greater, *far greater*, the socialising need is for the majority of these kids than I had imagined it was. And I wondered if this has always been the case or if I am just more sensitive to it today. The number and kinds of social interactions that have occurred with this one particular student that I'm watching and the others about him far exceed the numbers and kinds that I would have imagined would have occurred.

I believe at this point in the day that one of the friends of the eighth-grade boy that I was shadowing came up to me and announced that a bus driver had told the students on his bus that, 'A psychologist is going to follow somebody all day and he's going to be coming on this bus. We know it's either Mike or Doug.' It was at this point that I shifted my observation to a girl who was in the first and second hour classes that I had observed.

The next class was a very noisy one, the teacher alternating between shouting out directions and issuing comments on a lesson that she's following . . . virtually alone . . . and threatening the students who are laughing, playing around with little or no attention to the lesson. The teacher told the students that if they finished the lesson early they could go to the library. Sure enough the student that I was now shadowing goes to the library. . . .

The last class before lunch. Four minutes into the class my shadow student went up to the teacher and asked her . . . guess what! . . . Yes, could she go to the library? Off she went.

At this point I see, or maybe I sense more than see, a sameness, a continuity, as I go from class to class in respect to who this student is and what's expected of her. But the continuity is a social, interpersonal continuity and not an academic or intellectual one. The group provides the social continuity from class to class. So many classes: how can a student get him or herself together intellectually?

I wonder if the American dream of mass education can possibly make it with the powerful countervailing forces of sexual revolution, total deterioration of the concept of legitimate authority, emerging meaning of Blackness with no comparable meaning for whiteness, and a highly empathic steady desire to remove controls, regulations and needless restrictions by teachers and administrators?

Another quotable quote: 'Are you here to fix the carpets or to plant the grass? . . .'

Well, one more class. . . . The teacher greets me with 'Sit down, take out papers, grades. Quiet! The rules were yesterday that if you didn't bring your paper etc. . . . I usually have to tell you people five times anyway. . . .' (This is always a welcome relief for students because it means two minutes of chaos and they appear to like that. Perhaps their happiest moments are amidst anarchy; at least nobody is putting them down; and there's no strain; and they can just let it all hang out.)

The teacher is talking and so am I. The teacher doesn't care and neither do I.

*

I quit observing at this point. That was it. It was only 2.45 but this observer could walk out and he did. (But what of the student?)

I followed a kid to the john and he used it and stared at himself in the mirror for a couple or three minutes and then he tossed a paper on the floor and walked out.

I went to the Teachers' Lounge and there, as I have found so frequently throughout this year, I found teachers talking about *teaching!* This is an extraordinary phenomenon in my life as a school evaluator. Teachers rarely really talk about teaching in the Teachers' Lounge. And yet it characterises Illinois Junior High School's instructional staff.

Let me try to sum it up: this is a good school but I don't think I would be mature enough to be a student in it. The responsibility for self-control, for self-initiation and maintenance in purposeful activity is too great for my kind of student. Worse, I'm afraid I wouldn't become all that I could be. For those students who have been well-grooved, know what they're about, are skilful in learning, purposeful in their activities and who think well of themselves, this is a superior school. For those who have had six, seven, eight, lousy years of experience in schools complete salvation for them is unlikely. Not the usual hell, no, just—just a humane, steady, state of limbo. Paul Goodman said that may be good enough. I disagree. I found myself returning to my eraser analogy; it's so easy to see what you are *not* going to do—to remove the things that school ought not to be doing. But then what is to be done? The happy emphasis at Illinois Junior High School on personal development must be accompanied by skill learning, by attitude learning, by a systematic introduction to problem-solving on an individual and group basis. (These matters are discussed in the two other reaction papers.)

We don't know very much about that kind of curriculum. A purely self-discovery curriculum for young adolescents is a cop-out in my judgement. It's a dry well. I believe selves are created, not discovered. I think that the romantic view that the middle school or the junior high school student's personality is something precious, that it is uncovered like a leaf in a forest, is a bad metaphor. It's more the case that it's hewed out of solid granite.

I left with the feeling that this was one of the best schools that I had seen; and with an accompanying feeling that our best was not good enough. If I could confront the faculty with two questions they would be these: When a student needs a competent, compassionate, tough adult, where is she; where is he? When a student leaves Illinois Junior High after two years of classroom life, what will he be able to do that you can take some credit for?

My

My impressions will be very brief. I must confess that I am not so sure that I should have been functioning as an observer of what it is like for a black student to matriculate daily at Illinois Junior High. Very early in the day I changed my mission. I more or less began to look at the school as a whole but unconsciously so because I think that's how a student would be looking at it. I frankly found most of the things that I watched him do—like going to class, lunch, playing and this kind of thing—as being primarily irrelevant to my concern for the school as a whole.

Stated briefly, my concern is whether a school such as Illinois Junior High with the atmosphere that prevails there, with faculty members being trained as the faculty members there have been trained, with very diverse ideas and philosophies about how kids should be taught, can in fact maintain a school with that kind of atmosphere and impart much substantive knowledge to its students. As I said to the faculty, I think the situation that I observed (although I liked them a lot) really has made me think through the question as to whether or not they must in fact develop a new definition of school. I am wondering whether the people who are participating within that particular structure can continue to think and define school in the traditional historical definition and still maintain their sanity in the situation which exists in their school. I think we saw a lot of individual freedom which we all agree is necessary and in fact which is happening more and more in high and junior high schools today. We saw a lot of challenging of teachers on the part of the students but very little challenging of students on the part of the teachers. We saw a lot of black and white students challenging teachers; and, quite frankly, I was very disappointed in the inability of the faculty to meet the challenge of the students. Is this something which you can train a person to do as they pass through the educational curricula of our various colleges and universities? I think this speaks directly to the definition of a teacher; to the concept of teaching as it in fact exists in real life.

I was very much impressed by the facilities. I wonder, can better use be made of those facilities? I wish I knew more about this matter. The purposeful listlessness (it really wasn't a lack of purpose) on the part of the students and the seeming lack of ability to define purpose on the part of the faculty were very conspicuous. I really don't think I am being exceptionally critical, but in fact I am being very realistic in wondering whether or not the feeder schools that we were talking about (to prepare teachers to come into the atmosphere which prevails at Illinois Junior High) should not be also seriously examined — that is, a feeder system or some kind of a system which in a sense prepares faculty to deal with the kinds of situations which they will encounter in the emerging Illinois Junior High Schools across the country.

To be a black person in Illinois Junior High . . . I really don't know whether it's any more frustrating to be black at Illinois than it is to be white. I think what I saw there is a situation where the void between some faculty and many students is so wide that the white student at the school feels as alienated from the faculty (and in many instances I think more alienated) than do the black students.

I think this exists for at least one reason: and that is I think you saw at Illinois the bending over backwards by some teachers (some didn't) trying to be responsive to black students. I'm not saying that this is bad; I'm not saying that this form of 'compensation' is not necessary in critical cases. However, what concerns me is the lack of honesty in such a short-term effort which in a sense does not help anyone but merely 'colours' the situation and makes it bad for nearly everyone in the long run.

In closing, let me just say, somehow I am not impressed by teachers obsessed with an idea of freedom in the school. The main thing that they could point to was the fact that this is a 'fair', free atmosphere, that the kids are very free, that they play very freely. I must be old-fashioned (at 25!): *I still think that the imparting of substantive knowledge to the child which will enable him to compete in a very unfree world while developing an atmosphere within the school which will help him develop those characteristics which develop in an atmosphere of freedom is absolutely necessary.* I think in some way a school like this must continuously struggle with the issue of how to combine a free atmosphere with the very strenuous task of learning skills which will aid students in the many courses of action in which they (plan to) endeavour.

Occupational gossip: internal reports from the Keele Integrated Studies Project

Two short unpublished reports by David Jenkins, 'Saved by the bell' and 'Saved by the Army' [1969], come next. Again, narrowly defined, they were not perhaps evaluations. But they raise several interesting questions — for instance, about confidentiality. Both were written early in the life of the Keele Integrated Studies Project[1], at a time when Jenkins was one of a number of people monitoring the impact of the Project's philosophy and packs of curriculum materials in the trial schools.

The reports were originally intended for a limited audience, the Project team itself, and were classified as confidential.[2] The substance of both reports, in terms of the issues raised, was discussed with the teachers concerned. Nevertheless a problem remains, linked ultimately to the ethics of participant observation; what responsibility does the observer have towards those being observed? Section 4 features a paper by Barry MacDonald and Rob Walker which tries to establish a new ethic for evaluation studies within a democratic ideology. Jenkins' reports are clearly in breach of the spirit of that approach. But it could be argued that curriculum project team members, like co-fieldworkers engaged on an ethnographic study, need to work towards at least a provisional 'collective understanding' of the situation under review. In this light, internal reports can be regarded as equivalent to occupational gossip. Certainly the writing of 'strong' internal memos is rarely repudiated, even by outfits in zealous public pursuit of the 'democratic' model. Nevertheless the ethical problems need to be faced squarely: they do not simply go away because the documents are not technically 'public'. Put at its broadest, the question is whether teachers need to be protected against potentially damaging interpretative accounts of what goes on in classrooms. In the absence of a clear convention that a written report of any kind is first shown to those observed, it seems at least arguable that the only sensible course is explicitly to negotiate and understand, within every research situation, what the ground rules will be.

There is also the issue of methodology. Both reports take a single day's observation, and offer a selective account. They aim to unravel the day-to-day realities of a programme. In both situations there are unspoken but implicit questions about the nature of the school-project 'contract' and

1 For a full interpretative account of the Project by an independent participant observer, see M. D. Shipman (1974). *Inside a Curriculum Project.* London: Methuen.

2 The names of people and places have been changed so that the reports could be included in this reader.

247

the ways in which aspirations towards integrated studies *can be embedded in teaching and learning. The observer is seen to have his own agenda. Indeed if we read between the lines of these participant observation reports, further difficulties emerge. At Hardacre Lane the* ad hominem *ploys of the teacher suggest that he sought to weaken the threat posed by the observer's presence by offers of collusion. But we only have Jenkins' account of what happened, and it is easy to argue that its credibility is weakened by two considerations. In the first place David Jenkins was at that time a member of the Project directorate with a professional interest in seeing that the Project contract was at least being minimally fulfilled. This gave him a 'diplomatic' agenda capable of interfering with the kind of detachment that could reasonably be expected of a less role-locked participant observer. But also the social position of the observer determines what he is likely to see. This knowledge gives the reader the chance of speculating about possible counter-interpretations. Would another observer have given a substantially different account? What indeed would Bondine's own account have looked like? It is also interesting to note how uninhibited Jenkins is about abandoning his detached role in the Ethel Street Salvation Army Hostel. He appears to have played, without shame, at least a minor part in the discussion he reports. This is not only a clear example of 'measurement interference' but also reduces the credibility of the account.*

Another question concerns the style of reportage. Elliot Eisner has suggested that evaluation studies could usefully employ the techniques of literary criticism but we are short of clear and varied examples of the kind of thing he might have had in mind. Perhaps these succinct but somewhat over-vivid accounts would qualify. In place of summary statistics, they use the explanatory potential of metaphor, irony and humour. They aspire to be provocative. As such, they are far from the bland middle-of-the-road prose of scientific journals or government reports. Many may see fit however, to question the appropriateness of the style. Words that may come to mind are 'impressionistic', 'emotive', 'journalistic', 'over-personalised' and 'value-laden'. Indeed the author appears to realise this and avoids making extravagant claims of scientific rigour. But what are the truth conditions associated with assertions of the kind made here? Again, we lay down no strict orthodoxy: the reports should be read bearing in mind the circumstances of their production, and judged accordingly. Could Jenkins have spent his single day more profitably? It is possible that one or two readable [and 'literary'] mini-reports may be more pertinent, have more impact and be more illuminating than a more studied and drawn-out statement. Whether they should or not is another question.

5.2 David Jenkins
Saved by the bell

A report by DRJ on Mr Bondine teaching 'Exploration Man' to 1C at Hardacre Lane.

This report is written in a spirit of self-doubt. It records what the observer, scarcely neutral, regarded as significant events. An attempt is made throughout to distinguish between evidence and interpretation, and the descriptive parts are written in a broadly referential language. This is not to deny that the interpretation is occasionally, or even frequently, emotive.

It seemed to the observer for a number of reasons that the critical factor in this curriculum environment was the verbal interaction between teacher and class. This was recorded carefully (the quotations are as verbatim as the technique of direct note-taking will allow).

A few preliminary comments

(a) The observer had been made aware previously of the isolation felt by this particular teacher, who has not found colleagues willing to work with him in a team situation and is uneasily 'going it alone'. The question is bound to arise: is this still to be regarded usefully as a trial school?

(b) A further issue exercising the Keele Integrated Studies Project team at the moment is the need to identify a core (any innovation needs to answer the question: precisely what is it that you are recommending?). Hardacre Lane is open to question on this score as Mr Bondine claims only the most general kind of 'inspiration' from the pack he is using. Theoretical notions of 'flexibility' apart, what does this actually mean in terms of curriculum events? This itself called for a careful analysis.

(c) The concern is for the underlying curriculum assumptions of a particular way of teaching, not teacher effectiveness as such. For this reason the observer has concentrated on the verbal tactics displayed in the Humanities lesson in the hope that these tactics would offer some insights into the general problems of teaching integrated studies.

Source: D. R. Jenkins (1969). 'Saved by the bell'. Internal report from the Keele Integrated Studies Project, published here for the first time.

Observations

DRJ arrives at school in the middle of morning assembly, and is shown to the staffroom by the member of staff on duty. The staffroom is full. Conversation continues, by-passing DRJ (meticulously); on the welcome proximity of the end of term; football and babies. Mr Bondine arrives, warm and welcoming. Bondine takes DRJ to 'my place', a large room with grouped desks and curtained library shelves. Maps of Tristan are pinned to the wall, alongside accounts of the imaginary hurricane that felled Hardacre Lane.

The pupils (from 1C) drift in. Bondine is explaining his teaching strategy: *Right off the cuff, boy* (indicating outline scheme for 'Exploration Man' which he taps emphatically with his knuckle). *All I need is the front page. These ideas you see . . . it comes off the top* (presumably indicating that his management of the class is intuitive, inspirational). *Make yourself at home.*

The lesson begins abruptly with a recall of previous work:
What is the Industrial Revolution?
The response is uncertain, so Bondine dramatises . . .

Say this is a TV quiz programme. I am the interviewer and (he selects a child by calling a forceful *you* and pointing a finger) *you are being quizzed* (adopts TV interviewer's pose). *Now tell me what is the Industrial Revolution?* The boy finds the dramatisation unhelpful (*don't look at the camera, boy*) but manages a definition: *A complete circle of industry, sir.*

(A sudden doubt here. Is this definition useful? Or does it arise out of 'dictionary work' and a failure to distinguish between social 'revolutions' and r.p.m.'s?)

Bondine accepts the *complete circle of industry.*
Good. How does it affect us?
Various pupils list industrial artifacts (*potbanks, sir . . . canals, sir*). But the next moves have already been decided.
When we think of the Industrial Revolution what book comes to mind? (a few unhelpful suggestions).
I mean comes especially to mind?
'Oliver Twist' is tentatively suggested.
Right! Oliver Twist!
The books are duly handed out by monitors. The books themselves are tatty, one-between-two. Interest is low.

Bondine offers an option. Would the class like to read the play of 'Oliver Twist' aloud or dramatise the story? There is a chorus in favour of reading aloud, although the alternative is kept attractively open (*wouldn't you prefer . . .*). The result of the vote is greeted with applause.

At this point Bondine passes by your observer. *A quick move into literature,* he explains. This lapse in confrontation causes the class to renew private conversation. Two lads in the far corner (one recently absent) are talking about the fish floating dead in the green water of one of Bondine's tanks. It was later explained to me that the fish had terminated a project on 'fish' and initiated one on 'death and decomposition'.

You! What are you talking about?

The boy (with genuine feeling), *The fish, sir! The fish. It's dead!* (Chorus: *Didn't you know that!*). Bondine follows 'the flow of interest'.

It's stopped breathing hasn't it? But we don't want to go into the circulation of the blood just now.

(A little puzzling this; but evidently one of those opportunist moments through which it is legitimate to digress in quest of clarity.)

Could a really clever scientist bring that fish back to life? It's dead. (Chorus of doubt. DRJ wonders about the question as put. Just what would count as evidence?)

What is the most important . . . What do we associate with the brain? (Continued puzzled responses.)

What, so we are told, is the state of—the difference—so we are told, between man and, you know that, the animals?

(A confusing question. The double qualification *so we are told* suggested to your observer that Bondine was after the Christian doctrine of the soul.)

It's bigger, sir (ventured one lad).

It's bigger, yes there is that.

(What's bigger? At this point the logic eluded me.)

But what is man's chiefest advantage over an animal?

The pupils were willing to consider this question, judging by their expressions. Bondine finds the pause threatening and jumps in with an answer.

Man can make use of his surroundings!

(It seemed a curious way of distinguishing between man and animal, or did 'chiefest advantage' imply degree rather than kind?)

The next tactical target in the drift of the lesson was the 'soul', or perhaps it was a target before, lost in the previous exchange. As before the method was the dialogue. The idea has to come from the pupils, with Bondine as a kind of mental sheep dog, leading them towards the right pen.

Coming back to this death business. What happens to fish when they die? (a sudden dart; the stabbing finger) *You!*

Girl: *They rot away, sir.*

They rot away! Nothing else? You!

Boy: *They sink to the bottom, sir.*

(Evidently they needed more direct clues.)

Anybody here . . . How many think there is something after death?

(Pupils reconsider briefly their own theological position. Bondine declaring that they are free to decide themselves on this private matter, nevertheless, pulls out *you* and *you* for an instant conversation.)

Right! We're in the TV studios again! (He fingers his chin like the *Panorama* chairmen.) *Why do you believe in God?*

(Incongruously) *You!*

(Inaudible discussion at the TV studio. Boys examine the dead fish, girls read 'Oliver Twist' with flickering disinterest.)

The captive audience are enjoined to listen carefully. The dialogue at the front livens a little. A boy carefully and knowingly summarises a book he has read. A book of goodness, the salvation of souls, and an ordinary family confirmed in their faith by a coincidental happening attributed to the Almighty (probably a Sunday School prize).

As an argument for the existence of God it is unanswerable.

The ideological opponent was at loss for a reply.

Keep on! Keep on! Keep it up! urges Bondine (both glance up at him anxiously). *Not at me! At the camera.* (Bondine glances towards me questioningly.)

(At this point I asked a group of girls near the back of the class what arguments had been put forward. They did not seem to know.)

At this point there was a change in the tack in the actual ad hoc design of the learning unit. This was acknowledged openly. . . .

Just a change in plan before we come on to the 'Oliver Twist' . . .

(Pondering this afterwards, I concluded that Bondine was dissatisfied with the TV studio confrontation and was determined to present the class (or me) with a well-tried example.)

Just before we go on to 'Oliver Twist'; you are a Newcastle United supporter. Are there any Liverpool supporters here?

The lad from Newcastle was introduced by reference to the 'social revolution' that brought his father to work in Liverpool, and encouraged to sing 'Bladon Races' to rapturous applause. Bondine explained that we were to look for local dialect, and that the front of the class had become the terraces of the football stadium. A goal had been scored after an unnoticed foul on Clements.

These are two typical football supporters. The match is in progress. Now argue together!

(They do so, effectively at first. Bondine draws the moral, which has little to do with dialect.)

You know the trouble? (confidentially). *It's gangs. People are not prepared to reason.*

(My thoughts became confused again. How could a demonstration of dialect by two individuals end up as a diatribe on gangs?) A boy in the front row offers a further observation:

Gangs at Manchester. They use knives, sir.

(Alas, gambit declined, or postponed.)

We'll discuss that in five minutes.

(A promise to remain unfulfilled.)

At this point Bondine passes my vantage point and offers an evaluative aside:

We're getting a good lesson from this! Plenty of room for discussion and writing.

Meanwhile the drama at the front has degenerated into mutual abuse (*Get lost, you long-haired git*) and lapel-holding. This did not get in the way of the sought-after 'meaning'.

I, we, everybody, need to think about this. You can see from this how easy it is to be swayed by silly arguments. That is PREJUDICE. How many of you have heard of the word?

(Four hands go up.)

You.

Girl (interestingly) *There is a book called 'Pride and Prejudice'.*

(This suggestion brings no response.)

You!

Boy *Sir, sir, biased referees, sir.*

(Again not the hoped-for response.)

You!

(No answer. Any answer obviously isn't good enough. You must guess what Sir is thinking.)

Bondine decides to move the pen rather than manoeuvre the sheep.

Have any of you heard of the colour bar?

(A difficulty here: we have lost contact with the tentative introduction to prejudice, uneasily rooted in the football playlet, and the children are plainly uncertain about the meaning of the term.) Come to cold, it must be approached within its own terms. One boy ventures that it means *testing colours on the telly.*

Yes. Anything else?

Another boy suggests a *club for coloured people.*

(Bondine did not realise that both these attempts were based on the need to interpret the word 'bar', which was not linked in the pupils' minds with the idea of prejudice.)

We are getting near it now!

(And I hadn't realised!)

What is near to a club for coloured people? A girl suggests a pub for coloured people.

Bondine abandons the dialogue and explains prejudice, choosing the first example rather than the second (the boys are still standing sheepishly at the front of the class grasping each other by the lapel).

So you've got two people there. It's black and white. One supports one team and one the other, so you've got no questions asked, and its PREJUDICE; so lets turn now to a bit of 'Oliver Twist.'

(A round of applause, in which it was possible to detect traces of irony.)

But before we start, what connection did 'Oliver Twist' have with the Industrial Revolution?

(Clearly an integrative thread; and one which excited a thin stir of interest and comment.)

Then comes the naming of parts.

You. Master of the workhouse . . .

(At this point my eye caught the blackboard, on which Bondine had written from time to time the odd key word. It read: 'BRAIN HEAVEN HELL SHEEP INDUSTRIAL REVOLUTION FISH'. I wondered whether in any sense it could be cited as a testimony to integration.)

The reading was unexpectedly lively. For the first time Bondine used a pupil's name:

Hepworth! If you don't follow on, I'll . . . have you in the workhouse with Oliver.

(This wit brought forth a slight chuckle, and smiles all round.)

Presently the play became the thing. Although reading from shared books, pupils were enjoined to *make it live*. They were in danger of *losing the atmosphere*.

(I glanced down at a previously-proffered wad of 'creative writing' on 'Birth'. 'I was plucked by rude hands', remonstrated one little lass 'and so much wanted to return to my mother's womb'. The entire batch was based on a number of Freudian ideas originating in discussion, but a genuine personal feeling was coming through.)

At this point Bondine joined me at the back of the class while the reading continued. This was one of the number of indications that my presence was critical in the situation although I tried not to respond to the language of gesture that he was trying to establish (amounting at times to an attempt to implicate me by implied consent in the tactics of the lesson). Odd mixture of pride and defensiveness.

Right off the top! I follow their mood and judge accordingly.

(This interesting summary of the tactics of the lesson did not stand up to analysis. All the changes in direction, with the exception of the dead fish, began as links in the mind of the teacher. It is arguable whether these links at any point added up to an intellectual structure, crossing discipline boundaries or otherwise.)

(Meanwhile the play-reading was running out of steam.)

Right. We'll stop this now. Close your books and do some writing. 'The Christmas Scene'. I'm not stopping you making it rhyme, but avoid it if you can. Paint a word picture so that the reader gets on to the beam of your thoughts.

(When the bell came a few minutes later one girl had written her name, the title and 'snow falls'.)

After the lesson I questioned Bondine on his Humanities interest.

I was pushed into this creative stuff. Mind you, I like it.

Pushed?

Yes, pushed by the headmistress. I'm a geographer really but my geography was too progressive—fieldwork and all that. The headmistress did not understand my field approach. She wanted me to adopt a ship. I refused, so I didn't get the job. Now I'm English.

5.3 David Jenkins
Saved by the Army

A report by DRJ on the visit paid by Form 4B of Bolthole Secondary Girls School to the Ethel Street Salvation Army Hostel (Project pack being taught: 'Outgroups in Society'; supervising teachers: Mary Brown and Ivan Richards).

DRJ was invited because of the relevance of this particular visit to 'Outgroups in Society' pack material. The coach left at 1 p.m., driven by one Brian Hudson who exerts an interesting influence on the team. (Mary Brown — *I like the new pack enormously, and felt I could give it to Brian.* (!) *He's Salvation Army you know. I said, 'sort this one out and arrange some suitable visits for us'. He's got contacts, you see.*) Brian is in coach hire, is friendly and operates at low rates. In discussing his choice, Brian suspects that he is motivated by a desire *to protect the girls from the seamy side of life.* He *positively refused* (!) to arrange a visit to the Ramla Street Men's Hostel, possibly reflecting an Army preference for the more PRO-conscious Ethel Street outfit.

The outward journey is jovial. The teachers and DRJ sit at the front. Brian plays pop medium-loud on the coach radio. All admonition is done by Brian. (*Sit down girls, or I'll stop the coach.*) The girls file out at the hostel and are counted in case any decide to stay.

The hostel itself is uncompromisingly depressing. A decrepit building in a rundown and derelict slum area, it maintains an authentic 'brands from the burning' image — piety in the face of squalor. A board outside proclaims in lamb-blood red that this is the 'Rehabilitation' Centre of the Salvation Army's Men's Social Services. The place is run by Captain Robert Pring and Mrs Pring.

The physical organisation of the building lends itself to an interpretation of three symbolic levels. Upstairs are the cubicles and bedrooms. We are invited to tour these and view the cramped bunks with fleur-de-lys and buckled-belt blankets, that must remind the inmates that these are SALVATION ARMY and not personal possessions. Indeed, there is little evidence anywhere of a personal signature (contrast student rooms in colleges) and I wondered if in fact it was not untypical of the regime that the tour of the charitable works involved what in other circumstances would be a clear invasion of privacy.

Source: D. R. Jenkins (1969). 'Saved by the Army'. Internal report from the Keele Integrated Studies Project, published here for the first time.

The second symbolic level is the 'middle earth', lying immediately below the dubious heaven. This is taken up by an enormous chapel and a kitchen that services more temporary human needs. Above the table and the pulpit is an enormously repulsive sentimental Christ (later referred to by Mary as *that signed portrait of Jesus with eyes that follow you everywhere*). Around the walls are the jolly choruses uneasily reminiscent of my Welsh chapel days:

> My sins are gone, gone, gone
> Far far far away.

and incomprehensibly:

> Cheer up ye saints of God
> There is nothing to worry about (!)

This would possibly have offered some reassurance to the fragmentary personalities in care were it not for the symbolic ritual associated with the passage of time (ever a noncomformist preoccupation). The building is full of massive clocks, going quite beyond the questionable need to know the time in this twilight world. Each clock carries a card with the uncompromising message:

> Time gentlemen please!
> Time to turn to Christ.

This reference to the pub-culture is later to seem even stranger. Although DRJ did not see it himself, Mary later assured him that the actual numerals on one of these timepieces were replaced by the letters DECISION TIME.

Whether the 'saints' in fact had anything 'to worry about' was puzzlingly difficult to establish. One would be tempted to describe the descent to the lower sweathouse as a guided tour under the direction of Captain Guido de Montefeltro, but the metaphor would be lost on those either unfamiliar with Dante's *Inferno* or inhibited from using it in this context. The working conditions downstairs are incredibly cramped, squalid and overcrowded, and it would be difficult to imagine them not in breach of the Factory Acts. The men work with anything from manic intensity to total disaffection. They sit cheek-by-jowl, elbow-to-elbow on 'piecework' production of paper bags for a supermarket. Phrases from Tawney's *Religion and the Rise of Capitalism* flicker across the consciousness. There is a smell of unwholesomeness that one or two girls try to work back within their conventional understanding. (*Captain and Mrs Pring must be wonderful people to work and live in this smell.*)

The men themselves? They were clearly and visibly the flotsam and jetsam of our society, unkempt, shuffling, often with deranged or vacant expressions. Most had histories of mental illness or psychological breakdown. A number had come from Worrell Street Hospital under a questionable referral system. (*The doctor will ring up and say 'Captain Pring, we have some that you could take'.*) They are docile and friendly, and respond touchingly to the thin trail of pretty girls tripping innocently through their part of the human icefield. (*How is it then? Aye, Aye? Where do you come from, love? Is them students of yours?*) They had the kind of contentment that is born of resignation. (*Can't grumble. It's all right here; You know what I mean?*).

DRJ is going back to Bolthole School to talk about James Burke. Jimmy has added just a little to that aching 'hollowness within' that results from any contact with real human plight. He is not in the main workshop but DRJ catches sight of his hollow-eyed and stubbled face peering out of a coalhouse-like extension, and goes over to join him. What is his job?

I peel potatoes. I don't work for 'him up there' but work for the cook. He complained without emphasis of the regime, glancing around carefully before continuing:

They're religious fanatics, you know what I mean? I've been around you see. Different when you've been around. It's all right. I'm content, you know what I mean? It's good enough for such as me.

He earns 10/- per week, but some of those on piecework are able to earn up to 30/-. This ceiling figure was later defended by the management as being due to some MSS benefit complications. On the surface it seems wrong for mental defectives to be on piecework in nineteenth-century factory conditions and picking up 30/- per week, but normal notions of dignity and responsibility may not apply. One wonders about the purely commercial aspects. (How much are the bags sold for? DRJ resolves to ask Mary Brown to find out.) Does the alleged dignity of manual (and profitable) labour rule out art therapy, for example?

Jimmy Burke described the institutional setting very much in a 'management and men' framework. His 'definition of the situation' contrasted quite remarkably with the official account. 'The men' resent the 'exploitation' and see themselves working for less than fair reward, but on the other hand they need the security and are unwilling to venture out. Apparently, in some of them, this lack of confidence is pathological, but in no sense is rehabilitation a firm goal of the management. This worried Ivan Richards more than anything else.

(*Oh, just one or two leave us,* explained Mrs. Pring, *but that's usually when a cousin or somebody insists on taking them. It's stupid really, as they soon find out when they can't cope. The men get worse than ever and end up back in Worrell Street.*)

The impression that overwhelmed your observer, quite literally, could be summed up in the words 'captive congregation'.

Let Mr Burke continue his story. *He's not like us; him up there* confided Jim (he never referred to Captain Pring by name, let alone rank). *You know? He tells us we are working for the Lord.* (He looked down unbelievingly at the bucket of peeled potatoes.) *The men down here,* he confided, *ARE WORKING FOR THEIRSELVES.*

. . . And all this compulsory chapel, you know what I mean?

DRJ: *Are you sure it's compulsory?*

Jim (slyly): *Well, they say, you're expected to go. You know what I mean?*

DRJ: *You mean it's easier to go?*

Jim: *I mean you've got to go.*

By the time your lurker rejoins the main group, the chapel houses all the Bolthole Girls, and Captain Pring is 'putting them in the picture' about Army work in general. Mrs Pring stands near the door, but chips in when she feels a contribution would be useful. The effect is less of informality than a sort of tag-wrestling. Captain Pring is talking about the 'For God's Sake Care' campaign (a brilliantly effective advertising agency job) and drawing attention to the photograph of the pregnant thirteen-year-old whose condition (we were solemnly informed) *arose directly out of her own father's deed.* A phrase to savour. Captain Pring is an attractive personality, open and brisk. His wife is oddly paradoxical; warmly mothering and sharply narrow at one and the same time. They are both paternalistic in their attitude towards their duties:

These are weak, childlike personalities.

We have to think for them.

The girls ask a number of questions about the gift of shirts that the school had made, and obviously feel pleased that they had helped. DRJ very politely and tentatively asks if religious service is compulsory. Both answer immediately and together that it is optional, quite optional. *But we have a full house every Sunday. Everybody comes because they want to,* explained Mrs Pring. It was a helpful reply.

DRJ asks, again with care, whether fragmentary personalities may not actually be put under pressure by all the clocks and emphasis on the responsibility for repentance. *Is Salvationism in fact inappropriate in what must in some respects resemble a mental hospital?*

But apparently DRJ had got it wrong again. There is no pressure. They sing choruses. It is all warm and reassuring.

> (Cheer up ye saints of God
> There is nothing to worry about.)

What are they, up there? DRJ asks Jim, feigning ignorance.

They're salvationists, you see; that's what they are, salvationists.

DRJ: *What does that mean?*

Well, not like Catholics. You know what I mean? They take all the bits of the Bible. You know what I mean? The bits about the blood. They're fanatics, you see. You know what I mean?

(I think I know what he means.)

Later Mrs Pring bemoans the cramped premises. (Jim had previously told me that most of them crept over to the Cobblers Tavern for the odd evening drink.) She wishes that there were recreational facilities.

DRJ: *Aren't there any pubs around here that the men can go to?*

Mrs Pring treats the matter with contempt. (*Oh we discourage that kind of thing. Besides some of them are on tablets, and it wouldn't do if they saw the others going.*) When she talked of her vocation, actually living there on a pittance, one could excuse her General Booth-like attitude to the drink problem, itself 'traditional'. She is quite literally, in her eyes, surrendering her life to God. One felt genuinely sorry that so much of what we had seen was for other reasons disturbing.

Eventually the farewells. In the coach on the way back, Ivan Richards draws attention good-humorously to a seedy shop uncompromisingly labelled RICHARDS BANKRUPTCY BARGAINS. The laughter is polite, and the girls thoughtful.

Later Mary and I talked at the school gates to a group of girls. They said they felt 'very depressed' but couldn't quite explain why. When we gave our comments, they acknowledged recognition, almost with surprise (*Yeah, that's just how I felt*). The disturbing element had been without a doubt the quality of the lives of the inmates. If these were the saved, they did not want to be taken to see the lost.

Ivan goes about some business and I talk to Mary in the staffroom. She is a very perceptive and interesting person. Her depression about it all expressed itself in symbolic anger at the big Jesus with the staring eyes. She thought it dreadful that the men had to live under His constant reproach.

DRJ: *How do you get on with the Bolthole missionary zeal?*

Mary was glad that I asked. Mrs Crispin (the headmistress) and Ivan are *like that* (she indicated by crooked fingers a degree of cosy intimacy). *They are both very religious. I find it hard not to scream in agony, but I don't because they'd only think I was Antichrist or something, and Ivan is marvellous. There's this missionary friend of Mrs Crispin, a Miss Crabtree. They're always trying to drag her in, whether it fits into the scheme or not.*

This is interesting, and roughly corresponds with my own position. The continued spectacle of homo sapiens doing good to his fellow creature may be reassuring, but it lacks intellectual bite. What causes social problems in the first place?

(Enter Ivan Richards.)

Ivan's response is surprisingly similar. He confesses an almost identical disquiet.

Ivan: *I'm Church of England, you see. Now make no mistake about it, they're doing a wonderful job and one not easily done by people of other persuasions* (at this point, scribbling openly, I actually asked him to slow down, which he did obligingly and without question). *My own approach is liberal. . . .*

He then moves on to his own diagnosis. The Army is 'culturally deprived'. It attracts 'narrow people' who are 'trapped in an attitude of mind'. It all results in 'a denial of legitimate pleasure'. Why not (he wonders) art or music or decoration? Is the drabness really necessary?

We discussed total institutions and I tell them about Jim. Could the girls understand this kind of problem? They think that they could. DRJ will join the teaching team in the near future.

Some tentative conclusions

Well, obviously an educative experience, but what came out of it?

1   A teaching opportunity. The depression felt by the girls needs to be pinned honestly and courageously to what they actually saw and not what they were expected to see.

2   Art work already organised with Betty Cranfield to give a painting to every man as a gesture on behalf of light and colour.

3   A very serious and extended appraisal by DRJ and the teachers that went on long after 4 p.m. What are the educational purposes of this kind of exercise? How can the different insights be organised and assessed? Is Mary a cynic? Is Ivan being defensive about his own religious image in the school? (He denied this one.) Is DRJ a squalid nuisance, badgering the faithful? How can kids understand and test their own reactions? Why did different elements in the situation point so dramatically in different directions?

A pretty large ragbag of puzzles, and in the end they were left for another day. Oh, I forgot to tell you. *The men are not allowed to smoke, except in the Gents.*

Evaluation as portrayal: the T-City report

The T-City report by Robert Stake and Craig Gjerde represents a significant shift in style, purpose and scale of reporting. In contrast to the analysis of single events featured above, the T-City report is an evaluation 'portrayal' of a whole summer programme. Although we repeat the caveat that Robert Stake's reputation as an evaluation theorist should not stand or fall on a single practical exercise, it is nevertheless interesting and useful to trace the extent to which it embodies Stake's central concepts. Certainly T-City reflects Stake's belief that the task of the responsive evaluator is to assemble and process judgements for a wide range of audiences rather than present some final adjudication on the programme. The task is self-consciously one of effective communication to a variety of audiences. The report assembles facts, the impressions of people in or near the programme, opinions, judgements and ratings. This gathering together (all in one place, so to speak) serves as a distillation and general documentation of the programme. Even Stake's teenage son, Ben, was taken along for the ride. His comments are included as a 'participant observer's perspective' which description could be read as a nice comment on the mystique of social science methodology! But whereas Ben Stake clearly enjoyed the T-City programme, his father and Craig Gjerde bring a high degree of detachment to their task.

The 1971 session of the Twin City Institute for Talented Youth was held on the campus of Macalester College in St Paul, Minnesota. The Institute is fast becoming an annual event. The evaluation was designed both to be 'formative' (with the evaluators 'helping the staff raise questions, gather evidence, and solve procedural problems')[1] and also 'summative', in the sense of providing at the Institute's end a final document that served as a record and a collection of evidence. The authors describe the T-City report as providing 'a thorough description . . . of the background against which the Institute activities take place, the activities themselves, and the results'.[2] It is also seen to be relativistic, processing and articulating a number of judgements. As such it is presented as 'a statement of numerous personal judgements of the Institute'.[3] Such a report is likely to be used by its different audiences in different ways.

1 Robert Stake and Craig Gjerde (1971). *An Evaluation of T-City—The Twin City Institute for Talented Youth, 1971.* Center for Instructional Research and Curriculum Evaluation, University of Illinois, p. 2.
2 Stake and Gjerde, *op. cit.*, p. 2.
3 Stake and Gjerde, *op. cit.*, p. 2.

The T-City report was designed to accord with the circumstances of the programme, the evaluators' contract with the sponsors, the previous experiences and preferences of the investigators, the budget, the perceived audience and the time available. Given the brief duration of the Institute (from 14 June to 30 July, 1971), the limited resources available to the evaluators (2 per cent of the total operating budget) and the size of the Institute (823 students, 56 teachers and 23 different courses) it is obvious that an exhaustive evaluation exercise would have been impossible. Hence the economy, even terseness, of the evaluation 'display'.

Arising out of the wide range of audiences for the report, much attention went into its physical layout and presentation. Within the constraints of a small budget, they were able to produce an informal-looking document, in booklet form, with some simple artwork. Other attempts at experimental format have been more bold. The final report of the Illinois Gifted Programs, for example, consists of a bright orange folder with several small coloured booklets and leaflets inside, each dealing with separate aspects of the programmes ('Judgements of worth', 'Kids and teachers talk about gifted classes', etc.). While not going quite this far in modularising their report, Stake and Gjerde have nevertheless produced the T-City report so that it can be read in independent sections and not necessarily in consecutive sequence. Altogether there are twenty-one short sections in the report. We reproduce a selection.

Finally it may be useful to draw particular attention to two of the sections featured below. These are rather cryptically titled 'An advocate's statement' and 'An adversary's statement'. There is an immediate echo of Levine's ideas, discussed in Section 4, that the inferences derived from natural field situations are best tested by formalising claims and counter-claims, arguments and counter-arguments. The dialectic form offers some hope that evaluation may, in Stake's terms, initiate discussion as well as reflect it. Unfortunately the content does not begin to measure up to the form, although its potential is obvious.

Suggestive analogies to this dialectic approach are found in allegorical drama and the medieval disputation, as well as the principle of advocacy in a court of law. Given the imaginative strength of the genre it is easy to predict a growing future for such quasi-legal or quasi-literary devices in evaluation reports. But whether the illuminative evaluators press the metaphor back towards the courtroom or the theatre may depend on the relative weight that they give to the claims of analysis and portrayal. Also as the format becomes better understood it may become less necessary to go in for nervous disclaimers ('prepared by T. Denny, not to indicate his opinion of T-City in 1971, but as a summary of the most damaging charges that might reasonably be made').[4] The disclaimer can be judged nervous precisely because it falls between the two positions that would

4 Stake and Gjerde, *op. cit.*, p. 14.

appear the most defensible. Denny does not defend his report as a collection of definitions — he refrains even from suggesting that the programme had any real-life adversaries.

Equally he is not offering a justification based on the advocate-at-law analogy. The prosecuting lawyer does not mumble apologetically that the 'damaging charges' he is bringing just could be labelled 'reasonable'. Denny is either bluffing or not bidding the full value of his hand. His comment on the T-City summer school itself could serve ironically as a comment on his own 'Adversary's statement': 'it is both less than it pretends to be and more than it wishes to be'.[5]

Bob Stake's 'Advocate's statement' is embarrassing for other reasons, trapping its author into mouthing uncritically the plainly élitist sentiments of the T-City operation. Advocacy, at least in law, deals crucially in evidence, although it may allow value-loaded assertion as part of a plea in mitigation. If that's the point Stake was making, we at least found it too subtle. Whether or not the whole of the T-City report is an advocate's statement is another question.

It may be useful to point out that although the report appeared under the names of Stake and Gjerde, many of the sections within it are written by other contributors. Where the authorship of sections we feature is given, it is indicated in footnotes.

---

5 Stake and Gjerde, *op. cit.*, p. 27.

5.4   Robert Stake and Craig Gjerde
An evaluation of T-City (The Twin City Institute for Talented Youth) 1971

Goals

The primary objective of the Twin City Institute is to create an educational programme that has strong academic and social appeal for students who possess a variety of artistic, language, scientific and leadership talents. The programme is not designed to repeat the regular school experience, nor to repair it for the disenchanted. The Institute is designed to create a special experience, cutting across student interests, group identification, idea exploration and the traditional school curriculum.

The Institute is willing to take risks. Teachers will develop courses that have their locus in theory or intuition rather than in more conventional curricular constructs. The staff will recognise that any programme, traditional or experimental, that chooses to work in an atmosphere of freedom, where trust is extended in social relationships, and where new ideas are encouraged, is vulnerable to charges of aimlessness and confusion.

The Institute staff — particularly teachers involved in such areas as the arts and social sciences, where truths are more subjective and where curricular goals are disputed — will develop programmes that emphasise inquiry. To create a compelling and stimulating learning environment, TCI teachers will develop problem-centred courses which encourage thought, inquiry and creativity.

Finally, teachers will introduce students to a total Institute environment. The Institute campus will be open to the young, sensitive, inquiring mind. Students will share with each other — through conversation and exhibit — their productions and products: telescopes, dances, poetry, music, foreign language, fêtes, newspapers, etc. Against a background of computer programming, art, pottery-making, dance, athletics, folk dancing, games, canoe building, students will meet and talk and create.

Having come interested in maths, science, poetry or archaeology, students will leave more committed to understanding and appreciating the

Source: R. E. Stake and C. L. Gjerde (1971). An Evaluation of T-City — The Twin City Institute for Talented Youth 1971, *Centre for Instructional Research and Curriculum Evaluation, University of Illinois. The extracts reproduced here are taken from pp. 4, 6, 14, 18-19, 22-3, 26-7. The report has been reprinted in* Four Evaluation Examples: Anthropological, Economic, Narrative, and Portrayal, *AERA Monograph Series on Curriculum Evaluation, No. 7. Chicago: Rand McNally, pp. 99-139.*

total concerns of men. Success for the Institute will mean that students and teachers have infected each other with a personal honesty and will have demonstrated that learning can truly be humanising.[1]

Goal evaluation. Evaluators have an obligation to raise the question, 'Were the right goals pursued?' Different people have different ideas, of course, as to what the right goals are. Still, goals and priorities should be evaluated.

Many teachers and curriculum specialists endorse T-City's increased emphasis on humanisation, personal awareness and problem-solving, and decreased emphasis on skills and knowledge. Some teachers and many parents disagree, wanting the school experience to pay off in answers to the classical academic questions — the kind that get students employed, admitted to college, etc. In the eyes of the evaluators, the T-City goals are worthy goals, suitably discussed and reasonably operationalised.[2]

Calendar

A calendar of events for T-City, 1971

Fall	Course planning by master teachers.
Spring	Selection of associate teachers; screening of students.
15 April	Notice to applicants about acceptance.
15 May	Macalester College — classes met, planned their summer.
14 June	T-City opened with 823 students, 56 teachers.
21 June	All Physical Science classes left for two weeks at Tamarac.
22 June	German class students (12) flew to Germany for one month.
1 July	Dance and Music combined to present a programme; Russian classes crowned a czar, other classes joined in.
9 July	Sesame class visited a Minneapolis City Council meeting.
16 July	Language picnic; ragtime pianist in music class.
22 July	T-City Board Luncheon at Macalester; open house; AIM Indian group halted Archaeological dig at Welch, Minnesota.
26 July	Environmental Accounting on a three-day trip to Chicago.
28 July	Theatre show 'Rip-Off'; Dance production; Poetry reading.
29 July	Art display; Poetry reading; Music on the Mall; Interpretative dance; Evening theatre production for parents.
30 July	Institute ended; Language groups performed folk dances.

Monday, 19 July: A typical day at the Institute

Around 8 a.m. students started gathering in the bus area: the Sesame II class and combined French and German classes left for a Cannon River canoe trip with Wilderness class guides. Rest of Wilderness class left for

1   The above passage was written by Charles Caruson, Director, T-City.
2   The above passage was written by Robert Stake, Evaluation Specialist, CIRCE.

Isle Royale on an eight-day back-packing trip. Biology classes went to St Paul Ramsey Hospital for a series of physical tests.

About 8.15 or 8.30 other classes started in classrooms on the Macalester campus. Most of these classes took a short break about 10.30 and then continued until 12.00 or 12.30. Fifteen students started on a bike trip along the Mississippi River at 11.30. Some time during the morning, Basic Computer challenged Environmental Accounting to a volleyball game. A few students played tennis, frisbee, softball and went swimming later in the day.

After classes, opponents in the chess tournament started finding each other. At 1.00 Dr Mitra demonstrated the use of acrylics, and maths students began constructing a geodesic dome. At 2.00 Avi Davis' dance class met in the old gym.

Art rooms were busy with painting and pottery; astronomy students were grinding lenses for their telescopes; a few science students were finishing their redwood and fibreglass canoes. Poetry students were in the office duplicating their 'broadsides' for distribution to people in the streets, and there were other activities.

By 1.30 most of the 150 students who stayed for afternoon activities on campus had departed for home, except for the canoe builders who stayed until six or seven in their race against time.

Collective perspective (students)

The following was taken from the tally of the Student Final Critique Sheet. About 560 students filled out the sheet during the final week of the Institute.

We would like to know how the Institute *class activity* differs from the activity of classes of your regular school.

		No difference	Regular school	Institute
1	Which holds students more responsible for work?	12%	68%	20%
2	Which encourages students to 'show off' more?	36%	42%	22%
3	In which do students try out OWN ideas more?	9%	4%	87%
4	In which is more time wasted?	31%	47%	22%

And how do your *teachers* compare?

		No difference	Regular school	Institute
5	Which explain things better?	38%	11%	51%

6	Which know the subject matter better?	39%	7%	54%
7	Which understand students better?	28%	6%	66%
8	Which resist the urge to talk all the time?	42%	16%	42%

Rate the following features of the Institute as to how important they were to you:	Extremely important	A little important	Not important
27 Close contact with teachers	66%	29%	5%
28 Close contact with students	80%	17%	3%
29 Opportunity to study for extended period each day	46%	40%	14%
30 Trip to camp, canoe trip, etc.	46%	40%	14%
31 Exhibits, performances put on for 'outsiders'	36%	30%	33%
32 Diversity of students	60%	35%	5%
33 Afternoon symposia	28%	52%	20%
34 Concern that these people have for human problems	69%	26%	5%
35 Faith that these people have that these problems can be solved	69%	26%	5%
36 Being treated as a mature person	85%	13%	2%

Here are several goals of the Institute. Please rate the Institute on how well it met these goals, even if you only have a vague idea of what the whole Institute was doing.

	Excellent	Barely passing	Failed	Don't know
37 Provide an educational programme that is challenging, stimulating, relevant	86%	10%	0%	4%
38 Provide master teachers with the highest ability-to-teach	81%	9%	2%	9%
39 Provide younger teachers with a good opportunity to learn more about teaching	69%	14%	1%	16%
40 Develop curriculum ideas that can be used in regular schools	67%	13%	3%	17%

Collective perspective (faculty)

In the final week of the Institute all master and associate teachers were asked to complete a four-page questionnaire. About three-quarters of the teachers did so.

The master teachers listed the major satisfactions in T-City 71 as the opportunity to teach the way they wanted to; to work with highly motivated, able students; and to make the learning-experience a humanising encounter. The associate teachers emphasised these things plus the fact that the Institute was a major learning opportunity for them. Both groups were strong in their praise of T-City.

The least satisfactory aspects of the experience these teachers had were the administrative arrangements (too vague, too little pre-planning) and the workload (too much expected). Some master teachers objected to the large number of students enrolled in their classes. Almost all the associate teachers reported some unpleasant interpersonal experience during the summer.

Special features drawing approval were the May orientation sessions and Wilderness trips. New arrangements that teachers objected to were the admission of junior high students and the foreign language travel alternative.

Among the suggestions for improvement were the following:
1   Increase involvement of university students as teaching aides.
2   Better communication about T-City events, deadlines.
3   Less involvement in formal evaluation.
4   Extend the opportunities to suburban and out-state students.

By and large the faculty responses in 1971 were similar to what they had been in 1970. There seemed to be better communication across faculties in 1970 but better communication to and from the Directors in 1971. Communication remains as an important problem.

Most of the master teachers were pleased with what they had done, but still would like to offer a different course or teach the course differently next year. They strongly hoped that T-City could be located at Macalester again in 1972.

To detail their activities for the summer and to react more thoroughly to such evaluation issues, each master teacher submitted a synopsis called by Caruson 'The Gleanings'. These reports were loaded with recommendations for summer courses and Institutes.

The lighthouse school

The following is a partial consideration of the ways that T-City has influenced instructional programmes in Minneapolis schools. It is a personal statement based on my work as Secondary Social Studies Consultant for the Minneapolis Public Schools and my discussions with Institute teachers and social studies department chairmen.

It is especially appropriate to ask if social studies teachers not directly associated with the Institute are affected by T-City offerings in social science. This field involves virtually all secondary school students and some

300 teachers in the district. Furthermore, dissatisfaction with current social studies programmes has been expressed by students, teachers and administrators. National trends offer a variety of conflicting perspectives and approaches. In short, the need for change is felt, decisions about innovation in this field must be worked out locally and the Twin Cities Institute has engaged in structuring learning experiences that might serve as models for new social studies courses.

The quality of recent T-City work in the social sciences suggests that there would be merit in public school consideration of Institute offerings. The strong points in the T-City effort would appear to be —
— Students and teachers have actively explored the urban environment beyond the classroom.
— Special attention has been given to student interaction and inter-action between students and teachers.
— Questions dealing with values have been sensitively and deliberately explored as an integral part of the learning of concepts and skills of social inquiry.

Nevertheless, the impact of these efforts in Minneapolis high schools would appear to have been negligible because of the following factors:

1   The Institute has developed as a unique institution providing for the special needs of a particular group of young people. This goal has resulted in new approaches and roles different from those existing in the schools.

2   Public school personnel acknowledge the 'special' and valuable quality of Institute offerings. However, administrators and teachers have not seen the Institute as providing models of what might be done in their classrooms. Teacher knowledge of Institute offerings is minimal and interest in further information has not been expressed, even though there is interest in programmes from curriculum development centres.

3   Institute teachers tend to view their T-City experience positively and they thoughtfully explore the implications of this experience for their work in the schools. The autonomy and isolation of their regular teaching situations does not provide the exchanges that would encourage them to assume leadership in the reconstruction of departmental programmes. Several of these teachers are concerned about their inability to communicate their greater awareness of the complexity of teaching–learning processes to colleagues in ways that would further their own reflections and growth. The resulting frustration would appear in a few instances to have contributed to decisions to leave the regular classroom for graduate study and other positions in education.

4   Students who have been involved in the Institute apparently do not return to their schools as agitators for change. Students, like their regular teachers, apparently see the Institute as a unique experience separate from the standard school programme. It might be hypothesised that these talented students have learned how to be successful in the public school environment and they resume their previous student roles when they

return to the settings in which these behaviour patterns have proven successful.

It would appear that the culture of the schools and the unique features of the Institute tend to promote the separation of these experiences. Special programmes like T-City are isolated from the ongoing business of the schools because of expectations that students, school personnel and Institute faculty have for both the public schools and the Institute. Explicit efforts to use the Institute's experiences as models for improving the public schools must be devised if a development and demonstration function is desired. Even then success cannot be guaranteed. Efforts to use the regular Minneapolis summer school as a place to test new ideas and to serve as an in-service laboratory for curriculum development and the adaptation of materials from national social studies projects have met with very limited success.

If the Institute is to serve a more effective role in dealing with the urgent need for innovation in the social studies and in other curricular areas, detailed planning involving a range of persons — students, teachers, administrators, chairmen and consultants — must take place. It must be clear that any effort to use the Institute as a development and demonstration centre for curricular revision might very well compromise many of the unique qualities now included in the programme as it serves the special needs of talented students.

Again, it must be stressed that these are personal observations focusing on social science programmes. In those curricular areas such as computer mathematics the T-City experience may be a significant element in a broader innovative effort. The Institute teachers of computer maths also teach these courses in their schools and they instruct other teachers in staff development courses aimed at establishing similar courses. Also, their work has continued into the school year in ways that have significantly influenced their departments. However, the required social studies courses involving large numbers of teachers and all students in each school have not felt the impact of the T-City experience.[3]

An advocate's statement

No visitor who took a long, hard look at T-City 71 kept his scepticism. A young visitor knows how precious it is to discover, to be heard, to belong. An older visitor knows the rarity of a classroom where teachers and students perceive each other as real people. To the non-visitor it doesn't seem possible that a summer school programme can deliver on all these promises to over 800 kids, but T-City 71 did.

3 The above passage was written by Robert Berry, Curriculum Supervisor, Rochester Public Schools.

Every curriculum specialist fears that by relaxing conduct rules and encouraging student independence they may be saying goodbye to the hard work and hard thinking that education requires. T-City 71 teachers and students made learning so attractive, so purposive, that free-ranging thought returned again to curricular themes: awareness of the human condition, obstacles to communication, ecological interactions, etc.

T-City excels because of its staff. Its students give it movement. Its directors give it nurture. Its teachers give it movement, nurture and direction. It would be incorrect to say that Mr Caruson, Mr Rose, and the teachers think alike as to the prime goals and methods of education, but collectively, they create a dynamic, humanistically-bent, academically-based curriculum.

The quality of teaching this summer was consistently high, from day to day, from class to class. Some of the teachers chose to be casual, to offer 'opportunities', to share a meaningful experience. Others were more intense, more intent upon sharing information and problem-solving methods. Both kinds were there, doing it well.

The quality of the learning also was high. The students were tuned in. They were busy. They responded to the moves of their teachers. They improvised, they carried ideas and arguments, indignations and admirations, to the volleyball court, to the Commons, to the shade of campus elms and Cannon River oaks. The youngsters took a long step towards maturity.

True, it was a costly step. Thousands of hours, thousands of dollars and at least a few hundred aggravations. But fit to a scale of public school budgets — and budgets for parks, interstate highways and weapons of war — T-City 71 rates as a BEST BUY. Eight hundred kids, give or take a few, took home a new talent, a new line of thinking, a new awareness — a good purchase.

It cannot be denied that other youngsters in Minneapolis and St Paul deserve an experience like this. They should have it. Some say, 'T-City is bad because it caters to the élite.' But a greater wisdom says, 'Any effort fixated on giving an equal share of good things to all groups is destined to share nothing of value.' For less advantaged youth, a more equitable share of educational opportunities should be guaranteed. But even in times of economic recession, opportunities for the talented should be protected.

T-City 71 has succeeded. It is even a best buy. It satisfies a social obligation to specially educate some of those who will lead — in the arts, in business, in government, in life. The teachers of T-City 71 have blended a summer of caring, caprice, openness, and intellectual struggle to give potential leaders a summer of challenge.[4]

---

4   The above passage was written by Robert Stake, Evaluation Specialist, CIRCE; as he himself puts it, 'prepared by R. Stake, not to indicate his opinion of the Institute, but as a summary of the most positive claims that might reasonably be made'.

An adversary's statement

T-City is not a *scandalum magnatum*. But it is both less than it pretends to be and more than it wishes to be. There is enough evidence at least to question certain facets of the Institute — if not to return a true bill against it. Costly, enlarging, innovative, exemplary: these Institute attributes are worthy of critical examination.

How costly is this Institute? Dollar costs are sufficient to give each group of six students $1000 to design and conduct their own summer experience. Over 100 Upward Bound students could be readied for their college careers at Macalester. About twenty-five expert curriculum specialists could be supported for half a year to design and develop new curricula for the high school.

What is the cost of removing 800 talented leaders from the local youth culture? What is the cost of widening the experience gap between Institute students and their parents? . . . and their teachers in 'regular' high school? . . . and their non-Institute friends? Not enough here to charge neo-Fascist élitism. Enough to warrant discussion.

The Institute abounds with self-named innovators and innovations, with alternatives to the business-as-usual education of high schoolers. Note that the Institute is not promoted as an exemplary alternative *to* schooling. It seeks to promote the development of alternative forms of education *for* schools. And it is failing to do even that job. What is T-City doing to demonstrate that the T-City style of life could be lived in schools as we know them? Where in the regular school is the staff so crucial to the life of the Institute? . . . the money? . . . the administrative leadership? Where are the opportunities for the teachers, principals, superintendents to come and live that life that they might come to share in the vision? . . . and where are the parents? T-City should be getting poor grades on affecting the regular school programme.

There are other dimensions of T-City that puzzle the non-believer:

How long can in-class 'rapping' continue and still qualify as educative self-exploration? Are there quality control procedures in effect during the summer programme? For example: when one-third to one-half a class is absent from a scheduled meeting, should not that be seen as an educational crisis by the instructor?

What does T-City do to help students realise that the Institute standards are necessarily high; that the regular school norms and expectations do not count; that a heretofore 'best' becomes just a 'so-so'? There are unnecessarily disheartened students in T-City.

Is it unreasonable to expect that more than two of twenty-two teachers or associate teachers would have some clear idea or plan for utilising T-City approaches or curricula in their regular classrooms next fall?

Few students—or faculty—understand the selection procedures employed to staff the teaching cadre and to fill the student corps. Why should it be a mystery?

The worst has been saved for last. This report concludes with an assertion: the absence of a crucial dimension in the instructional life of T-City, that of constructive self-criticism, is a near-fatal flaw. The observation and interview notes taken by the adversary evaluator over four days contain but five instances of students engaging in, or faculty helping students to become skilful in, or desirous of, the cultivation of self-criticism. The instances of missed opportunities were excessive in my judgement. Worse: when queried by the writer, faculty and students alike showed little enthusiasm for such fare. Is it too much to expect from Institute participants after but four weeks? Seven may be insufficient. The staff post mortem, 'Gleanings', are a start—but it seems odd to start at the end.

The paucity of occurrence is less damning than the absence of manifest, widespread intent. Certain classes accounted for all the instances observed. They did not appear to be accidental. The intent was there. An Institute for talented high school youth cannot justifiably fail to feature individual and group self-criticism.[5]

5   The above passage was written by Terry Denny, Evaluation Specialist, CIRCE; as he himself puts it, 'prepared by T. Denny, not to indicate his opinion of T-City 1971, but as a summary of the most damaging charges that might reasonably be made'.

Your friendly neighbourhood evaluator: Center for New Schools at Metro High School

A very interesting evaluation strategy has been developed by Urban Research Corporation and Center for New Schools in Chicago. We look at their evaluation of Metro High School [The Chicago Public High School for Metropolitan Studies], an alternative school without walls operating from a down-town base in the Loop. It is in marked contrast to the necessarily condensed fieldwork that lay behind the T-City report.

Behind Urban Research Corporation and Center for New Schools is a continuity of personnel and a development of the ideas that now form the basis of the CNS evaluation model. Urban Research Corporation was founded in 1968 in response to the view that the 'private sector' had a role to play in averting the urban crisis — social, economic and educational. The educational division of Urban Research Corporation offered its services to schools undertaking curriculum development or extending the community role of urban schools. The URC consultants had a particular interest in curriculum evaluation and although they favoured a mixed model [that included conventional testing] the main thrust was within a social anthropology paradigm, and aimed both at formative feedback to the school community and writing an interpretative documentary account of the innovations. But their role-aspirations were towards closeness rather than detachment, seeking direct involvement as 'partner' in the planning, operation and evaluation of the programmes.

The school that is described in the evaluation reports we feature is interesting in its own right. Metro High School has been in its brief tempestuous years to date one of the most highly-visible educational experiments in the United States.[1] As one of the first-generation 'schools without walls' an immediate comparison is with the Parkway Programme in Philadelphia. But while Parkway was, at least in concept, more narrowly located [the Benjamin Franklin Parkway is a boulevard leading into the central business district of Philadelphia, along which many of the city's cultural institutions are clustered] Metro has created a diverse city-wide curriculum, using participating organisations and cooperating teachers as well as its own staff members.[2] Doctors, lawyers, astronomers, actors, social workers and very many others have worked in some capacity in the Metro programme.

1   See David Jenkins and Peter Raggatt (1974). *Alternative for Urban Schools,* Block 5 of the Open University 'Urban Education' course (E351). Milton Keynes: The Open University Press.

2   Metro High School began tentatively as the Summer School in the Loop, but when established spilled over into other parts of Chicago, including the southside black ghetto.

Urban Research Corporation was under contract to the Chicago Board of Education to help establish the Metro programme, but then phase out and allow the school to be self-sufficient. About this time Center for New Schools was emerging, marsupial-like, from the pouch of Urban Research Corporation and establishing its own style. When Donald Moore, Thomas Wilson, Richard Johnson and Steve Wilson joined the newly-established Center for New Schools, they worked out with their colleagues a 'CNS School Evaluation Model'[3] which stressed three underlying principles: [1] The school community as co-evaluator. [2] Evaluation as formative feedback. [3] An eclectic multi-method approach to evaluation. Center for New Schools continues the interest in illuminative evaluation.[4] The most striking feature of the CNS approach is its aspiration to combine an ethnographic research methodology with a willingness to operate as change agents in the situation under review. Indeed, Center for New Schools now sees itself first and foremost as a technical assistance group and has initiated research into TAG comparative methodology.[5]

Gordon Hoke made reference in Section 4 to Michael Scriven's comment on the interest that the literature on change-agency could hold for the professional evaluator. Change-agency apart, we have already argued that implicit in participant observation is the researcher's involvement in the situation under study. This may appear a self-evident truth, but it is an important one. Involvement is rarely simply a question of establishing entry into the research situation. The URC/CNS dilemma is that they want both to be 'honest friends' and retain external credibility, particularly as they have been under pressure to produce statements of endorsement, of the kind that satisfy school boards. The honest friend, like the honest clinical psychiatrist, needs a basis in reality for the advice, help and support he offers. It would be simplistic and misleading to regard an ethnographic research methodology and technical assistance as formally incompatible.

The overall design of the Metro research and evaluation had two parts:

1 A long-term comparison of 110 students randomly selected to attend Metro with 110 students still attending conventional schools. This included student questionnaires and in-depth interviews with a sub-sample. In May 1970 short interviews were conducted with the sub-sample concerning issues raised by the first semester of operation. In addition students were encouraged to keep journals.

2 A short-term formative study using a variety of techniques including anthropological observation, semi-structured and unstructured interviews, tape-recording of key meetings, student evaluation forms concerning tuition and counselling, and memo-writing around identified issues [e.g.

3 Center for New Schools (1974). 'The CNS school evaluation model', mimeo.

4 See Center for New Schools (1974). 'A review of the use of ethnographic techniques in educational research', mimeo, featured in Section 4.

5 See Center for New Schools (February 1974). 'On-site technical assistance as a facilitator of educational change: a comparative study of five technical assistance groups', mimeo.

student-initiated learning activity]. During this time there was also a case-study of a major crisis in the school [the loss of the school downtown headquarters].

It is tempting to generalise from the evaluation strategy for Metro High School, and suggest that alternative or illuminative evaluation techniques are particularly appropriate for atypical schools, not easily contained within framing assumptions other than their own. There are several reasons why this should be the case. Firstly, alternative schools like Metro are high risk innovations, and best evaluated in a climate tolerant of initial mistakes, and with a commitment to successive improvement. The question is whether commitment is possible without compromise. Secondly, specifically urban programmes [like Metro's programme of 'metropolitan studies'] can scarcely avoid a contextual emphasis, calling for an interpretative description of the school's educational milieu. Thirdly, any authentic attempt to involve the school community as co-evaluator, and work within its values and beliefs, demands the 'natural communication' of the ethnographer. The results of psychometric testing all too frequently have low accessibility to teachers and curriculum developers. Finally it can be argued that the sheer complexity of alternative schools and programmes viewed in a wide cultural and political setting needs an evaluation that validates a wider range of questions than is allowed by the conventional focusing of evaluative questions on student learnings.

We feature three presentations by the evaluation team. These were intended for different primary audiences. The first is an internal memo to the Metro staff; the second is written largely for educational administrators and those involved in policy decisions that may have some bearing on the continuation of the Metro experiment; the third report has as its reference group a community of research peers interested in the underlying problems of alternative schooling. The three presentations appear under the following titles:

1   'Internal memo to the Metro staff, 27 March 1970'.
2   'Metro High School: report on the third semester, February to June 1971'.
3   'Student involvement in decision-making in an alternative high school'.

5.5 Donald Moore and Thomas Wilson
Internal memo to the Metro staff, 27 March 1970

Students' reactions to learning units

Below we have presented some information that we have collected as part of the evaluation effort. This information comes from observations, interviews with students and student unit evaluation forms. Our purpose in collecting and presenting this information is to raise questions about what is going on in the school in the light of its stated goals. We hope that teachers will find this information useful to clarify the kinds of activities they want to undertake with students during the rest of this cycle and during the second cycle.

1 First, the information below is based on the unit evaluation forms that the students filled out.

The first question we asked them was *What do you like about the unit you like most?* They cited the following characteristics:
(a) Previous success in this area—they liked units where they had experienced previous academic success.
(b) New field—they liked work in fields where they had no previous experience so that there was no prior judgement on their part as to how well they could do in that area.
(c) One of the most common responses was that students like units where they have a definite sense of achievement; where they felt they were getting some place. There are two aspects to this response. In some cases students were perceiving organisation or disorganisation in a unit. In other cases students were reacting to the fact that the unit covered something that was unconventional. This is especially true in traditional academic areas where students had very well defined expectations as to what should go on in the unit.
(d) Related to (c) is a perception on the part of the students that the unit was cumulative from week to week. Even in cases where individual classes were well planned or interesting students became uneasy if they couldn't see a cumulative pattern of activity over a period of time.

Source: D. R. Moore and T. A. Wilson (1970). 'Internal memo to the Metro staff, 27 March 1970'. In D. R. Moore, T. A. Wilson and R. Johnson, The Metro School. A Report on the Progress of Chicago's Experimental 'School Without Walls', *Chicago: Urban Research Corporation, pp. 77-8.*

(e) Students liked units where they felt a strong personal attachment to the teacher who was working with them.
(f) Students liked units where they felt the teacher knew their individual strengths and weaknesses rather than only liking them in general as a person.
(g) Students liked units where they were working on individual projects.
(h) Students liked units where there was action and actual doing—not just talking. Many students react negatively to talking of any kind whether it be lecture or discussion. This includes discussions with individuals that many of the teachers and also many of the other students would perceive as being highly interesting.

What did students dislike about units that they liked least?
(a) They disliked units they perceived as being disorganised.
(b) They disliked units in which they felt there was too much talking. They responded especially negatively to lectures, but as was pointed out above, many students also responded negatively to long discussions.
(c) They disliked units in which they had experienced previous failure. For some students this factor was so important that they have not yet attended certain classes in which they have had negative experiences in their previous schools.
(d) As pointed out above, students disliked units which violated their expectations about what should go on in this type of academic activity.

What are some things the school doesn't offer now that the students feel should be offered in the next cycle? From the questionnaire and from talking with students, certain areas were mentioned by a large number of people:
1   The largest expressed desire was for work in various areas of physical education, ranging from baseball to swimming to skin diving to horseback riding.
2   Various aspects of psychology of interpersonal and social relations.
3   Home economics.
4   Auto shop.
5   Different types of volunteer activities, including volunteer work in hospitals and volunteer work in the tutoring of younger children.
6   Various aspects of mysticism and extrasensory perception.
7   Other areas mentioned by more than one student included modern dancing and radio production and broadcasting.
    In answer to the question 'What's your biggest gripe about the school?' the main impression that comes across is the students' general strong positive feeling towards the school. Even though we were trying to probe to get some negative statement about a particular aspect of the programme, about half of the students said nothing is wrong, nothing at all. This points to the fact that most students in the school have something they like about the school. It may be a course, it may be a particular teacher, it

may be the counselling group, it may be the relationship with their counsellor outside of their counselling group, it may be their job. But in any case, almost every student seems to have some strong point of contact with the school. Of those things which were complaints — in addition to the aspects of classes cited above — the most complaints were voiced about the all-school meeting and about other kids who don't work or who don't seem to understand the responsibilities that come with being part of the Metro programme.

2   These generalisations about the unit information forms for specific courses seemed to hold true across almost all units. First of all, students tended to dislike units strongly when they agreed that they *'didn't get much done in the course,'* when they agreed that *'things are pretty disorganised in this class'* or when they disagreed with the statement *'the course is well organised and all the teachers involved in it work closely together.'* On the other hand, students tended to like courses where they felt that *'the teacher had a very good idea about what my strengths and weaknesses are in this class.'* Few students checked this as being true about their particular classes, although almost all students said that *'the teachers are very friendly to students and talk to them outside of class.'*

Based on our observations up to the point when the unit information form was administered and on the results of the course information form, we found that relatively few classes have involved much cooperative student planning. Relatively few students agreed with the statement *'we have taken time in class in which the students have planned what we are going to do.'* Perhaps closely related to this is the fact that few students feel they can tell teachers what they don't like about a particular class. They feel that they can have a friendly relationship with a teacher, and yet they are reluctant to speak directly with him about matters that have to do with classwork and education. This seems to represent a specific barrier that must be broken down if there is to be effective cooperation and planning between students and teachers.

Relatively few students checked the statements *'I have a project of my own that I am working on in this class'* or *'the teacher has helped me find things I can learn about this subject outside of class.'* When students checked these statements as being true, they seemed to be generally quite satisfied with the course.

5.6 Urban Research Corporation
Metro High School: report on the third semester, February to June 1971

I Introduction

This report describes the development of the Metro programme during the school's third semester, February 1971 to June 1971. It attempts to be consistent with three crucial principles of the school:

1 The history of the school should be continuously and carefully analysed.

2 The programme of the school should be modified in light of that history so that it may continuously move closer to its goals.

3 The key people in terms of performing an analysis of the programme's history and in making useful programme modifications are the staff and students directly participating in the programme.

The commitment of the school to useful experimentation and to learn from its own successes and failures give the school great strength. This process requires frank discussions of what has happened and strong recommendations for what should happen.

This report comes at the end of an almost two-year period of contractual relationships between the Chicago Board of Education and the Urban Research Corporation. It will provide an overview of the school's development to this point, and indicate issues that are key to the school's continued success.

II The third semester: what happened

Despite the fact that the goldfish froze in their bowl during the first day of the semester, the staff and students at Metro looked forward to relative quiet and continued development of the school. . . .

On 18 March, 1971, at three o'clock in the afternoon Mr Blackman, Metro's Principal, received a phone call ordering him to vacate the Metro headquarters site because the building management was not in compliance with the City fire code. Metro operated without a headquarters site for thirty-seven days. The 'space crisis' became the most dramatic and probably the most significant event of the third semester. Other important

Source: Urban Research Corporation (October 1971). 'The Chicago High School for Metropolitan Studies: a report on the third semester, February to June 1971', mimeo. The extracts reproduced here are taken from pp. 1-3, 4-5, 6, 9, 10, 11, 12-13, 20-24.

events were the resignation of the physical education teacher; the establishment of the Student Support Services; the development of the Metro Parents' Action Council; the development of the Participating Organisations Council; the failure to receive accreditation; the debate about further expansion; the anticipated departure of the Urban Research Consultants; planning for the summer workshop and for the fourth semester; and the graduation of the first senior class. While many of these events and issues are closely intertwined, each will be treated separately.

A. *The resignation of the physical education teacher.* The resignation of the physical education teacher on 30 January raised several issues which were important to the third semester. The teacher left for a situation that promised him more support for an adequate physical education programme than had been available at Metro. The initial work of designing a programme for the diverse interests and talents of the Metro students had been completed. Scheduling and space problems were almost solved. The remaining problems were:

1   The lack of support for the physical education programme from the Central Office.

2   The fact that Metro's lack of accreditation was interpreted by the Central Office to exclude Metro teams from any kind of competition.

3   This teacher was very effective with many of the black students in the programme who had not been effectively reached by the programme. He felt that his attempts to get the staff to confront the issue of the educational needs of black students were not very successful.

His departure was difficult for the school because he was held in such high esteem.

B. *The Student Support Services.* The Student Support Services were designed by Richard Johnson, Urban Research Consultant, with the staff of the school. They were designed to make the Metro programme as effective as possible in dealing with each individual student. The Services concentrated on students who were judged from attendance records and/or teachers' reports to not be coping effectively with the educational programme. The Services were not designed to provide immediate solutions to the complex problems of individual student lives. Rather, the purpose of the Services was to provide an institutional and systematic response to students who were having difficulties adjusting to Metro. It was considered very important that the school make a response to individual students, and that that response be subject to continual development based on actual experience. The full system for the Student Support Services was described in *The second semester report.* . . .

C. *The space crisis.* While the space crisis temporarily distracted the school, . . . the net result of the crisis was to greatly strengthen the programme. A chronology of the crisis is presented in Appendix 1.

Analysis of this chronology suggests that the crisis had the following long-range effects on the development of the programme:

1   The staff emerged with a new confidence in its ability not only to run Metro on a day-to-day basis, but also to continually strengthen the programme.

The staff handled the crisis with great skill. Their first concern was to make sure that the school did not close, but to continue in its basic function of providing significant education for its students. The Herculean task of finding space for 111 class periods which had been held at the headquarters, of insuring effective communication with students by calling them weekly on the phone, of completing the registration process, of spending hours in discussions to make plans and decisions was performed while continuing their usual functions of teaching and working with cooperating teachers.

After the first week it became apparent that the school would remain open as long as the staff itself remained committed to that goal.

2   Strong city-wide support for Metro was demonstrated. Parents coalesced in support of the school. The participating organisations provided unexpected support in the form of temporary space and in the form of supportive statements to Dr Redmond about the school and about their participation in the programme. Friends of Metro who asked how they could help included many of the important community organisations in the city. The extended newspaper and television coverage was also supportive.

3   The school was successful in raising several important issues which were both important to the resolution of the crisis and which had plagued the school from its beginning. The two most important issues were: (a) The need for decentralised power so that programme participants could in fact make crucial day-to-day decisions. (b) The ineffective support, with some notable exceptions, which the school had received from the line administration of the Board. Workable solutions were proposed to these problems:

(i) Empower the Metro Policy Board to make decisions in designated areas. The role of line staff would shift from having to approve of every decision made at the school level before it could go into effect, to one of reviewing decisions of the Policy Board in light of the goals of the school.

(ii) Establish an experimental school's expeditor who would be accountable to the Deputy Superintendent and would aid experimental schools to secure meaningful support from the Central staff. . . .

While it is too early to assess the success in implementing these proposals, the school was successful in raising these issues so that they could be addressed by decision-makers.

When students returned to the headquarters building thirty-seven days after they had been evicted, they found that their school was stronger because together they had fought for its survival along with the staff, parents and participating organisations and they had won. Dr Joseph Hannon, Assistant Superintendent for Facility Planning, who provided much help to the school in the last two weeks of the crisis, wrote, 'Your buttons which have the inscription "Metro Lives" are appropriate only because YOU have kept it alive.'

D. *The Parents' Action Council.* Attempts by parents and by the staff to form a parents' organisation had basically failed before the crisis. At the parents' meeting on 25 March to explain the space crisis, the parents made a decision that they must develop an organisation that would be effective for the duration of the crisis and would be permanently organised to aid and support the school. An *ad hoc* committee on structure was organised and met regularly for several weeks developing structure and by-laws. . . .

The parents provided important resources to the school in terms of technical assistance, manpower and enthusiastic support during the crisis. They held that their main role was to support and to help the principal and staff of the school.

E. *The Participating Organisations Council (POC)*. The purpose of the POC is to develop and maintain the relationship between the school and organisations (business, community and cultural) directly involved in the school's programme, with the aim of providing continual developmental support to the school's educational programme. The Council serves in an advisory capacity to the principal of Metro. . . .

F. *Accreditation.* On 7 April 1971 Mr Byrd, Deputy Superintendent, received a letter from John A. Stanavage, Executive Director of the North Central Association, informing him that the Commission on Secondary Schools had been unable to take affirmative action on Metro because no formal application had been received from the Board of Education. While the Commission had considered ways to circumvent its own regulations for application procedures, it could find no legal way to certify Metro without the formal application. Mr Stanavage reiterated his strong interest in and support of Metro as 'a most worthy educational experiment'. . . .

G. *Expansion of the school in September 1971.* . . . During the five weeks that the school was operated on an emergency basis outside of the headquarters space, the question of expansion was shelved. The staff held three meetings when the school returned to the building to make a final determination as to whether the school should expand, and what shape that expansion should take. The recommendations, then, are the recommendations of Urban Research, but they have been developed and directly shaped by the Metro staff. . . .

H. *The planned departure of Urban Research Consultants.* The initial assumption behind Urban Research participation in the Metro programme was that Urban Research would provide aid to establish the programme and would phase out so that the school could become self-sufficient. . . .

In the final phase, from January to June 1971, consultants worked with the staff to insure that they could perform all the functions in the school which had been carried out by Urban Research. . . . Accordingly the President of Urban Research wrote the General Superintendent on 1 December 1970: 'We feel that after 30 June the existing programme can effectively function without our day-to-day assistance'. . . .

I. *Planning for summer workshop and the fourth semester.* Much staff effort during the last four weeks of the third semester was spent on planning a summer workshop, and refining the school's programme for the fourth semester. The staff made plans to deal directly with the problems of refining the educational programme so that its effect would be maximised on all of the students in the school. The issues which the staff isolated for planning during the workshop were:

1   Restructuring of counselling groups.
2   Modifications in the programme to insure the development of basic skills in all students.
3   The particular educational needs of black students.
4   The process of orientation for new students.
5   The process of training for new staff members.

During this planning period the staff established a system for interviewing new staff members in order to make recommendations to the Principal for staff positions to be filled for the fall. Interviews were conducted so that new staff could be on hand for the summer workshop.

J. *Graduation of the first senior class.* On 18 June the first class graduated from Metro in ceremonies held in Grant Park. All of the arrangements for the graduation, from securing permission from the Park District to carrying chairs, had been made by the senior class. The ceremony was brief, relaxed and a perfect Metro occasion. . . . Nate Blackman, Metro's principal, who continues to provide outstanding leadership to the school, awarded diplomas to the sixteen graduating seniors. Each senior then talked briefly about Metro and the meaning of his experience in the school. Several said that they would not have graduated from high school if they had not attended Metro. Several spoke of how the school had increased their skill, knowledge, ability to learn. Most spoke of the joy of being part of the Metro community. One black student talked about the appropriateness of the Metro programme for black students. Perhaps the moment that summed up the graduation, and the struggles and accomplishments of the graduates and of the school through its first three semesters was when one student stood quietly and then leaned toward the microphone and said: 'Rah'. . . .

Appendix I
Chronology of the major events of the space crisis
18 March 1971 to 23 April 1971

The incredible activity on the part of the staff, parents, students, participating organisations, Urban Research staff, community organisations, school board staff and building management to resolve the crisis cannot be adequately described in a chronology of this type. This chronology is not complete, rather it highlights the events of the crisis.

18 March. Mr Blackman received a phone call at 2.55 p.m. from Dr Bessie Lawrence informing him that the courts had evicted the school from its headquarters at 537 South Dearborn (due to violations of the fire code), and directing him to close the school. The formal notice was to be delivered on the morning of the 19th. No further information was available at this time.

Extraordinary meeting of staff and students held at 3.30 p.m. All students and staff who were in the building attended this meeting. The following decisions were made:

1   To move as fast as possible to secure more information about the eviction.

2   To call all students in the school that night to inform them that there would be no classes on Friday, and that they should attend an all-school meeting at 1.00 p.m. on Friday.

3   To prepare a written statement to read to students when they were called so that all students would have the same information to decrease rumours and misinformation.

4   To begin an immediate search for alternative classroom space.

5   To establish a Steering Committee of staff and students. This committee met immediately and worked out the written message to be read to each student.

19 March. Metro staff and URC consultants began intense search for space for the 111 class meetings during the week which had been held at the headquarters.

Information provided to students by phone, and staff members stationed at doors of the headquarters.

All-school meeting, Jones High School at 1.00 p.m. All information available was presented to students. Questions answered and appropriate action was discussed.

Very little new information available to the school regarding the nature of the violations. No formal eviction notice received by the school.

20-21 March. During the weekend, each teacher called each of the students in his counselling group to answer any questions and to tell him where classes would be held on Monday.

22 March. Classes resumed on schedule.

Statement of 'Recommendations for the acquisition of headquarters space for Metro High School' prepared as a result of staff and Steering Committee meetings. Statement urged the Board of Education to move to reoccupy the headquarters space at 537 South Dearborn. If this was not accomplished within thirty days the recommendation was to secure new headquarters space.

Staff meeting. Unanimously approved the recommendations.

Extraordinary meeting of the Participating Organisations Council. Recommendations endorsed and pledge of support given to the staff of the school.

All-school meeting at the Field Museum, 3.30 p.m. Students endorsed the recommendations. Further planning for carrying on the work of the school.

Class space had been found for all 111 class periods. Twelve organisations who had previously participated in the programme donated space and five new organisations donated space.

23 March. Memo from Direct Action Committee proposing a silent vigil at the Board of Education to demand resolution of the crisis.

24 March. Parents' Meeting, Jones High School Auditorium at 7.30 p.m. This meeting was highlighted by a moving speech from Mr Blackman on Metro's purpose, accomplishments and the importance of the school. Parents took the following action:

1   Elected a temporary chairman.

2   Unanimously endorsed the 'Recommendations for the acquisition of headquarters space for Metro High School'.

3   Decided to join with staff and students in a silent vigil at the Board of Education at 228 North LaSalle to demand action from the Board.

4   Appointed an ad hoc committee to work on the following:

(a) To propose a permanent structure of a parents' organisation.

(b) To work with staff and students to find alternative headquarters space.

(c) To prepare a parents' statement for the Board's policy hearings in early April.

(d) To develop a telephone chain to call the Board demonstrating support for the school.

25 March. Secured use of 1025 South Wabash from the Standard Oil Company.

Memo from W. E. Lloyd, a parent and an insurance underwriter. The

memo informed Mr Blackman that the building had twenty-nine violations, and that it would take a great amount of time and expense to bring
the building into accord with code. This was the first explicit information
on the violations received by the school.

A court hea·ing did not vacate eviction order. Based on fire department
inspections the building was not close to compliance.

Status report on the hunt for alternative headquarters space was made.
The Board had considered three or four sites, and had proposed one. The
staff, students and parents had visited seventeen sites and proposed three
for further consideration. The staff, parents and students held that the
space found by the Board was totally unsuitable for the school. The school
staff agreed to the *temporary* use of three classrooms.

Staff released 'Statement from the staff, 25 March 1971'. This statement
made two important points:

1   A shift in priorities from reoccupying 537 as the first priority to a
position that reoccupancy and the permanent occupation of a new site
be considered equally.

2   A position that issues beyond the space crisis which had contributed
detrimentally in the past and during the crisis to the effectiveness of the
school programme be resolved. . . .

Silent vigil of students, parents and staff at the Board of Education at
1.30 p.m. A newspaper reporter who has witnessed many demonstrations
at the Board was impressed that this demonstration was:

1   Asking for help from the Board to do something, rather than
protesting something the Board had done.

2   Integrated racially.

3   Had students, parents and staff well represented.

4   Was well organised and disciplined.

Letter presented to Dr Redmond by representatives of the school urging
him 'to take direct and complete authority in this crisis. We welcome you
as a friend to come to Metro and keep in close contact with us as we
progress'. . . .

26 March. Parents effectively tie up switchboard at the Board of
Education with statements of support for the school.

Staff, students and parents' space committee continue search for
alternative headquarters. The emphasis now is strongly on locating a
permanent new headquarters space for the school. Initially the hunt was
to find temporary headquarters space and to have space to fall back on if
537 could not be brought up to code. At this point, as the nature and
extent of the violations became clearer, it was almost a unanimous
conviction that it would be best to move permanently.

27-28 March. Each student in the school was again contacted by phone by his counselling group teacher to answer questions and to inform him of where classes would meet the following week.

29 March. Parents telephoning to the Board maintained.

1 April. Lee Botts, one of the leaders of the parents' space committee made a full report to that committee recommending that 1020 South Wabash become the new headquarters space.

Meeting of staff, students and parents to make final decision on headquarters space. Representatives of each of the staff, students and parents' space committees reported. After review and much talk, the meeting unanimously adopted the position that 1020 South Wabash was the best space and that action should be taken to facilitate a move there as soon as possible. Fire inspectors, invited to inspect the space by the parents, had already given a verbal OK to the space.

2 April. Metro Policy Board sent a letter to Dr Redmond. The Board is composed of two staff, parent, student and participating organisation representatives.

The letter emphasised the underlying problems of the space crisis:

1   Participants in the Metro programme do not have decentralised power to make crucial decisions affecting the programme's operation. While central staff has the power, it does not make effective decisions.

2   Central staff has not provided effective support for the school.

The letter proposed these solutions:

1   Empower the Policy Board to make decisions, with line staff having the power to review decisions in light of the school's goals.

2   Establish an experimental school expeditor who would report directly to the Deputy Superintendent.

The letter requested a meeting with the Superintendent by 6 April.

5 April. Evaluation of the third cycle and registration for the fourth cycle began. Metro's evaluation and registration process is complex. The complete process was carried out by school staff at sites away from the headquarters building. The process took the remainder of the week as planned.

6 April. Parents met with Dr Joseph Hannon, Assistant Superintendent for Facilities Planning. Dr Hannon stated that the resolution of the space crisis was his top priority. He was in favour of returning to the 537 building. He promised a letter outlining definite action.

8 April. Letter was received from Dr Hannon stating that:

1   The premises would be ready for occupancy by 19 April.

2   The building people agreed to maintain the building properly.

3   If approval was not secured by the 19th the Board would begin proceedings to terminate the lease.

While many expressed doubt that the building would be ready for occupancy on the 19th and questioned the priority of honouring the lease, most were pleased at the steps taken by the Board and Dr Hannon and that at last the Board was taking some action.

14 April. Parents testified at the policy hearings of the Board of Education.

15 April. Policy Board met with Dr Connelly and Dr Lawrence. While there was a good deal of dissension about specific examples in the April 2nd letter, there was general agreement that the solutions proposed in the letter were effective and should be implemented.

23 April. Metro reoccupied 537 South Dearborn.

5.7 Center for New Schools
Student involvement in decision-making in an alternative high school

This analysis is based primarily on participant observations and interviews. The attempt to justify each conclusion by relating it to data analysis is beyond the scope of this report. . . .

Although we will not attempt to review other research and theory in this outline, one distinction made by Etzioni[1] is extremely useful in understanding the students' initial orientations toward decision-making. Etzioni hypothesises that organisations develop two major realms of activity: the 'instrumental' realm, which is related to the official functions of the organisation, and the 'expressive' realm, which is related to people's personal concerns. In the school context, 'instrumental' activities deal mainly with the operation of the instructional programme, while 'expressive' activities centre around friendship, dating, athletics, informal 'rapping', etc. In many organisations, two different structures evolve to deal with these two realms, with the expressive realm having leaders, values and styles of action that may be at odds with the organisation of the instrumental realm. In the traditional school context, it is often the expressive realm in which the adolescent invests most of his energy, and it is leadership in expressive activities that determines prestige with other students. In strictly controlled high schools organised along traditional lines, administration and teachers often attempt to exert strict controls over not only the instrumental realm, but also the expressive realm. Traditional school rules touching the expressive realm regulate such areas as dress, social interaction, movement, eating and smoking. To defend their autonomy in the expressive realm, students have created separate expressive subcultures, and recently have directly challenged the school's right to regulate their expressive activity.

Coming from traditional school, the major concern of Metro students was to gain autonomy in the expressive realm. Metro staff strongly encouraged this direction, and they considered freedom of movement,

1   Amitia Etzioni (1965). 'Organizational control structure'. In James March (ed.), *Handbook of Organizations*. Chicago: Rand McNally.

Source: Center for New Schools (1971). 'Student involvement in decision-making in an alternative high school: a preliminary analysis'. Chicago: Center for New Schools. The extracts reproduced here are taken from pp. 9-12, 13, 14, 15. The footnote has been renumbered.

The analysis of student involvement in decision-making in this report is based substantially on the work of Steve Wilson, a member of the research team.

dress, expression, association, etc. fundamental to the programme's design from the beginning. Thus, in the areas that students cared most about, there was no need for participation in decision-making to gain desired ends. The battle had already been won. At the end of the first semester of operation, all students were asked what they liked most about Metro as compared with their old school. *The characteristic of the programme cited most often was freedom in the expressive realm: freedom to talk to friends, get up and leave if you were restless, wear what you wanted, eat when you wanted, etc.*

The characteristic cited second most often in this same series of interviews was the closer student-teacher relationship at Metro. The staff's willingness to grant freedom in the expressive realm established a degree of trust between teachers and students. . . . Staff members were sensitive to student concerns, and by the end of the first semester many students felt comfortable in openly criticising those aspects of the programme they wanted changed. . . .

Student: 'The way you got to do it is to make decisions. Then if we don't like it, we'll let you know. You do something and we'll react. Students don't dig sitting in meetings and stuff. You feel like teachers are talking about stuff and you don't have any idea what it means'.

The major concerns of students with regard to school policies might be described as follows:

1   To obtain as wide a field as possible for expressive activity.

2   To be able to complain to the staff about instrumental activities they disliked.

3   To establish the right to opt out of instrumental activity if they wished.

To a large extent the first objective was achieved. *In the few areas of expressive activity where freedom was not allowed (e.g. students were not allowed to smoke in the school headquarters because of a Board of Education rule), there was constant minor friction with the staff.* The second objective was also achieved almost completely; *almost all teachers were open to student complaints and effectively communicated this willingness to listen to students, even though they did not always solve the problems posed.* Many students initially felt that the third objective had also been achieved because of the staff's stated emphasis on freedom in the programme. Subsequent efforts by the staff to tighten up the attendance policy have been a subject of continuous controversy in the programme.

With their major objectives largely achieved, Metro students saw little reason to become actively involved in a formal decision-making process. *Staff members argued that students should carve out some formal decision-making role for themselves since the staff might not always act in the students' best interest. This argument, however, was extremely abstract, and most students were influenced much more by present reality. . . .*

One of the most powerful deterrents to the development of a formal mechanism for student participation in government was the students' strongly negative experiences with student governments in their old schools. . . .

Student: The student council was just puppets for the teachers. They pulled the strings and the student council did what they wanted.

Student: There was one clique that got involved. No one else paid any attention.

Staff and those students pushing student government were never successful in communicating an alternative image of what a government could be to the majority of the students.

Student: All government is is some guy going around telling you what to do. There are people here nobody is going to force them to do anything.

Student: If we have a student government, they'll start making rules and pretty soon we'll end up like the old schools.

Observer: Why don't you guys get together in some kind of student government and see what you can do about it [the lack of gym equipment]?

Student: A student government couldn't do that shit.

Especially in the Metro situation where students felt things were going well, many students cited local and national governmental structures with which they were dissatisfied in arguing against a government at Metro. Politically active 'youth culture' students cited the war policies of the national government. Many black students cited the actions of the police at a local level. In both instances, the form of the argument was the same: you're copying the kind of government that we already know doesn't work right. . . .

Further, when they did get involved, a small setback confirmed their belief that 'you can't fight the system'. . . . *The most many hoped for was a chance to complain. Staff attempts to get students beyond the complaining mode were largely unsuccessful.*

Closely related to their distrust of governmental structures, school-wide policies, etc., was a personal ethic that is summarised in two current clichés: 'do your own thing' and 'hang loose'. One of the strongest trends in our interviews and observations reflected student willingness to act on these concepts.

The ideal form of government for Metro, many students believed, was none at all. There would be no government, no rules; only 'people dealing with people'.

Student: We're going to have a beautiful anarchy. Everybody's going to do their own thing and leave everybody else alone. We decided we don't need a government.

The 'hang loose' ethic was also in strong conflict with the notion of a governmental structure. It glorified reacting to the feeling of the moment, and coping with each situation as it arose. It opposed planning, rules and long meetings. It led students to accept whatever happened with equanimity. If no one showed up for a scheduled meeting, 'We'll just have it another time'. If the person who was supposed to buy pop for a picnic came without it, the explanation 'I just couldn't get it together' satisfied many people. . . .

The evaluator as political journalist:
PLATO comes to the community college

At previous points in this section we have emphasised 'fitting' reports to particular audiences and their needs. This can entail, along with other precautions and procedures, carefully designating what the report attempts or does not attempt to do; for whom it is written; whether it represents a final, intermediate or preliminary account; how the reader should go about reading it; what reporting conventions it has adopted; and, most important of all, what types of data inform its judgement.

Perhaps every report needs a specific introduction devoted to such issues. Certainly many would benefit by having one. Plato Comes to the Community College *has an outstandingly clear and comprehensive introduction. We reproduce it partly to serve as* our *introduction to the passages from the report that we are able to include, partly as an example of the kind of reader-orientation to which we have just referred.*

House himself now looks back upon the report with some unease. The evaluators' access to the research situation was a general one, and the presence of the evaluators accepted as part of a PLATO 'package'. This resulted in a threatening situation, particularly as Ernest House became increasingly interested in the political problems surrounding institutionalisation. He reported not to the community colleges themselves but to the programme builders back in the university. It is safe to assume that some of the more damaging insights 'filtered back'. There was no negotiation of content, except with the funding agency, and very little information was considered too hot to handle.

But there are other points to make about this study. It has, first, a clear documentary function, amounting to a historical overview of an evolving major educational innovation, the introduction of what many believe to be the most advanced computer-based educational system in the world into the community colleges. It is not an official history duly toned down but a warts-and-all acount that gets behind the rhetoric of the operation and unravels some of its less comfortable truths. To this extent it accepts that a legitimate evaluation role may be the de-mythologising of the programme. It also discusses problems and how they were resolved, documents, personal reactions and behaviour, summarises attitudes and analyses what went right or wrong. In spite of this it remains within the format of the descriptive narrative. The authors do not, for instance, see themselves as expansive pedagogic theorists, seeking to comprehend the structure of computer-aided instruction. Nor do they flirt with management con-

sultancy or the various roles that come under the umbrella of technical assistance. Their main end-in-view is clearly the interpretative description.

But the study was not set up in conditions to encourage or even allow self-confrontation. The evaluators are less concerned with mediating between alternative perceptions of the programme, more with the honesty and perceptiveness of their own account. In this respect they raise questions about the ethics of the case study. Not surprisingly the exercise produced sensitiveness as well as sensitivity in the community colleges themselves.

Other difficulties are more mundanely practical. The documentary case study is likely to be long. It may tend to set down each and every significant event, and saturate the reader with a wealth of detail. This is doubtless good ethnographic methodology, but poor formative feedback. House and Gjerde are clearly aware of the danger and achieve a reasonable compromise. Nevertheless the report ended up longer than they would have wished. The dangers of the reverse situation are obvious. To increase the degree of selectivity can open the door to accusations of partiality and preference. To present conclusions or recommendations without detailed analysis weakens the link between data and interpretation. We have already noted the pressing need for clarity and brevity in evaluation reports. Perhaps more experimentation is required, say with back-up documentation available only on request, or specialist appendices. One difficulty with an anthology or book of readings is that readers are rarely in a position even provisionally to adjudicate these issues for themselves, since they are only presented with a selection.

Another issue strongly present in the House/Gjerde report is the tension between verisimilitude and confidentiality.

The authors write that it is 'conceivable' that a 'knowing' reader might be able to identify the source of some statements. This doesn't seem a very formidable task. The city's name is kept as Chicago, and PLATO is the real name of the programme. The tricks to preserve anonymity are frankly derisory. Even within particular institutions the procedures adopted offer, if not a 'dead giveaway', only a partial protection to those whose identity is ostensibly not revealed. This is, of course, an ever-present problem in the case study when pursued within an illuminative model. Relatedly, some of the arguments against the new paradigm have been that it 'drags in' irrelevant but potentially harmful personal or political details, at worst giving an unsavoury account of conflicts, failures and misunderstandings. Traditional psychometric evaluation manages to avoid these phenomena but at an obvious and severe cost: a divorce from real-world perceptions and perceived (and probably actual) relevance. This again relates to the obligations implicit in an exhaustive documentation. Single-day observations or looser reporting style (like the T-City report) can and do merely hint at incendiary material, nodding and winking in the direction of crucial inadequacies. The poor 'exhaustive documenters' cannot do so without accusations of timidity, gross bias, sloppy methodology or hired-hackmanship. They are expected to 'bite the bullet'. Again there are no golden rules or easy solutions. What is needed is a blend of common sense, openness about the difficulties and a willingness to acknowledge that some compromises may occasionally be required, as was obviously realised by House and Gjerde.

The extracts themselves show clear characteristics of an illuminative style, including touches of descriptive flair and a feel for the learning milieux in which the innovations have their day-to-day existence. One notices, too, the shifts in focus, between individuals, issues and conclusions.

It is right to pay attention, given the audience for this report and its political overtones, to the consequences of the style of reportage it adopts. But this must not be allowed to obscure the larger questions raised by House himself in the paper we have reprinted under the title 'Context and justification' in Section 4. What implicit values underpin the study? These values go beyond the value-position of the researcher and nudge into a consideration of the social role of this kind of study. It is one thing to value truths; it is another to assert, however indirectly, that others should live with the consequences.

5.8 Ernest House and Craig Gjerde
PLATO comes to the community college

Introduction: cautions to the wary reader

This paper is a revision of an evaluation report of an internal formative evaluation of the community college component of the PLATO project. Names and places have been disguised. PLATO is believed by many to be the most advanced computer-based educational system in the world. It has been under development by the University of Illinois for fifteen years. Descriptions of the system are available in many places and we will not repeat them here.[1]

This evaluation effort grew out of a three-year, $5 million National Science Foundation grant to the University of Illinois to develop, implement and demonstrate PLATO IV in public schools, an important part of which included community (two-year) colleges. The data collected here were to provide information to the community college development staff. It is *not* a summative evaluation of the project and did not gather any data to that end. Educational Testing Service has a separate $1 million grant to do the summative evaluation during the three years of the project. We strongly discourage interpreting our report as an evaluation of PLATO's effectiveness. It is not.

The evaluation was conceived as providing information to the programme developers, collecting data as situations and opportunities arose, similar to what Stake calls 'responsive' evaluation. Most data-gathering consisted of informal and formal interviews with community college personnel. The only prespecified part was to periodically sample attitudes of the entire faculty throughout the year. In providing the data we felt we were only moderately successful. It was a new role for us and we felt we were always trying to catch up to events. We did manage to respond to many anomalous events that characterised the year, such as the late arrival of terminals.

The community college development staff were very patient with us as we struggled with a new role, the helper/evaluator duality being rather

---

1   Allen C. Hammond (1972). 'Computer-assisted instruction: two major demonstrations'. *Science*, 176, No. 4039, June 9.

Source: E. R. House and C. L. Gjerde (1973). PLATO Comes to the Community College. *The extracts reproduced here are taken from pp. 1-3, 12-17, 37-8, 48-9, 51, 63-5. An extended version of this case-study appears in Ernest R. House (1974).* The Politics of Educational Innovation. *McCutchan: Berkeley, California.*

sticky. Another burden on the evaluation was the attempt to make it a little 'research-like' by deriving a few generalisations of middling abstraction. For example, we applied some microeconomic concepts to perceived PLATO benefits. Those generalisations are not represented in this evaluation report but did make us less responsive to the developers' needs than we might otherwise have been. This research was done of course only with the encouragement of the evaluation sponsors. The theory-construction was worthwhile but sometimes worked at cross-purposes with the evaluation function.

The upshot was that House concentrated on the social-political contexts of the community colleges and how faculty and administrators responded to the introduction of a major technological innovation over one year's time. Gjerde concentrated on the technical aspects of the authoring process, in itself a shift in emphasis away from measuring student responses, a shift necessitated because of delays in console deliveries. We studied what was available to study rather than waiting for something to become available as in a prespecified evaluation design.

Our substantive focus did concentrate exclusively on the reactions of community college personnel. We did not try to monitor, describe or evaluate the activities of the University personnel in any way. The University personnel are mentioned in the report only when someone mentioned them in our interviews. One of our fears is that since they are not always the centre of attention they will be perceived as inactive, which is far from the case. We could have evaluated their performance but we did not.

One of the impressions we do want to convey is that many events in the lives of the recipients of this innovation are outside the control of the University personnel. As the study progressed we found ourselves more and more explaining the world of the community college personnel to the developers and the PLATO staff. That is what this final report became.

Our own formative evaluation findings during the year were presented in a series of interview notes, brief written reports and oral sessions with the developers. At the beginning, we did not envision this as our final report form. Loaded at the end with numerous interview notes and reports, we decided to put them together to portray our overall impression of the year in order to share both the content and methodology.

The major concerns of the University developers in reading the report are its balance and confidentiality. They feel that interesting, dynamic events are pursued too much, dull ones not enough. Although we tried to correct these emphases, some imbalance remains. The serendipity of the method almost guarantees it. On the other hand, many events are expounded which would not otherwise be discovered. There is a temptation to pursue and report the interesting.

The other major concern is the confidentiality of the information. It is conceivable even using pseudonyms that a knowing reader might be able to identify the source of some statements. It is particularly perplexing in this type of evaluation which relies so heavily on honest judgements and personalisation. The direct incisive quotation which reveals so much is also likely to reveal the source's identity. His position in the structure, which determines so much of his behaviour, is often a dead giveaway. So we have regretfully sacrificed some verisimilitude for confidentiality. We have changed names and locations, merged people and sometimes created false facts to protect identities.

We have two major fears of being misread. One is that the reader unfamiliar with PLATO will take the problems discussed to be endemic only of PLATO itself. That would be grossly untrue. Through reading many study reports we have found the same problems must be faced by all technological innovations. The other fear is that the report will be dismissed by PLATO advocates in the belief that PLATO is above these difficulties.

So, the cautious reader is forewarned that the report is fragmentary, adventitious and in no way a summative evaluation of PLATO or the community college component, but rather a summary of our explorations. Nonetheless, we feel there are some worthwhile truths here. We cannot vouch for the validity of people's perceptions but are certain that they did say these things. . . .

One example: Muslem College

Muslem College lies along the Truman Expressway, a sleek black building two blocks long, in the middle of the West Side ghetto. Across the expressway it faces off against County Hospital and the massive medical complex. The area is one of the roughest in the city. No nurse can travel the underway passage to her quarters without a guard. During the King riots, this was the worst-hit part of Chicago.

Sitting in the midst of this decay is the beautiful black building of Muslem College designed by Mies Van der Roh. In front are three enormous 60-foot flag poles which fly the American flag, the white Illinois flag and the Black Liberation flag, the latter strikingly dissonant with its thick black, green, and red bars. When the building was dedicated, James Garvey, the President, explained for television why the Black Liberation flag flies there. 'At one time you couldn't fly the American flag in this neighbourhood. Now you can.'

Both at the Muslem parking lot and at the doors one must stop for security guards wearing black uniforms with orange Muslem insignias on the sleeve, all are reportedly ex-convicts. Inside, the building is handsomely furnished with heavy oak furniture and African art. In the lobby sits a black late 1950s Oldsmobile — an assassinated martyr's car.

At the time the terminals were introduced President Garvey was a political force to reckon with in Chicago. The student body was nearly 100 per cent black, the faculty 95 per cent so. The school was run on a tight, authoritarian basis. Garvey and the faculty were engaged in a tremendous protracted conflict over firings and reorganisation. The President placed his own people in all the top slots in the college and they exercised tight control. Teachers were afraid to be interviewed for fear that the rooms were bugged. Distrust gripped the school.

Garvey claimed that people were out to get him. Others claimed he had strong paranoid tendencies. Whether a self-fulfilling prophecy or not, in December 1972, a month after the arrival of the first PLATO terminals, irregularities were found in the financial books. Garvey resigned.

Garvey's views on PLATO were never recorded. Attempts to reach him were unsuccessful. The day of one interview visit, someone fired three shots in his office window early in the morning. Nonetheless, his actions had strong effect, not only on Muslem, but on the rest of CCC (City Colleges of Chicago). PLATO was one of many innovations that Garvey tried to implement at Muslem. He extracted the maximum publicity from them.

Internally, he disbanded the English department and established the Learning Resources Center. The task of the Learning Center was to teach basic reading and math skills. Learning skill instructors were ordered to have thirty contact hours per week with students. Garvey fired many instructors and hired the much lower paid 'non-contract' people who could be fired without cause since they had no contracts. These people were used to staff the Learning Center. Externally Garvey claimed they were individualising instruction. Internally the teachers claimed it was all publicity.

PLATO was introduced into Muslem as part of the Learning Center. At least three distinct groups could be identified vis-à-vis PLATO. The most directly affected people were the 'non-contract' personnel who comprised the bulk of the Learning Resources Center. Students who were unable to do regular college work were sent into the Learning Resources Center to pick up elementary reading and math skills. Ability levels varied tremendously, ranging as low as fifth grade. Any student was accepted, true to the philosophy of the school. The non-contract people were hired to 'tutor' these students. The faculty work load was exceedingly heavy — thirty contact hours per week and hundreds of students. Students were supposedly handled on an individual basis but much group work went on. The non-contract people, not having proper teaching credentials, had no job security and could be fired at any time.

In the fall of 1972, the non-contract people were most enthusiastic about PLATO. They could see PLATO helping them with their heavy work load. They would not have to take five or six students aside every class to tutor them. They were somewhat concerned about how their students would respond to an impersonal machine but were hopeful. They saw student response as being the critical element. Yet they knew little about PLATO. Their own major problem was not learning to use the machine, but time, they said. Many meetings and other duties were required, in addition to their thirty contact hours per week.

A smaller, older (thirty-ish) and more experienced group within the Learning Resources Center was the tenured, contract faculty. They had been around Muslem a little longer (three to five years) and could best be described as cynical, wary, weary. They had seen the 'innovations' come and go and as one put it, 'Muslem blew the groundwork for PLATO.' Like everything else in the school in their view, PLATO had been crammed down teachers' throats and would not receive a fair trial, they felt. Instead of being soft-pedalled as a supplement, which it might be good for, it was being forced on everybody.

According to the tenured faculty, the non-contract people were so enthusiastic because they had no choice. They had to reflect the administration line or be fired. The least secure people were the most enthusiastic and the most secure were the least enthusiastic. Although PLATO would be used in the Learning Resources Center because the faculty would be ordered to do so, it would be viewed negatively by teachers. The Learning Resource Center was the lowest status group in the college. According to them PLATO should have begun in the science group with Dean Dodd's division. They were the highest status group in Muslem, and if they had used it others would have followed. The reverse effect was achieved by installing it in the Learning Resources Center.

As early as the summer, the authors from Muslem had identified the teachers' union and the Science Division as the centre of resistance to PLATO. One would have predicted in advance on the basis of job threat that the science faculty would be most likely to use a technological innovation like PLATO while the non-contract people would feel the greatest job threat and resistance. In many ways, the Science Division (including math) was the most secure and best informed about PLATO. The faculty were almost all tenured professors who taught small seminar classes. They had technical backgrounds and were accorded the highest prestige in the school. They were distinctly unenthusiastic about PLATO.

Dean Dodd and his department chairmen were able to present a virtual catalogue of objections to PLATO. They contended that the PLATO materials were no different than what they taught their classes. The trained PLATO authors were from the Learning Resources Center and not from the chemistry and math departments. Instructors should have control over the content of their own classes. PLATO content was very weak, and had received minimal input from bonafide science instructors.

Their students needed real lab experiences, not simulated ones. Many never got a chance to handle lab equipment in their high schools because the teachers were afraid of breakage. Students who were to be nurses and technicians needed concrete experiences. The students might not respond to impersonal teaching. Some students, for example, even stayed around an extra year to take a regular class rather than take TV classes being offered.

Underlying these objections was a deep-seated suspicion that a technology like PLATO was used only for Blacks and other minority groups and not in top universities. 'What do the professors at Harvard and Yale think about this operation? Are they using PLATO? No, of course they won't use it. Technology like this is used to cheapen education and provide a poor education for Black and minority students as opposed to providing a good, small group kind of education for students at top universities.'

They saw the motivation behind PLATO as mainly a matter of financing, a way of providing cheaper education now that minorities had insisted on their rights. To provide a good education at Muslem would require doubling the cost. It was simply a matter of time until PLATO became a union problem, they felt. Yet they also expressed a willingness to give the thing a try, to be convinced. Some insisted on judging the device on currently available materials, not on potential.

A senior author's, Mike Hamilton's, explanation of the various attitudes toward PLATO was that PLATO did not threaten the non-contract people's jobs any more than usual since they were always insecure. On the other hand, it was a threat to the science faculty because they had an easy load already. PLATO promised to make a difficult job easier for the Learning Resources personnel and an easy job easier for the tenured faculty. On returning to Muslem College after his year at Urbana, Hamilton was named PLATO coordinator of Muslem. He worked in the office and very close to Carl Ellos.

Ellos, formerly the Director of Research at Muslem, was named by Dumas as city-wide coordinator for PLATO. He retained his office at Muslem College although he spent much time downtown at the central office. Physically, Ellos' office was located in the Learning Center and next to the non-contract personnel. Yet he and his group were somewhat outside the Muslem social structure. They seemed to keep to themselves and report to Dumas. They were predominantly non-black in an almost totally black faculty and student body.

Hamilton, acknowledged without question as the most proficient and imaginative author, was not perceived as being entirely legitimate within the Muslem structure. He helped Ellos with proposals for outside funding and, when asked, provided technical assistance for fellow authors at Muslem and elsewhere. According to some teachers, Ellos himself did not display very forceful leadership. Working well with University personnel, he exhibited a diffuse leadership within the college system. He had a difficult time keeping things together and meeting deadlines. Things always seemed out of hand. Teachers and others had a hard time gaining access to him. The administrative situation remained confused the entire year, according to these teachers.

The actual head of the Learning and the Instructional Resource

Division was Dean Wilma Osborne. In the authoritarian structure of Muslem, she was perceived by the teachers as the most authoritarian of all the administrators. She ruled by edict and threatened to dock personnel for not attending meetings, of which there were many, they said. In November, she felt the PLATO project was in a state of disarray. Since Hamilton was paid by the central office, she could not consider him to be working for Muslem. Therefore, she didn't ask him to do anything internally. The installation of the terminals was confused, roles were ill-defined, and there was nothing in writing.

Since she had no job descriptions for Ellos and Hamilton and didn't know what they were supposed to be doing, she appointed Bonnie Glenn to assume the duties of on-campus coordinator. Although she considered the management of PLATO within CCC to be a complete mess, the ultimate criterion of success was how much the terminals were used, she felt. She had thought the University personnel to be enthusiastic and competent, but since the mismanagement of the project, she had begun to wonder.

When she returned from Urbana, Bonnie Glenn was appointed Director of Tutorials and Self-Instruction, which meant that she spent most time coordinating and orientating faculty to PLATO. Although during the summer she expressed the least interest of all the authors in advancing her career, on returning she became an administrator. She had no time to author. Although less technically proficient than the other authors, Bonnie seemed to be better liked and more part of the social structure than the others.

When the terminals finally arrived in November, Bonnie oriented the faculty. She found more enthusiasm among the faculty than she had anticipated. Most teachers expressed an interest in writing their own programmes rather than in utilising present courses. (Even Dean Dodd became interested during his orientation and spent forty-five minutes checking out the system.) As far as Bonnie could see, the late arrival of the terminals had caused no diminution in enthusiasm. But they were months late in arriving.

A survey of teacher attitudes toward PLATO was conducted in the fall. As might be expected from the high publicity, the Muslem instructors were more aware of PLATO than the other CCC schools. They were also more inclined to believe that PLATO should be limited only to drill work and not extended to regular instruction. The Muslem faculty was more optimistic about PLATO than most of the other schools.

The PLATO terminals which were promised to Muslem for August were finally delivered in November. The authors with released time could not write lessons without the terminals. Shortly before Christmas, the Chicago papers began running headlines about Garvey's misuse of funds. The front page headline stories continued for about three weeks. Garvey was finally forced to resign.

During the year or so of the troubles at Muslem College culminating in Garvey's resignation enrollment declined from 6,200 students to approximately 4,700. Samuel Harrison, formerly vice-president of Ralph Bunche College, was appointed acting president of Muslem. The atmosphere around the school relaxed considerably. Although the security guards were still at their posts, they no longer wore uniforms. The faculty seemed relieved that the long siege with Garvey was over.

By spring there was a great deal of uncertainty. Many administrators, including Wilma Osborne, had been relieved of their jobs, although when they would leave was unclear. Harrison had also moved to eliminate the non-contract people, either by giving some contracts, as with one of the PLATO authors, or possibly by releasing them. So far, none had been fired but many were anxious.

Interest in PLATO was at low tide. The non-contract people were too busy or too anxious to do anything. A walk through the Learning Resources Center where the ten PLATO terminals were located indicated that, at most, two would be occupied while repairmen worked on another two. Two consoles had never worked. After the long delay in the fall in receiving the terminals, system downtime and terminal breakdowns had taken a heavy toll in whatever enthusiasm existed. Bob Rogers, another author, estimated the system was down 50 per cent of the time and it was not unusual for an author to lose material. Another major problem was the lack of educational materials available on the system.

By the spring, Mike Hamilton characterised the Muslem attitude toward PLATO as at best one of indifference and suggested that some of the terminals be put someplace else where there was more interest. The only group working on PLATO at Muslem were the three or four people around Ellos and Hamilton, all selected by Ellos. All were released full-time to author. Bonnie Glenn had been reassigned to non-PLATO duties. Rogers felt this might decrease utilisation since she was the only one talking to the rest of the faculty. Nobody else seemed to be interested. As one author said in explanation of the lack of interest at Muslem, 'You must understand the history of the last three years here'.

Dean Dodd seemed to be more positive now than before, yet no one from physical science was involved. The reasons he gave were varied: the training was inconveniently located at Ralph Bunche; there were not enough terminals; the terminals were inconveniently located. 'We want to get involved, but we need the proper orientation which hasn't existed.' Apparently Harrison had put some pressure on Dean Dodd to utilise PLATO. Dodd's ultimate defence was that the appropriate courseware was not available. Whether Dodd was defending the Science Division's lack of use or whether his price for using PLATO was to have terminals under his control was unclear.

During the course of those events, from the fall to the winter, Muslem suffered a severe drop in its optimism toward PLATO. True to Muslem's authoritarian structure, most of the faculty originally heard about PLATO through an administrator although this seemed to have no direct effect on attitude. As at other schools, fellow teachers were the main influences on attitude. The small group of people who were now interested in PLATO did not function much like a group. They worked more like individuals. Some felt that PLATO would not be given a long enough trial period in which to prove itself. All were in agreement that there would be no widespread use of PLATO in the foreseeable future, if ever.

In contrast to the great publicity which once attended PLATO, the faculty now seemed indifferent. Whether enthusiasm could be revived was dependent on the administration. Harrison had proven himself resourceful at Ralph Bunche College. Only bold new steps could now have any influence in resurrecting Muslem's interest.

In the spring, Stokely Carmichael brought his fiery pan-African socialism to Muslem. Although the enrolment was down, some enthusiasm was still there. 'America is not our home, Africa is our home,' he says. 'The black man is the victim of capitalism.' The students shouted, but they were confused. Chicago is a seedbed for Black capitalism. Is this the right way? Without Garvey, under a new president, they were confused. Let others worry about the reliability of the PLATO terminals. For both faculty and students there were larger issues. . . .

Personal portrait of an author

Mike Hamilton was one of the Muslem maths instructors who attended the PLATO III demonstration in the spring of 1971. He was released from his work in the Learning Resources Center to study PLATO in the summer of 1971 and during the academic year 1971-2. Later he became the PLATO supervisor at Muslem.

Since no one was really responsible for helping the community college authors, Mike's first two months on PLATO were extremely frustrating. After two months he could do some authoring, but only after eight months did he know the language well. Mike eventually became one of the most knowledgeable authors in Chicago. He did not work closely with any other authors in developing lessons, but he and Bob Rogers did divide up math areas before Elaine Hammer began coordinating the mathematics authoring.

His style of authoring was to start by thinking of the student goals for the lesson (behavioural objectives were determined *ex post facto*). About one-third of the time he flow-charted his lessons; i.e. he sketched out decision points, to avoid logical errors; other times he merely sketched out the decision points before he sat down to programme. Mike devoted about 10 per cent of his time planning his lessons and 90 per cent programming and reworking them at the terminal.

Mike admitted that he had strong notions about what good PLATO lessons should look like, but that he did not try to impose his ideas on other authors. He did not want his students to read text on the screen and then pick a, b, c or d. He preferred the student to be actively involved in what he was supposed to be learning; if the problem to be solved were $2X = 19$, the student should respond 'divide by 2' or '$D2$'.

He believed that PLATO design was not the same as class-teaching design — the strategies needed to be different. He felt that initially most people just translated their personal teaching style into PLATO and interjected a lot of multiple choice questions: lessons of this kind, he said, were a waste of space. In his opinion, the machine should be simulator, and text should not be the body of the lesson. Mike strongly felt that since PLATO authoring was not well coordinated and since authors choose their own lesson topics, many wrote textbook lessons and their programmes were inefficient — i.e. they made poor use of the PLATO medium and they did not employ the more powerful programming commands. After one and a half years of experience on PLATO, Mike judged that in the future he could keep up with programming and teaching if he had three quarters released time, i.e. if he taught one class a day and spent the rest of this time authoring lesson materials for that class. . . .

Lesson strategies

Firm opinions were held in regard to the best ways of utilising PLATO's unique potential. There was much live-and-let-live, but many authors were quite critical of the kinds of lessons their peers were writing and the learning strategies they employed.

The inductive example-rule format was probably the most commonly used teaching paradigm. Many authors espoused the philosophy of first providing the student with a successful learning experience and then telling him what he had done. The traditional English lessons (many of them not written as a part of the official PLATO project) were faulted for their rule-example-drill format and for being too linear and unimaginative.

A senior author observed that most authors tried to translate their personal teaching style into a PLATO format by programming their discussions in multiple-choice response format. Such lessons were a waste of space on the system, he felt. By his standards, simulation was the proper use for PLATO; how well the lesson simulated a situation was his criterion for a good lesson. He believed that because there were few external standards imposed on the authors, several authors were programming text and writing 'inefficient' programmes. Those adept at programming TUTOR, he says, wrote his way.

Although no analyses of the finished lessons were made, it was obvious that authors used a variety of strategies and that the lessons were of irregular quality. . . .

Incentives

Released time was an incentive to authors, but it was considered a necessary — not a sufficient — condition. Instructors believed that no one would want to or be able to author without released time. Personal satisfaction was the most frequently cited incentive for becoming associated with PLATO. Authors were curious about PLATO, liked the creative challenge and liked problem-solving. Some thought it might help them advance in their careers; others sought potential summer employment. A few wanted the graduate credit. One author saw PLATO as a threat to his job survival and decided that to keep his job he had better learn to use PLATO. A secondary motivation was related to students; PLATO would expand the teachers' tools for teaching, increase student learning and help direct students into constructive channels. The prospect of authoring royalties was not an important motivation.

Most authors believed that PLATO would prove to be an educational benefit in the long run, but felt that currently there was little fame or prestige associated with being an author. In a few cases authors were able to identify some possible risks from their being associated with the PLATO project. First, since PLATO in Chicago was managed by the Central Office which had once bragged about the number of teachers it would be able to replace by educational television and which had sought to cut expenses by using PLATO to simulate science laboratory experiments, some authors were concerned that their colleagues might think that they had sold out to the administration.

Secondly, most authors had held administrative or teaching positions before they were released to work on PLATO; some feared that they might not get their jobs back or that their administrative units and students would suffer in their absence. . . .

Some conclusions, predictions and challenges

The comments in this paper have been based on interview and question-naire data. This section goes beyond the data and draws conclusions, some of which require a greater inferential leap than others.

1 PLATO was not meant to be ready as an operational system by 1973-4. It should be noted that it was indeed not ready. The hardware was expensive, slow in production and unreliable in the natural setting. The software (TUTOR) was constantly changing and difficult for teachers to learn without considerable effort. The courseware was limited in quantity and quality and proved to be more difficult and time-consuming to write than anyone had imagined.

All these deficiencies exacted a heavy toll in the enthusiasm and involvement of teachers and one assumes in the eventual acceptance of

PLATO. Solutions to these problems seem prerequisite to successful widespread use. On the other hand, we feel that the project will be able to meet the demands of the NSF/ETS evaluation eventually, i.e., eventually, to have courseware in selected schools up and running.

2   Institutional acceptance of PLATO was hampered by conflict over short-range and long-range goals. Continuous changes in the system may have made for a better system over a long period of time but greatly frustrated the teacher-authors in the community colleges and discouraged other teachers from getting involved. These effects might not be remedial. There seemed to be a time when each institution and possibly each teacher was ready to attend to the innovation. If PLATO could not deliver at that time, interest waned and was often difficult to revive.

Likewise, the long-range strategy of training teachers as authors might pay off handsomely in winning teacher acceptance of PLATO, slow, difficult and laborious as the strategy was. Yet the pressures of the ETS evaluation, the short-range goal, forced central development of curricula which might well be rejected by teachers eventually.

3   Individual and institutional acceptance was also very much organisationally dependent. Bringing PLATO into a highly politicised atmosphere like Muslem College necessarily imbued the innovation with meanings of that setting. Past events were important. The whole history of the organisation had a strong effect on how PLATO would be utilised. Larger events also tended to decrease the importance of PLATO. Few teachers at Muslem could have got excited about PLATO during the Muslem scandals. These larger events, which are not as uncommon as supposed, tended to submerge the innovation. PLATO was simply not a central focus of life at any place other than CERL.

4   The tangible incentives for learning about and using PLATO were few. Released time to author seemed to be a major attraction. Course credits through extension courses were a major motivation enabling teachers to move up the salary and promotion schedule. Only those teachers who were very ambitious, who got released time or credits, or who had very heavy work loads tended to get involved. Those who had a great number of students of very different abilities were also interested. Most teachers faced exerting much effort to learn TUTOR without clear chance of recompense.

The colleges had a similar problem. On the one hand, they had to share courseware for PLATO to be affordable, yet teachers were not amenable to using centrally developed courseware which they saw as unresponsive to their needs. So far the colleges have used PLATO as a basis for writing proposals for state and federal grants. It is difficult to see what the University could do to change the economic structure of the school, but it does present a severe limitation.

5   Within the currect setting, the 'soft sell' and trimming down of promises has worked best. Low-profile approaches have caused less

trouble, the most notable exemplar being Bunche College. Within Bunche an interest group developed based on previous social contacts. At Downstate several groups have emerged which are tied into the PLATO social system at the University. The enthusiasm and involvement are maintained through formal ties. Only these groups seem really capable of surviving over time.

As mentioned above, there does seem to be an optimal period of time for introducing PLATO terminals within each college. If the opportunity is not seized, the faculty turns indifferent. Reviving the enthusiasm at Muslem may not be impossible, particularly since the most resourceful administrator is there. A viable strategy might be to reintroduce PLATO through the Science Division, the most technically competent and highest prestige part of the college. To do so would require meeting some of the Dean's terms, such as offering extension courses at Muslem and even placing some terminals under his control.

For the ETS evaluation, the best strategy would be to continue to work in science and business with Downstate, Bunche and Miller. Downstate has the greatest likelihood of success because of the composition of its student body and the proximity to the University. The other three schools offer some promise, particularly the Vocational. However, it would be advisable to keep them simmering on the back burner until the capacity and problems of the system are improved. They could be brought to a boil quickly by publicity and many terminals, but they will be greatly disappointed and frustrated under current conditions. A good strategy would be to give them a few terminals and let them do their own in-service training at a very slow, deliberate speed, which all are inclined to do anyhow.

6   Many people involved with PLATO saw considerable potential in it as a supplemental learning aid, particularly those with a great range of student abilities. Its main advantage was perceived as the capacity for specialised instruction, such as simulation training. No teachers or administrators saw it as a potential replacement for regular instruction.

While most saw an important specialised potential, all saw formidable problems that had to be solved before PLATO could ever become widely used. These problems included the full range of hardware, software, courseware, cost and institutional acceptance. Overselling of the system was a major difficulty. The main challenge to the PLATO staff was whether these problems could be overcome so that PLATO's potential could be fully realised.

Evaluator on the flight-deck: pilot trials of the Aesthetic Education Program

This is an altogether differently-focused report. It is lengthy, involved and tries to achieve a variety of goals. Smith's year-long study of the Aesthetic Education Program [AEP] is one of a series of studies that he completed working with CEMREL, Inc., a private, non-profit making corporation devoted to curriculum development and implementation of educational innovations.[1]

Like the Stake and Gjerde report, Smith and Schumacher are writing for multiple audiences. The authors discuss this in their introduction:

One of the basic truths of education and evaluation is that different groups of people pose different questions for the educational evaluator. These varying questions demand different data. And, finally, theoretical interpretations will vary in cogency among these different groups. In part, the evaluator is faced with a very old problem in communication, knowing the audience to whom he is writing. In this report, we are caught in the middle of this dilemma. Among the several audiences for whom our comments have relevance are those practitioners in curriculum development, teaching, administration and State Departments of Education and those theorists in diffusion, measurement and the psychology of aesthetic education.

While our findings will be woven into a consistent fabric each section will shift slightly in perspective as a new audience comes into focus, and prior audiences recede into the background. Under circumstances of more time and resources we might have prepared separate documents directed toward each of the relevant groups.[2]

These various constituencies can find in this report what they are looking for. However, compared with the T-City report, it is not easy to skip-read. Altogether it is a more heavyweight document, addressing fundamental, theoretical, methodological and pedagogic issues.

Not surprisingly, it is difficult to extract parts of this report for reproduction here without feeling that one is destroying a carefully woven-together fabric of argument. Rather than draw on all the various segments, attention is given especially to the description and analysis of the classroom use of the curriculum material. A large part of the report is

---

1 We have already featured extracts from 'Some further aspects of fieldwork methodology', Appendix 1 of the report, in Section 4.

2 L. M. Smith and S. Schumacher (August, 1972). *Extended Pilot Trials of the Aesthetic Education Program: A Qualitative Description, Analysis and Evaluation*. CEMREL, Inc., p. 1.

devoted to the presentation and extended interpretation of a model of aesthetic education, and the implications for the future development of the programme.

The first extract is a section that describes the six packages used in the Aesthetic Education Program curriculum. Reference, in later extracts, will be made to these packages.

It is indicative of prevailing attitudes towards evaluation in general that Smith and Schumacher feel called upon, in Chapter 3 of their report, to state the following:

It seems reasonable that part of our descriptive and analytic effort might well go toward recounting experiences we saw occurring.[3]

They go on, quoting a memorandum which they wrote to the AEP staff and their evaluation staff colleagues, to argue for the 'vignette' as a 'means of casting the data':

One of the very real problems we have faced in Pennsylvania is the development of a mode of reporting on the way the package materials are being used. The thought occurred that a series of vignettes might be useful. From our notes we will try to reconstruct a descriptive account of the classroom scene, a picture of the reality. For the moment, no attempt will be made to develop causal analyses: the children were (or were not) dull, the teacher didn't (or did) understand the materials, the classroom was hot and crowded (or cool and spacious), and so forth.[4] Hopefully, the vignettes will be useful for later purposes of process assessment, programme implementation, teacher training and product revision and dissemination.[5]

A number of these vignettes, along with short discussions of classroom issues and problems, difficulties for the teacher and observations of pupils studying the curriculum material, are included here. They have been chosen to be intelligible without all the supporting text. In each of the small extracts that follow, a concern with discussion and interpretation of classroom phenomena comes through very strongly. As such, their work is of enormous interest to sensitive teachers, thoughtful curriculum developers and classroom researchers. It is definitely within the anthropological paradigm. At the same time, Smith and Schumacher make few concessions to the rapid reader or the busy bureaucrat. There is a rich yield, but it is not always as accessible as it might be. There is at times a ponderous tone, an over-careful explication of the ordinary and the unremarkable. This could be because Smith and Schumacher repudiate the dazzling pyrotechnics of Elliot Eisner's 'thick description' and attempt instead to spark across between the rather referential accounts and the driving theory. There are

3 Smith and Schumacher, op. cit., p. 43.
4 In the final report itself, Smith and Schumacher went beyond these constraints.
5 Smith and Schumacher, op. cit., p. 43.

times when the clutch slips a little. This interest in theory precludes Smith and Schumacher from having an ideological commitment to work within the framing assumptions of the teachers. However, when one considers the intellectual poverty of so much evaluation research, the wealth of their insights is impressive.

It will be no surprise, therefore, that aside from this realm of detailed reporting at classroom level, Smith and Schumacher develop certain theoretical notions concerning aesthetic education. They introduce and develop a complicated model of aesthetic education, pointing out how it can provide a common set of referents for curriculum developers, teachers, and developmental psychologists; they show how the different implicit models held by teachers and developers can be delineated more clearly and show how ideas of 'aesthetic sophistication' and 'aesthetic development' can be clarified and drawn out; and how considering the model and its relationship to the AEP leads to questions concerning basic conceptions of human nature and personality. Here we find extension of the role of evaluator into being pedagogic theoretician. Unfortunately, lack of space precluded the reproduction of this part of the report.

Smith and Schumacher, in the final paragraph of their report, lay out what their perception is of the role of evaluation in the development and implementation of curricula:

One of the most intriguing findings concerns the confluence of diffusion theory and practice, organisation theory and practice, and curriculum theory and practice in an enterprise such as these extended pilot trials. AEP is an interdisciplinary arts curriculum which is being introduced into organisations with idiosyncratic structures (specialist vs generalist; central office vs building control, etc.), through a complicated cooperative interorganisational effort. The descriptions and analyses we have included add to the cumulating traditions and literature in educational programme and policy development. Our intent is to increase the practicality of theoreticians and increase the theoretical in practitioners. [6]

The last chapter of Smith and Schumacher's report on the AEP consists of the summary, conclusions and recommendations. We reproduce the first section of the last chapter in which the authors present three general conclusions as a result of their study. This strikes us as a model of clarity, brevity and straightforwardness.

6   Smith and Schumacher, *op. cit.*, p. 156.

5.9 Louis Smith and Sally Schumacher
Extended pilot trials of the Aesthetic
Education Program: a qualitative description,
analysis and evaluation[1]

A brief description of the AEP curriculum and the six packages

For purposes of clarity, we present a brief overview of the AEP curriculum, the object of study in the evaluation inquiry. Each teacher's guide presents this statement as an introduction to the programme.

Traditionally, all of the arts have not been a part of the education of elementary and secondary students. In an attempt to remedy this situation, the Aesthetic Education Program at CEMREL, Inc. is developing a materials resource in aesthetic education that presents aesthetic qualities of all the arts and deals with the impact of these qualities on our daily lives.

This package is one in a group of instructional units for use in the primary grades. Designed to be taught by the classroom teacher as well as the arts specialist, the package introduces students to one aspect of the arts and the environment on which they can build an aesthetic awareness. The package can be used in conjunction with other aesthetic education packages in a sequence appropriate to the needs and capabilities of students. The needs and capabilities of the students also determine the grade at which the package is taught. The correspondence between levels, as used in these packages and grades, is as follows:

AEP package level	Grade
1	K
2	1
3	2
4	3

Packages for the primary grades are organised around four themes. Series 1, Introduction to Aesthetic Phenomena, contains packages that acquaint students with basic physical elements of the arts—light, sound, motion, time and shape. Packages in the second series, Elements in the Arts Disciplines and the

1 The research reported herein was supported in part by CEMREL, Inc. (formerly the Central Midwestern Regional Educational Laboratory, Inc.), a private non-profit making corporation supported in part as a regional educational laboratory by funds from the United States Office of Education, Department of Health, Education and Welfare. The opinions expressed in this publication do not necessarily reflect the position of policy of the Office of Education, and no official endorsement by the Office of Education should be inferred.

Source: L. M. Smith and S. Schumacher (August 1972). Extended Pilot Trials of the Aesthetic Education Program: A Qualitative Description, Analysis and Evaluation, CEMREL, Inc. The extracts reproduced here are taken from pp. 5-6, 8-9, 43-5, 48-52, 64-6, 71-2, 76-7, 79-83, 154-5. The footnotes have been renumbered.

Environment, focus on elements within the arts, such as texture in music, shape in the visual arts, patterns of conflict in theatre. Series III, The Process of Transformation, contains packages that lead students through the creative process of synthesising aesthetic and physical elements into a work of art. People in the Arts packages (Series IV) contain materials and activities to help students come to an understanding of what an artist is, what he does, and how he does it. (Teacher's Guide, Relating Sound and Movement, p. 5.)

Eventually the curriculum will encompass kindergarten through Grade 12. . . .

During this first year of the extended pilot trial six of ten anticipated packages were delivered during the year. Because this analysis rests entirely upon these first six packages and because the reader needs a clear perception of the formal programme we present a short description of each package, again from the teacher's guides. Later, and in considerable detail, we will extend the meaning of each package in a discussion of its use by teachers and pupils and in our inferences regarding a broad conception of aesthetic education.

Creating Dramatic Plot

One of the aesthetic phenomena of theatre is dramatic structure. The ability to perceive any portion of this structure increases the student's capacity to experience this phenomenon. As dramatic plot is a significant aspect of dramatic structure, the exploration of this component should increase the students' aesthetic perceptions of the theatrical experience.

Relating Sound and Movement

Relating Sound and Movement is designed to provide third-level students with a vehicle for exploring and experiencing continuums within pitch, tempo and amount of intensity in sound; within amount of space, amount of time and amount of force in movement. The seven lessons are arranged to refine the student's ability to differentiate among high-low, fast-slow, loud-soft/strong-weak sounds and movements. The student explores possible relationships between sound and movement: matching sound with movement, contrasting the two and, finally, integrating his experiences with sound and movement and sharing with other students and the teacher the evaluation of his progress.

Metre

In this package the student will be introduced to the concept of metre and its functional relationship to musical composition. Through exposure to recorded musical selections, he will learn to identify and execute simple metres. Nine lessons, ranging in length from ten to thirty minutes, include introductions to the musical terms 'accent', 'barline', 'metre', 'measure' and 'theme'. Student involvement will require listening to the recording, perceiving metrical notations on the charts, clapping metres heard and notating simple duple and triple metres on response sheets.

Creating Word Pictures
This package is designed to increase the abilities of students at the third, fourth and fifth levels to communicate effectively and imaginatively in the English language, both orally and in writing. The package is divided into five major parts: a brief diagnostic activity that can be used both prior to and after instruction, and the four sections of the Word Book. The Word Book and its activities provides opportunities for students to reach these goals: creating novel word combinations, describing the sensuous connotations of words and drawing specific and meaningful analogies.

Creating Characterisation
One of the aesthetic phenomena of theatre is characterisation. Characterisation may be defined as the actor's process of selection, synthesis and expression of personality traits, emotional and intellectual, of a character. In preparing a part an actor will identify specific mental and emotional characteristics of a personality. The characteristics chosen must then be organised and related to other facets of the character's personality. Finally, the actor's body and voice must be made to express those characteristics for the audience. The ability to perceive any portion of the actor's portrayal increases the student's capacity to experience this phenomenon.

Texture: Visual and Tactual
The unit is designed to provide kindergartners and first grade students with the means to identify and understand texture in the environment and in visual art referents through sensory tactual experiences, verbal and tactual relationships, kinesthetic and tactual relationships and correlation of tactual and visual stimuli.

   This then is the curriculum being tried out in extended pilot. Half a dozen packages were finished and made available during this first year. Mostly they were directed to second and third grade children. They were those packages which were ready, that is, those that had been conceived, tried out in a 'messing around' stage, revised, survived through 'hot house' and 'pilot trials' and received their 'near final' editing and been accepted by a commercial publisher for limited production. . . .

Classroom experiences

An illustrative vignette

This morning at 10.25 a.m. I observed my first class using the Metre package. For a musical illiterate, it proved to be a fascinating experience. The twenty-eight children (second and third graders in an open environment class) were grouped in two semi-circles with centre stage shared by Chart 4, the phonograph and two children, each with what looked like a homemade drum head. The teacher, who seemed comfortable with the materials, explained 'accents' as 'louder or stronger' beats and indicated that the children should make a fist for the hard beats and use an open hand for the soft taps. Her directions blended with explanations as she indicated 'bar lines', 'measures' and 'duple' and 'triple' metre. The two children had little trouble reading the music and performing as musicians. This activity was rotated through several pairs of children, each of whom selected his successor. Spliced into the activity was a total group performance. The children clapped the several lines of music in duple and triple metre with appropriate accents. Throughout, participation and involvement were high. The facial expressions were of pleasure. The teacher made almost no comments of a disciplinary sort. (In a later part of the lesson, considerable contrast occurred.)

The teacher flowed in and out of the lesson in what might be called 'goal facilitation interventions', that is, when some problem occurred which hindered accomplishment she found a way to move in, momentarily help and move out. The best example occurred with a child or two who couldn't use the drum head. As though she were teaching a psychomotor skill, she reached around the child, held the drum and the child's hand, and started the appropriate duple or triple metre. When the child caught on, she carried on alone. Later illustrations of the same sort occurred in the total group clapping. For instance, the teacher would clap in exaggerated fashion, particularly with each new line and new beat. In the middle section of activities she went from table to table where the children were having difficulty. As she said 'Listen!' she would tap on the table with exaggerated and obvious motions, the beats and accents. As the children understood, even momentarily, she would move on.

The middle part of the day's activity consisted of listening to Activity 7 and recording on Response Sheet 3. Once the response sheets had been passed out, the teacher began the record. The children had difficulty following the directions, hearing the metre and getting responses recorded on the sheets. The teacher (and the principal who was visiting) moved about helping the children, as indicated earlier. The kids seemed puzzled, their faces and actions were not of clarity, they looked at each other and each other's papers, they raised their hands for the teacher. Progressively, as they worked through the three illustrations, more playing with pencils, reading library books and chattering occurred. Concurrently, through this twenty minutes, more teacher comments, 'shushes' and 'sit right in your seat' directions appeared.

The final fifteen minutes took the form of a total class review, 'go over the materials so you understand', of the record and identification of the metre and noting of accents. This turned out to be a 'mild disaster'. The teacher drew the metre charts on the blackboard. She tried to stay ahead by alternating between two boards, one on the south wall and one on the west wall. She had a pupil go to the board and indicate metre and accent for each. They had some problems. In spite of several reprimands, two girls persisted in playing with the drum heads; they alternated in reading Chart 4 and trying to keep time with the music on the record. The teacher's comments, 'Listen carefully, boys and girls. Most of you aren't listening', seemed both accurate and necessary. She did the last part 'once again' over the growing distraction and resistance of the children for she was concerned that they understood. Her last comment was 'I think we'll have to do it over again. Some of you haven't got it yet'. At 11.13 they started to set up for an ETV science lesson about the moon. . . .

Performing and observing re affective content

The Creating Characterisation package arrived late in the year; consequently, some of the teachers did not try it during the last few weeks of school. As we observed those that did, we found it opened several new domains of experience. For instance, one class, a group of eighteen to twenty children in a small room were using the masks and a projector which threw the various colours from the theatrical gels upon a screen. The children had some minor troubles with the elastic strings which were to hold the masks on their faces, eagerly volunteered for turns and busily selected by themselves the mask, the emotions and the mode and content of expression that went with the emotion. The teacher gave simple instructions to 'listen, watch arms, body, etc.'. The first three children were sad, happy and surprised in turn. The sad girl rubbed her eyes, commenting 'Oh, I'm so sad'; the happy boy exuberantly jumped up and down and commented 'Oh, I'm so happy. The sun is out'. Later, anger and fright entered the parade.

Among the complex array of implications suggested by the episode is the dual nature of the activity. Some children engaged in 'performing behaviour' and others engaged in 'audience or observing behaviour'. All were part of the substantive discussion or 'ideational behaviour' which tied the two together. The content of these three clusters was 'affect' or 'emotion'. In general it was cloaked as drama and theatre; however, it spilled over into the classroom more generally as we indicate in a later discussion of 'pupil–classroom roles'.

Conversations later in the day with the teacher indicated that over the years she has been involved in a variety of creative teaching activities. One of these paralleled the nature and intent of the emotion book. She would bring in magazines and have the children cut out pictures of people. With these the class would talk about the way the people felt and what had happened to them in the pictures. She related this then to creative writing. . . .

Converting perceptions to expressive performances

Nuances of aesthetic learning appeared in all of the packages. In Characterisation, the development of performing skills were built on to perceptions and ideas.

> Teacher: *Look at that picture* (of the composite which they had created) *and try to make yourself like the picture.*
> They do.
> We (teacher, aide and observers) go around.
> (Obs: *Great Fun!*)
> Teacher: *Is it as easy as you thought?*
> Pupils: *No!*
> Teacher: *Want to do another one?*
> Pupils: *Yes!*
> Teacher: *Select another face, emotions, whole body. Help each other if they need a little.*

Finally, the focus shifted ever so slightly, from figural cues for performances to verbal cues. The children are in pairs and the teacher comments:

> Teacher: *Each of you think of an emotion word.*
> *See how good you are at expressing an emotion. Just use your face, head, neck.*
> They do those.
> (Obs: *Some very well.*)
> Teacher: *Now try just hands and arms.*

Once again while our point is quite simple, the processes are quite complex. The children are involved with covert internal processes. In this instance, emotions. They then were trying to convert these feelings into overt 'expressive' behaviours. They have constructed, synthesised, emotional reactions using the picture composite activity. They tried to 'act' out the representation. They think of new emotions. They try to represent these with limited parts of the body. They help one another — which is a very complex perceptional, social, emotional skill in itself.

Difficulties in performing expressive acts

The evaluative observer has the continual analytic task of pulling apart items that tend to be integrated in most life situations. In this manner distinctions and emphases can be built rationally into the programme. Late one day late in the year, the observers reflected on several aspects of the day's observations:

Another outcome of observing Characterisation this morning involves the distinction between the kids' social intelligence in knowing what some of the signs mean, which is one set of problems and being able to perform or express them. The latter fits very nicely in the performance role. It poses the problem of the 'for real' approaches as opposed to the 'acting' point of view. The perception of the issues might well be in the appreciator role.

In the same sense, watching the kids in Sound and Movement during the early afternoon raises more of the issue of the kids who can very simply make cognitive discriminations and comparisons between high and low, fast and slow, etc., and those kids who somehow are not able to actually perform the actions. In this sense not only perform them but also do it with some style, *élan* or imagination. For at least some of these items you've got to be aware, you've got to know, before you can behave. In other situations, you may well be able to engage in the expression of the emotion or of the activity without really being aware of how it's being done or being able to talk about it. The kids also seem to have some of that problem today when the teachers, for whatever reason, wanted them to explain what they would do before they came up on the stage. Often the kids couldn't explain it even though some of them could do it.

A similar observation had occurred a month earlier as another group began work on the Characterisation package.

For instance, in watching a Characterisation package, for the first time, yesterday, the children were very keen on the materials themselves and enjoyed working with the composite as well as the brief review of the emotion book. They seemed to be able to identify very quickly emotions of anger, surprise, happiness that the dancer in the composite was expressing. Later, when the teacher had them try to show the illusion by acting it out, some of the children had great difficulty getting the placement of hands or feet or face or arms. One little chubby girl sitting in the back was quite beautiful at this. The teacher told me later that she was a 'real actress' and this was quite evident in the Dramatic Plot game when they acted out some of their materials. Some of the boys as well as the girls were quite stiff and unable to use their bodies to convey and represent the emotions being expressed in the materials from the composites. Again, the point I want to make here is that the perceptual, cognitive understanding of the expression of emotions in non-verbal ways from pictures, cards, etc. is very different from the expression of the materials with one's own hands or face or body.

One of the problems this suggests is the relationship of the domain of 'tacit knowledge' to aesthetic education. As Polanyi, who has tried to develop a point of view about tacit knowledge, explains it:

. . . We can know more than we can tell. This fact seems obvious enough; but it is not easy to say exactly what it means. Take an example. We know a person's face, and can recognise it among a thousand, indeed among a million. Yet we usually cannot tell how we recognise a face we know. So most of this knowledge cannot be put into words.[2]

In some instances the children seem to 'know' more than they can express verbally. In addition, at times the motoric expression is almost as difficult

2   M. Polanyi (1966). *The Tacit Dimension*. Garden City, New York: Doubleday, p. 4.

as the verbal expression. In other instances the programme seems to be stressing a kind of knowledge which is very difficult to assess and thereby provokes extreme difficulty in evaluation.[3]

Selfconsciousness

Several of the teachers spoke of 'selfconsciousness' of children as they engaged in aesthetic activities such as drama, music and graphic arts. While it was difficult to pin them down they seemed to be saying several things:

1   As children progress from kindergarten through the primary grades they become conscious of themselves in an embarrassed way when carrying out performing kinds of tasks or roles.

2   The teachers see this as inhibiting and as not desirable.

3   This embarrassedness can be minimised by varied activities and considerable experience carried out with the children in smaller groups and away from 'centre stage'.

4   The CEMREL materials should be useful in this regard.

At this point, the four propositions are mostly conjectural. They are testable. The ultimate goal of more open and expressive interaction in the classroom — and more generally — would probably be seen as desirable by most teachers and parents. The children's willingness to volunteer in characterisations with the masks, to 'acting out' their brief dramatic plots, and to try novel variations in movement, and to lead the clapping or marching to various metres in music attest to the viability of the fourth hypothesis, the role of the AEP curriculum. . . .

Teachability

Perhaps the best way to introduce the emphasis on the teacher concerns the degree to which the materials can be used by the teacher. The summary notes reflect on a full day of observation when all of the first five packages were being used.

A number of generalisations have come up, some very broad and some very narrow. I'll try to talk about a few of those.

First, one of the most general conclusions is that the programme is teachable. That may not be a very incisive one but it is a very important one. Yesterday I saw parts of all the packages . . . Metre, Sound and Movement, Dramatic Plot, Word Pictures and Characterisation. Some of the lessons were review lessons and a return to the materials after some four, five or six weeks. This was the case with Word Pictures and also with Dramatic Plot. Some of it was very new and at the beginning, as in the case of Characterisation, particularly, and Sound and Movement to some degree.

3   Polanyi's illustrations of the police use of picture composites might be an interesting way of testing understanding as well as AEP's use in developing and teaching in this area.

In effect, on that day, the materials were in all stages of introduction: initial lessons to long-term review. Seven different teachers were involved with five different packages.

A related point, variability in teacher utilisation, extends the teachability idea. The notes continued:

Another item concerns the immense variability in the way the programme is utilised from classroom to classroom and school to school. Yesterday's field notes, for instance, contain extended description of a team teaching of a Metre package which seemed to go very well. The two girls meet the criterion of a 'swinging team' as we have used it before. They seem to work very well together, enjoy each other's company, and are interested in the materials and the kids and what is happening. There also seems to be a 'school building factor' in the use of the materials. I don't know whether I'm hung up on the group norm conception or whether it is a reality that I am seeing. But from building to building some packages seem to go well and other packages don't. We speculate a little bit in the field notes proper about that as to whether it is abilities and backgrounds of the kids or whether it is an evolving common perception by the teachers. This group, for instance, was quite down on Word Pictures and quite high on Dramatic Plot which is a contrast with the teachers from yesterday. Actually, as I watched a Word Pictures Lesson, which was a three-week to six-week later review kind of thing, the kids seemed to do very well, seemed to enjoy the game and seemed to be creating quite imaginative responses.

In short, the materials were in a variety of classrooms. The teachers were inventing ways to use the materials with their children in their social setting. They were usable, that is teachable. As discussion develops we will indicate sub-concerns in this overall viewpoint.

Contrasting cases of teacher response to AEP

As we have indicated elsewhere, a new curriculum comes into a complicated structure of school organisation, faculty cliques and curriculum reorganisation. As might be expected, individual teachers responded quite differentially to this 'new opportunity' or 'new demands'. In a few instances, they used the materials infrequently, found fault with specific aspects of a package 'the children don't like to be forced to put elements in (Dramatic Plot)' or 'the carry-over has been much less than other teachers (in the building) have found', and used the late arrival of a package (Characterisation) in the spring as a reason for putting it aside until next fall.

In other instances, the materials have fit the teacher's style, methods and purposes like the proverbial glove. Then the materials became a major class activity during the year. In at least one instance it led to a major climactic teaching activity, a Christmas drama and hence pervaded all aspects of the teacher's class activity, her visibility and reputation among other teachers and parents, and her own self-conception and esteem.[4]

The specific generalisations are these: (1) there is high variability among teacher reception; (2) some of this is package-specific and (3) the general reaction was favourable. Perhaps the best evidence for the favourable reaction was the offhand unsolicited comments that came unexpectedly. For instance, while sitting in a teachers' lounge the observer had a chat with the school librarian which the notes caught this way:

Had a brief conversation with the school librarian; several unsolicited comments:
(1) Teachers are all excited; talk about it at odd times all the time.
(Obs: very important data.) . . .

A caveat for developers who sometime live in a cloistered setting of true belief is that one's shining lovely creative product is not viewed that way by everyone. The corollary is that classroom teachers are caught with background, talent and ability limitations and in their own worlds of stress and multiple demands, with children who are sometimes recalcitrant as well as creative. . . .

Flair

Webster defines flair as a natural talent or ability. Some of our teachers seemed to find the materials so isomorphic or congruent with their teaching style that they moved with the materials as though they were born to it. It was as though they had a tacit understanding of the curriculum. In the notes we speculated this way.

Another one of the experiments that needs to be run is to take a teacher like Mrs Johnson and have her teach the AEP stuff and also have her teach comparable groups with the regular stuff. That would be an interesting part of the degree of implementation problem, it would also raise some real questions about what happens when the teachers with the enthusiasm and the flair go at the problem with any set of materials. Maybe partly what I am asking is to scale teachers in terms of something that might be called flair and watch them take on different kinds of materials such as AEP and such as the Silver Burdette or other materials. In a sense then, one could get middle level teachers on flair and non-flair type teachers. That would give you an interesting interaction with the materials themselves.

In a sense we are raising the aptitude-treatment interaction problem at the level of the teachers and the materials in contrast to the usual discussion of pupils and materials interaction. . . .

4 Parenthetically, it's difficult to convey in the words of a final report the quality of expression of voice, face, eyes of a teacher as the teacher recounted with emotion the details of 'What happened' to the itinerant evaluator who inquired 'How'd it go?' in his best non-directive stance.

Two major problems in teaching the AEP curriculum

Classroom control: a common concern

One of the educational partial truths, if not a fallacy, which curriculum developers are prone to believe is that 'good' materials, such as theirs eliminate all problems in discipline, deviancy and lack of work-involvement. Our data suggest that the AEP materials pose some very interesting and important problems in management and instruction. The first of these problems might be labelled 'teaching a non-recitational curriculum'. The second problem we have called 'Arousing complex emotions and expressive behaviour in the classroom'. Both are linked through one of the classic dilemmas of our time, freedom and control, as that dilemma plays itself out in the classroom. It is also our contention that the programme in its workshops, teacher's manuals and other formal documents has barely touched these complexities. This section of our report lays out some of the issues as we observed them and have begun to analyse them. In keeping with our general approach, the ideas are hypotheses and questions presented to further the developing theoretical, practical and research basis of the programme.

In the public schools, at least as they are currently organised, large numbers of children and teachers share limited space, materials and facilities. Children are required to attend. Many classroom activities are determined by forces other than the children and their teachers. Teachers and principals are in *loco parentis* and are legally responsible for the supervision of the children; superintendents are hired to carry out school board policy; and school boards are elected to represent the will of the public. These realities exist[5] and underlie all attempts at school reform and innovation at the organisational, instructional and curricular levels. Elements of control, coordination, impersonality and rules follow, if not like night after day, almost as probably and unchangeably.[6]

Into this set of assumptions, we would make the observation that in any group of teachers and their classes variability exists in 'classroom control'. By classroom control we mean simply that the children respond readily and agreeably to teacher requests, instructions and directives. For the moment we need not concern ourselves with the sources of control, the kind of power involved, but for purposes of discussion assume that it's reasonably benevolent in most instances. The point we wish to make is that for those teachers with limited control the package programme introduces some interesting complications. . . .

5   Many variations appear; much discussion and activity is currently underway to alter these societal-school relationships as well as the more manifest characteristics.

6   For exciting if somewhat pessimistic recent efforts at attempts to alter schools see L. M. Smith & P. Keith (1971). *Anatomy of Educational Innovation.* New York: Wiley.

Teaching a non-recitational curriculum

Methods of grouping was a recurrent problem to many teachers. The variations included pupil choices, lottery, partial ability grouping, socio-metric choices, teacher judgement and so forth. Some alternatives were very time-consuming, some the pupils didn't like initially, others they accepted initially but later when they couldn't work productively they rejected. As one teacher reported:

Mrs Koster told me that friendship groups break down if at least one of the children is not able. They've tried grouping this way.

The fact of having eight to ten subgroups operating at the same time was a new experience for many teachers. Most had experienced the classical three reading groups pattern, and some typically had four or five groups. This posed serious problems when the materials were too difficult for several of the groups (e.g. reading the Dramatic Plot cards), when the instructions indicated that the teacher was supposed to monitor, question or evaluate the children's production, or when the children had to be instructed in the game. When the rules and the mode of operating had to be taught continuously as opposed to the format of playing a game which had been played before and everyone knew 'how to do it', then a very different set of circumstances arose. The interrelationship of this to the usual educational tasks which progressively increase in difficulty is an under-investigated phenomenon.

In some instances the children presented serious problems in being able to work cooperatively in small groups. This led to a much more intensive analysis of the dimensions in cooperation; we presented that elsewhere . . .

The line between 'humour' and 'silliness' is very fine. Creative materials, whether in word pictures, dramatic plot or characterisation, have an irrevocable tie with humour. On occasion, with classes with minimal control or with pupils with personal problems the materials would set them off, the noise level would increase, the excitement would contage and soon their behaviour would lose any kind of focus intended by the package, and the teacher would struggle with the chaos.

Additional difficulties arose with any class with a larger than usual number of children with 'discipline problems', 'mental health problems' or 'situational difficulties'. Granted that these categories are difficult to define conceptually, the realities were real. The situational problem included children who recently lost a parent through death, or whose parents were in the middle of a divorce. Teachers mentioned several such incidents to us. Children who were receiving psychiatric care or counselling were present in some of the classes. Finally, the children who constantly called out, moved from group to group 'bothering other children' and who 'weren't interested' in the AEP materials, or anything else according to their teachers, presented a problem.

Other problems concerned the 'differential finishing' of plots and word pictures. The transition out of the activity was difficult for several classes. Trying to get all groups to finish (rather than letting some return later in the day or week), trying to have all groups record their dramas, or trying to get more than two or three to report to the entire class, seemed to provoke difficulties. For instance:

As groups terminate at different times, there is no easy transition. Some kids write them out (Dramatic Plot). Others wait to read them to the teacher. Some get playful as they explore around.

And in another class:

11.10 Attempts to read story are inhibited by too much noise. Half of class gathers around close to hear. Problem in keeping kids quiet. She speaks to the class several times. Through all this the group at my table rushes to finish.
11.17 Continues oral reading. Kids are a bit quieter after the more noisy ones have really been put in their seats. Tempo ebbs and flows this way.
(Obs: Some feeling on my part that the children are hyperstimulated or bored, no simple medium.)
Lion and tiger story sets off a few of the children.
11.22 Finally finishes last story.

Later, at lunch, the notes pick up a final comment:

The teacher comes over. Raise problems for workable style in oral reading. Reading, writing, taping, etc. Apologises for 'losing her cool'.[7]

Most of the teachers tried oral reporting of dramatic plots (as well as word pictures and characterisation). After observing and talking with teachers from three different schools the following notes were made:

Oral reporting of all groups full of problems:
  1   kids don't talk loud enough,
  2   often facing away from others; need desks pointed in,
  3   some stories aren't interesting enough,
  4   some kids unfinished; consequently still talking,
  5   scattered in awkward decentralised space,
  6   once a group has reported it's off into other activities,
  7   oral reading problems; some can't read cards very well,
  8   detail often missing; who quizzes, teachers or pupils?

In one sense, all this says is that the children need to be taught performing and audience skills. So it is. While they are learning the skills, they produce some problems in group management.

7   On other occasions we were observers of more traditional total class language arts and spelling lessons. These moved along with much less conflict.

In summary, there seemed to be a variety of barriers to 'effective utilisation' of the packages. Specifying the problem spots often suggests some immediate solutions. Some of the issues are tied to more fundamental styles of the teacher, interactional skills and pupil personality. These remain important areas for experimental variations and for teacher training research and workshops.

Hyperactive or excitable classes contrast with one we labelled, 'the lethargic class'. Labelling or typing classes has its hazards. If the labels reflect critical dimensions, then the process can help produce the careful thinking or the muted cues that contribute to successful teaching. One of our groups was described as 'below average in ability and difficult to arouse emotionally'. The teacher seemed to be doing several things as she taught a lesson in Creating Word Pictures.[8] First, she let them organise themselves into groups of fours which took about six minutes. As she said 'if I let them find themselves it works easier'. Second, she had monitors come up for books, cards and large layout sheets. Third, she told them to turn to page 28. Fourth, she presented the guiding idea with a reference back to 'grasshopper wallpaper' and 'wallpaper grasshopper'. Fifth, she read the first page or two to the children. Sixth, she made sure everyone could find the 'spot with the spider'. Seventh, she finished reading. And finally, the teacher starts to move around among the children giving help and suggestions. The observer noted 'Through all this the kids are quiet, attentive, interested'.

Late in the year in talking with two teachers—one of whom had tried Dramatic Plot and the other who was about to start—the control issue arose concerning the kids' introduction to the materials. The discussion went back and forth and around several points. The difficulties, the non-school gamelike format, the excitement of the children and so forth. In the course of the conversation the possibility arose of partially combining the two classes and introducing the new children to the materials much as children's games are learned in the home and neighbourhood. The older and more experienced children play, show, tell and explain the rules and procedures to younger, less experienced children and thereby gradually induct them into the experience.[9] If this is half as successful as it seemed in planning it could help considerably with the control problem.

Successful art teachers report their surprise that management problems exist with the curriculum. They are used to living in the 'orderly chaos' of higher noise levels, multiple kinds of materials (paints, paper, brushes, water, etc.), pupils scattered everywhere each doing his own thing in some

---

8   The management skills in her reading the materials to offset the pupil's limitations, the clarity of directions and in this instance leisurely pace illustrate the possibilities in thinking through the teacher's skills in management.

9   Seldom have we found an occasion where team teaching and peer tutoring, two of the current icons, made as much sense as in this episode. How it works we don't know; but the teachers were enthused to try.

kind of total class context, and so forth. Since we have not been arts teachers, have not been exposed to the conventional wisdom in the principles of teaching art and the apprenticeship programmes, nor have we conducted research in such settings, the problem strikes us as one open to codification and possibly empirical investigation. Whichever tack, the knowledge seems a high priority on the agenda of a number of AEP teachers whose experience tends to be dominated by total group recitational activities in the three Rs.

Arousing complex emotions and expressive behaviour in the classroom

The second issue, the arousal of complex emotions in a classroom, is a very complicated and real problem also. For many teachers the possible gains are not worth the costs of their own anxiety, of possible loss of classroom controls, and in moving into an area where the professional guidelines are less well worked out than in reading, 'riting, and 'rithmetic. Since AEP moves directly into this area, some discussion and clarification seems warranted of this aspect of classroom utilisation.

During a very brief observation of an activity from the characterisation package, we were privy to several fragmented comments which suggest the array of issues in expressive behaviour in the classroom. The children are engaged in improvisation sessions built around Raef, Egar and Har on a picnic. The fragments are these:

1   As the children are thoroughly in their roles the teacher comments 'All right. There is a fine line between staying in the character and acting silly.[10] Don't overdo it.'
2   Two children commenting to each other, *sotto voce,* said, 'Billy's acting is not his real self; Joey's acting his real self.'
3   In describing and critiquing Joey's performance of Egar the children indicate 'Everything was good, powerful voice feeling of anger building up.'
(Obs: Kids are worked up; difficult to control selves. Once again expressiveness running loose.)
4   Later, a boy who had been playing Raef sought the teacher's attention. He did not get it. He engaged in a variety of attention-getting behaviours.
(Obs: Boy who was Raef is ticked off. He wants commentary on his acting. He also seems like a problem child. Her move to the next activity is a very bad move on above grounds.)

Our vignette suggests a simple hypothesis or two such as role playing or dramatic improvisation in contrast to textbook learning is more apt to generate emotional and attitudinal reactions and involvement. Secondly, that turning off the emotional reaction is not as simple as shifting from arithmetic to spelling. In the case of the boy playing Raef, who the

---

10   The acting 'silly' came up with almost every package at one time or another in one classroom or another.

observer saw as a 'problem' in the class, mainly in his calling out, his attempts to gain the teacher's attention, and his disturbing other children, the problem was very real. He was so 'jazzed up' by the activity that he could not settle down.

Insofar as emotional reactions have a respondent rather than operant basis, to use Skinner's terminology, (and Mowrer's framework as well), then a very different set of procedures and principles apply. Insofar as expressive behaviour involves a mix of the respondent and operant (or the affective with the cognitive and psychomotor to use another framework) the problems are doubly difficult. In addition, if teachers define these kinds of pupil reactions as involving counselling rather than teaching, a further issue is created. All of which is to say, the curriculum has some pervasive, difficult and only partially analysed problems in this area. In a sense the curriculum seems involved in these issues whether we like it or not. . . .

Summary and conclusions

This evaluation project was the first step of a five-year summative evaluation of the extended pilot trials of a new curriculum. In a few short paragraphs it seems appropriate to state briefly and pointedly: what we did, why we did what we did, what we have found out and what recommendations we would make.

We have come to these conclusions through direct observation of the programme. The mode of inquiry goes by such names as 'participant observation', 'qualitative field study', 'ethnography' and case study research. It is practised by a wide range of social scientists in education, psychology, sociology and anthropology. In our view it is admirably suitable for investigating complex social phenomena, i.e. social systems, for developing concrete descriptions of those phenomena and for generating conceptualisations, hypotheses and theories.

A number of substantive results occurred from our observational research. First and foremost perhaps is that the materials are 'teachable'. By that we mean that most teachers, after a two-day teacher workshop, some review on their own, some support (coordinator and from local district supervisors and/or its specialists) can present the materials and involve the children in ways that seem relevant to the rationale. That such a statement is made by two investigators who are relatively independent[11]

11   We accent the 'relatively' aspect of independent evaluation. Elsewhere we spoke to the issues of cooptation and independence. A major analysis of this is needed in the context of R & D, federal support and the social science establishment. For openers, the statements by Mills (1959) and Gouldner (1968, 1971) suggest the magnitude and the seriousness of the problem: see C. W. Mills (1959). *The Sociological Imagination.* London: Oxford University Press; A. W. Gouldner (1968). 'The sociologist as partisan: sociology and the welfare state', *American Sociologist,* 3, 103-16; A. W. Gouldner (1971). *The Coming Crisis in Western Sociology.* New York: Basic Books.

of the programme, of the laboratory and the State Department seems significant.

Secondly, and related to the teachability concept, the children responded positively to the materials. For the most part they enjoyed the sub-activities. They seemed to take part in creating, implementing and critiquing activities; all behaviours which seem essential to a conception of aesthetic education. In addition, their performances in music and theatre, to pick the two most relevant illustrations, and their ability to 'talk aesthetic education' regarding the half dozen packages, suggest that learning has occurred.

Thirdly, in our judgement, the most serious weakness in AEP has been a theoretical conception of aesthetic education viable for children, teachers and evaluators, if not for developers also. In part, this is contradictory to our first comment regarding teachability of the materials; our hypothesis is that further understanding would enhance the teachers' ability to improvise and use the materials and related activities more creatively.

Evaluation as vivisection:
two experiments at MIT

*The final selection of extracts comes from a report commissioned within
the Massachusetts Institute of Technology on two experimental undergraduate programmes.*[1] *The two programmes studied were USSP [the
Unified Science Study Program] and ESG [the Experimental Study
Group]. In 1971, when Malcolm Parlett and his associates made the study,
these two programmes were in their third year and there was a growing
sense that some of their fundamental premises needed to be re-examined
in the light of experience.*

*The experimental programmes were set up at a time when radical
innovations were fashionable throughout American higher education.
Their rationales reflect some of the predominent themes — not to say
preoccupations — of the reformist movement in the late 1960s; there was a
concern to redefine student/teacher roles, to remove restrictions and lessen
the academic and social control exercised by 'power groups' in the
universities, to encourage individual and independent enterprises. USSP
and ESG were established at MIT mainly for first-year students. Each
provided an alternative freshman year, a total experience [short of living
together] that was designed to encourage individual initiative, in a climate
of supportive freedom. The two programmes developed independently of
one another. There was even some hostility and rivalry between them for a
long while. However, this did not prevent their encountering similar
difficulties, many of which derived from their particular — isolated but
dependent — institutional status within the university.*

*A good deal of scepticism about the two programmes existed among the
rest of the faculty at MIT. The faculty Committee on Educational Policy
was responsible for 'evaluating' the programmes and for making a
recommendation to the whole faculty at MIT concerning whether they
should be continued and institutionalised or phased out. Parlett was
commissioned to make a study that would inform members of this
committee. Although the report was open to all members of the
community, and though he intended that the report should be of interest
and perhaps use to members of the programmes themselves, his chief
purpose, defined by his brief, was to report to the committee. He took
pains to ensure that they understood that he was not going to make their
decisions for them, but give them as full an account as possible of what*

1 Malcolm Parlett (1972). *A Study of Two Experimental Programs at MIT.* Report to the Committee on Educational Policy, MIT, Cambridge, Mass.

had transpired in the programmes, what the programmes did and what they didn't do, what their problems were, and how they had overcome them.

The study was completed in six weeks and written up in another six. For a quick study it is both lengthy and relatively comprehensive, but of necessity it lacked the capacity to observe directly changes over time, where secondary sources had to be relied upon. Somewhat surprisingly, there is little shift in the style of reportage between the face-to-face situations and those in which the information has been mediated through other accounts.

Parlett's report, like the PLATO study, begins with an explanatory scene-setting memorandum-cum-foreword. It takes the form of a memo from Parlett to Hartley Rogers, Jr. and Dan Kleitman which, as Parlett remarks, 'can be regarded as a Foreword to the report'. In this foreword he makes it clear to the policy-makers that he is not 'evaluating' the special programme in the sense of 'assigning value', but rather has the more modest aim, 'to study each programme . . . "with a view to describing them; exploring pedagogic issues they raise, distinguishing between their central and peripheral features; and detailing what participants and others regard as their advantages and disadvantages relative to the normal MIT programme" '.[2] *A brief extract from the 'foreword', together with an extract from a further memorandum from Parlett to Dan Kleitman, chairman of a coordinating sub-committee of the CEP at MIT, is included before the selections from the report proper. The second memorandum, written in advance of the study and included in an abbreviated version in the report as Appendix 1, throws light on the 'contract' between the evaluator, his client and sponsors. It also confirms the agreement, by committing Parlett's understanding of it to writing.*

One of the main functions of an evaluation report within the new paradigm is to document 'what happens'. The first extracts from A Study of Two Experimental Programs at MIT *are a clear example of this, tracing what the changes of the Unified Science Study Program were and why they occurred, and pulling together, in a single account, a whole variety of occurrences and developments whose significance had not generally been appreciated. One point, however, needs to be made: since Parlett is writing for members of a single institution, there is much that he can take for granted among the readers that may not be fully comprehensible to outsiders. This raises yet again the general issue of whether such 'close-up' reports are of compelling interest to outsiders. We feel that they are, although it may be necessary to remind ourselves that we are often eavesdropping on internal intelligence operations. Parlett is less interested than Lou Smith in pursuing generalisations, or advancing pedagogic*

2   M. Parlett (1972), *op. cit.*, p. i.

theory, from case-study data. His report is in a much more exact sense a 'portrayal' of the programmes under study.

This is not to say that Parlett approaches his authentic situations in a state of innocence, shorn of all theories. A major concern in his writing is with the learning milieu. This includes far more than the physical surroundings, buildings, classroom layout and so on. Yet 'milieu', as a word, does denote place, albeit place imbued with a style, a social climate, expectations, norms and so on.

It is the locality in which people live and work, fight, worry or teach; it is the environment-as-experienced. Although Parlett appears only minimally influenced by Barker's ecological psychology, he pays considerable attention to the physical dimensions that 'frame' the educational activities. To speak of milieu in Parlett's terms necessarily implies relating social processes and events in part to physical plant. But the descriptions of place are not in any way narrowly referential. The 'space imagery' moves easily within an emotive vocabulary of 'enclaves' and 'wombs'.

The chapter titles of A Study of Two Experimental Programs at MIT *reflect one of the intents of the 'responsive' evaluator, to address the questions raised by the audience to whom his report is addressed. There is some tension in Parlett's writing between the conflicting needs to back his own acute sensitivity and judgement (i.e. to offer an interpretation) and his methodological commitment to represent alternative perceptions and viewpoints in and around the programme fairly at the same time as facing the questions and issues raised by his primary audience. Parlett's report is easily seen as a compromise between these tensions, but one leaning perceptibly in the direction of the quasi-authoritative personal account. This is not how Parlett sees himself, although he acknowledges the dilemma which is a persistent one, endemic to this kind of study. A careful reading of the MIT report, however, suggests that Parlett's main goal in the exercise was to weave a wealth of collected 'quotes' into the fabric of a single comprehensive interpretation. There are implicit problems, and it is right to ask whether Parlett manages to avoid them.*

Readers of future evaluation reports, however, may rightly learn to suspect the formula 'I've heard it said' which is in danger of becoming the democratic evaluator's way of conferring legitimacy on some of his own hunches! Not that Parlett is other than meticulous in giving his sources, and the concern for fairness, aided by the slightly detached stance, comes through. On the other hand there is some ambivalence in Parlett's claim that the report is organised around specific questions that his audience is likely to ask. True, his chapter headings adopt the grammatical form of questions, but they include a number of purely rhetorical queries like 'what is floundering?'. 'Floundering', it turns out, was a word frequently used by members of the programmes and by those outside them to explain the disorientated and unproductive behaviour of students, confronted with free choice in the academic sphere. Like 'glop', 'floundering' clearly took

Parlett's fancy. But as the term originally offered an explanation, *not a question, it cannot easily be cited in support of Parlett's claim to be Stake's 'responsive evaluator', addressing himself to the questions of others. But the section on 'floundering' is, for other reasons, a clear example of interpretative evaluation at work.*

'Floundering' was a construct and concept already in existence, and one that allows Parlett a way of organising a number of comments and quotations from programme members. 'Floundering', like many other phenomena at MIT, was not restricted simply to one of the programmes and could be seen in ESG as well as USSP.

Finally a number of issues raised by the programmes are featured. These concern such matters as the personal rewards and frustrations of faculty members in the programmes, interactions between teachers and taught and role relationships in relatively undefined settings. These focused observations represent what Parlett considered to be some of the more fundamental underlying problems that had led to the widespread disaffection and unease felt by a lot of students.

Malcolm Parlett's style is an interesting and idiosyncratic one; it is not easily contained by simplistic summaries like 'a mixture of description and interpretation', although this phrase does contain a basic truth. Like Stake and Gjerde at T-City, Parlett is a collector and hoarder of viewpoints and perspectives. But he binds these together into a portrayal that is coherent in its style, format and organisation. And yet it is possible to claim that this study, written to a time-scale that scarcely gave time to reflect, is the most 'clinical' of the alternative evaluation reports featured, in the sense of seeking interpretations and explanations for phenomena, problems, trends and events observed, and also the 'thickest' in its description. It also comes nearest, as one might have expected, to the model put forward by Parlett himself and David Hamilton in 'Evaluation as illumination', with which we set the ball rolling in Section 1.

5.10   Malcolm Parlett
A study of two experimental programmes at MIT

Memo to Hartley Rogers, Jr. and Dan Kleitman, 15 December 1971

. . . Throughout the report I try to keep my personal views and opinions in the background. This is not to say I have no opinions, nor that they do not influence my work. They are bound to, and I acknowledge this. But the researcher has deliberately to minimise their impact on his perceptions and judgement. Otherwise he is in trouble.

In this memorandum I am partially freed from this constraint. And I can make the following statements of personal opinion.

1   I consider that ESG and USSP have contributed in a highly significant way to a major change in attitude (for both faculty and students) toward what is possible at MIT.

2   I think it would be an unfortunate state of affairs if it were taken for granted that Special Programmes need to be studied, and that somehow the regular programme does not need to be. It implies that one is 'deviant' and the other is 'normal'. The regular programme, in my view, is in need of a very great deal of searching study.

3   I believe that whatever is decided about these two particular programmes, avenues of experimentation should continue to exist at MIT. New programmes should be developed and enterprising and concerned faculty members should be supported if they wish to innovate. Difficult though it is to question educational assumptions in an effective and active way, it is precisely what MIT should continue to do. I consider it would be a disaster for MIT to cease to innovate and to experiment.

Having said all this makes it easier in the report that follows to be frank, searching and detached. It is not written in the guarded, euphemistic style of committee minutes. The need to understand the detailed operations of educational systems has an importance and urgency that leaves no room for the bland, for the vacuous or for the anodyne. . . .

Source: M. Parlett (1972). A Study of Two Experimental Programs at MIT. Report to the Committee on Educational Policy, MIT, Cambridge, Mass. The extracts reproduced here are taken from pp. iv-v, 7-15, 20, 28-31, 40-2, 45-6, 65-7, 73-4, 75-6, 77-8, 79.

Memo to Dan Kleitman, 16 June 1971

Preamble

There seems to be general agreement about the aims of the proposed study:

(i)   To examine the two programmes, USSP and ESG, with a view to describing them, exploring pedagogic issues they raise, distinguishing between their central and peripheral features and detailing what participants and others regard as their advantages and disadvantages relative to the normal MIT programme.

(ii)   To emphasise throughout, to all concerned, that my function is to 'illuminate' rather than to 'evaluate'. My task is not to suggest policy but to provide information and insight that can contribute to discussion and decision.

(iii)   To provide, by actually doing this study, an example of one way in which educational innovations can begin to be appraised and understood; to demonstrate that there is perhaps more to evaluating than reading grade-point averages off print-outs.

(iv)   To include, as a subsidiary study, a preliminary outline description of Concourse.

(v)   To produce a report (or, perhaps preferably, two separate reports) on USSP and ESG, which after submission to the CEP should be made freely available to all members of the MIT community.

General outline

The general aim will be to examine the programmes at three different levels:

1   The aims, ideologies, learning models and assumptions that underlie each programme;

2   Each programme's organisation, practices, conventions, prohibitions, faculty - student and student - student relations, resource management and decision-making processes;

3   Participating students' coping strategies, methods of study, academic activities, work records and perceptions of experiences. . . .

Report

What were the origins of these programmes, and What did they set out to do?

Unified Science Study Program

. . . The programme evolved out of several earlier projects considered by ERC, one of which was to set up a pre-medical programme for disadvantaged students. USSP had several different elements. It was to be an experimental programme at MIT; but also 'Once under way and successfully operating', a model for programmes, 'at other institutions in this and other countries'. 'We are undertaking to design, test and proliferate teaching materials and educational strategies to audiences of varied composition and sophistication'.

The driving force was dissatisfaction with 'the traditional constraints of American higher education'. It was *not* directed at MIT as such, but at college teaching in general. USSP would 'question all the assumptions of form and strategy: credentials, certification, style, scope, topic, pace, technique and organisation'. . . .

'It requires only guidance, observation, inquisitiveness and the willing-ness to dig patiently for clues and answers, for the complex and truly multi-disciplinary nature of our environment to emerge — an environment that presents us, ready made, with all the illustrative teaching material that anybody could ever want.' The programme would 'deliberately blur the boundaries which commonly separate our departmental disciplines', and concentrate on projects or problem-centred studies, that were 'recognisable and representative examples of phenomena and problems taken from nature as man finds it or makes it'. Many students 'do not acquire skills and knowledge best in the conventional classroom atmosphere'. . . .

Interdisciplinary projects, 'can appeal to audiences that vary widely in sophistication, prior training and vocational or professional aspirations'. They permit 'many entry points, many routes through, and many exits from, the formal educational experience. The choice of entry point, path and exit point for each student should be a function of his style, and ability, not limited by artificial constraints'.

The unit was to be both a topic, and a package of learning aids: 'background information about the phenomenon, relevant equipment and audio-visual material, suggestions for further studies, and an extensively annotated bibliography'. The unit was to be the basic component of the curriculum, and starting point for projects. 'The problem, phenomenon or idea the unit represents is recognisable and manageable at first.' The units, on such topics as mouldy bread, soap bubbles, water pollution, were to form a 'pivot' for a student's 'deep excursions into the sciences and the humanities'. For instance, 'by isolating moulds and finding out how and where they grow, he could reach topics in microbiology, biochemistry, pathology, nutrition, cross-cultural food processing methods. From there he might study problems in enzymology and chemical thermodynamics, or genetics and perhaps even anthropology'. . . . USSP hinged on a specific theory of instruction: cross-disciplinary project-based studies which start with some everyday phenomenon and lead the student into deeper, more sophisticated and more abstract study. It could almost be regarded as a higher order exercise in curriculum reform. . . .

Certain common expectations

Despite their differences there was certainly one shared expectation between the two new programmes: that the entering students would want to engage in intellectual activity of some sort. Not only this, but there was also the confident hope that a good many would 'take-off', 'catch fire', 'get turned on' or 'get locked (or latched) on to something'[1], that they would go into depth, and do a sustained piece of work. . . .

Associated with the general anticipation of intellectual vitality were several subsidiary predictions: that students would be around and would be seen; would use resources available; form interest groups and attend discussions, seminars and meetings if there were any; follow suggestions from faculty and do assigned work if asked to.

It is not surprising, given these ideas, that the organisers of the programme, when they began, were uncertain what precise procedures they would use for handling certification and credit. Surely they thought, these issues would look after themselves, except, perhaps, for a small minority. It is also not surprising that when these predominant expectations were by and large *not* fulfilled, it should have led to rethinking, to staff anxiety, to many of the preliminary ideas undergoing transformation.

What are the facilities and characteristics of the two programme areas?

One thing visitors to the programmes always seem to agree about. The two programmes look different, and somehow feel different — fundamentally so.

USSP is housed in the ramshackle labyrinth of Building 20, occupies 11 190 square feet,[2] and has the atmosphere and appearance of a research lab. ESG is much smaller — 2970 square feet, and its image is that of a comfortable reading room: carpeted, easy chairs, people sitting around reading and chatting. The discrepancy in the overall size of the programmes space is, first, because most of the USSP staff have their offices within the programme area, whereas only the chairman and administrative assistant have offices in ESG; and, second, it arises because USSP has several sizeable labs. ESG has only a small workshop/lab, which seemed to be used, at the beginning of this term, mostly for bicycle repairs. (USSP also has the use of the Education Research Centre Workshop facilities.)

They differ not only in size and furnishings, but also in their layout. ESG has its rooms (e.g. library, music-listening room, seminar rooms, office, lab, etc.) clustered around a central lounge area which forms a definitive focus and communal centre. Anybody entering ESG must go

1   All these metaphors were heard in the course of our study.
2   This does not include the area of general ERC facilities (e.g. shop, Xerox room, conference room) that are used by USSP.

through it. It would be difficult to avoid all communication. It is easy to see whether people are in or not. USSP is quite unlike this. Rooms it uses are spread along four corridors on three floors. 'Have you seen Harry?', 'No, have you seen Don?' is an instantly recognisable USSP corridor encounter. While Edna Torgerson in ESG could tell you at once whether a particular student or faculty member was around, her counterpart in USSP would find it impossible. USSP is diffuse, its boundaries uncertain. It's just sections of corridor and numerous little rooms. ESG is an intimate little enclave, distinct, intraregarding and secure. Its members' descriptions reflect this: ESG is 'a home', 'a private club', 'a refuge', 'a type of commune', 'a womb', 'a fraternity without the artificial garbage'. The most common metaphor is 'a home' (and, as one visitor remarked, 'a middle-class home at that'). ESG has a kitchen, used privately and for preparing group lunches; most of the ESG area is open twenty-four hours, and there is an extensive night life.[3] In addition, there are organised social activities—e.g. excursions to the beach. In fact, ESG set out to be home-like ('comfortable, colourful, almost child-like' *ESG faculty member*), providing facilities more often associated with living groups than with academic programmes.

USSP is not like this, and even if it wanted to be (which it does not) it would be severely hampered by Building 20. USSP has no kitchen; it designates less than 2 per cent of its total space as 'lounge area' (the lounge in ESG is 37 per cent of its total); it is not generally open and in use much after office hours; its social activity is sporadic and limited (the Friday afternoon beer parties seem to have dried up). This is not to say that USSP is against informality and pleasant surroundings. Visually speaking, USSP is by far the most cheerful area in Building 20. (It was instrumental in getting some of the corridors painted in non-grey.) However, for USSP, its labs, workshop and computer room—in the best tradition of Building 20—are seen as its most significant facilities.

Different values and orientations
It is fascinating to see other differences between the two programmes that are entirely compatible with their contrasting physical environments: differences in their value systems and general orientations. This is speculative; and I am not suggesting an architectural determinism. Nevertheless, the connections are there. Of course, each programme could

3   My colleague Ellen Ehrenfeld stayed late one night and subsequently filed this report on 'ESG after 5 p.m.': 'ESG has a distinctly different atmosphere from 7 p.m. on. Several people who never are there during the days are regular frequenters, and many old ESG-ers drift in, some of them at least four hours a day. Atmosphere is like a private club—several groups stand out, yet everyone's presence is acknowledged and anyone can join in a conversation. Activities range from purely theoretical physical or math discussions, to studying, to doing crossword puzzles. One ex-ESG-er made a spaghetti dinner for anyone who wanted it, a group of five went for ice-cream, people were sleeping, a game of "Go" was continuously going, others were studying in corners, on couches and in the library. I left at 11.45 p.m., and there were about twenty people there at that time, with no signs of anyone else leaving.'

also use its space in a varied number of ways, each could create its environment to some extent.

What are these differences in orientation? Well, ESG seeks to soften the division between academic and non-academic, between intellectual and personal. 'The ESG offers the opportunity to concentrate on this absorbing task . . . finding their own goals' (*ESG report*). This has led to immense concern with counselling, caring and showing sympathy and concern. The move towards 'nurturitive' values is customarily linked with female influence. It is interesting, therefore, that ESG argues, in one of its reports, that 'there should be more opportunities for students to talk with and be advised by mature women'. Already, in ESG, such counselling exists. Edna Torgerson, the administrative assistant, spends half her time at it. She is warmly regarded and has a very central position.

If the imagery appropriate for ESG tends to be 'female' and 'maternal', it is certainly not so for USSP. There it is consistently male. Various familial relationships were proposed: Judah Schwartz was 'a father figure' with 'Zach as the grandfather'; or 'Zach is the absent father, Judah is the eldest son'; or 'the staff see themselves as elder brothers'. While behaviour and expression in ESG were those permissible in a home, here, in USSP, 'you require an active front, a coolness . . . if you are confused you are supposed to get over it' (*USSP faculty member*). There was nowhere near so much tolerance of psychological confusion as there was in ESG: 'I was his adviser—I was a bad thing for him—I kept away from psychological problems. If I could get him to do *work* I knew it would be good for him' is a remark typical in USSP, but would not be at all typical in ESG.

There are other contrasts of a similar type. Thus, humanities, one suspects, should have been less prominent in USSP than in ESG. This was so. The humanities staff were very influential in ESG; much less so in USSP, where until this year they were under-represented.[4] Another difference—in the planning of the first year: ESG had been absorbed in how they would put freshmen at their ease (and in the event provided 'a sort of pampering experience' (*ex-faculty member, ESG*); whereas USSP had been 'totally curriculum-oriented' (*ex-faculty member, USSP*) in their planning.

The most vivid contrast came, though, from discussions with senior staff members in both programmes. We asked them about the characteristics of students they judged to be 'successes' in the programme. Their criteria and certainly their imagery were distinctively different: at ESG we heard of students who had 'opened up', 'were happier now', 'become somewhat less

4 Students were aware of what they called 'an anti-humanities bias' in USSP. One said: 'USSP needs physicists, chemists, engineers. Otherwise it sinks. If USSP becomes a collection of weirdos, it's had it.' Whether there was a strong bias of this sort is an open question. What *is* clear is the faculty supply/demand problem for programmes like these: in the first year of USSP there were a number of students who would have benefited by more humanities faculty. This year there are more such faculty, but fewer students are interested in the humanities.

convergent'. At USSP we were told of students who 'had done a lot of work', 'had done things', 'had written a paper'. A similar contrast emerged in considering 'unsuccessful' characteristics. In ESG there were comments of the type: 'just as confused as ever', 'didn't make any friends', 'no more mature'; and at USSP there were remarks such as: 'never pulled things together', 'did little to justify his time', 'around but didn't make good'.

Naturally this is only a sample, and there were many other types of comments made. But there was certainly a difference in emphasis: ESG concerned more with personal development, USSP more with intellectual productivity. In line with this there was a far higher incidence in ESG than in USSP of remarks such as 'we did something for him', or 'he didn't come around here enough for us to do much for him', or 'getting him to think rationally — but didn't get through to him'. It seemed that ESG was almost anxious to assume a wider responsibility. USSP talk was more robust, and left responsibility more with the student: 'he didn't make it here', 'he had problems here but now he's found himself', 'he never faced up to the problem of how he can do something on his own'. . . .

What happened in the first year?

By general acknowledgement the first year of each programme (1969-70) was tumultuous, the second pale by comparison. So formative were the first-year experiences that inevitably attention must be paid them. To jump straight from the proposal to the present would simply bewilder. The first year was the decisive time, and it provides the link.

There is another reason: the majority of those we spoke with, themselves made reference to the first year. Even those — both faculty and students — who had joined a programme in its second year (1970-1) were deeply conscious of what had happened in the first. Consistently, the first year was the base line for comparison. . . .

USSP in the first year: projects and contracts, enthusiasm and evaluation
. . . During the summer preceding the first entry of students (summer 1969) twenty students (mainly upperclassmen) were employed. Each was to produce a unit. This did not work out. The term 'fiasco' has been used by several USSP staff members:

The 'summer workers' didn't know what they were supposed to be doing . . . they got conflicting demands. . . . Many of them were screwing ERC . . . coming in only on Fridays to collect their pay-cheques. Others were trying desperately to produce, but seemed lost. Several attempts were made . . . to draw things together and organise the summer . . . [but] were not what I call successes' (*ex-staff member, USSP*).[5]

5 Surprisingly no careful or searching post-mortem ever took place: 'If the summer experience had been adequately analysed and hashed over immediately afterwards . . . we could have crystallised the problems, and proposed solutions which might have made the first year of USSP somewhat easier. . . . We could have learned more about how much structure is necessary for people to actually accomplish a task and could have learned from the failure to communicate' (*ex-staff member*).

It is not clear how many units were actually completed. But it is certain that neither students nor staff liked or used them. 'The idea was OK . . . [but] there was nothing there, no substance—the cupboard was bare' (*staff member*).

In the absence of units, how did students get started on projects? One retrospective account was this: 'When the students arrived we said, "What would you like to do?" They said, "We don't know what to do".' [6]

In general, students did not find it easy to fasten on to a project. The effect of this on the programme was substantial. While a number of students, possibly about ten, did get immediately involved in projects, the majority did not. It was the first inkling of 'floundering'. There were some who did nothing. There were others who looked for a project to latch on to but did not find one. A third group dipped into numerous different projects, collected commitments, but seldom focused long enough to do a sustained piece of work. This latter syndrome was regarded by the staff as a defence mechanism—the appearance of productivity without the hazards of in-depth study. It was known as 'smorgasbording'.

The first month or so was a time of considerable confusion. A gulf loomed between the expectations and plans couched in general terms on the one hand, and the detailed day-to-day business of running a full-time programme on the other. In retrospect, staff members comment on how naive they were at the beginning. Others spoke of 'a lack of communication' between senior and junior staff, as well as between staff and students. Particularly, some felt, there had been a lack of certainty about the programme's precise objectives; others, however, had regarded the formulation of any such list as 'failing to keep one's options open'.

The staff—many of them anxious about the obvious uncertainty of many students (one said: 'I felt guilty that the kids were not getting more out of it')—met regularly to discuss the programme. Discussion ranged over policy and organisation, but also students' progress and problems.

This latter aspect predominated at first: 'At the very beginning we were very uptight about what was happening, about what we were doing. It was very important to us to go through in detail each of the students and assure ourselves that each one was spending his time productively.' These came to be known as evaluation meetings. A student would be discussed and any staff member who had contact with this student would add his comments. After the meeting transcripts of the discussion were prepared and the part relating to a student was given to him. At least one staff member was critical of this: 'A crude evaluation . . . anecdotal, off the top of our heads . . . the transcripts that have resulted have been very crude approximations.' Nevertheless it reflected the keen desire of staff to

---

6 At least one faculty member, however, adopted a different approach. Instead of saying 'Tell us what you want to do', he said 'I am interested in . . .' and mentioned a research project he was engaged in. He was described to me as a 'very good teacher—charismatic, enthusiastic'.

keep a closer eye on what the students in the programme were doing, and to monitor their progress.

Students, however, regarded closed faculty meetings as contrary to the spirit of the programme: 'somehow it didn't bother you in high school that they talked about you, [but] it did upset you here' (*Junior, ex-USSP*). The staff had been at pains, explicitly, to diminish the barriers between themselves and students. The evaluation meetings, the student went on, led to 'disappointment that things they said were going to happen weren't really happening'.

After students had urged 'a USSP-wide meeting'[7] to discuss the matter, it was decided that students would be admitted in future.

Although some staff members argued that they could not be sufficiently candid at an open meeting, the students' view that closed meetings were contrary to the spirit of the new experiment in education prevailed (Report by Judah Schwartz).

From then on these evaluation discussions were conducted with students present, though attendance was low. Sometimes the student himself was brought into the discussion. It is not, perhaps, altogether surprising that one student at least was still dissatisfied: 'You always had the feeling they weren't being honest'.

The issue of evaluation emerged again at the end of the first semester. How was credit to be awarded? Some thought credit should be based on work completed — the better the work, the more credits. Others believed credit was a 'false currency', that small discriminations were impossible, and that a fixed number of credits should be given for a 'completed satisfactory term's work'. The latter view prevailed. A student was given an 'Incomplete' grade, or a 'Pass' — in which case he or she received fifty units of credit — 'the average load carried by an MIT student during a traditional first term'.[8]

The basis for evaluation of students' work was to be the report. Again there had been a general expectation that students would naturally document their work. A number of students claimed they had been given inadequate warning that they would have to do so. There was a flurry of activity at the end of the first term. There is ambiguity as to whether they had been sufficiently warned. One staff member said:

7 At the same meeting another issue was discussed, that of colloquia. These had been set up to promote the sharing of experiences and to provide foci for students' efforts. But '. . . staff and student expectations about the function of a colloquium proved significantly different. While students viewed it as an opportunity to share . . . experiences . . . some staff members appeared to use the colloquia as oral examinations' (Report by Judah Schwartz).

This led to another student recommendation: 'We, the students, suggest that colloquia be voluntary and non-hostile, i.e. explanatory and not investigatory' (*ibid.*). Colloquia were subsequently 'presented when the individual student felt ready' (*ibid.*).

8 This procedure meant that several students, given Incompletes, received no credit for the term. The Committee on Academic Performance had to consider some of these students. Members of the CAP pointed out to me that the USSP scheme meant that 'when there is a failure, it's a catastrophic failure'. They merely observed this — it was not a criticism, they were at pains to say.

As I recall, we never mentioned to them that they would be responsible for documentation of their work at the end of the semester or year—we weren't clear on that ourselves.

More probably, however, it was a case of, 'We had said the words but we didn't communicate it', as another staff member put it.

The high level of concern with evaluation of students' work signified, perhaps, the staff's lack of certainty as to whether students had accomplished as much as they could or should have done. It was concern over this that led to two staff members writing a memo which led to a day-long closed staff meeting in March 1970, at Endicott House.[9] It contained a number of issues for discussion. Some referred to students: 'failing to keep appointments without notifying anyone'; projects often had 'no clear short-term goal'; 'ultimata' were ignored. Other points concerned staff: 'What's bothering us? . . . What am I (specifically) doing? What kinds of responsibilities for which students do I have?'

The Endicott House meeting resulted in several plans for the future particularly the notion of formal 'contracts' between students and staff: 'People weren't working enough, we didn't know what people were doing, people were getting lost. . . . [We] came up with a number of strategies to deal with it . . . proposals and documentation'. The student would produce a proposal, and with his adviser, 'work out how he was to spend his time . . . what he would do for the term' (*staff member*). The full effect of these procedural changes was not felt until the programme's second year. They represented a shift towards defined structure and explicit demands on students.

This fleeting and selective survey cannot do justice to the complexity and excitement of USSP's first year. For the staff members it was demanding. Some had never taught before, and some had no idea, when they joined USSP, that they would be teaching. There are specific difficulties, even for an experienced teacher, in a programme like USSP: e.g. 'There was no real reason to prepare your thoughts . . . because you didn't know what they were going to be doing'.

In addition there was a good deal of staff anxiety. For those at the Endicott meeting, the most memorable feature was a startling intervention by Judah Schwartz. He brought up what he, and others, considered the underlying cause of staff anxiety—namely the joint issue of their being untenured, and the 'marginal nature of education research and innovation at MIT'. There was also a deeply-felt concern (it seems strange in retrospect) that the CEP might abruptly terminate the programme at the end of the first year, if the programme did not make a satisfactory impression. In addition there was the initial apprehension that attends the inauguration of almost any new venture ('I felt we had created a monster',

9 A country house owned by MIT.

staff member). These various worries were undoubtedly known to students, and in fact contributed to feelings of unease that they, too, experienced.

However, significant though the confusion and anxiety was, it is by no means the full story. USSP also maintained a unique brand of exuberance and vitality throughout. Overall there was general informality, good humour, and a refreshing lack of bureaucratisation and regulation. Judah Schwartz exercised strong and optimistic leadership. In many ways he served as a role model: one staff member supposed that they had wanted students to 'turn out like miniature Judahs'. He was charismatic and friendly. One student, asked who his close friends had been among students and staff, listed 'Judah — he was everybody's friend, I guess'. There was a good deal of irritation too: e.g. he was 'a hierarchy of one'; 'he is an idealistic type who doesn't want to be bothered with administrative detail'. But it remains true that he was the inspiration of the programme and kept long-term self-confidence to a high level, preserving the feeling that they were pioneering a revolutionary new approach.

There were other factors. The staff were informal and enthusiastic, most were professionally committed to educational reform. One student, now a Junior, though critical of USSP, looked back nostalgically: 'It was really nice . . . the staff were bright and liberal people. You had the feeling you could always find somebody who knew about a particular topic or would talk to you about it.' Staff were seen as friendly and open; most of them were young and this helped too. Sandy Morgan, as adminstrative assistant, counselled, befriended, sorted out muddles and knew what was going on. Another staff member could be relied on to crack jokes and reduce tension. There was staff disagreement, but discussions never became embittered. . . .

How has USSP developed since the first year?

'USSP has become a new way of doing the same things as opposed to a new way of doing new things' *(Junior, ex-USSP).* This student puts into words what has been realised by many: that the programme's orientation has shifted from the 'project idea . . . to "lots of different ways to study the same subject" ' *(Sophomore, USSP).* Of course, 'they know they *can* do a project' *(Senior staff member in October 1971, at USSP staff meeting).*

The first year's experiences led to changes in the second. The faculty thought too little had been accomplished ('it had never occurred to us that there would be a group of people who didn't want to do anything', *USSP staff member),* and they resolved to 'figure out ways to get them to do more'. In particular there was a sharpened awareness of the time limitations:

I don't have the guts to let people flounder for a year and then come up with something good. I wish I did, but I don't have the guts' (*Staff member, USSP*).

When you operate on a Summerhill basis, you have to have Summerhill time constants . . . I think the Summerhill concept that is willing to let the student fuck around until he finds something that he is interested in, which is still the USSP concept . . . undermines the student because we don't have an infinite amount of time per student to prepare for this (*Former staff member*).

There was concern for the students. Staff were aware of reactions of the type:

It's very discouraging to spend an entire semester or year supposedly working only to find you haven't produced anything at the end of the year (*USSP Junior*).

There was also concern for the programme, not only for its survival at MIT, but for the idea, which they hoped would be proliferated:

We didn't think a programme could be built if that sort of phenomenon is widespread (*Staff member, USSP*).

In short, the staff wanted to ensure, in the second year, that there was no 'general atmosphere of people not turning up', and no 'flopping around'. They therefore instituted, in a much more systematic way, required formulation of proposals, to serve as contracts between advisers and advisees, and subsequent 'documentation' of work completed. 'Useful work', they emphasised, 'is something that is communicable, can be documented, and criticised by other people' (*Staff member*). . . .

What was 'floundering'? Why did it arise? How was it handled?

'To flounder' comes from a Dutch word meaning to splash through mire or to flop about. It was a term used in both USSP and ESG, and was used in various ways. For some it meant a short-lived phenomenon — the initial uncertainties of a student entering the programme; for others it referred to longer-term personal or intellectual disarray. Theories abounded as to its causes. There was a disagreement on how, and even if it should be handled. Mark Levensky has defined 'general floundering' as:

Aimless activity, vacant stares, starts and stops, unrecognised fantasies, unpredictable forgetfulness, some non-academic work but a strong reluctance to do any academic work on their own or to work with other students on traditional academic subjects, self-deception about what they were or weren't doing, too much sleep.

Whether lesser degrees of disorganisation are also defined as floundering is unimportant. To some extent nearly every student floundered — though there were a very few in each programme who seemed to be sure of what to do and where to go.

Floundering and 'self-realisation'

For some, floundering reflected profound self-questioning, introspection and concern with long-term goals. Partly this arose because, in the words of one ESG faculty member, 'the aim in life for these students is to get into the best college. Now he's in the best college, what's his aim in life now?' Students also spoke of this:

Imagine that you are a freshman. You have been tracked and moulded and disciplined to the Ivy League Express but since you dug science you want to come to MIT. Thoughts about the future always ended up at the point where you would leave home and go to College. Then you got there and it is all big and exciting. And then you get into the ESG and no one puts the huge iron lid back on you the way it was in High School. At last, a breathing space, but what do you do? You don't know, you are too bewildered.

There were several other references to 'the twelve years of being bull-dozed'. 'Certainly it gave me my first opportunity in over twelve years to really think about what I learn, to be introspective, and to be human as opposed to being a "good student".' These and other students 'were anxious . . . to figure out who, exactly, they were, how, miracle of miracles, they happened to be at MIT, and what, on earth, they wanted or at least were going to do now' (Mark Levensky's Report).

Were the programmes the right places for students to confront these issues? Certainly ESG thought that it was. One of their publications says that ESG should not only serve those who know their goals, but others 'who are preoccupied in finding their own goals'. Among other things, 'they need help in exploring possibilities of self-commitment in life'. Some faculty outside also thought so, but others did not. Thus, one department head argued that the problem should not arise:

A student should not have doubts; he should be highly motivated if he comes to MIT . . . many should be counselled out of coming here.

But the more general view was that students *did* 'need a self-assessment procedure' (*Professor, management*). A department head thought it was acceptable if it was a 'functional self-realisation' of the type—'What am I going to work on for the next couple of years?' It would *not* be acceptable, however, if meant in 'a mod sense . . . we don't want poets and potheads . . . hopefully a man matures here. But our principal focus should not go away from getting to do things well' (*Department head*).

Clearly a good number of students did go beyond this narrower definition of 'self-realisation'. 'The kids are infected with the psychological literature. Finding their identity is an enormous challenge', was the view of one mathematics professor. (He added, wryly: 'I always thought ESG was for people who *know* they like an unstructured environment. But it seems as if it's full of kids who are trying to *find out* whether they like it'.)

An even more basic question seemed to be raised: should questions of

348 Alternative evaluation

the variety 'What shall I do with my life?' be considered early or late? Some thought freshmen were too young to be absorbed in these issues.

I seriously question the ability of a seventeen-year-old to say this is what I want to do with my life. Even to say that this is what I would like to do with my life in the next three months. Because you are just coming out of adolescence and you are not quite sure what you want from one moment to the next (*USSP staff member*).

A mathematics professor, unconnected with either programme, recalled how he had had to write an essay, at age sixteen, on 'My Philosophy of Life'. His comment: 'How absurd that now seems'. A former faculty member of ESG: 'It is a criticism of both programmes: people of this age are too likely anyway to become introverted. . . . I felt uncomfortable to see students paying so much attention to these matters'.

The contrary view was that it was a bad thing for students to be swept along, straight from high school, through a set of experiences which left them no time to address central questions, and which simply put off, until a much later stage, basic questioning about life-style, career choice and so on. (I heard it said that many MIT faculty had addressed these problems only when they were middle-aged.)

I asked a senior faculty member in ESG: 'Is it the right time to go through this, when they first get to college?' His reply: 'I don't know . . . [pause]. There are some people who do it after graduation. It is hard to justify the situation that allows *that* to happen — even on economic grounds'.

A view expressed by an ESG student is by no means unrepresentative:

This experience has not been particularly pleasant . . . I have had to go through a great deal of painful self-evaluation . . . I think that this is the proper time in my college career for this to happen. Otherwise I could have slid through four years without ever having examined my real motives, desires, etc. This could have led to a great deal of pain if I had suddenly discovered that the whole enterprise had been a waste . . . it has been most valuable in forcing the issue . . . ESG has greatly speeded my maturation process.

The controversy, Early or Late, is one for which there may be no simple answer. Seventeen-year-olds have to make important decisions, yet clearly they have a limited set of experiences on which to base them.

One view, for which there was widespread enthusiasm, was that many more students should take a year off between high school and coming to MIT. Fifteen students, admitted to MIT in 1971, arranged to do this. One ESG staff member wondered whether these students might not have gravitated toward ESG, had they been here this semester ('Take their year off in ESG instead' — was his mock-serious comment). . . .

Good and bad effects
Numerous positive and negative features of floundering were cited. Only

some can be considered here. One prominent USSP faculty member wrote the following:

A prominent ingredient of the phenomenon is the sudden discovery . . . that the removal of an external driving force leaves them far less intellectually motivated than they would like to be.

This, however, is only part of the story. He goes on:

It is painful to discover truths about oneself. When that discovery makes personal reassessment necessary, some time, energy and support are required to deal with the problem.

Asking a student, in other words, 'to do his own thinking about his own course [can] cause a hell of a lot of commotion in the kid's mind for a while. . . .' (*USSP staff member*). People in USSP 'have been forced to think and figure out what they are doing and why they are doing it, or what they are *not* doing and why they are *not* doing it' (*ex-staff member, USSP*].

These experiences, perhaps uncomfortable at the time, were likely to be formative ones. But they did not proceed in isolation: they were often accompanied by anxiety or feelings of guilt. There was also an interesting tendency to hive off 'motivation' as a reified concept and to bemoan the lack of it. 'I was turned off by my lack of motivation' (*ex-ESG student*). 'USSP I think is really a wonderful thing. If I was motivated to do work I think it could have been the best thing that ever happened to me. But I couldn't get myself to do the work' (*Sophomore, ex-USSP*).

An MIT psychiatrist, who strongly believed that the programmes had been 'actually detrimental for certain persons' described how one or two students he had seen 'got alarmed at their capacity to let things go'. They had had 'a nice feeling of freedom . . . it was like a temptation offered and taken . . . in retrospect, they would feel very sad and bitter about it'. Another psychiatrist, when it was suggested that one of the programmes' aims was to take 'the Institute pressure off', replied: 'Sometimes it *increases* the pressure — lack of structure produces anxiety, guilt that they are not getting anything done which produces depression'. One professor, outside the programmes, argued that they 'put too big a psychological burden on the student. "Remember the choice is yours", they say. "It will show you what sort of person you are — if you can't manage it here then get back to the regular programme".'[10] This is almost certainly an exaggeration, but the idea that these programmes are a soft option for playboys, a theme we heard from time to time, is equally untrue. The regular programme causes certain types of strain, these programmes cause others. One

---

10   One USSP student, according to a staff member, got particularly worried 'about not being able to find one thing which turned him on more than anything else'.

freshman joined ESG this term because he saw it as 'a challenge' — it was almost a trial of strength which he was making for himself. This is in contrast to the view of one MIT alumnus, whose nephew was in USSP. He told his nephew: 'Be a man, go into the regular programme. . . .'

What have been the advantages and disadvantages, both professional and personal, for those who have taught in the programmes?

Personal rewards and frustrations

One professor, outside the programmes but knowing them well, thought that teaching in programmes like ESG and USSP . . . was ultimately 'immensely unrewarding and frustrating, with no internal or external rewards'. The 'internal' rewards, at best, are intangible and nebulous: 'If you manage to get students motivated and educated, the millenium has arrived'; and the 'external reward system — remuneration, rewards, tenure — largely calls the tune. . . . [It] is more powerful than any internal reward system that operates'. He concluded with a statement common in the MIT Commission: 'Hard values drive out soft values'.

The internal rewards (of 'soft' value) outweighed the internal frustrations. At least, the great majority of those who had taught in one or other programme did not regret having done so. Even the critical and pessimistic acknowledged how much they had learned: about teaching, students and their fellow faculty. Several suggested that all faculty members at MIT should have experience of teaching this way at some point in their careers. Many different learning experiences were cited. This was one of them:

Teaching now seems to me to be redefined as helping someone figure out what he wants to do, and not so much showing how to do something, but showing them how to go about finding out how to do something. You don't teach facts and figures, you teach techniques. That's what I found out (*USSP staff member*).

During the beginning year, the staff in the programmes were intensely involved. They were anxious:

I remember the terror of the first year — thrown in, thinking 'my God, is it going to work?' It was like a space probe . . . we wondered, 'have we shot something up that will never come back?' . . . I went round saying everything was OK. But underneath I was very frightened (*ESG faculty member*).

They were also unsure what they were supposed to be doing: if the situation was unstructured for students, so it was for staff. One USSP staff member made the following connection: 'We floundered and they floundered for the first so many months'. And an ex-ESG staff member reported that he felt he had been operating 'in a vacuum': 'I had a feeling of helplessness; what can I do? How can I be useful?'

But the sense of exhilaration and new opportunity felt by students in the first year was shared by many of both faculties. As the second year progressed, this faded somewhat: it became less exciting; they were 'coasting' (*ESG faculty member*).

The 'teaching' was, of course, quite unlike conventional teaching. Moreover, it was more difficult. 'It is a very erratic business . . . everyone wants to know something different — in the regular programme you know what you want to be wise about' (*ESG senior faculty member*). He characterised his previous teaching as 'handling elementary physics in rote fashion'. When he began teaching in ESG he 'simply couldn't do it, made outrageous mistakes'. The successful staff member had to get used to admitting not knowing the answer, or that he had forgotten a point, or that he needed time to work it out. This almost certainly helped to make faculty 'more human' in students' eyes.

The time demands were heavy. One phenomenon is of interest. One faculty member reported: 'Somehow time disappears in ESG. . . you are not sure you have done enough, you always want to invest more time'. Another put it differently: that 'the number of intellectual quanta transmitted per unit hour is very low'. The uncertainty and lack of formality of the teaching left many staff questioning, when they went home, whether they had achieved much that day.

In USSP the time problem was magnified. Their offices were in the programme area itself (unlike ESG) and (unless they took determined action) were always available.

Interactions with students in programmes where 'education is in the personal mode' (*sophomore, USSP*), inevitably draw more heavily on the teacher's emotional resources. A USSP faculty member described how both disappointments and achievements were felt more deeply than in the regular programme. A student breaks an appointment and it is a cause for concern. But, in the regular programme, 'If a fellow drops out of recitation, I don't even notice'. The best rewards, likewise, are felt personally. The 'greatest reward' for one ESG faculty member was 'to see individual students, one at a time, slowly loosen up, turn on, behave more adventuresomely with regard to their work. . . .'

Could the programmes have been more 'successful'? If so, how?

Interaction between teacher and taught
At the heart of any form of instruction is an interaction — between someone who knows more, or who has more experience, or more institutional responsibility, and someone else. The relationship between teacher and student varies with the instructional context, differences in age and status of the two parties, and so on.

The conventional system of MIT instruction has modes of interaction between faculty and students that have evolved into relatively standard forms. They may be partly renegotiated or redefined by individuals: some faculty are vastly more approachable than others, some more naturally authoritative and so on. But there is a framework of common expectation and accepted ritual.

These programmes, USSP and ESG, lie outside this framework:

Outside the framework they are grappling with souls. The beauty of the normal system is that you don't have to grapple with souls, which is also why (as a teaching programme) it is mediocre (*Professor, Faculty of Science*).

In the programmes the normal rules and conventions cannot be relied on. Inevitably there is strain on individuals involved, as they seek to redefine roles and relationships in a situation of flux. In the programmes . . . both sought as a central objective to redefine the faculty/student relationship itself.

Faculty ambiguities
It is my view that for both programmes their chief difficulty lay in certain unresolved ambiguities: some concerning this relationship directly, some deriving from the programme but profoundly affecting this relationship. These were present from the beginning; were exacerbated by the programme's difficulties of the first year, and by the additional strain of that particular academic year; and are perhaps still present, though each programme has learned to live with them.

One such ambiguity seemed to arise in conflicting messages signalled to students. In blunt, summary form these were: first, 'do what you like'; and second 'match up to our expectations'. The 'expectations' were themselves not simple: one of them was 'do not ignore studying conventional academic subjects'; another was 'study unconventional things and don't be a tool'. (I emphasise that this is an exceedingly complex area, and that I am certainly oversimplifying.)

Another ambiguity—or area of uncertainty—arose from considering the actual role of the faculty member. Was he 'friend', 'pal', 'parent figure', 'elder learner', 'teacher', 'tutor' or 'supervisor'? Or all at the same time? Should the staff member encourage, cajole or leave the student alone? If he actively encourages or makes suggestions, is he curtailing the student's freedom and abrogating a principle? Or is he fulfilling an important staff responsibility? Outside the framework the faculty member is grappling not only with souls, but also with all the inherent conflicts of teaching: e.g. achieving depth without sacrificing coverage; criticising without discouraging; encouraging students to come and talk without its absorbing all his time: all these and many more.

It is not that such profound educational questions are absent in the standard system, but that they do not obtrude to the same degree. There are usually precedents and mechanisms and catalogue regulations. The edifice is there—you live within it. . . .

Evaluation of students' work
The ambiguities are most acute when it comes to evaluation of students'

work and staff feedback generally. There was a general and pervasive feeling among students in both programmes that it was 'very hard to know when you have accomplished anything' (*Junior, ex-USSP*). He went on: '[there are] no hard and fast three-hour finals. No way to compare my work *vis-à-vis* the Institute'. There was often a lack of certainty about what was good work, what was not; what could reasonably be expected per month; what was a competent standard; and so on. Evaluating (and going through the procedures of testing before a waiver for an Institue requirement was granted by a programme faculty member), brought these matters to a head. Not surprisingly there were elements of tension, occasionally misunderstandings and a good deal of ambivalence. We heard two separate views in USSP: from students who complained that there had been 'too little evaluation of their work'; from advisers that, if they evaluated a student, he was likely 'not to come back for three weeks'.

Underlying the conflicting feelings towards evaluation were two other factors, each of which was highly significant. The programmes were different from the regular system of instruction by being personal and by a merciful lack of bureaucratic procedures. This had numerous effects, of which I shall mention two.

(i) Had the faculties of the programmes been inclined to pressure or coerce their students—which of course they were not—it would have been immensely difficult. The conventional system, by comparison both heavily bureaucratised and impersonal, permits a good deal of pressure to be put on a student without face-to-face encounters between individuals. If, in the regular programme, all assignments were collected together and presented by a single individual (say a personal tutor) across a desk, the work load on the student might well appear to be too heavy an imposition. In the programmes there were face-to-face encounters, fewer divisions of responsibility between faculty members, and far less opportunity to say: 'I'm sorry, it's the regulations'.[11]

(ii) It is well known that in college education generally there are any number of strategies used by students for coping with the demands made on them by their professors. Many of these strategies may be necessary for survival (see *The Hidden Curriculum*, Benson R. Snyder, Knopf, 1971). Often they have an element of deception, faking or 'bullshitting'. A number of students made remarks of the type, 'I got by at High School—just slop off the work . . . not really doing the stuff.' 'Getting by', or pulling the wool over the instructor's glasses, is an entrenched part of student academic practice. Because the instructor is assigned a distant role, which is defined by the system, the undergraduate's deception is not seen in personal terms: he is cheating the system, not an individual

11 An ex-USSP junior remarked: 'In the second year, the staff were going to be Fascist if necessary to get some work out of the students.' It is interesting to note that this trend (incidentally a trifle exaggerated by this student) was accompanied by the introduction of certain 'mechanisms', impersonal 'rules' that applied to every student, etc.

professor. In ESG and USSP, however, this does not apply. Teachers are not distant figures whom you meet in formal situations. Students are also grappling with souls. Faking, bullshitting or getting by are now seen differently. They *are* deceiving an individual; it *is* personal; it is no longer a ritualised and widely accepted institutional phenomenon.

The evaluating exchanges between faculty and students had to cope with these factors. Most of the staff found it difficult, for instance, to demand that students reach a particular standard, or complete an assignment *without fail* by a certain date, even when they wanted to. Similarly, the students—who were often worried about completing the Institute requirements—were greatly tempted to 'get by' and do only enough to appear, to the programme faculty member in question, that they knew the stuff. Some, inevitably, did fake: 'do less and get by—you still want to maintain this . . . the ethic here was work; if you appeared to be doing work it was OK' (*Junior, ex-USSP*). 'Bullshit, sheer bullshit. I got 18.02, 5.41 and 18.60. They thought I knew my stuff, but I didn't' (*Junior, ex-ESG*). But to a greater extent than for many students in the regular programme, students who did this had feelings of considerable guilt. They also felt that their interaction with their instructor had been subtly undermined—and by them. They had cheated their friend. . . .

'You need to overcome glop'
One ESG faculty member described 'glop' as more or less 'defensive inactivity'—a heavy, rather resentful and unenergetic state that characterised a number of students in ESG (and a great many more in his classes in the standard programme). He thought glop had multiple causes: 'it is resentment at being in school, at society, at parents', but is obviously more besides. In some sense it seems to serve as a self-protecting withdrawal from being involved in group or institutional activity. The paucity of questions from students and the lack of intelligent and lively discourse in recitations are perhaps further indications of this state. Whatever its complex tangle of roots, the phenomenon is well known in numerous educational settings—not only at MIT of course.

Glop (I use the term because I can find no better) often involves a show of lack of any defined interest. Enterprising teachers attempt to provide interesting and enjoyable experiences, one of which they hope will 'turn their students on'. (The imagery of drugs is revealing—they locate the source of interest in a particular topic or curriculum arrangement.) When such attempts to spark interest fail, there is a ready explanation to hand: 'Their previous unsatisfactory school experiences have been too deadening'. Most deliberate attempts within the programmes to 'interest a group of students in something' were not successful. Setting up seminars, for instance, however 'interesting', generally failed to overcome glop.

Teaching involves human interaction. This may be anathema to many educational technologists and system analysts, but it remains true. Just as telling a person to 'be spontaneous' or 'be amused' and expecting them to be so, is laughable; so is telling a person to 'be interested'. Yet that is the thinly disguised message that many teachers pass to their students.

There are clues to an alternative: successful actors, novelists and lovers for instance. They do not ask directly for response; they win us over, court us, capture our involvement. Overcoming glop involves winning the student over to the point that he lets himself become vulnerable to opportunities beyond it. It is not merely attempting to interest him, but persuading him to let himself become amenable to being interested.

How is this accomplished? There are no glib formulae or pat answers. But I can briefly describe what the most successful faculty members seemed to be doing when they overcame glop. They did not all do it in the same way. They were *not* all 'charismatic', nor were they always the most experienced teachers. What they shared was having a context or style of interaction with their students that was free of many ambiguities recorded earlier in this section.

One or two had students working on their own research with them. This immediately removed a lot of uncertainty: the student was treated as partner and as apprentice; the student knew what he was doing and saw it as being worthwhile. It was a situation that encouraged commitment and often won it. The faculty member may well have been serving as a 'role model' for the student, someone with whom the student identified. The key factor was that they were working together. They were not always successful, of course. One USSP staff member, who consistently had students working on his research with him, remarked: 'They are very hesitant about making commitments to anything. They are convinced that once they do that the road to the end of their lives has been paved'.

Some faculty members worked alongside students in joint learning activities within a new area. These, too, seemed to cut through the ambiguities and have a closer and franker relationship. They were consistently singled out as being 'good advisers' or 'really interested in you'. These faculty, along with those with research apprentices, commented on their *own* personal interest in the outcome of the student's efforts, over and above their interest as teachers or advisers.

Finally, there were one or two individuals, who were seen as 'tough' and demanding teachers. They would get angry and show it, if suggestions were not followed up or reading had not been done. One of these was described as 'more honest somehow . . . you know where he stands'. Again, this teacher had established a way of relating to students that was free of many of the ambiguities usually present. Like the other mentioned he largely overcame glop. His manifestly great concern for students' well-being was something they responded to with their commitment — tough or not. . . .

Bibliography

Numbers in bold type refer to page on which reference occurs

Adams, R. N. & Preiss, J. J. (eds.) (1960). *Human Organization Research*. Homewood, Illinois: Dorsey Press. **19**

Atkin, J. M. (1963). 'Some evaluation problems in a course content improvement project'. *Journal of Research in Science Teaching, 1*, pp. 129-32. **75**

Atkin, J. M. (1967-8). 'Research styles in science education'. *Journal of Research in Science Teaching, 5*, pp. 338-45. **78, 118**

Atkin, J. M. (1968). 'Behavioral objectives in curriculum design: a cautionary note'. *The Science Teacher, 35*, No. 5, pp. 27-30. **82, 85**

Atkin, J. M. (1970). 'Curriculum design: the central development group and the local teacher'. *In IPN Symposium 1970 uber Forschung und Entwicklung naturwissenschaftlicher Curricula*, Kiel: Institut fur die Padagogik der Naturwissenschaften an der Christian-Albrechts-Universitat. **84**

Bassham, H. (1962). 'Teacher understanding and pupil efficiency in mathematics: a study of relationship'. *Arithmetic Teacher, 9*, pp. 383-7. **154**

Beals, A. (1972). *Field Work in Eleven Cultures*, (ed. G. Splindler). New York: Holt, Rinehart and Winston. **183**

Becker, H. S. (1958). 'Problems of inference and proof in participant observation'. *American Sociological Review, 23*, pp. 652-60. **169**

Becker, H. S. (1971). *Sociological Work*. Harmondsworth: Allen Lane. **184**

Becker, H. S., Geer, B. & Hughes, E. (1968). *Making the Grade*. New York: Wiley & Sons. **13, 170**

Becker, H. S., Geer, B., Hughes, E. & Strauss, A. (1961). *Boys in White*. Chicago: University of Chicago Press. **200, 209, 213**

Bell, C. (1969). 'A note on participant observation'. *Sociology, 3*, No. 3., pp. 417-18. **169**

Bellman, R. (1957). *Dynamic Programming*. Princeton, N.J.: Princeton University Press. **48**

Bellman, R. & Dreyfus, S.E. (1962). *Applied Dynamic Programming*. Princeton, N.J.: Princeton University Press. **48**

Black, S. & Geiser, K. (1971). *The Watertown Home Base School Evaluation Methodology Report*. Watertown, Massachusetts. (mimeo) **222**

Bloom, B. S. (ed.) (1956). *Taxonomy of Educational Objectives, Handbook 1: Cognitive Domain*. New York: Longmans, Green. **27**

Blyth, W. A. L. (1959). 'School groups and neighbourhood groups: a study of predictive sociometry'. Paper read to the Education Section of the Fourth World Congress of Sociology, Stresa. **178**

Box, G. E. P. (1957). 'Evolutionary operation: a method for increasing industrial productivity'. *Applied Statistics, 6*, pp. 81-101. **49**

Bruyn, S. T. (1966). *The Human Perspective in Sociology: the Methodology of Participant Observation*. Englewood Cliffs, N.J.: Prentice-Hall. **195, 209**

Butcher, H. J. & Rudd, E. (eds.) (1972). *Contemporary Problems in Higher Education*. London: McGraw-Hill. **7**

Caro, F. G. (1971). 'Issues in the evaluation of social programs'. *Review of Educational Research, 41*, pp. 87-114. **6**

Center for New Schools. (1971). 'Student involvement in decision-making in an alternative high school: a preliminary analysis'. Chicago: Center for New Schools. (mimeo) **277, 291**

Center for New Schools. (1974). 'A review of the use of ethnographic techniques in educational research'. Chicago: Center for New Schools. (mimeo) **193, 276**

Center for New Schools. (1974). 'On-site technical assistance as a facilitator of educational change: a comparative study of five technical assistance groups'. Chicago: Center for New Schools. (mimeo) **190, 276**

Center for New Schools. (1974). 'The CNS school evaluation model'. Chicago: Center for New Schools. (mimeo) **276**

Cicourel, A. V. (1967). *Method and Measurement in Sociology*. New York: Free Press. **16**

Clark, D. L. & Guba, E. G. (1965). 'An examination of potential change roles in education'. Columbus, Ohio: Ohio State University. (mimeo) **155**

Collingwood, R. J. (1946, 1961). *The Idea of History*. London: Oxford University Press. **184**

Cronbach, L. J. (1957). 'The two disciplines of scientific psychology'. *American Psychologist, 12*, pp. 671-84. **43**

Cronbach, L. J. (1963). 'Evaluation for course improvement'. *Teachers' College Record, 64*, No. 8, pp. 672-83. **49, 127**

Cronbach, L. J. & Gleser, G. C. (1965). *Psychological Tests and Personnel Decisions*. Urbana, Illinois: University of Illinois Press. **43, 47**

Denny, T., Cotton, C. & Storm, G. (1971). 'Three reflections'. Center for Instructional Research and Curriculum Evaluation, University of Illinois. (mimeo) **237, 240**

Dewey, J. (1934). *Art as Experience*. New York: Minton, Balch & Co. **96**

Dollard, J. (1940). *Caste and Class in a Southern Town*. New York: Harper **183**

Downing, J. (ed.) (1967). *The i.t.a. Symposium.* London: National Foundation for Educational Research. 8

Duncanson, J. P. (1964). *Intelligence and the Ability to Learn.* Princeton, N.J.: Educational Testing Service. 44

Eggleston, S. J. (ed.). (1971). *Paedagogica Europaea VI,* Braunschweig: L. C. G. Malmberg N. V./Georg Westermann. 115

Eisner, E. W. (1967). 'A response to my critics'. *School Review, 75,* No. 3, pp. 277-82. 90

Eisner, E. W. (1967). 'Educational objectives: help or hindrance?'. *School Review, 75,* No. 3, pp. 250-60. 88

Eisner, E. W. (1969). 'Instructional and expressive educational objectives: their formulation and use in curriculum'. In W. James Popham (ed.), *Instructional Objectives,* AERA Monograph Series on Curriculum Evaluation, No. 3. Chicago: Rand McNally, pp. 1-18. 91

Eisner, E. W. (1972). 'Emerging models for educational evaluation'. *School Review, 80,* pp. 573-90. 95

Eisner, E. W. (1975). 'Applying educational connoisseurship and criticism to educational settings'. Unpublished paper. 97

Emans, R. (1966). 'A proposed conceptual framework for curriculum development'. *Journal of Educational Research, 59,* pp. 327-32. 117

Etzioni, A. (1965). 'Organizational control structure'. In J. March (ed.), *Handbook of Organizations.* Chicago: Rand McNally. 291

Feuer, L. S. (1965). 'Causality in the social sciences'. In D. Lerner (ed.) *Cause and Effect.* New York: The Free Press. 217

Fleishman, E. A. (1965). 'The description and prediction of perceptual-motor skill learning'. In R. Glaser (ed.), *Training Research and Education.* New York: John Wiley & Sons, pp. 137-76. 43

Freire, P. (1970). *Pedagogy of the Oppressed.* New York: Herder & Herder. 217

Freud, S. (1953). *Collected Works (Standard Edition)* Vol. 2. London: Hogarth Press and the Institute of Psychoanalysis. 182

Frye, N. (1947). *Fearful Symmetry: A Study of William Blake.* Princeton, N.J.: Princeton University Press. 116

Gagné, R. M. (1967). 'Curriculum research and the promotion of learning'. In R. E. Stake (ed.), *Perspectives of Curriculum Evaluation,* AERA Monograph Series on Curriculum Evaluation, No. 1. Chicago: Rand McNally, pp. 19-38. 27

Gallagher, J. J., Nuthall, G. A. & Rosenshine, B. (1970). *Classroom Observation.* AERA Monograph Series on Curriculum Evaluation, No. 6. Chicago: Rand McNally. 15

Gallaher, Jr., A. (1964). 'The role of the advocate and directed change'. In W. C. Meierhenry (ed.) *Media and Educational Innovation.* Lincoln, Nebraska: University of Nebraska Press, pp. 33-40. 217

Glaser, R. (1963). 'Instructional technology and the measurement of learning outcomes: some questions'. *American Psychologist, 18,* pp. 519-21. 27

Glaser, R. (1970). 'Evaluation of instruction and changing educational models'. In M. C. Wittrock & D. E. Wiley (eds.), *The Evaluation of Instruction: Issues and Problems.* New York: Holt, Rinehart & Winston, pp. 70-86. 37

Glaser, B. & Strauss, A. (1967). *The Discovery of Grounded Theory.* New York: Aldine. **16, 196, 206, 209, 213**

Gouldner, A. W. (1968). 'The sociologist as partisan: sociology and the welfare state'. *American Sociologist, 3,* pp. 103-16. 329

Gouldner, A. W. (1971) *The Coming Crisis in Western Sociology.* New York: Basic Books. 329

Grobman, H. (1968). *Evaluation Activities of Curriculum Projects,* AERA Monograph Series on Curriculum Evaluation, No. 2. Chicago: Rand McNally. 204

Groen, G. J. & Atkinson, R. C. (1966). 'Models for optimizing the learning process'. *Psychological Bulletin, 66,* pp. 309-20. 48

Guba, E. (1969). 'Significant differences'. *Educational Researcher, 20,* pp. 4-5. 223

Guttentag, M. (1971). 'Models and methods in evaluation research', *Journal of Theory of Social Behaviour, 1,* pp. 75-95. 8

Hammond, A. C. (1972). 'Computer-assisted instruction: two major demonstrations'. *Science, 176,* No. 4039. 298

Hammond, P. E. (1964). *Sociologists at Work.* New York: Basic Books. 231

Hanley, J. P. *et al.* (1969). *Curiosity, Competence, Community.* Cambridge, Massachusetts: Educational Development Center Inc. 10

Henry, J. (1971). *Essays on Education.* Harmondworth: Penguin. 7

Herndon, J. (1965). *The Way It Spozed to Be.* New York: Simon & Schuster. 22

Hirst, P. H. (1963). 'The curriculum'. *Western European Education, 1,* i, pp. 31-48. 115

Hoke, G. (1972). *Goodbye to Yesterday.* Center for Instructional Research and Curriculum Evaluation, University of Illinois. 217

Holt, J. (1964). *How Children Fail.* New York: Dell. 22

Homans, G. C. (1950). *The Human Group.* New York: Harcourt Brace. 209

House, E. R. (1972). 'The conscience of educational evaluation'. *Teachers' College Record, 73,* pp. 405-14. 219

House, E. R. (ed.) (1973). *School Evaluation.* Berkeley, California: McCutchan. 8

House, E. R. & Gjerde, C. L. (1974). 'PLATO comes to the community college'. In E. R. House, *The Politics of Educational Innovation.* Berkeley, California: McCutchan. **295, 298**

Hyman, H. H. *et al.* (1954). *Interviewing in Social Research.* Chicago: University of Chicago Press. 16

Jackson, P. W. (1968). *Life in Classrooms.* London: Holt, Rinehart & Winston. **7, 172, 174**

Jenkins, D. R. (1969). 'Saved by the Army'. Internal report from the Keele Integrated Studies Project. **247, 256**

Jenkins, D. R. (1969). 'Saved by the bell'. Internal report from the Keele Integrated Studies Project. **247, 249**

Jenkins, D. R. and Raggatt. P. (1974). *Alternatives for Urban Schools*, Block 5 of the Open University 'Urban Education' course (E351). Milton Keynes: The Open University Press. **275**

Jensen, A. R. (1967). 'Varieties of individual differences in learning'. In R. Gagné (ed.), *Learning and Individual Differences*. Columbus, Ohio: Charles E. Merrill, pp. 117-35. **44, 47**

Judd, W. A. & Glaser, R. (1969). 'Response latency as a function of training method, information level, acquisition and over-learning'. *Journal of Educational Psychology Monograph*, *60* (Part 2). **46**

Kleine, P. (1968). *The Interrelation of Psychological and Cognitive Differentiation in Two Experimental Tasks in an Educational Setting*. Unpublished PhD dissertation, Washington University. **205**

Krathwohl, D. R., Bloom, B. S. and Masia, B. B. (1964). *Taxonomy of Educational Objectives, Handbook II: Affective Domain*. New York: David McKay. **27, 119**

Kuhn, T. S. (1970). *The Structure of Scientific Revolutions*. (2nd edn.) Chicago: University of Chicago Press. **7**

Leach, E. R. (1962). *Rethinking Anthropology*. London: Athlone Press. **183**

Light, R. J. & Smith, P. V. (1970). 'Choosing a future: strategies for designing and evaluating new programs'. *Harvard Educational Review*, *40*, Winter, pp. 1-28. **6, 8**

Lindquist, E. F. (ed.) (1951). *Educational Measurement*. Washington, DC: American Council on Education. **147**

Lindvall, C. M. & Cox, R. C. (1970). *The IPI Evaluation Program*. AERA Monograph Series on Curriculum Evaluation, No. 5. Chicago: Rand McNally. **7**

Lubin, A. (1961). 'The interpretation of significant interaction'. *Educational and Psychological Measurement*, *21*, pp. 807-17. **47**

McCall, G. J. & Simmons, J. L. (1969). *Issues in Participant Observation*. London: Addison-Wesley. **15**

MacDonald, B. (1971). 'The evaluation of the Humanities Curriculum Project: a wholistic approach'. Paper presented to the AERA Annual Meeting, New York, 1971. **8, 179**

MacDonald, B. (1976). 'Evaluation and the control of education'. In D. Tawney (ed.), *Curriculum Evaluation Today: Trends and Implications*, Schools Council Research Studies. London: Macmillan Education, pp. 125-36. **186**

Mager, R. F. (1962). *Preparing Objectives for Programmed Instruction*. San Francisco: Fearon. **27, 151**

Malinowski, B. (1922). *The Argonauts of the Western Pacific*. London: Routledge. **201, 209**

Messick, S. 'Evaluation of educational programs as research on educational process'. Princeton: Educational Testing Service. (n.d.) **8**

Metcalf, L. E. (1963). 'Research on teaching the social studies'. In N. L. Gage (ed.), *Handbook of Research on Teaching*. Chicago: Rand McNally. **106**

Mills, C. W. (1959). *The Sociological Imagination*. London: Oxford University Press, **171, 172, 208, 329**

Moore, D. *et. al.* (1972). 'Strengthening alternative high schools'. *Harvard Educational Review*, *42*, No. 3, pp. 315-50. **190**

Moore, D. R. & Wilson, T. A. (1970). 'Internal memo to the Metro staff, 27 March 1970'. In D. R. Moore, T. A. Wilson & R. Johnson, *The Metro School. A Report on the Progress of Chicago's Experimental 'School Without Walls'*. Chicago: Urban Research Corporation. **277, 278**

Morrisett, I. (ed.) (1966). *Concepts and Structure in the New Social Science Curricula*. Lafayette, Indiana: Social Science Education Consortium, Purdue University. **152**

Myrdal, G. (1969). *Objectivity in Social Research*. New York: Random House. **220**

Nuthall, G. A. (1970). 'A review of some selected recent studies of classroom interaction and teaching behavior'. In J. J. Gallagher, G. A. Nuthall & B. Rosenshine, *Classroom Observation*, AERA Monograph Series on Curriculum Evaluation, No. 6. Chicago: Rand McNally, pp. 6-29. **15**

Parlett, M. (1967). *'Classroom and Beyond: a study of a sophomore physics section at MIT.'* MIT: Education Research Center. **17**

Parlett, M. (1969). 'Undergraduate teaching observed'. *Nature*, *223*, pp. 1102-4. **10**

Parlett, M. (1972). *A Study of Two Experimental Programs at MIT*. Report to the Committee on Educational Policy, MIT, Cambridge, Massachusetts. **17, 331, 335**

Parlett, M. (1972). 'Evaluating innovations in teaching'. In H. J. Butcher & E. Rudd (eds.), *Contemporary Problems in Higher Education*. London: McGraw-Hill. **7, 8**

Parlett, M. & Hamilton, D. (1972). 'Evaluation as illumination: a new approach to the study of innovatory programmes'. Occasional Paper 9, Centre for Research in the Educational Sciences, University of Edinburgh. **6**

Parlett, M & King, J. G. (1971). *Concentrated Study*, Research in Higher Education Monograph No. 14. London: Society for Research in Higher Education. **10, 12**

Perry, W. G. (1968). *Forms of Intellectual and Ethical Development in the College Years*. New York: Holt, Rinehart & Winston. **13**

Polanyi, M. (1966). *The Tacit Dimension*. Garden City, New York: Doubleday. **320**

Popham, W. J. (1972). 'Must all objectives be behavioral?'. *Educational Leadership*, *29*, No. 7. **53**

Popham, W. J., Eisner, E. W., Sullivan, H. J. & Tyler, L. L. (1969). *Instructional Objectives*, AERA Monograph Series on Curriculum Evaluation, No. 3. Chicago: Rand McNally. **6, 91**

Price, D. J. de S. (1963). *Little Science, Big Science.* Columbia: Columbia University Press. **6**

Rosenthal, R. (1966). *Experimenter Effects in Behavioral Research.* New York: Appleton-Century-Crofts. **18**

Russell, H. (ed.) (1969). *Evaluation of Computer-Assisted Instruction Program.* St. Ann, Missouri: CEMREL. **204**

Scheffler, I. (1967). *Science and Subjectivity.* Indianapolis, Indiana: Bobbs-Merrill Co. **219**

Scriven, M. (1967). 'The methodology of evaluation'. In R. W. Tyler, R. M. Gagné & M. Scriven, *Perspectives of Curriculum Evaluation,* AERA Monograph Series on Curriculum Evaluation, No. 1. Chicago: Rand McNally, pp. 39-83. **6, 13, 126, 148, 219**

Scriven, M. (1971). 'Current problems in philosophy and practice of evaluation'. Informal memo, June 1971. **217**

Scriven, M. (1971). 'Curriculum problems: philosophy and practice of evaluation'. A paper produced for ETS Product Evaluation Pool, Draft VII. **132**

Scriven, M. (1971). 'Goal-free behavioral objectives'. 11-71 NIE 2D (mimeo) **140**

Scriven, M. (1971). 'Goal-free evaluation, Part 1'. 11-71 NIE 2A. (mimeo) **134**

Scriven, M. (1971). 'Goal-free evaluation Part II'. 11-71 NIE 2B (mimeo) **134**

Scriven, M. (1971). 'Legitimate and illegitimate cases of evaluating the treatment rather than the effects'. 11-71 NIE 2C. (mimeo) **139**

Scriven, M. (1972). 'Goal Lib (the GFE's manifesto)'. NIE 3A. (mimeo) **141**

Scriven, M. (1972). 'Prose and cons about goal-free evaluation'. *Evaluation Comment: The Journal of Educational Evaluation, 3,* No. 4, pp. 1-4. **130**

Shipman, M. D. (1974). *Inside a Curriculum Project.* London: Methuen. **247**

Short, E. C. & Marconnit, G. D. (1968). *Contemporary Thought on Public School Curriculum.* Dubuque, Iowa: Wm. C. Brown, **122**

Simons, H. (1971). 'Innovation and the case-study of schools'. *Cambridge Journal of Education, 3,* pp. 118-24. **178**

Smith, B. O. & Meux, M. O. *A Study of the Logic of Teaching.* Bureau of Educational Research, University of Illinois. (n.d.) **149**

Smith, L. M. (1971). 'Participant observation and evaluation strategies'. A paper presented to AERA symposium on 'Participant Observation and Curriculum: Research and Evaluation', New York, February 1971. **6, 203**

Smith, L. M. & Brock, J. A. M. (1970). *Go, Bug, Go!: Methodological Issues in Classroom Observational Research.* Occasional Paper Series: No. 5. St Ann, Missouri: CEMREL. **208**

Smith, L. M. & Brock, J. A. M. *Teacher Plans and Classroom Interaction.* St Ann, Missouri: CEMREL (In process) **201**

Smith, L. M. & Geoffrey, W. (1968). *The Complexities of an Urban Classroom.* New York: Holt, Rinehart & Winston. **191, 201, 205, 208**

Smith, L. M. & Keith, P. M. (1971). *Anatomy of Educational Innovation.* New York: John Wiley. **15, 202, 208, 324**

Smith, L. M. & Kleine, P. F. (1969). 'Teacher awareness: social cognition in the classroom'. *School Review, 77,* pp. 245-56. **205**

Smith, L. M. & Pohland, P. A. (1969). 'Participant observation of the CAI program?'. In H. Russell (ed.), *Evaluation of Computer-Assisted Instruction Program.* St Ann, Missouri: CEMREL. **10, 203**

Smith, L. M. & Pohland, P. A. (1974). 'Education, technology and the rural highlands'. In *Four Evaluation Examples: Anthropological, Economic, Narrative, and Portrayal,* AERA Monograph Series on Curriculum Evaluation, No. 7. Chicago: Rand McNally, pp. 5-54. **201, 203, 208**

Smith, L. M. & Schumacher, S. (1972). *Extended Pilot Trials of the Aesthetic Education Program: a Qualitative Description, Analysis and Evaluation.* St Ann, Missouri: CEMREL. **208, 311, 312, 313, 314**

Snyder, B. R. (1971). *The Hidden Curriculum.* New York: Knopf. **13**

Spears, H. (1950). *The High School for Today.* New York: American Book Company. **122**

Stake, R. E. (1961). 'Learning parameters, aptitudes and achievements'. *Psychometric Monographs,* No. 9. **44**

Stake, R. E. (1967). 'The countenance of educational evaluation'. *Teachers' College Record, 68,* No. 7, pp. 523-40. **63, 146**

Stake, R. E. (1972). 'An approach to the evaluation of instructional programs (program portrayal vs. analysis)'. A paper delivered at the AERA Annual Meeting in Chicago, 4 April 1972. **161**

Stake, R. E. (1972). 'Comments and conjectures: the seeds of doubt'. *The Educational Forum,* January 1972, pp. 271-2. **158**

Stake, R. E. (1972). 'The seven principal cardinals of educational evaluation'. Handout for presentation by R. E. Stake, AERA Annual Meeting, Chicago, 1972. **160**

Stake, R. E. (1973). 'Measuring what learners learn (with a special look at performance contracting)'. In E. House (ed.), *School Evaluation.* Berkeley, California: McCutchan. **8, 17**

Stake, R. E. 'Formative and summative evaluation'. (mimeo n.d.) **156**

Stake, R. E. 'To evaluate an arts program'. (To appear in a forthcoming issue of the *Journal of Aesthetic Education.*) **163**

Stake, R. E. & Gjerde, C. L. (1974). *An Evaluation of T-City, the Twin City Institute for Talented Youth, 1971.* In *Four Evaluation Examples: Anthropological, Economic, Narrative, and Portrayal,* AERA Monograph Series on Curriculum Evaluation, No. 7. Chicago: Rand McNally, pp. 99-139. **170, 262, 265**

Stenhouse, L. (1970). 'Controversial value-issues in the classroom'. In W. G. Carr (ed.), *Values and the Curriculum,* Report of the Fourth International Curriculum Conference. Washington DC: National Educational Association Center for the Study of Instruction, pp. 103-15. **104**

Stenhouse, L. (1970). 'Some limitations of the use of objectives in curriculum research and planning'. In S. J. Eggleston (ed.), *Paedagogica Europaea VI, 1970/71*. Braunschweig: L. C. G. Malmberg N. V./Georg Westermann, pp. 73-83. **115**

Stenhouse, L. (1972). 'Defining the curriculum problem'. (mimeo) **122**

Stenhouse, L. (1973). *The Design of the Project*, SSRC Project: Problems and Effects of Teaching about Race Relations, Working Paper No. 1. Internal project working paper. **113**

Stenhouse, L. (1973). 'The Humanities Curriculum Project'. In H. J. Butcher & H. B. Pont (eds.), *Educational Research in Britain 3*. London: University of London Press, pp. 149-67. **99, 100, 107**

Stenhouse, L. (1975). 'Problems of research in teaching about race relations'. In G. K. Verma & C. Bagley (eds.), *Race and Education Across Cultures*. London: Heinemann Educational Books, pp. 305-21. **109**

Suchman, E. A. (1967). 'Principles and practice of evaluative research'. In J. T. Doby (ed.), *An Introduction to Social Research*. New York: Appleton-Century-Crofts, pp. 327-51. **37**

Taylor, L. C. (1971). *Resources for Learning*. Harmondsworth: Penguin. **8, 14**

Travers, R. M. W. (1963). *Essentials of Learning: an Overview for Students of Education*. New York: Crowell-Collier & Macmillan. **44**

Trow, M. A. (1970). 'Methodological problems in the evaluation of innovation'. In M. C. Wittrock & D. E. Wiley (eds.), *The Evaluation of Instruction*. New York: Holt, Rinehart & Winston. **10**

Tyler, R. W. (1949). *Basic Principles of Curriculum and Instruction*. Chicago: University of Chicago Press. **29**

Urban Research Corporation (1971). 'The Chicago High School for Metropolitan Studies: a report on the third semester, February 1971 to June 1971'. (mimeo) **277, 281**

Urofsky, M. I. (ed.) (1970). *Why Teachers Strike: Teachers' Rights and Community Control*. Garden City, New York: Anchor Books. **218**

Walker, R. (1974). 'The conduct of educational case study: ethics, theory and procedures'. In B. MacDonald & R. Walker (eds.), *SAFARI. Innovation, Evaluation, Research and the Problem of Control: Some Interim Papers*. Norwich: Centre for Applied Research in Education. **181**

Waller, W. (1961). *The Sociology of Teaching*. New York: Russell & Russell. **171, 172**

Webb, E. J., Campbell, D. T., Schwartz, R. D. & Sechrest, L. (1966) *Unobtrusive Measures: Nonreactive Research in the Social Sciences*. Chicago: Rand McNally, **3, 14**

Whyte, W. F. (1955). *Street Corner Society* (2nd ed.). Chicago: University of Chicago Press. **183, 209**

Wild, D. J. & Beightler, C. S. (1967). *Foundations of Optimization*. Englewood Cliffs, N.J.: Prentice-Hall. **49**

Willower, D. J. (1969). 'Schools as organizations: some illustrated strategies for educational research and practice'. *Journal of Educational Innovation*, October 1969. **178**

Wilson, S. (1974). 'The use of ethnography in educational evaluation'. (mimeo) **190**

Wiseman, S. & Pidgeon, D. (1972). *Curriculum Evaluation*. Windsor: NFER. **60**

Woodrow, H. A. (1946). 'The ability to learn'. *Psychological Review, 53*, pp. 147-58. **44**

Young, M. F. D. (ed.) (1971). *Knowledge and Control*. London: Crowell Collier-Macmillan. **7**

Zeaman, D. & House, B. J. (1967). 'The relation of IQ and learning'. In R. Gagné (ed.), *Learning and Individual Differences*. Columbus, Ohio: Charles E. Merrill, pp. 192-212. **46**